The Flea Market Shopper's Companion

The Flea Market Shopper's Companion
is authorized by the
Independent Dealers Association of America, Inc.,
the association of vendors and concessionaires
who set up and sell at the markets throughout North America.

THE FLEA MARKET SHOPPER'S COMPANION

• • • • • • • • • • • •

A Complete Guide
for Buyers and Sellers Coast to Coast

James Goodridge

CITADEL PRESS
Kensington Publishing Corp.
www.kensingtonbooks.com

CITADEL PRESS books are published by

Kensington Publishing Corp.
850 Third Avenue
New York, NY 10022

All Kensington titles, imprints, and distributed lines are available at special quantity discounts for bulk purchases for sales promotions, premiums, fund raising, educational, or institutional use. Special book excerpts or customized printings can also be created to fit specific needs. For details, write or phone the office of the Kensington special sales manager: Kensington Publishing Corp., 850 Third Avenue, New York, NY 10022, attn: Special Sales Department, phone 1-800-221-2647.

First printing

10 9 8 7 6 5 4 3 2 1

Printed in the United States of America

Library of Congress Cataloging-in-Publication Data

Goodridge, James.
The flea market shopper's companion : a complete guide for buyers and sellers coast to coast / James Goodridge.
p. cm.
"A Citadel Press book."
ISBN 0-8065-2085-X (pbk.)
1. Flea markets—United States—States Directories. I. Title.
HF5482.15.G66 2001
381′.192′02573—dc21 99–22732
CIP

CONTENTS

HOW TO USE THIS BOOK

This book is for those who want to buy *and/or* sell at flea markets. The markets are categorized by state and are alphabetical by town.

The name, mailing address, street address, and phone numbers are listed with the stern recommendation that you should *call the flea market* before embarking on a visit. Also listed are the days and hours the market is open (most flea markets are open all year and from 8 a.m. until dark unless specifically indicated).

An itemization of what is sold at each particular market is listed for those who want to buy or sell goods. Food vendor availability, handicap accessibility (abbreviated h/a in the listings), entertainment, and parking information is included. For those who need trailer accommodations, information on electricity and water accessibility is noted.

Author's Note

Important Notice. Every effort has been made to ensure that the information contained in this directory is accurate. However, due to the size and scope of the publication and the fluid nature of the industry, market information is subject to change. The publisher and author assume no responsibility for errors or omissions in content or composition.

AUTHOR'S GUIDE TO THE WORLD OF FLEA MARKETS

Flea Market Shopper's Quiz

by Georgia Goodridge

Before you get started, take this quiz. Test your flea market shopping savvy. Take our "Flea Market Shopper's Quiz" and find out if you are: (a) *a novice shopper* who needs a few more lessons before you enter the big league of bargain hunting; (b) *a middleweight,* with promise, who with a few more shopping bouts under your belt will be able to go the distance with anyone; or (c) *a seasoned pro* whose skill at finding treasure, haggling, and outmaneuvering the competition makes you a candidate for this year's "Flea Market Shopper's Hall of Fame." Check the statements that apply. Scoring information can be found at the end of the quiz.

1. Your local flea market opens at 7 a.m. on Saturday. You make plans to go.

____ a. You arrive early and are one of the first people in the parking lot.

____ b. You don't arrive until 9 a.m. so you can have breakfast with your spouse first.

____ c. You go flea marketing with a group of friends but don't arrive until well after noon.

2. You find a "thingamajig" that you simply can't live without. However, it's priced $5 more than what you have left in your purse/wallet.

____ a. You offer the seller $7 less than the asking price, so if he agrees, you will still have money left over after your purchase.

____ b. You show the seller a small flaw in the item, hoping he will lower the price, but you never outright ask for a discount. When he doesn't budge, you give up and borrow money from your eight-year-old to buy it.

____ c. You ask the seller if he takes credit cards. You are surprised when he doesn't and cry as someone else steps up with cash.

3. You decide to travel to a new flea market that is located 50 miles from home. You are really into fashion and are dying to wear the new sandals you just bought.

____ a. You leave them at home in the closet and wear a pair of comfortable, well-cushioned shoes.

____ b. You wear your sandals but take an extra pair of comfortable walking shoes to change into if the need arises.

____ c. You wear your sandals because you believe that looks make the shopper.

4. You have just discovered a ring marked 14k in a cigar box of miscellaneous trinkets and costume jewelry. Box and contents are marked $4.95 Takes All.

____ a. You stifle the urge to yell "Whoopie" out loud, pay for the box and all its contents, then leave with your prize.

____ b. You are so excited at your discovery that, with the ring on your finger, you ask the seller if the price marked on the box is right. You've just tipped your hand. Thinking something's up, the seller comes over to examine it. The price goes up 10 times, and you are left to decide how much it is worth to you.

____ c. You ask the seller is he knows he has a 14k gold ring in his box of miscellaneous because you want to impress him with your shopping smarts. You then discover he won't sell it to you for $4.95.

5. You have found something that you really like. The price seems fair. The overall condition is good. It is small enough that you won't have any trouble getting it home in your car.

____ a. You buy it on the spot before someone else sets their sights on it.

____ b. You think it over for a minute and step down the row to the next booth. In the minute it takes you to ponder, the item gets broken beyond repair. You buy a Snooze and Lose bumper sticker before you go home.

____ c. You talk to the seller for 20 minutes about the item and how much you want it. The seller says he can't hold it for you without something down.

Convinced it will still be there after you and your family have lunch, you tell him you'll be back. When you return, you discover the item has been sold.

6. You buy several pieces of very fragile, breakable goods. The seller has no extra boxes or packing materials.

____ a. You go to your car because you always come to the flea market prepared. Your trunk holds: a cardboard box, blankets, a small stack of old newspapers, masking tape, string, and scissors.

____ b. You go to your car but find only a couple of rags and a Styrofoam ice chest. You're forced to make do. All's well in the end.

____ c. You pay an arm and a leg for an empty banana box from a vendor, buy a couple of overpriced T-shirts you'll never wear for padding, and grit your teeth as you listen to your items clank and chink all the way home

Scoring the Quiz

If you answered the letter (a) most often, then consider yourself a flea market shopping expert. You can hold your own with the best of them. Keep up the good job. You have learned the truth in the old adage, "To the victor belong the spoils," and you are sure to continue to get your share. Have fun and happy hunting!

If you answered by checking the letter (b) most often, you have shown a clear grasp of the basics of savvy flea market shopping but need some more field research. Experience is the best teacher. So with your eyes on the prize, get out there and shop! It won't be long before you're a pro and find yourself in the Flea Market Shopper's Hall of Fame.

If most of your answers fell under the letter (c), stay after school and write on the blackboard 100 times: *Flea market shopping is an art, and I will practice, practice, practice.* Have fun, keep shopping, and you'll graduate to pro league in no time at all.

FLEA MARKET BUG SHORTS

by Georgia Goodridge

YOU KNOW YOU'VE BEEN BITTEN BY THE FLEA MARKET BUG IF...

- You plan your vacations to include frequent stops at flea markets along the way.
- You receive an I Brake for Flea Markets bumper sticker for your birthday, and instead of explaining why the sticky stuff will ruin your paint job, you rush outside and proudly slap it on.

- You get to the flea market early enough to shop by flashlight.
- You find yourself trying to haggle over the price of cereal with a bewildered checker at the grocery store, citing the nearness of the expiration date, and a few obvious box dents.
- You plan your honeymoon to include shopping at a new flea market you just heard about, explaining to your bride that this is what all newlyweds do in the '90s!
- The favorite possession left to you by your late Aunt Sadie is her big-wheeled shopping cart.
- You see nothing wrong with commandeering your husband's favorite fishing vest and turning it into the ultimate flea market shopper's fashion accessory with pockets containing: a tape measure, magnifying glass, fountain pen, scratch paper, change, penlight, pocketknife, cell phone, and other various shopping necessities.
- Wrestling with the rear seat of your minivan to remove it for more shopping cargo space has become a Friday night ritual.
- You draw a map of bank ATM locations nearest to the flea market.

Tenets of Shopper Courtesy

Everyone appreciates a courteous shopper, and this is especially true at flea markets. Because of the freewheeling spirit at markets, buyers often forget that the dealers selling their wares are not there for enjoyment but are in their place of business.

Sellers and shoppers alike can get the most from the flea market experience if everyone will follow these tenets of shopping courtesy:

- Don't open or reach inside display cases. Ask for assistance.
- Sealed boxes should never be opened. Ask dealers to assist you if you want to get a closer look at something.
- If you knock something off a table, pick it up.
- If you break something, offer and plan to pay for it.
- Never walk into blocked-off areas of a booth.
- Don't make rude comments about a person's booth or insult the merchandise.

- When shopping with children, keep them under control. Do not let them handle or grab merchandise. Be prepared to help them yourself. Never allow horseplay in and around booths. Be prepared to pay for anything your children might damage.

Bargaining is a part of the flea market scene but be reasonable and courteous when making an offer.

Bargaining Savvy for the Beginner

It is perfectly acceptable at a flea market to try to negotiate a lower price on an item. Most dealers expect bargaining and have built maneuvering room into their prices. Here are some tips that may improve your results.

1. If you have never tried haggling over a price before, now is your chance. The first thing to do is to walk around at your local market, window-shop a bit, and try to eavesdrop on others. Pay particular attention to what they say and how the dealer reacts. When you are ready, try it yourself. Remember the adage, "Nothing ventured, nothing gained."

2. Make sure your offer is reasonable. Don't expect a dealer to accept $2 on a $50 item. This is a surefire way to get your feelings hurt.

3. Make more than one offer if you want the item. Allow the seller to make a counter-offer. Try to find a price that is acceptable to both of you. The more practice you get, the better you will become at bargaining.

4. If a seller goes to the trouble to haggle over price with you, show him the courtesy of buying the item right then. Do not ask him to hold it until later, unless money changes hands. It is unfair to expect him to pass up other sales opportunities only to have you change your mind after leaving his stand and not returning. If you are sure you want the item, be prepared to do business then and there.

5. Look carefully at the item you are interested in. Does it have a price tag? If it does, is it marked with the word *firm*? If it is, don't even ask for a discount; the dealer is not willing to negotiate on this particular item. You will appear naive, rude, or both. However, you won't find this situation too often at flea markets. It is something usually reserved for valuable items at antique shows and collector malls.

6. If you come across a dealer who acts insulted when you try to dicker over price, move on to another booth. Chances are that this dealer is new and

doesn't understand that bargaining is part of traditional flea market sales. It might also be that he has not bought wisely for resale and can't bargain without taking a loss. In either case, he has a lot to learn about flea marketing. You needn't waste your time in this booth; there are plenty of other dealers who will wheel and deal.

7. Finally, resist the urge to knock an item's worthiness in order to make your offer stand. It is a bit insulting to a seller and actually makes the buyer doing it look silly for wanting an item of such inferior character.

Bargaining can be fun and profitable, and with experience a beginner can quickly become savvy.

Shopping Tips—Dress for the Hunt

1. *Dress in layers.* Weather is changeable and unpredictable, and you don't want to have to cut your trip short because you are too hot or too cold.
2. *Wear comfortable shoes.* A *must* due to the amount of walking it usually takes to cover a flea market. Also, a lot of the terrain at markets is unpaved, with only gravel to walk on.
3. *Take some sort of tote bag for carrying your purchases,* even if you don't plan on buying anything.
4. *Be prepared.* Keep a blanket, empty cardboard box, and a few newspapers in the trunk of your car in case you need to pad something you buy, or to protect small items. Nylon cord or a piece of clothesline can also come in handy.
5. *Glasses or magnifying glass.* Don't forget to bring them for inspecting prospective purchases.
6. *Dress for comfort.* Casual is the name of the game when shopping at flea markets.

Barter

Almost every flea market dealer likes to trade, especially if you can trade stock for stock. The rule of thumb I use in a trade is that both traders have to be using the same "dollar." For example, my wholesale price should equal your wholesale price, or retail should equal retail.

Over the years, I have traded for real estate, dental work, gold, silver, coins, fine jewelry, lodging, food, restaurant credit, and different kinds of merchandise that I can resell. The opportunity for trades is always present at a market.

I always put up three signs: 1. Buy, Sell, Trade; 2. Wholesale-Retail; 3. All Sales Final.

All Sales Final

For any item, examine, handle, smell, and taste (if necessary) the item, and then make a decision. If you want it, pay the price and take it home with you.

If you like to buy items that have guarantees, then you should shop at Sears or Wal-Mart. For the most part, items sold at flea markets are sold the same as at auctions, "Where is, as is."

If you are buying electric items, most markets have an outlet where you can go and plug the item in and test it. It is your responsibility to check out the item.

With new items, especially items that are factory sealed in boxes, most dealers will exchange the item for you if there are hidden damages. If the item is damaged by misuse, they won't. The rules are not the same as at the discount house.

Green Cash

In the world of flea market selling, a cash sale is only one that is paid in U.S. currency, what I like to call "Yankee greenbacks."

When I am negotiating with a customer for very expensive items, I always ask, "What kind of funds are you going to pay with?" Credit cards cost the dealer money to process, and if you are selling on the road, both the credit card and the check have to be sent home to be processed, delaying you in obtaining the funds.

Rare Items in Poor Condition

Quite often, all of us find some real treasures at the flea market. However, there is one that I can't caution you too much against, and that is a truly rare item or a very unique item that is in very poor condition.

Sure it may be listed in the book as worth a lot of money in "poor to bad condition," but keep in mind that "books don't buy." I have yet to have a book come up to my booth and buy a single item from me.

The majority of collectors want items in nice to excellent condition. Battered, torn-up, rusty, or generally unpresentable items do not sell well.

Buying Toys at a Flea Market—Safety Check Tip 1

There are always a lot of toys to be found when shopping the markets. Especially if your little ones are with you, it is hard to resist the temptation to buy. Most of us can't do it. A consumer safety tip, however. The same precautions should be taken with used toys that are taken when buying new ones at the store. For example, be sure to buy a toy that is age-appropriate for the child. Also remember no loose pieces or tiny wheels to pull off, for instance, that a baby or toddler would be likely to put in their mouth and perhaps choke on.

Here's a good idea. Take the empty cardboard tube from a roll of toilet tissue along with you on your shopping trip. Before you buy a toy for a young child, make sure that none of the pieces can fall through the tube. The tube is approximately the size of a child's airway passage. If the toy or any piece of it falls through the tube, for your child's safety, don't buy it.

Buying Toys at a Flea Market—Safety Check Tip 2

There are many new toys to be found when shopping at flea markets, and you may want to take advantage of the great buys. For your children's safety, however, you should know that many of these toys are imports and do not meet American standards for child protection. Boxes are not always marked with the age of the child the toy is intended for, for example. Also, foreign manufacturers often use materials for their toys that can cause safety hazards for children: hard plastics, for example, in such things as projectiles, or warrior battle gear that encourages fighting and could actually cause injury if a child is hit with it.

As a parent, use your best judgment when buying toys at flea markets. Inspect the item thoroughly. Consider the children who will be using the toy and how they will be using it. Take their age, their physical development, as well as their maturity into consideration. If it meets your tough safety standards, buy it!

Handicap Shopping at Flea Markets

While we have listed the flea markets that have indicated that they are handicap accessible, I do want to caution our disabled friends about some of the physical realities inherent to the industry. There are certain physical site restraints to note. The majority of flea markets have an outdoor area where dealers set up their booths. Though often flat, the terrain can be uneven with small hills and valleys, often roughly covered with such surfaces as gravel or chat. There are hazards such as potholes, mud, ruts, and sand; all the things you would find in a barren field. Though many of the larger markets are paved, for the most part, the parking areas are either dirt or gravel and can be very difficult to navigate.

A great number of the indoor facilities used by flea markets are older buildings. Most of these buildings, because of their physical age and construction, are simply not handicap friendly. The markets that will provide you with the easiest access may be those held in convention centers, arenas, or fairgrounds where most buildings have been brought up to federal, state, and local standards.

For easy shopping, your best bet might be markets that are located in newer buildings such as former grocery stores, discount houses, or furniture stores. These buildings are usually built on one level. They are also likely to have a nice paved parking lot and handicap-accessible rest rooms.

Flea markets are for everyone. If you have difficulties shopping at a market, don't hesitate to make suggestions to the management. I have always found the people involved in this business—dealers, management, customers—to be friendly and helpful. Chances are others have also encountered the same problems. I also strongly recommend that you call the markets in advance of your visit in order to find out specifics about their facilities so you won't be frustrated.

Shopping for Your Pet

Shoppers can find almost anything they need for the family pet at a flea market—aquariums, terrariums, dog houses, kitty cushions, even rhinestone-studded collars and leashes. Pet supplies are a popular line among vendors, and you may be able to find shampoo, toys, flea collars, pet food of all brands and descriptions, and practically everything to keep your pet happy and healthy. At some markets, dealers sell personally engraved name tags for pets made to order while you wait.

We know of one market where a veterinarian holds periodic immunization clinics and does pet identification tattooing!

Many great buys for your pet await you at the flea market, and for bargains and variety, this is the place to shop

Try It Before You Buy It

Most dealers will tell you that the electric appliance they are selling "works all the way." Reputable ones will advise you of any defects or quirks. However, a rule of thumb is to ask to try it out before you buy it.

Ninety-five percent of all flea markets will have an electrical outlet somewhere designated for this purpose. If a dealer refuses to allow you to test an item, pass on it. That defective microwave you fail to check out first could become an awfully large bookend in your kitchen and a hard reminder.

Flea Market Return Policy

When making a purchase at a flea market, be aware that most dealers do not accept returns. Before buying, see if the dealer has posted his policy on a sign. If you don't see one, don't be afraid to ask. Many dealers will accept exchanges on items, but there is usually one hard and fast rule at a flea market—Buyer Beware.

Trading With Traders!

Wheeling and dealing. Old-fashioned "horse trading." It can be fun *and* profitable. If you have something you'd like to trade that would be of value to a dealer and a dealer has something you're interested in, ask if he'll swap. Remember, the value of the two items must be comparable.

Swapping, after all, is the very essence of the open-air marketplace. A lot of barter is still going on today, and like anything else, there is a certain skill to it that comes with practice and experience.

A shrewd trader can come out making a good profit from his dealings. One sign that I always put up is "Offers Welcome—Some Accepted!"

Beware of Reproductions

Tip 1

In the world of antiques and collectibles, reproductions have become a real problem. Many times, unsuspecting buyers think they are purchasing an original item and are really getting a copy. For the most part, reproduced antiques are quite legal—the manufacturers are not breaking any patent rights or copyright infringement. Ethical dealers will tell you that an item is a reproduction. If you are not sure, ask, and decide if you can trust the dealer or not. Rely on your gut instinct and knowledge of the item in question. If you are really not sure, you are always safe to refrain from making the purchase.

Tip 2

Price is a good measure of whether an item is an original or a reproduction. Again, you will have to be somewhat knowledgeable about the general category.

If you find a piece of pink depression glass on the market for $40 and in the same booth find another for $12, the odds are the lesser-priced item is either a broken original or a reproduction. If you don't discover damage, you probably know the answer.

Flea Market Treasure Hunting

by Georgia Goodridge

It may not be quite the same as combing shipwrecks on the ocean floor for treasure chests laden with long-lost gold and precious antiquities. But the well-worn adage, "One man's trash is another man's treasure," quite aptly describes the lure of flea markets. Thus the legions of modern-day treasure hunters who comb through a veritable sea of merchandise, each and every week, at marketplaces across the country, all in search of their version of the "prize."

What is it about flea markets that brings out the spirit of "gold fever" in otherwise well-grounded individuals? The answer to that question is as varied as the people who are drawn back to them week after week. It is also in the very nature of flea markets themselves.

Swap meets, trade days, or flea markets have always been outside of traditional retail establishment ranks, which is one of the primary reasons for their attraction.

At a department store or typical mainstream retail business you can count on consistency in product, presentation, and pricing. There is a status quo that varies little from one store to the other.

There is a certain vagabond nature to flea markets, even the most well-established institutions, that creates a constant air of the unknown. Merchandise, and the sellers who peddle it, are in a constant state of flux. Variety and diversity is the name of this game.

From time to time we have all read newspaper accounts of remarkable flea market finds: rare photos and valuable autographs of celebrities; artwork produced by great American artists; museum-quality, historical documents found hidden behind old pictures. These are the stories that bring out the treasure hunter.

This is not to say, however, that everyone expects to run across such rare and elusive finds. For most of us, the "prize," the thing that gives us a charge, is more attainable but no less exciting. It is like a game of bargain-hunting hide and seek.

There is nothing quite like the thrill of running across an addition to our collection of this or that, buried amid the rows of bric-a-brac. If we can buy our cookie jar or our baseball card or our diamond ring for a price below market value, that's our treasure bounty. But if we find a seller unaware of what he has, and we can buy our quarry for a steal—we've just struck gold! That's modern-day flea market treasure hunting in its finest hour.

Believe that treasure can be found and keep your eye sharp for it when shopping the flea markets, and you are as likely as anyone else to find a jewel.

And lest you think that all sellers are omnipotent: Even the writer of this flea market guide was caught unaware recently. He had rejected a tarnished tray stamped Made in Mexico as junk and put it out for sale for $2. Then I, his wife, came along with some silver polish. And behold! Beneath the layers of grime appeared the numbers .925—the designation for sterling silver. The tray was repriced and sold for $25. Had a sharp buyer come along before we discovered what we had under that blackened metal, he would have reaped the reward, instead of us.

"There's gold in them thar flea markets." Why not find some for yourself!

Tips for Selling at Flea Markets

First, the obvious. Dress in layers. It gets a lot warmer after dawn. Bring a chair, a visor or hat, sunglasses, some sunscreen, and fluids to drink. And get to bed early the night before. Most markets start ridiculously early, and you might not get a spot if you show up late.

Next, if the market doesn't provide tables, bring anything resembling a table; I use wooden planks that I lay over some cardboard boxes. Customers are reluctant to pick up merchandise if it's not displayed at arm's length.

Don't forget to bring bags. This surprised me when I first started. People ask vendors at flea markets for bags? Yeah, they do all the time. If I don't have enough bags in my cupboards, I go to the supermarket and get some from the recycling bin to take with me.

Another item to tote along is tiny labels (available at office supply stores) to mark prices on your items. For one thing, it gets annoying to repeat prices to each casual passerby who inquires. But more important, I've found buyers are less likely to bargain a price down if it's printed on a tag.

Remember change. If all you've got to sell is garage sale merchandise, a roll of quarters plus $20 in singles and fives is usually enough change to start.

Don't worry about paying rent on your table when you arrive. Just claim a spot and ask around to other dealers to make sure it isn't reserved (often there's no indication of which tables are reserved; the regulars just know by consensus). Then, once the market is under way, the flea market manager will come around to collect rent from you.

Finally, be prepared to be approached by people looking to buy before you even unpack your stuff. These are usually owners of retail shops looking for items they can resell. Make sure you stand your ground on a price with them—if they won't pay the price you're asking, don't back down. There's plenty of time to reduce the price later in the day if an item isn't selling.

Now, about pricing. I usually price items at one-tenth of their purchase price when new. That's a little lower than what regular vendors charge for comparable items, but it guarantees that I have nothing left over at the end of the day.

Exceptions to this pricing rule of thumb are, of course, antiques and collectibles. And remember that people will collect anything. For example, I bought a little plastic bust of Michael Jordan emblazoned with the *Space Jam* logo and filled with gumballs for $1. I added that item to my own growing "tacky Americana" collection, and would have paid up to $7 for that little thrill.

Make sure you sell much more than you buy. You'll be tempted to buy other people's cast-offs while trying to sell your own, but resist the urge. It feels wonderful to go home with a full wallet and an empty vehicle. Well, almost empty, except for maybe a little plastic bust of Michael Jordan.

And then there's flea market etiquette. When your neighbors excuse themselves to go to the rest room, watch their tables for them; you're bound to need the favor returned. When customers try to bargain the price down, be courteous, even if they are offering $2 for that Ming vase. And when it's time to pack up and go home, don't leave anything behind for others to clean up. Most flea markets have large Dumpsters—if you don't want your leftovers, put them there.

Except for flea markets that specialize in antiques, most markets will allow you to sell anything. In fact, Al Minguez, Sr., manager of the Bensalem Lions Club flea market, remembers a woman who put a For Sale sign on her car at the flea market, sold it that day, and called a cab to go home.

But no flea market will allow you to sell weapons (even collectible guns and knives), fireworks, pornographic materials, drug paraphernalia, name-brand counterfeits, bootleg videos and tapes, and items with serial numbers defaced. Many won't allow food to be sold at all, but some will allow it if the vendor has proper licensing for that county. If you're unsure, call the market for information.

Great New Retailing Opportunity for Flea Marketers!

For those in the flea market business, the hottest trend in the country today is the advent of antique and craft malls. Just imagine selling your merchandise for 7 to 10 times markup and sometimes a lot more. Now imagine no flea market shoppers to have to contend with. You may never even have to come into contact with the customers.

The mall concept is a tremendous, yet very simple one. It combines the excitement and variety of an antique show or craft festival with the permanence and convenience of a store.

During the 1980s antique and craft malls came into their own on a national scale as a legitimate arm of retailing. The 1990s have seen an explosion in the mall concept of marketing fine antiques, collectibles, handcrafted items, as well as new merchandise, secondhand items, and general flea market merchandise.

The public's seemingly insatiable appetite for quality items of yesteryear seems to be fed by the hunger of today's affluent shoppers to possess a piece of their heritage, their childhood. This desire is driving the entire mall industry. The majority of malls feature antiques, collectibles, and crafts. Yet almost every mall has a fair share of new and used (vintage) merchandise. This is where the clever dealer can make a great profit.

I am in three different malls, and in one of them I have two separate booths. I have schooled myself slightly on antiques and some of the collectible fields. I purchase my older pieces at the flea market, at auctions, and garage sales. There are still a lot of treasures out there to be found every week. Don't forget, I love garage sales.

I also have been successful at purchasing small pieces of what I call used furniture (junk), such as: desks, vanities, chairs, and end tables. After I clean them up and do the "Old English" bit on them, I put them in my booths and voilà, "vintage furniture." Pieces that I paid $4 or $5 for at an auction or garage sale, now bring $45 to $55 in my mall booth.

In each booth I try to run in as much new merchandise as I can get away with. There are plenty of new collectibles and decorator items on the market. The Associated Surplus Dealers (ASD) shows and the *ASD Trade News* provide a great source for these items. Marcasite jewelry and knives (under glass) in each booth do well for me, along with vintage replica costume jewelry.

Some other great lines to add are cast-iron items, especially toys and banks. Replica depression-era glass is also a good item to add to a mall booth. The new or reproduction metal advertising signs do very well at malls as do newer tobacco items, especially Joe Camel items. Your experience from the flea market will pay you handsome dividends here in picking merchandise to place in a mall.

Though specifics vary from mall to mall, most charge a flat rate for exhibit space plus commission on sales—10 to 20% is common in most parts of the country. Rates vary from about $65 for an 8×10 booth to upward of $200 depending on the mall's popularity and customer traffic.

Most malls are open daily. You do not need to be present to sell your merchandise, which is perhaps the most appealing aspect of this business. The mall personnel will handle advertising, show your merchandise, sell it, collect for it, and pay the sales tax as well as provide security. In other words, a complete turnkey operation can be had for as little as $25 to $50 per week. All you must do is keep the booth well stocked.

Look in the classified section of your local Sunday paper under "antiques" and you will find the antique malls in your area. Go and visit a few. Pay particular attention to the price tags of merchandise. Remember, you won't find flea market prices at an antique mall. What would have been marked at the flea market for $1 you will find marked at up to $5 at the mall. Of course, it will be properly described all on a neat little tag. You will find much of the same merchandise you are already selling but commanding premium prices.

I try to visit each of my booths at least once every two weeks to add new stock, rearrange the booth, and shuffle some items that have sat too long between malls. Sales will fare a lot better if you visit your booth each week.

Week after week, as dealers bring in new and different merchandise, shoppers can find all the diverse and interesting items that were heretofore available only at shows. Every trip to the mall is an adventure to see "what's here today."

By sheer numbers, the Midwest is the leader, with far more multidealer malls than the rest of the country. However, the South and the West Coast are not far behind, as new malls are springing up daily. The East Coast (with the exception of Pennsylvania, which is mall heaven) is beginning to follow suit as the collectible field booms.

One thing is certain: You will not find the same boring and uninteresting franchises and groups of young hooligans roaming the aisles that you now find in the large shopping center malls.

AUTHOR'S NOTE TO THE LIST

Having spent most of my adult life in and around flea markets I can say without any reservation at all that I truly love flea marketing. Many of my fondest memories are of days set up at a flea market.

Often people will ask, "What is your favorite market?" "Which is the best market?" Always the most-asked question is, "What's the biggest market?"

Those are some very difficult questions. I have set up and sold from coast to coast and almost all points in between. Fond memories and great days abound. Some days not so great—no sales, rain, all are part of the deal.

What are the best? The colorful, trendy markets of southern California? The wide-open markets of Texas? The big commercial markets of Florida? The solid markets of the Midwest? The fast-paced markets on the East Coast?

I have never been able to give a clear and concise answer to any of those questions.

Flea marketing is a very personal thing, whether you are a buyer or seller or as I am a mixture of both. I buy, sell, and trade. Each market, each day stands uniquely on its own.

I am always being asked to rate markets. I have just not figured out a way to do this satisfactorily. If I am selling at a market and having a good day, then it is a good market. If I am having a great day, then it's a great market, and, of course, if I am having a bad day, then it's a bad market. (We always blame the market.)

The same is true for buyers. If you are finding bargains or treasures for your collection and having a great time, then it certainly is a great market. Don't find anything at a market, and you won't particularly care for it. (Again we always blame the market.)

I've had a couple of unhappy experiences in which I have driven 300 miles to set up at markets that were closed. At one the property had been sold and the other had burnt down. I could have saved myself a lot of grief by simply calling first.

I can't urge you too strongly to always call ahead before traveling long distances. Keeping up with flea markets is like keeping up with a flock of rabbits. They come, they go. Things change. Call first.

Also remember that most markets are open on major holidays—Labor Day Monday, Memorial Day weekend, Fourth of July, etc. Also a lot of markets have extended seasons during the Christmas season, especially indoor markets and ones in the sunbelt states. Markets that are held at places like fairgrounds, dog tracks, racetracks, etc. will be closed during the particular season of that facility, such as when the fair is running.

When the days of the market are shown as first weekend, third Sunday, etc., that means the first weekend of the month or third Sunday of the particular month. It also means that in the example of the first Monday, the market will be open the Saturday and Sunday of the weekend in front of the first Monday. If there is a market that you have a question about, be sure to call the market before traveling a long distance.

These first Mondays, second Mondays, etc., are common in Texas and a lot of the southern states. Why, I don't know, but I agree they can be confusing, so just call the market in advance.

Keep in mind that by their very nature flea markets are early-running events. They open early, and the good buys and special items are available to the early shopper. As a rule, by 1 p.m. most markets are winding down, and the stock is pretty well picked over. Remember the old saying: "The early bird gets the worm."

A special note here on reading the addresses. The first address shown is the local address, such as 123 Main St. The second address is how the market will show up on the state highway map, such as 123 Hwy. 57. The directions are literal, behind Wal-Mart, next to McDonald's, two miles south of town, etc.

Here's to happy flea marketing. Hope you enjoy this book and feel free to submit articles, listings, and your opinion.

ALABAMA

ATHENS

Limestone Flea Market
U.S. Hwy. 72 and Burgreen Rd., between
Athens and Huntsville
Eight miles east of I-65
(205) 233-5183

Saturday, 8 a.m.–5 p.m., Sunday, 9 a.m.–5 p.m. Indoor market, 62,000 square feet, 360 indoor spaces, outdoor spaces available. Well-stocked market with a wide variety of new, used, antiques, collectibles, primitives, memorabilia, and crafts. Clean rest rooms and good food concession, h/a.* Ample bus and RV parking. Space from $40 per 10×10 for the weekend. *Contact* Rosa Isbell, 30030 Hwy. 72W, Madison, AL 35756 (256) 233-5183, fax (256) 233-1415.

ATTALLA

Mountain Top Flea Market
11301 U.S. Hwy. 278
West of Gadsden
(800) 535-2286 or (205) 589-4119
E-mail: mtopflea@hopper.net

Sundays only, 5 a.m. until dark. Average attendance 30,000 with over 1,000 dealers. Parking and walking here can be a nightmare as there are over 2.5 miles of booths. Market covers over 96 acres and is located on a mountain in a rural area. This market is a treasure hunter's bonanza: antiques, produce, crafts, new merchandise, secondhand items. If you are a dealer or a decorator, this is a don't miss. Overnight parking, rest rooms, showers, and nine food concessions. Space from $7. Inside and outside space available.

BESSEMER

Bessemer Flea Market
1013 8th Ave. North
Exit 112 off I-59, behind McDonalds
(205) 425-8510

Friday, Saturday, Sunday, 8 a.m.–5 p.m. Average attendance 10,000 for the weekend, averages 450 vendors. Wide variety of goods at this market: crafts, collectibles, new merchandise, and great bargains can be found here, from electronics to sportswear. Food and beverage concessions. Rest rooms, ample parking, h/a. Inside and outside spaces from $6. Camping available with electricity. Motels nearby. To reserve space *contact* Beverly Morton, Box 805, 35020.

BIRMINGHAM

Quality Antique Flea Market
2331 Bessemer Hwy.
Alabama State Fairgrounds
(205) 787-2641

Friday, Saturday, Sunday, every third weekend. Admission charge. Excellent market for quality antiques and good collectibles, Food, rest rooms, h/a, ample paved parking.

Dixie Land Flea & Farmers Market
3000 Hwy. 25 South
(205) 672-2022 or (800) 440-4125

NOTE: Please note that the abbreviation h/a is used for handicap accessible throughout this directory.

Friday, Saturday, Sunday. Average weekend attendance of over 25,000 with approximately 300 dealers. Indoor and outdoor market with covered spaces. New merchandise, sportswear, housewares, antiques, collectibles, country items, and crafts. Snack bars, rest rooms, ample parking. Space from $6. Overnight camping available $2. Showers on grounds.

The Flea Market
2331 Bessemer Hwy.
Alabama State Fairgrounds
(205) 786-3532 or (800) 362-7538

Every first weekend, Friday, 3 a.m.–9 p.m., Saturday, Sunday, 7 a.m.–6 p.m. Free admission. One of the South's most popular markets with an average weekend attendance of 25,000 and approximately 500 vendors. Lots of quality booths that are well stocked and manned by professional dealers. Antiques, vintage clothing, crafts, dolls, jewelry, produce, collectibles; a good mix of antiques and new items. (Market is also open on special dates; call for current schedule of special days.) Food, rest rooms, h/a, ample parking. Inside space from $45, outside $25 per weekend. *Contact* The Flea Market, Box 39063, 35208.

BUCKSVILLE

Tannehill Trade Days
Tannehill State Park (Birmingham)

Every third weekend, 7 a.m.–5 p.m. Admission charge. Excellent attendance with over 450 dealers. One of the South's larger and better flea markets, interesting market with a little bit of everything. Wide-open market, from fine antiques to new imports. Lots of primitives, country and farm-related items. Good market for the wholesale buyer and the serious collector, many quality collector fields are represented. This is an all-day or entire weekend stop. Good food, rest rooms, ample parking, but a lot of walking that can be difficult for the handicapped due to terrain. Camping and lodging nearby. *Contact* Helen Riggins (205) 447-5711.

COLLINSVILLE

Collinsville Trade Day
Hwy. 11 South
(256) 524-2536 or 524-2127

Every first Monday, 4:30 a.m.–2:30 p.m. Market is strong on quality antiques and collectibles, coins, new merchandise, livestock, plants, fresh produce, and poultry. Lots of crafts, primitives, and decorator items here, also. Good market for the wholesale buyer. Plenty of food, rest rooms, h/a, ample parking. Lots of walking at this market. Space from $8 inside and $3 outside. Overnight camping available, showers on grounds. *Contact* Manager, Box 560, 35961.

Jim's Flea Market
Hwy. 68
East on Hwy. 68 to Hwy. 11 South
(205) 524-2565

Saturdays only, 6 a.m. until dark, open on holidays. This market averages 200 dealers. New and used merchandise, crafts, antiques, furniture, housewares, produce. Good selection of country and farm items. Snack bar, rest rooms, h/a. Ample parking available. Inside and outside space available. *Contact* Charles Cook, Box 257, 35961 (256) 524-2536 or (888) 524-2536.

CULLMAN

Cullman Flea Market
I-65, Exit 308 on Hwy. 278
(256) 739-0910

Saturday, Sunday, 8 a.m.–5 p.m. Indoor/outdoor market with approximately 300 dealers. Crafts, fine art, jewelry, coins, new and used merchandise, antiques, books, collectibles, two food concessions. Market has several specialty shops located in an old bar that are open on weekdays. Market has a lot of special events and attractions. Ample parking, overnight camping available. Space from $20 for the weekend. *Contact* Gene Bates, P.O. Box 921, 35055 (256) 739-0910, fax (256) 739-5352.

DECATUR

Southeastern Flea Market
Sports Arena
(205) 353-5313

Every second weekend. Large, well-attended market with good selection of antiques, collectibles, and some new merchandise. Market is primarily composed of high-quality collector lines. Food available, rest rooms, h/a, ample paved parking. Nice indoor facility.

DOTHAN

Sadie's Flea Market
7990 Hwy. 231 South
Five miles south of town
(334) 677-5138

Friday, Saturday, Sunday, 8 a.m.–5 p.m. Approximately 150 dealers participate. Good selection of merchandise, antiques, collectibles, new and used merchandise, sportswear, electronics, toys, craft, junk. Nice market to poke around at because amongst the junk are some real treasures. Friendly, fun market. Snack bars, rest rooms, h/a, ample parking. Overnight camping available. Space from $6. *Contact* Sadie's Flea Market, Rte. 11, Box 165, 36301.

Jed's Country Mall & Flea Market
Hwy. 231
Ten miles south of town
(334) 677-7234

Saturday, Sunday, 9 a.m.–6 p.m. Indoor space, 23,000-square-foot building and outdoor space available. Antiques, lots of crafts, electronics, jewelry, housewares, new and used merchandise, produce, collectibles. Snack bar and good restaurant on premises. Rest rooms, h/a, good security. Ample parking available. Market conducts many special events, usually country and western or gospel-themed. Space from $3 per day. Overnight camping available. *Contact* Jim Easterly, Rte. 1, Box 223, Cottonwood, 36320.

DUTTON

Ta-Co-Bet Trade Days
Three miles southeast of Scottsboro on Rte. 1

Saturday, Sunday. Approximately 175 dealers. Antiques, collectibles, new merchandise, and flea market merchandise. This is a real pleasant country market. Always lots of interesting booths and dealers here. Snack bars, rest rooms, h/a. Ample parking. Inside and outside spaces available. Reservation required. *Contact* Russell DePaul, Box 198, Valley Head, 35744.

ELMORE

Bargain Place Flea Market
Hwy. 143 and 14
Off I-65, Exit 186, go six miles north
at the railroad overpass
(334) 514-0336 or 567-7731

Friday, Saturday, Sunday, 9 a.m. until dark. There are 50 inside dealers. An everything-goes market: new and used, collectibles, primitives, crafts, tools, toys, and advertising items. Food concessions, rest rooms, h/a. Ample parking. Inside and outside and some covered spaces. Overnight camping available. *Contact* Marty Greer.

FALKVILLE

Lacon Trade Days
Old Hwy. 31
South between Birmingham and Huntsville
(205) 784-5091

Saturday, Sunday, dawn until dark. Approximately 400 dealers occupy outside and covered spaces. Interesting market with wide range of dealers, new and used merchandise, produce, livestock, antiques, toys, jewelry, collectibles, and crafts. Food, rest rooms. Camping available. Space from $2.50. *Contact* T. C. McGee, Box 179, 35622.

FLORENCE

Uncle Charlie's Flea Market
Hwy. 72 West
Five miles west of Florence
(256) 757-1771 or (800) 542-2848

Saturday, Sunday, 8 a.m.–5 p.m., open on holidays. Average attendance is 15,000 for the weekend with approximately 300 covered spaces. Tools, leather, antiques, books, livestock, produce, crafts, furniture, and new merchandise are sold as well as sportswear, electronics, and imports. Kids' pony rides. Good market for the commercial vendor. Plenty of food, rest rooms, h/a. Free and ample parking. Space for the weekend starts at $25 for 8×10. Camping available. *Contact* Tom Mabry, Box 190, Killen, 35645.

FOLEY

Foley Flea Market
Hwy. 59
(334) 943-6349

Friday, Saturday, Sunday, 8 a.m.–5 p.m. Indoor and outdoor market with approximately 175 dealers. Snack bars, rest rooms, h/a, ample parking. *Contact* Pam Harding.

GADSDEN

Rainbow Trade Day
Highway 77 and Steele Station Rd.
(205) 442-9928 or 442-3474

Saturday, Sunday. Across from the Kmart in the old Pontiac/Cadillac building. Daily attendance averages 500 with approximately 75 dealers. Good selection of used and new merchandise, housewares, sportswear, electronics, crafts, collectibles, primitives, glassware. Snack bar, rest rooms, h/a. Ample parking, space from $5. *Contact* Wayne Kern, 503 Country Club Dr., 35901.

431 Trade Days
Hwy. 431

Saturday, Sunday. Inside and outside spaces. Approximately 150 dealers. Lots of stuff here, new, used, collectibles, antiques, new, used and antique furniture, country and primitive, crafts. Snack bar, rest rooms, h/a, camping available. Ample parking. Spaces for $2. *Contact* Mona Hyatt, Rte. 9, 35905 (205) 538-5238.

GUNTERSVILLE

All American Trade Days
1190 Hwy. 431 South
(205) 582-0385

Saturday, Sunday, 8 a.m.–5 p.m. Average weekend attendance is 20,000 with approximately 350 dealers. Indoor and outdoor market. Lots of secondhand and new merchandise: tools, collectibles and primitives, livestock, produce, toys, jewelry. Market has live entertainment on weekends and many special events are also held here. There is a restaurant and antique mall on premises; mall is open Tuesday through Sunday. Nice selection of antiques and collectibles in the mall. Rest rooms, h/a. Ample parking. Camping available, showers on grounds. Space from $5 outside and $10 inside per day. *Contact* Gladys Cornelius, Trade Days, 11190 Hwy. 431 South, 35976.

HAMMONDVILLE

I-59 Flea Market
I-59, Exit 231, Hammondville
(256) 635-6899

Saturday, Sunday, 8 a.m.–5 p.m. Large outdoor commercial market with approximately 350 dealers. Antiques, collectibles, new and used merchandise, lots of garage sale items, locally made crafts and produce. Snack bars, rest rooms, h/a, ample parking.

HARPERSVILLE

Evans Flea Market
Hwy. 280
Four miles from Childersburg
(205) 672-2022
Fax (205) 672-2203

Saturday, Sunday. Approximately 50 dealers selling antiques, crafts, produce, and new merchandise. Snack bar, rest rooms, h/a. Ample parking. Camping available. Space from $1 per day. *Contact* Manager, 33985/Hwy. 25, 35078.

Dixie Land Flea & Farmer's Market
3000 Hwy. 25 South
(205) 672-2011 or (800) 448-4155

Friday, Saturday, Sunday, 9 a.m.–5 p.m. Average weekend attendance 30,000 with over 300 dealers inside and outside. New, old, and collectible merchandise, including furniture, glassware, and miscellaneous, are available. This is a real down-home country market, very friendly and pleasant place. Good variety of food here, rest rooms, h/a. Ample parking. Space from $6 per day. Overnight camping, electricity available, showers, and 24-hour security.

HUNTSVILLE

Tennessee Valley Swap Meet & Trade Days
North Pkwy. and Winchester
Hwys. 231 and 431
(256) 852-9700 or 536-8492

Friday, Saturday, Sunday, 8 a.m.–5 p.m. Approximately 30 dealers offer new and used merchandise, tools, country and farm items, and crafts. Snack bar, rest rooms, h/a. Ample parking. Spaces $3. Overnight parking. *Contact* John Behman, 603 Dallas St., 35801.

Limestone Flea Market
U.S. Hwy. 72
(256) 233-5183

Saturday, 8 a.m.–5 p.m., Sunday, 9 a.m.–5 p.m. This is one of the area's largest indoor markets; outdoor space is also available. New and used merchandise, imports, gifts, collectibles, sportswear, housewares, electronics, and tools available. Indoor market is a 62,000-square-foot building situated on 40 acres. Plenty of parking for buses and RVs.

I-565 Trade Mart
Corner of University Dr. and Washington St.
(256) 534-7960

Wednesday–Sunday. Indoor and outdoor market, has commercial vendors with large loads of new merchandise. If you are looking for deals on new merchandise, this is the place to bring a big truck and lots of cash. Market also conducts many special events. Food available, rest rooms, h/a. Ample parking. Camping available, showers on grounds.

Madison Flea Market
8600 W. Hwy. 72, I-65, exit Hwy. 72, nine miles east

Saturday, Sunday, 8 a.m.–5 p.m. Approximately 200 vendors. Indoor and outdoor market. Books, new and used merchandise, clothing and furniture. Antiques, collectibles, produce, crafts, tools. Snack bar, rest rooms, h/a. Space from $10. *Contact* Jim Case (256) 837-1880.

JASPER

Kelly's Flea Market
Hwy. 78, 3 miles east of town

Wednesday, Saturday, Sunday, dawn to dusk. Outdoor market with approximately 40 dealers. New and used merchandise, garage sale items, gifts, imports, crafts, produce. Space from $44. Snack bar, rest room. *Contact* Ray Fowler, 10016 Hwy. 78, 35504 (205) 483-6045.

KILLEN

Uncle Charlie's Flea Market
Hwy. 72 West, five miles east of Florence

Saturday, Sunday, 9 a.m.–5 p.m. Indoor market with approximately 400 dealers. Reservations required. Space from $25 for the weekend. Snack bars, rest rooms, h/a. *Contact* Tom Mabry, Box 190, 35645 (800) 542-2848.

LACON

Lacon Trade Days
Hwy. 31 South
(205) 784-5091

Saturday, Sunday. Good range of merchandise here from lots of new and imports to second-hand items. Some collectibles, primitives, country items, memorabilia, and crafts. Snack bar, rest rooms, h/a. Ample parking.

MADISON

Limestone Flea Market
Hwy. 72 at Burgreen Rd.

Saturday, Sunday, 9 a.m.–5 p.m. Indoor market with approximately 200 dealers. Antiques, collectibles, new and used merchandise. Space from $40 for the weekend. Snack bars, rest rooms, h/a. Overnight camping. *Contact* Manager, 30030 Hwy. 72, 35756 (256) 233-5183, fax (256) 233-1415.

MIDLAND CITY

Alabama Flea Market
Hwy. 231
Across street from Jimmy's Smoke House
(334) 983-1795 or 983-4371

Friday, Saturday, Sunday, 8 a.m. until dark. The market averages over 50 dealers, indoor, outdoor, and covered spaces. New and used merchandise: bric-a-brac, housewares, collectibles, primitives, and crafts are available. Snack bar, rest rooms, h/a. Ample parking. Space from $3 outside. Overnight camping available.

MILLBROOK

Bonanza Farmers & Flea Market
I-65 North, Exit 179
(334) 285-5145

Saturday, Sunday. Lots of flea market merchandise, plus antiques, collectibles, furniture, country and farm items, and locally made crafts. Food available, rest rooms, h/a, ample parking. Inside and outside space available from $5 inside and $3 outside. *Contact* Mrs. Chris Norris, Box 485, 36054.

MOBILE

Traders Village Flea Market
9700 Cleste Rd.
Five miles west of I-65, Exit 15, North Mobile
(334) 675-5569

Saturday, Sunday. Average daily attendance is 2,000. New and used merchandise, collectibles, tools, primitives, crafts. Snack bar, rest rooms, h/a, ample parking. Space from $20 per weekend.

Flea Market Mobile
Airport Blvd., Exit W to 401 Schillinger Rd. North
(334) 633-7533 or 633-7571
Fax (334) 639-0570

Saturday, Sunday, 9 a.m.–5 p.m. The average weekend attendance is 20,000 with over 450 dealers in lots of covered spaces. Great selection of antiques and collectibles, including nice selection of antique furniture. New and used merchandise, coins, crafts, produce. No snakes allowed. Clean rest rooms and snack bar, h/a. Ample parking. Space from $20 for weekend, $2 for electricity. Reservations recommended. Camping with showers and electricity available. *Contact* Flea Market Mobile, Daryl Thompson, 401 Schillinger Rd. North, 36608.

Malfunction Junction
7721 Hwy. 90
At 15A mile marker on I-10
West at Hwy. 90
(334) 653-5549

Daily. New and used merchandise with lots of good collectibles at this market. Snack bar, rest rooms, h/a. Ample parking. Spaces from $3 per day, tables and electricity available. Camping available on grounds. *Contact* Malfunction Junction, 7721 Hwy. 90, 36601.

Fairgrounds
(601) 939-8596

Every second weekend. Antiques, collectibles, new and used merchandise, crafts. Food available, rest rooms, h/a. Ample parking. *Contact* Larry Emery.

Po Boy Flea Market
5250 Moffat Rd.
(334) 343-2722

Thursday–Sunday. Approximately 50 dealers offer lots of flea market merchandise, some new merchandise, collectibles, crafts. Rest rooms, snack bar, h/a. Ample parking. Space from $5 per day. Camping available.

South Alabama Flea Market
I-10, Exit 13, south 1 mile
(334) 653-4736 or 653-5483

Daily. This market averages 40 dealers using indoor and outdoor spaces, some covered. Some new merchandise, mostly used and secondhand items, good selection of primitives, collectibles, and advertising items. Clean rest rooms and snack bar, h/a. Ample parking. Food concessions welcome. Overnight camping available. *Contact* Marie Massengill, 6511 Highmount Dr., Theodore, 36582.

MONTGOMERY

Washington Ferry Flea Market
Washington Ferry Rd.
Two miles from Hwy. 31
(334) 262-4608

Every second Saturday, March–December. Approximately 300 dealers offer a wide range of goods new and used, collectibles, antiques, crafts, primitives, memorabilia. Good market to look for treasures. Food available, rest rooms, h/a. Ample parking and lots of walking. Space from $10. Overnight camping available.

Montgomery Flea Market and Arts & Crafts Shows
Alcazar Shrine Temple
(334) 279-9174

Last Saturday of each month, April–September, call to confirm dates. Antiques, collectibles, memorabilia, decorator items, lots of quality crafts. Food available, rest rooms, h/a. Ample parking.

ALWAYS CALL BEFORE TRAVELING LONG DISTANCES!

Montgomery's Gigantic Indoor Flea Market
2270 E. South Blvd., one block west of Wal-Mart

Friday, noon–6 p.m., Saturday, Sunday, 9 a.m.–6 p.m. New market, opened in 1999. Approximately 200 dealers. Antiques, collectibles, new and used merchandise. Snack bar, rest rooms, h/a, ample parking. Space from $10 per day. *Contact* Barbara Butler, 2270 E. south Blvd., 36116 (334) 286-5005, fax (334) 281-2404.

MOODY

Smith Trade Days
Hwy. 441 North
(205) 640-6444

Friday, Sunday. Wide range of merchandise here, lots of secondhand items, tools, housewares, collectibles, and country and farm items. Snack bar, rest rooms, h/a. Ample parking and lots of walking.

MUSCLE SHOALS

North Alabama Flea Market
North Alabama Fairgrounds, Hwy. 43 South
(800) 672-8988 or (256) 764-6400

Every second weekend. Antiques, collectibles, memorabilia, primitives, farm items, used merchandise, bric-a-brac. Snack bar, rest rooms, h/a. Ample parking. *Contact* Michael Epperson, 254 Seville St., #3, Florence, AL 35360.

PHENIX CITY

Valley Flea & Farmers Market
3864 Hwy. 80 West
(334) 291-1496 or 298-3728

Wednesday, Friday, Saturday, Sunday. Indoor and outdoor market with over 100 dealers with lots of secondhand merchandise, tools, clothes, crafts, and new items. Pony rides. Clean rest rooms and snack bar. Ample parking. Market is themed more like a carnival than a flea market. Space from $5. Camping nearby. *Contact* Gene Stafford, 3864 U.S. Hwy. 80 West, 36869.

PRATTVILLE

T & G's Flea and Antique Mall
742 E. Main St.
I–65 North to Exit 179, left on Cobbs Ford Rd. (becomes Main St. about 4 miles on left, just past Hwy. 31)
(334) 361-4500
e-mail: thebrock5@bigfoot.com

Monday–Saturday, 9 a.m.–5 p.m., Sunday, 1 a.m.–5 p.m. Indoor, permanent booths. Antiques, collectibles, new and used merchandise. Over 225 vendors. Snack bar, rest rooms, ample parking, h/a. Space from $1.20 per square foot—reservations required. *Contact* Tina or Gloria.

ROBERTSDALE

First Weekend Trade Days
(205) 947-5932

First weekend of each month, 8 a.m.–5 p.m. Average attendance of 2,500 with over 100 dealers. Excellent market for collectibles, antiques, antique furniture, and quality decorator items, although no new merchandise is allowed. This is an excellent market for the shopkeeper, dealer, serious collector. Good food, rest rooms, h/a. Ample parking and lots of walking is required. Spaces from $7. Electricity available. Camping nearby. *Contact* Chamber of Commerce, Box 587, 36567.

SCOTTSBORO

First Monday Trade Days
Downtown, Courthouse Square
(256) 574-4468
Fax (256) 574-4339

Sunday, Monday, dawn until dark. There are about 250–300 dealers. This is one of the South's oldest and largest trade day events. Antiques, crafts, lots of secondhand merchandise, antique furniture, collectibles, primitives, and other interesting things. This market can easily be a two-day adventure. If you are looking for some quality items at a fair price, then this is a market for you. Lots of good food here, rest rooms, h/a. Ample parking but a lot of walking is required at the market, and you may have to park a good distance from the market. Space from $5 per day. *Contact* Chamber of Commerce, Gayle Swafford, 409 S. Broad St., 35768.

SELMA

Selma Flea Market
Hwy. 80 and River Rd. (Selma Bypass)
(334) 875-0500

Saturday, Sunday, 5 a.m. until dark. This market has approximately 400 vendors. Covered spaces and outdoor spaces featuring antiques, furniture, toys, crafts, produce, collectibles, and livestock—a wide range of goods here. Clean, friendly, well-managed market. Snack bar, rest rooms, h/a. Ample parking. RV park next to market. Space from $8 per day under cover, $5 outside. *Contact* Gary Maluda, 606 River Rd., 36703.

SMITHS

Lee County Flea Market
431 N. 280 at Lee County Hwy. 87
Old West Point Rd. Exit 62 from I-85
(334) 291-7780 or (800) 835-0498

Sunday only. Average daily attendance 2,500 with approximately 50 exhibitors. New merchandise, housewares, sportswear, antiques, and collectibles available with lots of advertising items, primitives, and farm items. Snack bar, rest rooms, h/a. Ample parking. Space from $3 to $12. Camping available. *Contact* Ruth or Bryant Williams, Box 471, 36877.

SUMMERDALE

Highway 59 Flea Market
Intersection of Hwys. 59 and 32
Between Robertsdal and Foley
(334) 989-6642
Fax (334) 989-6809

Friday, Saturday, Sunday, dawn to dusk. Average attendance 9,000 with over 300 dealers.

Wide variety of merchandise with a friendly country atmosphere. This is a market that is fun for both the buyer and seller. Travel trailer park, mobile home park on premises. Discount furniture store and antique shops on premises open daily. Good selection of antiques and collectibles in the shops. Good food, rest rooms, h/a. Ample parking. Year-round market. Over 1,200 square feet of covered tables, with electricity for each. Twenty-three acres and space for dealers who wish to bring their own tables or displays. *Contact* Jeff Smith, 804 S. Hwy. 59, 36580.

TACOBET

Tacobet Trade Days
Hwy. 40
(205) 477-5711 or 845-4725

Sundays only, 6 a.m.–6 p.m. Almost 7,000 attendees are here with approximately 250 dealers participating. Wide range of goods at this market: antiques, collectibles, crafts, new and used merchandise, and lots of farm and country primitives. Food available, rest rooms, h/a. Ample parking and lots of walking is required. Space from $3. *Contact* Russell Paul, Rte. 40, 35744.

TUSCALOOSA

Tuscaloosa County Flea Market
Kicker Rd.

Friday, Saturday, Sunday, 8 a.m.–5 p.m. Indoor market with approximately 25 dealers. Mostly used merchandise, imports, locally made crafts. Rest room, ample parking. *Contact* Orman Corbin (205) 533-9206.

WESTOVER

Highway 280 Flea Market
Hwy. 280 and Westover St.
Mile marker 21.5
(205) 678-6729

Friday, Saturday, Sunday, 8 a.m.–6 p.m. New and used merchandise, collectibles, primitives, crafts, country items, tools. Food available, rest rooms, h/a. Ample parking. *Contact* Jeff Boomhower.

WETUMPKA

Trading Post Flea Market
Hwy. 14 West
(334) 567-7728

Friday, Saturday, Sunday. New merchandise, closeouts, surplus, used merchandise, collectibles, crafts, produce, gifts, imports, country items, primitives. Snack bar, rest rooms, h/a. Ample parking. Space from $5 per day. Campground with electricity. Auction on Friday night.

Santuck Flea Market
Twenty-five miles north of Montgomery,
Rte. 231 North to Hwy. 9, then 6 miles to the right
(334) 567-7400

Every first Saturday, March–December. New and used merchandise, tools, collectibles, crafts. Snack bar, rest rooms. Ample parking. *Contact* Jack Johnson, 662 Dexter Rd., 36092.

WINFIELD

Monkey's Flea Market
Hwy. W
(205) 487-6802

Saturdays only. New and used merchandise, garage sale items, bric-a-brac, crafts, primitives, collectibles. Snack bar, rest rooms, h/a. Ample parking.

INFORMATION IS SUBJECT TO CHANGE—ALWAYS CALL FIRST!

ALASKA

ANCHORAGE

Downtown Saturday Flea Market
Third and E Sts., parking lot, across from the Hilton Hotel

Saturdays from Memorial Day to Labor Day weekend, 10 a.m.–6 p.m. Outdoor market with approximately 250 dealers. Reservations required. Antiques, collectibles, new and used merchandise, produce, locally made arts and crafts. Space from $25. This is considered the largest market in Alaska. Rest rooms, food available, ample parking. *Contact* Bill Webb, Box 102440, 99510 (907) 272-5634. E-mail: Saturdaymarket@alaskalife.net.

Downtown Wednesday Flea Market
On Fourth Ave. from C to F Sts. and on D and F Sts.

Wednesdays, from early July to the end of August, 10 a.m.–8 p.m. Outdoor market with approximately 100 dealers. Antiques, collectibles, new and used merchandise, produce, locally made arts and crafts. Food available, rest rooms, ample parking. *Contact* Diana Arthur, Box 102440, 99510 (907) 272-5634.

Note: Anyone having information about Alaskan flea markets, please send the information to us at Jim Goodridge, P.O. Box 744, Arnold, MO 63010. E-mail: fleamktusa@aol.com.

FAIRBANKS

Fairbanks Flea Market
Tanana Valley Fairgrounds
(907) 452-3750

Monthly, call for dates. This is probably Alaska's best regular flea market. New and used merchandise, sportswear, tools, electronics, toys, antiques, collectibles, jewelry (both fine and costume). Many quality booths here. Snack bar, rest rooms, h/a, ample parking.

KENAI

Kenai Flea Market
Downtown
(907) 283-7501

Monthly, call for dates. New and used merchandise, lots of secondhand and garage sale items. Snack bar, rest rooms, h/a, ample parking.

SEWARD

American Legion Flea Market
402 5th Ave., American Legion Building

Thursday–Saturday, noon–4 p.m. Indoor market. *Contact* Helen Nelson, 402 5th Ave., 99664 (907) 224-5440.

ARIZONA

APACHE JUNCTION

Apache Park-N-$wap
2651 W. Apache Trail
(480) 288-0571

Friday–Sunday, October–April; Monday, Friday, May–September, 7 a.m.–4 p.m. There are approximately 900 dealers with average attendance of about 20,000 per weekend. One of the West's better markets. New and used merchandise, lots of western and Indian items and jewelry. Great selection of merchandise at this market, virtually every category covered by quality dealers. No food vendors. No guns, ammunition, pornography. Good food, rest rooms, h/a, ample parking. Reservations recommended. Space from $10. *Contact* Bud Gray, 13480 West Hwy. 84, Casa Grande, 85222.

United Swap Meet
950 E. Baseline Rd.
(480) 983-2524

Thursday–Sunday. Indoor market with air conditioning. New and used merchandise, housewares, sportswear, lots of new collectibles, jewelry. Snack bar, rest rooms, h/a, ample parking. Spaces from $5 per day.

BLACK CANYON

Black Canyon Park-N-Swap
Hwy. 17

Saturday, Sunday. There are about 100 dealers who offer western clothes, Indian jewelry, new and used merchandise, sportswear, collectibles, and farm and ranch items. Snack bar, rest rooms, h/a, ample parking. Space from $2. *Contact* Jack Sipe, Box 25, 85324 (602) 374-5434.

BULLHEAD CITY

Bud's Highway 95 Flea Market
5005 Hwy. 95
(520) 768-3103

Monday–Saturday. Indoor/outdoor market with antiques, collectibles, crafts, furniture, new merchandise. There are approximately 150 dealers during the winter and about 25 dealers in the summer. Space is rented by the month. Snack bar, rest rooms, h/a, ample parking. *Contact* Jean, 5005 Hwy. 95, 86426.

CASA GRANDE

The Shopper's Barn Swap Meet
5650 N. 55th Ave., Exit 10, Hwy. 84, west two miles

Saturday, Sunday, 5 a.m.–3 p.m. Admission 50 cents. Approximately 125 dealers. Lots of nice antiques and collectibles here. New and secondhand merchandise, western items, farm and ranch items, produce. Snack bar, rest rooms, h/a, ample parking. Space from $5. Camping available. *Contact* Bud Gray, Box 10250, 85239 (520) 836-1934.

CHANDLER

Manufacturers and Merchants Flea Market
670 N. Arizona Ave. 85224

Friday, Saturday, Sunday, 10 a.m.–4 p.m. Lots of new merchandise, surplus, closeouts. Some collectibles, western items, crafts. Snack bar, rest rooms, h/a, ample parking.

FLAGSTAFF

Big Tree Swap Meet
6500 N. Hwy. 89
(520) 526-2538

Saturday, Sunday. Lots of new merchandise, Indian jewelry, and Indian art and collectibles. General line of collectibles, used merchandise, farm and ranch items. Snack bar, rest rooms, h/a, ample parking.

GLENDALE

Thunderbird Swap Meet and Bargain Jamboree
5533 N. 59th Ave.

Wednesday, Saturday, Sunday. Average daily attendance of 5,000. Approximately 300 dealers. Large well-stocked outdoor market. Lots of new merchandise, imports, and electronics, as well as used merchandise, housewares, tools. New sportswear, western wear, and Indian jewelry and art. Rest rooms, snack bar, h/a, ample parking. Spaces $7 to $12. *Contact* Buddy Goodman (602) 934-SWAP or 931-0877.

Glendale Swap Meet
5630 N. 55th Ave.
Glendale Drive-In Theater

Friday, Saturday, Sunday. Admission 50 cents. Average daily attendance 5,000 with over 300 dealers. New and secondhand merchandise, crafts, antiques, collectibles, produce, toys. Snack bars, rest rooms, h/a, ample parking. Camping available. Space from $20 for the weekend. *Contact* Charles Barone (602) 931-0877 or 230-7922, fax (623) 981-8135.

GOODYEAR

Goodyear Park N Swap
W. Van Buren and Cotton Lane
(602) 853-9300

Saturday, Sunday. New and used merchandise, farm and ranch items, Indian jewelry, collectibles and art, western wear, and western items. Snack bar, rest rooms, h/a. Covered spaces from $4. Ample parking.

Goodyear Market Place Swap Meet
17605 W. McDowell
(623) 853-1488

Friday, Saturday, Sunday. New indoor market. Snack bar, rest rooms, h/a.

HAVASU CITY

Flea Market
Smoketree and McCullough Sts.

Saturday, Sunday. Approximately 100 dealers. Well-rounded variety of merchandise here, new merchandise, sportswear, housewares, electronics. Used merchandise, tools, toys. Collectibles, crafts, Indian jewelry and art, western wear and western items. Food available, rest rooms, h/a. Ample parking. *Contact* Claypool and Co., 725 Broadway, Needles, CA 92363 (714) 326-2109.

KINGMAN

Route 66 Flea Market
off I-40 on eastbound Rte. 66
(520) 692-1428

Friday, Saturday, Sunday, 8 a.m.–4 p.m. Outdoor market with approximately 50 dealers. New and used merchandise. Western wear and ranch items. Indian jewelry and Indian collectibles. Rest rooms, snack bar, ample parking.

MESA

Mesa Market Place Swap Meet
10550 E. Baseline
East on Hwy. 60 to Exit 193 and Signal Butte Rd. Make a right at light to Baseline Rd. and then turn right, entrance is on right.

Friday, Saturday, Sunday, 7 a.m.–4 p.m. Swap meet with covered spaces and totally paved. Antiques, collectibles, new and used merchandise, produce, crafts, Indian jewelry. Food facilities with free parking and free entertainment, rest rooms, h/a. *Contact* Tricia Curran, 10550 E. Baseline, 85208 (480) 380-5572 or 380-7467, fax (480) 380-5578.

MOJAVE

Mojave Swap Meet
5005 Hwy. 95
Twelve miles south of Laughlin, Nevada, or 12 miles north of Needles, California.

Daily, 7:30 a.m.–4:30 p.m. Open every day except Monday. Outdoor/indoor market with approximately 150 dealers in the winter and down to about 25 during the summer months. *Contact* Manager, 5005 Hwy. 95, 86426 (520) 768-3103.

PARKER

Claypool Shopping Center Flea Market
Claypool Shopping Center
(520) 326-2101

First and third Saturday. New merchandise, used merchandise, Indian jewelry, art and artifacts, western wear, and collectibles and antiques. Snack bar, rest rooms, h/a, ample paved parking.

PEORIA

Peoria Swap Meet
12040 N. 91st Ave.
(602) 979-1003

Wednesday, Saturday, Sunday. Average daily attendance is 5,000. Large well-stocked outdoor market with lots of new and used merchandise, imports, closeouts, clothes, tools, Indian jewelry, art and artifacts, western wear and western and ranch collectibles, crafts, and produce. Food available. Rest rooms, h/a, ample parking; 350 spaces starting at $4. *Contact* Peoria Swap Meet, 12040 N. 91st Ave., 85345.

DAYS, DATES, AND MARKETS ARE SUBJECT TO CHANGE!

Grand Avenue Swap Meet
Old Glendale Airport
Corner of 79th Ave. and Grand Ave.
(602) 230-7927

Friday, Saturday, Sunday. Large outdoor market with approximately 350 dealers in the winter and 75 during the summer months. New and used merchandise, lots of garage sale dealers, crafts, produce, collectibles. Snack bars, rest rooms, h/a, ample paved parking. Space from $10. *Contact* Bob Whittington, 7855 N.W. Grand, 85345.

PHOENIX

Fairgrounds Antique Market
1826 W. McDowell (Fairgrounds)
(602) 943-1766 or (800) 678-9987
Fax (602) 997-4686

Every third weekend, Saturday, 9 a.m.–5 p.m., Sunday, 9 a.m.–4 p.m. There are approximately 100 dealers. Excellent collectibles market with many fine antiques, coins, collections, and crafts. Snack bar, rest rooms, h/a, ample paved parking. Camping available. Space from $75 for 10×16. Reservations advised. *Contact* Jack Black, Box 61172, 85082.

Paradise Valley Swap Meet
2414 E. Union Hills Dr.

Friday, Saturday, Sunday, 5 a.m.–3 p.m. Antiques, collectibles, new and used merchandise, clothing, produce. Space from $10 per day. Snack bars, ample parking, rest rooms, h/a. *Contact* Viola Cirio, 2414 E. Union Hills Dr., 85024 (602) 569-0052.

Phoenix Indoor Swap Meet
5115 N. 27th Ave.

Friday, Saturday, Sunday, 8 a.m.–6 p.m. Admission charge. Indoor market with approximately 300 dealers. Lots of new merchandise, gifts, imports, western items, Indian jewelry and Indian collectibles. Crafts, produce. Snack bars, rest rooms, h/a. Free parking. *Contact* Michelle Leslie (602) 246-9600.

Phoenix Trade Fair
3839 W. Indian School Rd.
(602) 278-6221

Friday, noon–9 p.m., Saturday, Sunday, 8 a.m.–5 p.m. There are approximately 100 dealers. Lots of new merchandise, closeouts, overruns, used merchandise, collectibles, crafts. Snack bar, rest rooms, ample parking, h/a. Inside and outside spaces. Outside starts at $6 for 10×15. Inside varies. *Contact* Kathy Cline, 3839 W. Indian School Rd., 85019.

Swap-A-Rama
75th and W. Southern
(602) 237-9915

Saturday, Sunday. New merchandise, sportswear, electronics, housewares, collectibles, artifacts and art, western wear, and western collectibles. Snack bar, rest rooms, h/a, ample parking. Spaces from $3. Camping available. *Contact* Edie Roer.

Swap-O-Rama
3636 S. 48th St.
I-10 and 48th St.
(602) 968-8609

Saturday, Sunday. There are approximately 500 dealers with a wide variety of merchandise—good place to buy at wholesale. Good market to acquire Indian jewelry and art for resale. Outdoor market. Snack bars, rest rooms, h/a, ample paved parking. Acres of walking required. Space from $5. Reservations recommended. *Contact* William Stevens Sr. 3636 S. 48th St., 85040.

American Park-N-Swap Flea Market
3801 E. Washington St.
One mile north of Sky Harbor International Airport
(602) 273-1259 or (800) 772-0852
Fax (602) 273-7375
e-mail: ppns0010@aol.com

Wednesday, 4 a.m.–10 p.m., Friday, 6 a.m.–2 p.m., Saturday, Sunday, 6 a.m.–4 p.m. Admission $1. Average attendance 30,000 per weekend with 1,000 dealers. This is one of the largest and most diverse markets in the area. Wide variety of merchandise at this market including good Indian jewelry. Plenty of good food here. Rest rooms, h/a, ample parking for $2. Much walking is required at this market. Camping available, reservations recommended. Spaces start at $10 for Saturday and Sunday and $5 on Friday. *Contact* Richard Hogue, 3801 E. Washington, 85034.

7th Street Trade-Save-Swap Meet
709 E. Broadway
(602) 276-7183

Wednesday–Sunday. Approximately 80 vendors. New merchandise, used merchandise, collectibles, antiques, crafts, produce. Snack bars, rest rooms, h/a, ample parking. Spaces from $4 Wednesday to $8 for Saturday and Sunday. Electricity available. Reservations recommended. *Contact* Dick Jones, 709 E. Broadway, 85050.

PRESCOTT

Peddler's Pass Flea Market
2201 Clubhouse Dr.
Six miles east of Prescott on Hwy. 69
(520) 775-4117

Friday, Saturday, Sunday, 8 a.m.–4 p.m. Average weekend attendance 9,000 with 200 vendors. Clean, friendly, well-attended market with good selection of merchandise, lots of fine Indian jewelry. Very nice food concession, rest rooms, h/a, ample parking. Space from $8 to $20. Overnight privilege on all spaces. *Contact* Bob Scott, 2201 Clubhouse Dr., 86301.

QUARTZSITE

Annual Gemboree and The Main Event
I-10 at mile marker 17
(520) 927-5213

Scheduled periodically, call or write for dates. One of the largest winter and spring markets in the country. This is truly a unique American event with 1,500 exhibitors and thousands of customers from around the world. It takes two or three days to cover this market; many high-quality items here. This stop takes up an entire vacation. Lots of Native American entertainment, wide variety of food, special events. Parking can be difficult, and there is a lot of walking required. Camping and everything you need is available here. Company has 16-page brochure available. Spaces are 18×32 from $230. *Contact* Howard Armstrong, Box 2801, 85346, fax (520) 927-4496. E-mail: mainevent@redrivemet.com.

Garden's Swap & Show
Frontage Rd., off I-10, Exit 17
(520) 927-6848 or 927-5555

Friday, Saturday, Sunday. Approximately 200 spaces for vendors. New market with jewelry, collectibles, new merchandise. Market has restaurant, antique car and mining museum. Market hosts Native American ceremonies on weekends; 200-unit mobile home and RV park next door. Rest rooms, electricity, and water.

SAFFORD

Safford Swap Meet
Fairgrounds, Hwy. 666
(602) 428-6341

Friday, Saturday, Sunday. Outdoor market with approximately 300 dealers. Large, well-stocked market with lots of new and used merchandise, collectibles, crafts, primitives, western collectibles. Good buys on quality Indian jewelry and art here. Snack bars, rest rooms, h/a, ample paved parking. Camping available.

SCOTTSDALE

Scottsdale Swap Meet
8101 McKellips St.
Scottsdale Drive-In Theater

Friday, Saturday, Sunday, 5 a.m.–3 p.m. Admission 25 cents. Average daily attendance is 3–4,000 with approximately 200 dealers. Good selection here, some antiques, lots of collectibles and bric-a-brac, new and secondhand merchandise, good selection of Indian and costume jewelry, produce. Snack bar, clean rest rooms, h/a, ample parking. Camping nearby. Space from $5. *Contact* Ed Nezelek or Barbara Klein (602) 994-3709.

SOUTH TUCSON

South Tucson Park N Swap
2601 S. 3rd Ave.
(520) 623-4012

Saturday, Sunday. Outdoor market with approximately 350 dealers. Large well-stocked market with many quality dealers. New, antique, crafts, collectibles, and produce sold here. Food available, rest rooms, h/a, ample parking. Space from $4. *Contact* Dan Martiniz, 2601 S. 3rd Ave., 85713.

SURPRISE

Surprise Swap Meet
12912 Santa Fe Dr.
(623) 583-1616

Thursday 3 p.m. until dark, Saturday, Sunday, 5 a.m. until dark. Average daily attendance 4–5,000 with approximately 200 dealers. Lots of new merchandise, good collectibles, and interesting junk. Good food on premises, h/a, ample parking. Call for reservations. Spaces from $5. *Contact* Convention Center Swap Meet, 12912 W. Santa Fe Dr., 85374.

TUCSON

Wilmot Bazaar & Swap Meet
Wilmot St. and I-10
Exit 269 from I-10
(520) 574-2772 or 574-0191

Friday, Saturday, Sunday. Outdoor market with approximately 400 spaces averaging 125 dealers. New market. Good selection of items here with new, secondhand, antiques, books, crafts, Indian items, and collectibles. Camping available, showers on grounds, convenience store, cafe and beer garden on premises; h/a, ample parking. *Contact* Wayne Dennis, 7011 E. Rosewood, 85710.

Tanque Verde Swap Meet
4100 S. Palo Verde Rd.
Palo Verde exit from I-10
(520) 294-4252

Thursday, Friday, Saturday, Sunday, 7 a.m.–11 p.m. Approximately 750 dealers in this large outdoor market. Lots of southwestern and Indian jewelry and collectibles related to the West. New merchandise, crafts, some antiques and collectibles. Good variety of food here, rest rooms, h/a, ample parking. Space from $12. *Contact* Ken Fiore, Box 19095, 85731 fax (520) 294-2358.

MarketPlace USA
3750 E. Irvington Rd.
I-10, Palo Verde Exit, east to Irvington
(520) 745-5000

Friday, Saturday, Sunday. Large indoor market approximately 300 dealers. New merchandise, electronics, housewares, several specialty shops, some antiques and collectibles. Great prices on hot new merchandise and super bargains on closeouts, surplus, and overruns. Food, a sports bar, rest rooms, h/a, ample paved parking. Space rental by the month and reservations are required. Note: This market produces a lot of special events; call for current schedule. *Contact* Brian Weeks, 3750 E. Irvington Rd., 85714.

YUMA

Arizona Avenue Swap Meet
1749 Arizona Ave.

Daily, 8 a.m.–5 p.m. Outdoor market with approximately 75 dealers. Antiques, collectibles, new and used merchandise, garage sale and bric-a-brac items. Space from $6. Snack bar, rest rooms, h/a, ample parking. *Contact* Bob Butcher, 1749 Arizona Ave., 85365 (520) 343-1837.

Avenue 3E South Swap Meet
4151 S. Ave. 3E
(520) 344-2399

Saturday, Sunday, October–June. The average attendance is 3–5,000 daily. There are over 250 spaces for vendors. New merchandise, used merchandise, tools, farm and ranch items, crafts, produce, Indian jewelry, western wear, and western collectibles. Food, rest rooms, h/a, ample parking. Dealers can set up at noon on Friday for the weekend.

Yuma Park-N-Swap
4000 4th Ave.
(800) 722-6811 or (520) 726-4655
Fax (520) 344-0115

Saturday, Sunday, 6 a.m.–4 p.m. Average attendance 7,500 with approximately 250 dealers. New merchandise, imports, surplus, used merchandise, tools, housewares, Indian jewelry and art, and western wear. Snack bars, rest rooms, h/a, ample parking. Excellent winter market. Spaces from $5 per day. *Contact* Bill Gresser, 4000 S. 4th Ave., 85365. E-mail: bill@gresser.com.

ALWAYS CALL AHEAD TO VERIFY DATES AND INFORMATION

ARKANSAS

BATESVILLE

America's Flea Market
310 W. Main St.
Lower end of downtown
(870) 793-7508

Friday, Saturday, Sunday, 9 a.m.–6 p.m. There are approximately 150 dealers with indoor and outdoor booths. Antiques, collectibles, advertising items, glassware, memorabilia, and new merchandise are offered. Food available, rest rooms, h/a, ample parking. Advance reservations required. Space from $25 for the weekend. *Contact* Mark Davis, 310 W. Main St., 72501.

CONWAY

Pickles Gap Craft & Flea Market
Hwy. 65 North
(501) 327-6028 or 327-8049

Saturday, Sunday. New and used merchandise, garage sale items, bric-a-brac, collectibles, good selection of locally made crafts. Rest rooms, h/a, ample parking.

DAMASCUS

Ozarks Traders Weekend
I-40, Exit 125
(501) 45-CRAFT

Every second weekend. Antiques, great selection of locally made crafts, collectibles, primitives, used farm items, vintage clothing. Rest rooms, food available, h/a, ample parking.

DOVER

Linker Mountain Flea Market
Four miles north of I-40
(501) 967-2480

Friday, Sunday. There are approximately 30 vendors. Market is mainly used merchandise, antiques, collectibles, and primitives. New merchandise welcome. Rest rooms, ample parking. Space from $3 outside and $5 inside. *Contact* Don Sehorn, Rte. 7, Box 117, Russellville, 72801.

FAYETTEVILLE

Highway 62 Flea Market
Hwy. 62 West
One mile west of 71 bypass
(501) 442-6818

Friday, Saturday, Sunday, 9 a.m.–5 p.m. Indoor and outdoor market with new and used merchandise, housewares, tools, electronics, sportswear, farm items, collectibles, advertising items. Food available, rest rooms, h/a, ample parking.

FT. SMITH

Zero Street Flea Market
2425 S. Zero St.

Friday, Sunday. Good selection of new merchandise and used items. Primitives, collectibles, crafts. Food available, rest rooms, h/a, ample parking. *Contact* Tom McGovern, 72902 (501) 783-9909.

Fort Smith Flea Market
3721 Towson Ave.
(501) 646-1502

Friday, Sunday, 9 a.m.–5 p.m.. There are over 50 dealers offering new and used merchandise, antiques, collectibles, sportswear, and tools. Snack bar, rest rooms, h/a, ample parking.

At Simon Etc. Flea Market
923 Louisville
(501) 646-3710

Friday, Sunday, 8 a.m.–6 p.m. This indoor market offers Indian artifacts, coins, jewelry, tools, crafts, dolls, kitchenware, silver, and books. Snack bar, rest rooms, h/a, ample parking.

GREENBRIER

Springhill Flea Market
Hwy. 65, north of the junction of Rtes. 65 and 287

Daily, 10 a.m.–5 p.m. Small indoor market with approximately 20 dealers. Lots of collectibles, gifts, crafts here. Rest room. *Contact* Bill Wisler (501) 679-9106.

HOT SPRINGS

Hot Springs Flea Market & Antique Mall
2138 Higdon Ferry Rd.

Daily, 10 a.m.–6 p.m. There are approximately 80 dealers offering lots of antiques, a good selection of antique furniture, collectibles, glassware, and unusually large amounts of country crafts at this market. Good food, rest rooms, h/a. Camping available. Antique mall section of market is open daily. Space $7.50 per day. *Contact* Doyce Garner, Higdon Ferry Rd., 71913 (501) 525-9927, fax (501) 525-9304.

Snow Springs Flea Market
3628 Park Ave.

Friday, Saturday, Sunday. Outdoor market with approximately 25 dealers. Snack bar, rest rooms. *Contact* J. L. Long (501) 624-7469.

LITTLE ROCK

Giant Flea Market
8610 New Benton Hwy.
I-30, Exit 130 or 132

Saturday, Sunday, 8 a.m.–5 p.m. Average daily attendance 3,500 to this indoor/outdoor market that hosts approximately 75 dealers. Lots of new merchandise, bric-a-brac, and collectibles. Snack bar, rest room. Spaces $22.50 per weekend. *Contact* Hall Purses (501) 565-9915.

Flea Market
Arkansas State Fairgrounds

Every second and fourth weekend. Admission $1. Antiques, collectibles, crafts, new, and used merchandise. Food available, rest rooms, h/a, ample paved parking. *Contact* Jim Hembree (501) 455-1001.

Carrie's Flea Market
8717 Geyer Springs Rd.

Monday–Saturday, 8 a.m.–5 p.m. Contact Henrietta Grainger (501) 562-8088.

MOUNTAIN HOME

The Alko Flea Market
Hwy. 62 East
(870) 425-9942 or 424-2815

Friday, Sunday. This indoor/outdoor market has approximately 40 dealers. New merchandise, sportswear, housewares, used merchandise, crafts, produce. Snack bar, rest rooms, h/a, ample parking. Space from $5. Camping available. Electricity and water available.

PINE BLUFF

I-270 Flea Market
8112 Sheridan Rd.
I-270 to Pine Bluff Exit
(870) 247-9957

Sundays only. Antiques, collectibles, vintage jewelry, clothing, and glassware. Rest rooms, h/a. *Contact* Francis Lewis.

PLEASANT PLAINS

Pleasant Plains Flea Market
Hwy. 167
6830 Batesville Blvd.

Friday, Saturday, Sunday, 7 a.m.–6 p.m. Indoor/outdoor market with approximately 50 dealers, offering collectibles, toys, vintage clothing, books, used merchandise, and tools. Food, rest rooms, h/a, ample parking. Clean, friendly market. Camping available. *Contact* Lonnie Bolden, P.O. Box 201, 72568 (501) 345-2720 or (870) 668-3434.

POTTSVILLE

Pottsville Flea & Farmers Market
Hwy. 64
(501) 968-3235

Friday, Sunday. New and used merchandise, collectibles, produce, livestock, and farm items available. Snack bar, rest rooms, h/a, ample parking. Inside and outside spaces from $3 per day.

ROGERS

Rose Hall Flea & Craft Market
2875 W. Walnut St.

Daily, Monday–Saturday, 9 a.m.–5:30 p.m., Sunday, 11 a.m.–4 p.m. Antiques, collectibles, crafts, and new and used merchandise. Ample parking. Market is located in a very scenic city with many fine specialty shops, and it hosts one of America's major craft events: "War Eagle Days." *Contact* Wanda Duffin (501) 631-8940.

SPRINGDALE

Oak Grove Flea Market
Corner of Elm Springs and Oak Grove Rd.

Saturday, Sunday. Indoor/outdoor market with approximately 50 dealers. Snack bar, rest rooms, h/a. *Contact* Bob Wallis (501) 756-0764.

Discount Corner Flea Market Mall
418 E. Emma
(501) 576-0764

Daily, 10 a.m.–5 p.m. Indoor market with new merchandise, crafts, gifts and imports. Snack bar, rest room, h/a. Ample parking.

WEST MEMPHIS

West Memphis Flea Market
557 E. Broadway

Thursday, Sunday, 10 a.m.–6 p.m. Indoor/outdoor market with an average daily attendance of 3,000 with approximately 75 dealers. Auction held Thursday and Saturday. Lots of new merchandise, collectibles, used merchandise, and tools. There is a sister market across the street at 512 E. Broadway, which has the same hours. Restaurant, rest rooms, h/a, ample parking. Camping and casino boats nearby. *Contact* Juanita Moxier (870) 735-9332 or 735- 1644.

WHITEHALL

Flea Market
Hwy. 65, Exit 34
(870) 247-9957

Sundays only. New and used merchandise, crafts, produce, tools. Rest rooms, ample parking.

INFORMATION IS SUBJECT TO CHANGE—ALWAYS CALL AHEAD TO AVOID DISAPPOINTMENT

CALIFORNIA

ALAMEDA

Alameda Swap Meet
4501 S. Alameda St.

Weekdays, 10 a.m.–7 p.m, weekends, 8 a.m.–7 p.m. Indoor year-round market featuring all new merchandise. Approximately 300 dealers. Wide selection of merchandise from clothes to jewelry. Great buys here for the serious shopper. Does not rent to traveling dealers. Ample parking. *Contact* Romeo Ramos, 4501 S. Alameda St., 90058 (510) 233-2764, (510) 233-2688. E-mail: ramos6953@aol.com.

First Sunday Flea Market
(510) 522-7500

Every first Sunday.

ANAHEIM

Anaheim Swap Meet
1520 N. Lemon St.
(714) 680-0986

Saturday, Sunday, 8 a.m.–5 p.m. Admission $1. Ample parking.

ANDERSON

Jolly Giant Flea Market
6719 Eastside Rd.

Saturday, Sunday, 6 a.m.–4 p.m. Admission 50 cents. Large indoor/outdoor market with approximately 150 dealers. Antiques, collectibles, new and used merchandise, wide selection of goods here. One of the area's better markets. Space from $6. Snack bar, rest rooms, h/a. Ample free parking. *Contact* Pattie or Jim Smith, 6719 Eastside Rd., 96007 (530) 365-6458, fax (530) 365-6450.

ANTIOCH

Antioch Fairgrounds Flea Market
Corner 10th and L Sts.
(510) 778-6900 or 706-0502

Friday, Sunday. This is a large well-stocked market with 300 dealers. This open-air flea market is for new and used merchandise, crafts, tools, housewares, and collectibles. Snack bars, rest rooms h/a, ample parking. Lots of walking required. Space from $10 per day. *Contact* Manager, 1201 W. 10th St., 94509.

ARCADIA

Edward's Drive-In Swap Meet
4469 Live Oak Ave.
Edward's Drive-In Theater
(818) 447-8179

Saturday, Sunday. Approximately 1,000 dealers show at one of the area's better markets for all types of sales. Lots of new and California-type merchandise. An excellent market to purchase merchandise for resale. Good attendance at this market. Food available, rest rooms, h/a, ample parking. This market requires a lot of walking.

ARLINGTON

Van Buren Cinema Swap Meet
Van Buren Cinema
3035 Van Buren Blvd.
(909) 688-2829

Saturday, Sunday, 8 a.m.–4 p.m. Admission charge. Outdoor market, new and used merchandise, some collectibles, garage sale items, crafts, produce. Snack bars, rest rooms, h/a. Ample parking.

AROMAS

The Big Red Barn Flea Market
1000 Hwy. 101
Seventeen miles North of Salinas
Seventeen miles South of Gilroy

Saturday, Sunday, 7 a.m.–5 p.m. Should have called this market the 17-mile market. Approximately 300 dealers. Indoor/outdoor market, antiques, collectibles, lots of new merchandise. Space from $10. Snack bars, rest rooms, h/a. *Contact* Debra Hagan, 1000 Hwy. 101, 95004 (831) 422-1271 or 726-3101.

AZUSA

Azusa Swap Meet
Foothill Drive-In Theater
675 E. Foothill Blvd.
(626) 334-0263 or (714) 640-4603
Fax (626) 334-4813

Sunday only, 5 a.m.–4 p.m. There are approximately 500 dealers in this excellent outdoor market. Market features new merchandise and everything from A to Z in the U.S.A. at severely discounted prices. Snack bars, rest rooms, h/a, ample parking. *Contact* Jim Edwards, 91702.

BAKERSFIELD

Swap-O-Rama
4501 Wible Rd.

Saturday, Sunday. Admission charge 75 cents. Approximately 500 dealers offer a wide variety of goods such as antiques, collectibles, crafts, new and used merchandise, and tools. Food available, rest rooms, h/a, ample parking. Market features several carnival rides. Space from $12. Reservations required. *Contact* Tom Ballard, 93307 (661) 831-9346.

South Union Swap Meet
2546 S. Union St.
Corner of Ming and Union Sts.

Saturday, Sunday. Admission charge. Over 300 dealers offer a wide range of new merchandise, used merchandise, jewelry, collectibles, crafts, and produce. Rest rooms, food available, h/a, ample parking. Camping available. *Contact* Walt Roe (661) 831-8700.

Bakersfield Fairgrounds Swap Meet
Fairgrounds, Union Avenue Parking Lot
(661) 833-1733 or 397-1504

Saturday, Sunday, 6 a.m.–3 p.m. Admission charge 75 cents. This outdoor market with approximately 500 dealers is where new and used merchandise, tools, antiques, collectibles, even autos and RVs are sold. Snack bars, rest rooms, h/a, ample parking. *Contact* Ed Murphy, 312 Stable Ave., 93304.

BERKELEY

Berkeley Flea Market
Martin Luther King Way and Ashby
BART station parking lot

Saturday, Sunday, 7 a.m.–7 p.m. Outdoor market, antiques, collectibles, lots of unusual and unique items here. Very trendy market. Where the "cool" folks shop. Space from $20. Limited parking. *Contact* Charisse, Community Services, 1937 Ashby Ave., 94703, (510) 644-0744, fax (510) 540-6970. E-mail: findme@berkeleyfleamarket.com.

CAMPBELL

Second Saturday Flea Market, Campbell Center
1769 S. Winchester Blvd.

Every second Saturday. Outdoor market with approximately 50 dealers. Snack bar, rest room, h/a. Ample parking. *Contact* Karl Miller (408) 374-1415.

CANOGA PARK

Valley Indoor Swap Meet
6701 Variel Ave.
(818) 340-9123

Friday, Saturday, Sunday, 8 a.m.–4 p.m. Admission charge. Snack bar, rest room, h/a. Ample parking.

CERES

Ceres Flea Market
1651 E. Whitmore Ave., off Hwy. 99

Saturday, Sunday, 6 a.m.–3 p.m. Admission $1.50 per carload on Sundays, Saturday is free. Outdoor market with some covered spaces. Approximately 300 dealers. New and used merchandise, sporting goods, general flea market merchandise. Space from $5 per day. Snack bar, rest rooms, h/a. *Contact* Joann Fluharty, Box 35, 95307 (209) 537-9827.

CHICO

Silver Dollar Flea Market
Fairgrounds
Corner of Fair St. and Park Ave.
(530) 892-9205

Saturday, Sunday, 8 a.m.–4 p.m. Indoor market with approximately 50 dealers. Snack bar, rest rooms, h/a. Ample parking.

CHINO

Maclin Swap Meet
7407 Riverside Dr.
(909) 984-5131

Sunday–Tuesday. Approximately 250 dealers. Large colorful market with lots of new merchandise, collectibles, produce, and plenty of used merchandise. One of the area's better attended markets. Snack bars, rest rooms, h/a. This is a clean, well-managed market that is always a pleasure to shop at. Ample parking.

CLEARLAKE

Clearlake Flea Market
16080 Davis St.
(707) 995-7070

Friday, Saturday, Sunday, 7 a.m.–3 p.m. Indoor/outdoor market with approximately 75 dealers. New and used merchandise, crafts, some antiques and collectibles, gifts, imports, jewelry, sportswear. Snack bar, rest rooms, h/a. Market has approximately 30–35 antique and gift shops that are open daily. Ample parking.

COLTON

Maclin Open Air Market
1902 Valley Blvd.
(800) 222-7467 or (909) 877-3700

Thursday, Saturday, 5:30 a.m.–3 p.m. Admission charge 50 cents. Average attendance 10–12,000 each day with over 250 dealers. One of the area's better markets with large amounts of quality items. Good food here. Lots of walking. Rest rooms, h/a, ample parking. Space from $25. Reservations required. *Contact* Maclin Markets, 7407 Riverside Dr., Ontario, 91761. Auctions on Thursday.

CONCORD

Solano Swap Meet
1611 Solano Way
(925) 687-6445 or 825-1951

Saturday, Sunday, 6 a.m.–4 p.m. Admission charge $1. Average daily attendance 7,000 with approximately 500 dealers for this well-stocked market with new and trendy merchandise, and a good selection of quality collectibles and crafts. Fully stocked booths make shopping enjoyable. Plenty of food, rest rooms, h/a, ample parking. Space from $5 on Saturday to $15 on Sunday. Camping nearby.

COSTA MESA

Orange Count College Swap Meet
2701 Fairview Rd.
(714) 432-5880

Saturday, Sunday. Colorful and trendy outdoor California market. Snack bar, rest rooms, h/a.

Costa Mesa Swap Meet
Orange County Fairgrounds
(949) 723-6660

Saturday, Sunday, 7 a.m.–4 p.m. Admission charge $1. One of Los Angeles's leading marketplaces. With a little bit of everything, this market is strong on new merchandise. This is a great market for the shopper, especially if you're looking for deals on new merchandise, but this market has what is probably the crabbiest management in the entire industry. Food available, rest rooms, h/a, ample parking. Space is usually at a premium. Strong attendance, reservations recommended. *Contact* Tel Phil Enterprises, 88 Fair Dr., 92626. E-mail: telphil@earthlink.net.

CUPERTINO

Flea Market
De Anza College
21250 Stevens Creek Blvd.
(408) 864-8946 or 864-8414

Every first Saturday, 8 a.m.–4 p.m. Approximately 750 dealers use this outdoor market. New and used merchandise are offered. Some dealers set up here with large well-stocked booths of antiques, collectibles, fine art, crafts, and new sports items. Food available. Rest rooms, h/a. Parking charge $3. Space from $25. Reservations required. *Contact* Flea Market Manager, 21250 Stevens Creek Blvd., 95014.

CYPRESS

California Outdoor Market
Los Alaitos Race Course
(714) 220-0251

Sunday. Admission charge. Over 300 dealers offer worlds of new merchandise, everything from computers to can openers. Includes used merchandise, collectibles, crafts, and produce. Food available, rest rooms, h/a, ample paved parking.

DALY CITY

Geneva Swap Meet
607 Carter St.
Next door to the Cow Palace

Saturday, Sunday, 7 a.m.–4 p.m. Admission charge 75 cents. Over 250 dealers offer new and used goods, trendy imports, produce, jewelry, some antiques, sports items, and collectibles. Snack bar, rest rooms, h/a. Space from $12.50. Reservations required for space. *Contact* Lance Edwards, 607 Carter St., 94014 (650) 587-0515 or 587-4606.

Doelger Senior Center Flea Market
Doelger Senior Center
101 Lake Merced Blvd.
(650) 991-8012

Every second Saturday. Indoor market with approximately 50 dealers. Snack bar, rest room, h/a. Ample parking.

EL CAJON

Aero Drive-In Swap Meet
1470 E. Broadway

Saturday, Sunday. Approximately 400 dealers. New and used merchandise, lots of garage sale items, farm items, crafts, collectibles, vintage clothing, and produce. Sale of new merchandise requires city license. Snack bar, rest rooms, h/a, ample parking. Space from $3. *Contact* Art Ashcraft (619) 444-8800.

EL MONTE

Starlite Drive-In Swap Meet
3559 N. Chico Blvd.
Starlite Drive-In Theatre

Saturday, Sunday. Approximately 600 dealers. One of the San Gabriel Valley's better markets. This large classic California market has acres of new and trendy merchandise, lots of used items, crafts, collectibles, and other goods. Snack bars, rest rooms, h/a, ample parking. Lots of walking here. Reservations recommended. Space from $47. *Contact* Rodger Mansfield (626) 448-2810 or 401-3489.

ESCONDIDO

Escondido Swap Meet
635 W. Mission Ave.

Wednesday–Sunday. Indoor/outdoor market. Admission charge. Snack bar, rest rooms, h/a. Ample parking. *Contact* Lee Porter (760) 745-3100.

EUREKA

Flea Mart By The Bay
1200 W. Del Norte

Friday, Saturday, Sunday, 8 a.m.–8 p.m. Indoor market with approximately 50 dealers. Antiques, collectibles, glassware, used merchandise. Space from $5 per table. Market is located in a very scenic area with great fishing. Snack bar, rest rooms, h/a. Ample parking. *Contact* Lea Patton, 1200 W. Del Norte St., 95503 (707) 443-3103.

FONTANA

Belair Swap Meet
15895 Valley Blvd.

Wednesday, Saturday, Sunday, 6 a.m.–3 p.m. Admission charge. Approximately 400 dealers on weekends. Good selection here, new merchandise, trendy and California items, imports, some antiques, collectibles, vintage clothing. Lots of jewelry. *Contact* James Kwak, 15895 Valley Blvd., 92335 (909) 355-3000 or (213) 754-3000, fax (909) 355-3044.

FREMONT

Ohlone College Super Flea Market
436000 Mission Blvd.

Every second Saturday, 8 a.m.–3 p.m. Parking $1.50 per car. Approximately 200 dealers. Outdoor market. Used and new merchandise, general flea market items. A very pleasant and colorful "California" market. Space from $25 per day. Snack bars, rest rooms, h/a. *Contact* Elaine Nagel, 436000 Mission Blvd., 94539 (510) 659-6285, fax (510) 659-6264.

FRESNO

Cherry Auction & Swap Meet
4640 S. Cherry Ave.

Tuesday, Saturday, Sunday, 6:30 a.m.–5 p.m. Admission charge. Approximately 500 dealers. Antiques, collectibles, produce, new merchandise of all types. Food available, rest rooms, h/a, ample parking. Space from $10 on Saturday; it varies on other days. *Contact* Frank Meyer, 4640 S. Cherry Ave., 93706 (559) 266-9856, fax (556) 266-9439.

Wood Park Antique Flea Market
7150 N. Abbey
Fax (556) 266-9439

Every fourth Sunday. Admission charge. No new or flea market merchandise allowed—strong antique and collectible market. Quality items, furniture, silver, jewelry, and fine collectibles available. Food available, rest rooms, h/a, ample parking. Space from $12.50. Reservations accepted. *Contact* Neil Burson, 4640 S. Cherry Ave., 93706.

ALWAYS CALL BEFORE TRAVELING LONG DISTANCES!

GALT

Galt Flea Market
890 Caroline Ave.
Corner of Caroline and Walnut Sts.

Tuesday, Wednesday. Average attendance 5,000. Over 200 dealers on Tuesday and 400 dealers on Wednesday. Market features lots of new merchandise, imports, used, antiques, and collectibles. Tuesday is wholesale market and Wednesday is retail market. Space from $25 on Tuesday and $15 on Wednesday. Reservations required. Camping and electricity available. Snack bar, rest rooms, h/a, ample parking. Seller's permit required. *Contact* City of Galt, P.O. Box 97, 95632 (209) 745-2437 or 745-2961, fax (209) 745-9794.

GLENDALE

Glendale Community College Swap Meet
1122 E. Garfield Ave., Glendale to Freeway at the Mountain Street exit

Every third Sunday, 8 a.m.–3 p.m. Outdoor market. Antiques, collectibles, new and used merchandise, crafts, furniture. Space from $35. Snack bars, rest rooms, h/a. Ample parking. *Contact* Jane Harris, 1122 E. Garfield Ave., 91205 (818) 240-1000 or 548-0864, fax (818) 548-6216. E-mail: jharris@glendale.cc.ca.us.

GOLETA

Santa Barbara Swap Meet
907 S. Kellogg Ave.
Twin Drive-In Theater

Sundays only, 7 a.m.–2 p.m. Admission charge $1. Outdoor market with over 225 dealers offering new merchandise, trendy California items, imports, vintage clothing, jewelry, secondhand merchandise, and lots of junk. Space from $17. Snack bars, rest rooms, h/a, ample parking. *Contact* Robert Strojek, 907 S. Kellogg Ave., 93117 (805) 964-9050.

HANFORD

Kings Swap Meet
14th and Lacey

Saturday, Sunday. Over 250 dealers offering new merchandise, electronics, housewares, tapes, sportswear, tools, used merchandise, crafts, collectibles, antiques, and primitives. Snack bar, rest rooms, h/a, ample parking. Space $4 to $8. Reservations recommended. *Contact* Winston Newby (209) 292-8116.

HAYWARD

Chabot College Flea Market
25555 Hesperian Blvd.

Every third Saturday, 8 a.m.–4 p.m. Outdoor market. Lots of collectibles and locally made crafts, used merchandise, sporting goods and lots of sportswear. Space from $20 per day. Snack bars, rest rooms, h/a. Ample parking. *Contact* Joanne Simonson, 25555 Hesperian Blvd., 94545 (510) 786-6918, fax (510) 265-5739.

HUNTINGTON BEACH

Golden West College Swap Meet
College parking lot on Golden West St.
(714) 898-2289 or 898-7927

Saturday, Sunday, 7 a.m.–4 p.m. Outdoor market. Snack bar, rest room, h/a. Ample parking.

INDIO

Sunair Swap Meet
84245 Indio Spring Dr.
Next to Indio/Fantasy Springs Casino

Tuesday, Sunday, May–September. Outdoor market with approximately 250 dealers. New merchandise, crafts, furniture, used items, produce. Snack bars, h/a, ample parking. Space from $18 per day. *Contact* John Blazej, Box 10170, 92202 (619) 347-9479, fax (619) 347-9790.

Maclin's Indio Open Air Market
46-350 Arabia St., behind the Riverside County Fairgrounds

Wednesday, Saturday, 4 p.m.–10 p.m. Outdoor market. Approximately 100 dealers. New and used merchandise, lots of bric-a-brac and garage sale items, produce, locally made crafts. Space from $15. Ample parking. *Contact* Manager, 46-350 Arabia Ave., 92201 (800) 222-7467 or (909) 984-5131.

LA CIENEGA

La Cienega Manufacturers Outlet Indoor Swap Meet
3485 S. La Cienega Blvd.
Next to Fedco
(714) 838-2109

Daily. This is the market for the bargain hunter, or for the person looking for merchandise to resell. Mountains of all types of new, hot, and trendy stock. Bring a big truck and plenty of money, and you can make some real deals. Snack bar, rest rooms, h/a, ample parking.

LANCASTER

Lancaster Chamber of Commerce Flea Market
Antelope Valley Fairgrounds
Division St. and East Ave. I
Exit Freeway #14 (north of LA), turn east two miles. Fairgrounds on left.

Every first Sunday. Five hundred spaces, 10,000–11,000 paid attendance. Vendor friendly, $25–$70. spaces. Inside and outside space available. One of California's oldest and largest. Bring own tables. Reservations required 10 days before event, more helpful and better choices of spaces. Electric available. No overnight camping. New, used, antique, and collectibles. Event open first Sunday in May and October. *Contact* Ramon Ortega, 554 W. Lancaster Blvd., 93534 (661) 948-4518, fax (661) 949-1212. E-mail: ram.on@lancasterchamber.org.

LONG BEACH

Outdoor Antique Market
Long Beach Veterans Stadium
Lakewood Blvd. and Conant St.
(323) 655-5703

Third Sunday, 8 a.m.–3 p.m. Admission charge. Outdoor market with approximately 600 dealers. One of the largest antique and collectible markets on the West Coast. Lots of furniture, plus decorator and period items. If you are a serious collector, shopkeeper, or decorator, this is a market not to miss. Food available, rest rooms, h/a; parking can be difficult, lots of walking. Reservations required. Space from $50. *Contact* Americana Enterprises, Box 69219, Los Angeles, 90069.

LOS ALTOS HILLS

Foothill College Flea Market
12345 El Monte Rd.
Foothill College parking lot F

Every third Saturday, 8 a.m.–3 p.m. Outdoor market. Parking $2. New and used merchandise, collectibles, crafts, produce, jewelry, garage sale items. Snack bars, rest rooms, h/a. Space from $15. *Contact* Charlotte Davis, 12345 El Monte Rd., 94022 (650) 948-6417.

LOS BANOS

World's Faire
1725 W. Pacheco Hwy.
(209) 826-6779

Saturday, Sunday. Average daily attendance 4,000 to see new merchandise, electronics, tools, housewares, sportswear, and trendy and upscale merchandise. Good food, rest rooms, h/a, ample parking. Camping nearby. Good produce market here, open daily. Space from $20 per day.

INFORMATION IS SUBJECT TO CHANGE—ALWAYS CALL FIRST!

MARIN CITY

Marin City Flea Market
147 Donahue (at Drake)
Marin City, Sausalito, Exit off Hwy. 101
(415) 332-1441
Fax (415) 332-9225

Saturday, Sunday, 8 a.m.–3 p.m. Outdoor market with over 500 dealers offering lots of high-grade antiques and collectibles. Some very well-stocked booths of fine merchandise. Great overall selection of items from garage sale to museum quality. Rest rooms, food available, h/a, parking charge $2. Space from $420. Food vendors welcome. City license required. *Contact* Gene Clark.

MARYSVILLE

Marysville Flea Market
1468 Simpson Lane, off Hwy. 20

Sundays, 6 a.m.–4 p.m. Outdoor/indoor market. Antiques, collectibles, locally made crafts, produce, new and used merchandise, livestock, lots of flea market merchandise. Space from $5. *Contact* Betty Foster, 1468 Simpson Lane, 95901 (530) 743-8713.

MORGAN HILL

Morgan Hill Flea Market
140 E. Main Ave.

Saturday, Sunday, 7:30 a.m.–6 p.m. Approximately 75 dealers. Antiques, collectibles, new and used merchandise, crafts, produce. Snack bars, rest rooms, h/a. Space from $12. Ample parking. *Contact* Jim Ahlin, 140 E. Main Ave., 95037 (408) 779-3809.

NAPA

Napa Valley Antiques and Collectibles Market
3285 California Blvd.
(707) 253-1599

Every third Sunday. Seasonal market open May–October. Admission charge. Quality antiques, collectibles, and smalls. Snack bar, rest rooms, h/a. Ample free parking.

NIPOMO

Nipomo Swap Meet
263 N. Frontage Rd.
101 Freeway, exit Tefft St.

Friday, Saturday, Sunday, 6 a.m.–6 p.m. Indoor/outdoor market with approximately 250 dealers. Antiques, collectibles, jewelry, furniture, produce, new and used merchandise. Snack bars, rest rooms, h/a. Space from $3 on Friday, $6 on Saturday and $9 on Sunday. Paid parking. *Contact* Carnival Marketplaces, 263 N. Frontage Rd., 9344 (805) 929-7000, fax (805) 929-7007. E-mail: swapmeet@calcoa.com.

NORTHRIDGE

Northridge Antique Flea Market
Cal State University Northridge

Every fourth Sunday, 8 a.m.–3 p.m. Outdoor market. Admission $3. Approximately 200 dealers. Quality antiques, lots of antique furniture, great quality collectibles here, also crafts are allowed here. Space from $50. Snack bar, rest rooms, h/a. Ample free parking. *Contact* Antique Attractions, 17041 Lakewood Blvd., Bellflower, CA 90706 (562) 633-3836, fax (562) 408-0496.

OAKLAND

Coliseum Flea Market
5401 Coliseum Way
(510) 534-0325 or 533-1601

Thursday, Sunday, 6:30 a.m.–4 p.m. Admission charge. Average daily attendance 5–6,000, with approximately 400 dealers in an outdoor market. New and used merchandise, electronics, sportswear, produce, antiques, collectibles, and crafts. Food available, rest rooms, h/a, camping nearby. Good market for the commercial vendor. Space from $10 per day. *Contact* Coliseum Flea Market, 5401 Coliseum Way, 94601.

Nor Cal Swap Meet
Laney College
7th and Fallon Sts., parking lot

Saturday, Sunday, 7 a.m.–4 p.m. Outdoor market. Admission 50 cents per person. Antiques, collectibles, great selection of locally made crafts, new merchandise, produce, lots of new sportswear. Space from $16. Snack bar, rest rooms, h/a. Free ample parking. *Contact* Manager, 1150 Ballena Blvd., #250, Alameda, CA 94501 (510) 769-7266.

Antiques Mart
Jack London Square at the waterfront
(510) 652-5728

Every first Saturday, 8 a.m.–4 p.m. Outdoor market with approximately 100 dealers. Antiques, collectibles. Snack bar, rest room, h/a.

OCEANSIDE

Oceanside Swap Meet
3480 Mission Ave.
(760) 757-5286 or 745-3100

Friday, Saturday, Sunday, 7 a.m.–3 p.m. This outdoor market has approximately 1,000 dealers and a wide range of goods; recommended for commercial dealers. Large selection of new merchandise, trendy California items, imports, and sports-related merchandise. Lots of food here, rest rooms, h/a, ample parking. Space from $6 on Friday, $13 for Saturday, and $16 for Sunday and holidays. *Contact* Howard Morgan, 3480 Mission Ave.

ONTARIO

Maclin Swap Meet
7407 Riverside Dr.
(800) 222-7467 or (909) 984-5131

Tuesday, Saturday, Sunday, 5:30 a.m.–3 p.m. Admission charge. Approximately 250 dealers offer lots of new and trendy merchandise, sports-related merchandise, jewelry, produce, and some good collectibles. Restaurant and bar, kiddie rides. Auction on Tuesday. Good food, bakery, and fish market. Rest rooms, h/a, ample parking. Space starts at $7.

OROVILLE

Oro Dam Flea Market
1141 Oro Dam Blvd. West
(916) 533-1324

Saturday, Sunday, 7 a.m.–4 p.m. Approximately 50 dealers. New and used merchandise, lots of garage sale items, produce, crafts. Space from $8. Ample parking.

PALMDALE

Four Points Swap Meet
5505 Pear Blossom Hwy.
Intersection of Hwy. 138 and Pear Blossom

Saturday, Sunday, 6 a.m.–3 p.m. Admission charge $1. Average weekend attendance of 8–10,000 with approximately 350 dealers. This market has a wide-open, everything-goes atmosphere. It has been in operation over 10 years and features live country and western entertainment on Sunday. Pony rides, clean rest rooms, ample parking. This swap meet has lots of good food, especially Mexican. Inside and outside space available from $10 on Saturday and $15 for Sunday. Camping available. *Contact* Joyce Bruce, Box 901807, 93590, fax (805) 273-5465.

PALO ALTO

Music Boosters Flea Market
50 Embarcadero Rd.
Corner of El Camino Real, across from Stanford Stadium

Every second Saturday, 9 a.m.–3 p.m. Approximately 100 dealers. Used merchandise, crafts, some collectibles, Space from $20. Snack bars, rest rooms, h/a. Ample parking. *Contact* Phyllis Smith, 920 Boyce Ave., 94301 (650) 321-0725 or 321-6783.

PANORAMA CITY

Valley Indoor Swap Meet
14650 Parthenia St.

Wednesday–Monday, 10 a.m.–6 p.m. Indoor market with approximately 250 dealers offering new merchandise, collectibles, clothing, crafts, used items, furniture. Snack bars, rest rooms, h/a, and ample parking. Rates by the month from $500. *Contact* Deanna McLintock, 14650 Parthenia St., 91002 (818) 892-0183, fax (818) 884-9405. E-mail: info@indoorswap.com.

PARAMOUNT

Paramount Swap Meet
14711 S. Paramount Ave.

Daily. Approximately 600 dealers. Excellent wholesale market as well as market for new merchandise. If you are looking for large loads of new merchandise to resell or if you're furnishing a new house, this is a market for you. Prices here are dramatically less than at the discount houses. Space from $15 per day. Ample parking. *Contact* Darren Kurkowski, 14711 Paramount Blvd., 90723 (562) 633-0741.

PASADENA

Pasadena City College Flea Market
1570 E. Colorado Blvd.
(626) 585-7906

Every first Sunday, 8 a.m.–3 p.m. Excellent outdoor market held on college's parking lot; a very fun and colorful market to attend, either as a shopper or a seller. Good sales and good buys at this market. This market is operated by the college students and is always a pleasure to attend. It is one of my favorite stops. Food available, rest rooms, h/a. Parking can be difficult.

Rose Bowl Flea Market
Rose Bowl

Every second Sunday, 9 a.m.–3 p.m. Admission charge $5. One of the country's largest and best-attended selling events. This market has it all and is a surefire don't-miss event. Approximately 1,500 vendors show with an average attendance of 30–40,000. This market is heavy on antiques, collectibles, crafts, and high-quality items. Good variety of food. Many celebrities and stars can be seen shopping this market. (When the Cabbage Patch dolls were so hot they were unobtainable, I purchased a load of them from a vice president of Coleco—the manufacturer—who was running a booth at this market. And Coleco was the company that was making the dolls. Sure liked running across that booth.) *Contact* R. G. Canning, Box 400, Maywood, 90270 (323) 560-7469 or 587-5100, fax (323) 560-5924. E-mail: rgc@rgcshows.com.

PETALUMA

Petaluma Fairground Flea Market
Fairgrounds at the junction of East Washington and Payron Sts.

Saturday, Sunday. Indoor/outdoor market with approximately 100 dealers. Antiques, collectibles, new and used merchandise, gifts, imports, crafts, produce. Snack bars, rest rooms, h/a. Ample parking. *Contact* John Letinich (707) 763-0931 or 763-1242.

PICO RIVERA

Fiesta Swap Meet
8452 E. Whittier Blvd.

Saturday, Sunday, 8 a.m.–4 p.m. Outdoor market. *Contact* Chamber of Commerce (562) 949-5918.

POMONA

Mission Drive-In Swap Meet
10798 Ramona Blvd.
Mission Drive-In Theater

Saturday, Sunday. Admission charge. This is one of the area's better flea markets. Lots of new and used merchandise, collectibles, crafts, and produce. Good assortment of dealers, both professional and amateur. Snack bar, rest rooms, ample parking. This market involves a lot of walking. Inside and outside space from $4. Reservations recommended. *Contact* Ronald Bacon (909) 627-3565 or 628-7943.

PORTERVILLE

Porterville College Swap Meet
900 S. Main St.
Porterville College parking lot

Sunday, 5 a.m. until dark. This outdoor market with approximately 350 dealers offers new and used merchandise, lots of garage sale items, crafts, antiques, collectibles, and jewelry both fine and costume. Good food, rest rooms, h/a, ample parking. Very nice market with friendly dealers and management. Space from $10. *Contact* Bill Roucher, Porterville Swap Meet, 900 S. Main St., 93257 (209) 781-3130 or 784-9161.

REDDING

Epperson Brothers Auction and Flea Market
End of Fig Tree Lane, off Airport Rd., one mile south of the Municipal Airport.

Saturday, Sunday, 7 a.m.–5 p.m.. Large indoor/outdoor market. Admission $1. Antiques, collectibles, produce, furniture, lots of new quality merchandise, crafts. Space from $5 on Saturday and $10 on Sunday. One of the better markets in the area. Rest rooms, snack bars, h/a. Ample free parking. *Contact* Keith Bloom, 21005 Fig Tree Lane, 96002 (916) 365-7242 or 378-1266.

ROSEVILLE

Denio's Roseville Farmers & Flea Market
1551 Vineyard Rd.

Saturday, Sunday, 7 a.m.–5 p.m. One of the largest markets in northern California. Approximately 1,500 dealers in summer increasing to 2,000 in winter. Wide range of merchandise: antiques, furniture, collectibles, crafts, new and used merchandise, housewares, electronics, sportswear, and much more. Many high-quality dealers here with large well-stocked booths and quality collector lines. Food available, rest rooms, ample parking, (although it can be difficult), h/a. Space from $15 per day. Reservations recommended. *Contact* Ken Denio, 1551 Vineyard Rd., 95678 (916) 782-2704.

SACRAMENTO

Auction City & Flea Market
8529 Folsom Blvd.

Tuesday, Friday, 7 a.m.–5 p.m. One of the area's original markets with approximately 400 dealers. Antiques, collectibles, stamps, coins, new and used merchandise, crafts, produce, and toys are available. Good food, rest rooms, h/a, ample parking. Market also conducts several special events. Space from $20. Reservations recommended. *Contact* Emil Magova, 8521 Folsom Blvd., 95826 (916) 383-0880 or 383-0950.

49'er Flea Market
4450 Marysville Blvd.

Thursday–Sunday, 7 a.m.–4 p.m. Admission charge 25 cents. Average daily attendance is 2,000 for this outdoor market with approximately 100 dealers. New merchandise, lots of used items, clothing, furniture, and bric-a-brac are available. This is the kind of place where you are sure to find treasures. Snack bar, rest rooms, h/a, ample parking. Space from $4 on Friday, $8 on Saturday and Sunday. *Contact* Bill Brancamp, 4450 Marysville Blvd., 95838 (916) 920-3530, fax (916) 920-3530.

SALINAS

Salinas Flea Market
Skyview Drive-In Theater
925 N. Sanborn Rd.

Saturday, Sunday, 6 a.m.–4 p.m. Large outdoor market. Admission 50 cents. Approximately 100 dealers. Lots of used merchandise, some antiques and collectibles, crafts, furniture, produce. Space from $15. Snack bar, rest rooms, h/a. Ample free parking. *Contact* Art Jackson, 925 N. Sanborn Rd., 93905 (831) 757-3532 or 424-7490.

SAN BERNARDINO

San Bernardino Outdoor Market
National Orange Showgrounds

Sunday, 6 a.m.–3 p.m. Average attendance is 15–18,000 with approximately 800 dealers. This is an excellent market, as well as a fun event to attend. Offerings are unusually heavy on new merchandise and garage sale merchandise; there are limited numbers of antiques and collectibles. If you are thinking about starting out in the business, this market is great. Snack bars, rest rooms, h/a, ample parking. Miles of walking at this swap and shop. Space starts at $8. *Contact* R. G. Canning, Box 400, Maywood, 90270 (909) 795-1884. E-mail: rgc@rgcshows.com.

SAN DIEGO

Kobey's Swap Meet
3500 Sports Arena Blvd.
Sports Arena parking lot
(619) 523-2700

Thursday–Sunday, 7 a.m.–3 p.m. Admission $1. This is the largest market in the area with approximately 800 vendors. Outdoor market with lots of variety—antiques to computers, new merchandise to Hummels, crafts to rare books. Good food here, rest rooms, h/a, ample parking. Space starts at $25. *Contact* Chris Haesloop, Kobey's, Box 81492, 92138; 24-hour message line (619) 226-0650, fax (619) 523-2715.

Spring Valley Swap Meet
6377 Quarry Rd.
(619) 463-1194

Saturday, Sunday. Large outdoor market with lots of new merchandise, Mexican imports and crafts, garage sale items, tools, housewares, and toys. Snack bar, rest rooms, h/a, ample parking.

SAN FERNANDO

San Fernando Swap Meet
585 Glen Oaks Blvd.
(818) 361-1431

Saturday, Sunday.

SAN FRANCISCO

Aleman Flea Market
100 Alemany Blvd.
Intersection of Hwy. 101 South and 280 North

Wednesday, Sunday, 7 a.m.–3 p.m. Outdoor market with some covered spaces. Approximately 100 dealers. Antiques, collectibles, crafts, lots of new and "in style" merchandise. Very trendy market. Space from $30. Snack bars, rest rooms, h/a. Ample parking. *Contact* Sid Baker, 501 Cesar Chavez, Room 109A, 94124 (415) 647-2043 or 285-5011.

San Francisco Flea Market
601 Tunnel Ave.
(415) 467-4849

Saturday, Sunday. Approximately 150 dealers offer new merchandise, antiques, collectibles, trendy decorator items, and crafts. Food available, rest rooms, h/a, ample parking. Inside and outside space available.

San Francisco Flea Market
140 S. Van Ness
(415) 646-0544

Saturday, Sunday, 6 a.m.–4:30 p.m. Outdoor market. Admission 50 cents. Approximately 100 dealers. Space from $25 for the weekend. Food available off premises, rest rooms. Limited parking.

Geneva Swap Meet
607 Carter St.
Geneva Drive-In Theater
(916) 587-4606

Saturday, Sunday. Admission charge. Average daily attendance 4,000 with over 200 dealers in this outdoor market. Lots of new merchandise, trendy hot new items, decorator finds, art, crafts, and collectibles available. Good snack bar, clean rest rooms, h/a, ample parking. Camping nearby. Space starts at $10 per day.

SAN JACINTO

Maclin Open Air Market & Auction
22124 Lyon Ave.
Corner of Lyon and De Anza St.
(909) 654-2546 or (800) 222-7467
Fax (909) 988-8041

Saturday, Sunday. This outdoor market has spaces for over 400 dealers. There are antiques, crafts, collectibles, new merchandise, and a lot of sporting goods at this market. This is a clean, well-managed market that is always a pleasure. Good food, rest rooms, ample parking, lots of walking. Space from $15. *Contact* Maclin Markets, 7407 Riverside Dr., Ontario, 91761.

SAN JOSE

Capitol Flea Market
3630 Hill Cap Ave.
Capitol Drive-In Theater
Hwy. 101, Capitol Expwy. exit

Thursday–Sunday, 6 a.m.–5:30 p.m. Admission fee. Large attendance with over 1,000 dealers. Lots of local garage-sale-type sellers. Secondhand and new merchandise. Auto and truck sale on the first Saturday of every month. Snack bars and cafe, rest rooms, h/a. Large farmer's market. Space from $15. *Contact* Glen Norris, 3630 Hill Cap Ave., 95136 (408) 225-5800.

The Original World's Largest Flea Market
12000 Berryessa Rd.
Northeast corner of Santa Clara Valley
(408) 453-1110
Fax (408) 437-9011
E-mail: rich@sjfm.com

Wednesday, Thursday, Saturday, Sunday, dawn to dusk. Admission fee charged. 120 acres of sellers' spaces for approximately 2,600 vendors. The average weekend attendance is 80,000. Said to be the nation's original flea market and the fourth largest attended attraction in the United States. Market conducts many special events and also has special promotions with name entertainment. Electricity available and 24-hour security. Indoor and outdoor spaces approximately 14×20. Space available on a daily, weekly, or monthly basis. Market has 35 restaurants, 60 roving snack/beverage carts, a carousel, live music, and two arcades. Ample paved parking. Market also open on major holidays. Closed Friday. Major media advertising.

SAN LUIS OBISPO

Flea Market
Sunset Drive-In Theater
Elks Lane

Wednesday–Sunday. Outdoor market. *Contact* Larry Rodkey (805) 544-4592.

SAN YSIDRO

San Ysidro Swap Meet
2383 Via Segundo

Wednesday, Thursday, Sunday. Approximately 250 vendors in this indoor/outdoor market offer lots of new merchandise, gifts, imports, antiques, collectibles, crafts, silver, coins, sports-related merchandise, produce, and auto supplies. Space from $5. *Contact* Joseph Garcia, Jr., 2388 Via Segundo, 92173 (619) 690-6756.

SANTA CLARA

Santa Clara Flea Market
5500 Lafayette St.
(415) 467-4849

Saturday, Sunday. Approximately 200 dealers offer new and used merchandise, crafts, collectibles, produce. Many fine dealers at this market with large well-stocked booths. Good market to shop for the budget-conscious.

Snack bar, ample parking with charge, rest rooms. Inside and outside space from $5. Carnival rides are a special attraction of this market.

Orange Coast College Swap Meet
Rancho Santiago College parking lot on Fairview St.
Hwy. 17 and Bristol St.
(714) 432-5866 or 432-5880

Sundays. New merchandise, imports, gifts, used merchandise, tools, housewares, toys, sporting goods. Crafts, collectibles, produce. Food available, rest rooms, h/a. Ample parking.

SANTA CRUZ

Skyview Flea Market
2240 Soquel Dr.
(408) 462-4442

Saturday, Sunday. Admission charge. Over 350 dealers offer a good variety of new merchandise, overruns, closeouts, surplus. Great place for shopping for your personal and home needs, crafts, art, collectibles, lots of used merchandise, tools, bicycles, and toys. Snack bars, rest rooms, h/a, ample parking, and lots of walking. Space from $2.50. *Contact* Marcy.

Santa Cruz Antiques Fair
Lincoln and Cedar Sts.

Every second Sunday. Outdoor antiques and collectibles market. *Contact* Santa Cruz Downtown Association (408) 429-8433.

SANTA FE SPRINGS

La Mirada Theater Drive-In Swap Meet
13963 Alondra Blvd.

Wednesday, Saturday, Sunday, 5 a.m.–10 p.m. One of the area's better commercial markets with over 250 dealers. Lots of new merchandise, gifts, imports, sports-related merchandise, decorator items, collectibles, and antiques are available. Ample parking. Space from $48. Reservations required. *Contact* La Mirada Swap Meet, 13963 Alondra Blvd., 90670 (562) 921-4359 or 921-9996.

SANTA MARIA

Hi-Way Drive-In Theater Flea Market
3170 Santa Maria Way, Santa Maria exit from 101 Freeway

Sundays, 6 a.m.–noon. Admission 25 cents. Approximately 100 dealers, new and used merchandise, crafts, produce, lots of bric-a-brac. Space from $8. Snack bar, rest rooms, h/a. Ample parking. *Contact* Bob Gran, 3170 San Maria Way, 93455 (805) 934-1582.

SANTA MONICA

Outdoor Antique and Collectibles Market
Santa Monica Airport
(313) 933-2511

Every fourth Sunday. Outdoor antique and collectible market.

SANTA ROSA

Forty and Eight Flea Market
Santa Rosa Veterans Memorial Building
Maple Ave., from Hwy. 12.
Across the street from the Sonoma County Fairgrounds

Sundays, 7 a.m.–3 p.m. Seasonal market open from May through September. Outdoor market with approximately 200 dealers. Used merchandise, lots of garage sale items, produce, crafts, some new merchandise. Space from $15. Snack bars, rest rooms, h/a. Free parking. *Contact* Manager, Box 9191, 95405 (707) 522-9391.

SANTEE

Santee Swap Meet
10990 Woodside Ave. North
(760) 745-3100 or (619) 449-7927

Saturday, Sunday, 8 a.m.–3 p.m. Admission charge. Outdoor market with approximately 50 dealers. Ample parking.

SAUGUS

Saugus Swap Meet
22500 Soledad Canyon Rd.

Sundays only, 7 a.m.–3 p.m. Admission charge $1. The San Fernando Valley's leading marketplace, with over 750 dealers. Antiques, collectibles, produce, and lots of flea market items. Excellent market for commercial vendors. Market is on the grounds of former movie star Hoot Gibson's ranch. Good food, fun shopping, interesting market with upbeat dealers. Rest rooms, h/a, ample parking with lots of walking. Space from $20. *Contact* Ray Wilkings, Box 901, Santa Clarita, 91380 (805) 259-3886 or (818) 716-6010.

SEBASTOPOL

Midgley's Flea Market
2200 Gravenstein Hwy. South

Saturday, Sunday, 6:30 a.m.–4:30 p.m. An outdoor market with some covered areas for over 600 dealers. This market is loaded with stuff—antiques, great selection for collectors, new merchandise, imports, and gifts. Snack bars, rest rooms, ample parking, h/a. Come prepared for a lot of walking if you want to see this market. You will find this to be a very interesting and most pleasant market to shop. It is clean and well managed. Space from $10. *Contact* Rosalie Midgley, 2200 Gravenstein Hwy. South, 94572 (707) 823-7874 or (800) 800-FLEA.

SLAUSON

Slauson Indoor Swap Meet
1600 W. Slauson Ave.
(323) 778-6055

Daily, 9 a.m.–4 p.m. Indoor market with approximately 140 dealers. Lots of used merchandise and garage sale items here, new merchandise, crafts, gifts and imports, Snack bar, rest rooms, h/a.

SOUTH LAKE TAHOE

Tahoe Flea Market
Elks Lodge
2094 Hwy. 50

Sundays, 8 a.m.–5 p.m. Outdoor market. Admission charge. Antiques, collectibles, new and used merchandise, vintage clothing, produce, tools, toys, standard flea market items. Space from $12. Free parking. *Contact* Randy Mundt, Box 10645, 96158 (530) 541-3967.

SPRING VALLEY

Spring Valley Swap Meet
6377 Quarry Rd.
(619) 463-1194
Fax (619) 472-1435

Saturday, Sunday, 7 a.m.–3 p.m. Admission charge. Approximately 1,000 dealers. Giant classic outdoor California market with never ending variety of dealers from the professional to the garage-salers. There is a little bit of everything at this wide open market. Space from $7. Food available, rest rooms, h/a, and miles of walking required. Ample parking.

STANTON

Stanton Indoor Swap Meet
10401 Beach Blvd.
Corner of Beach Blvd. and Cerritos;
near Knotts Berry Farm

Daily, 9 a.m.–5 p.m. Indoor market with approximately 75 dealers. New and used merchandise, some collectibles, gifts, crafts and imports. Snack bar, rest rooms, h/a. Ample free parking. *Contact* Jila Ilami (714) 527-1234.

STOCKTON

Flea Market
Fairgrounds
Corner of Airport Way and Charter St.
(209) 467-7355

Friday, Saturday, Sunday, 5 a.m.–3 p.m. This indoor and outdoor market has approximately 400 dealers offering new merchandise, electronics, sportswear, collectibles, crafts, used merchandise, autos, and boats. Snack bars, rest rooms, h/a, ample parking.

Stockton Flea Market
2542 S. El Dorado

Saturday, Sunday. New outdoor market. *Contact* Tae Oh (209) 465-9933.

Stockton Open Air Mall
3550 N. Wilson Way

Saturday, Sunday. Contact Glen Marzion (209) 465-1544.

TEMECULA

Weekly Flea and Farmers Market

Wednesday, 8 a.m.–1 p.m., Saturdays, 8 a.m.–1 p.m.

THORNTON

The Barn Yard
I-5 and Walnut Grove Rd.

Saturday, Sunday. Approximately 200 spaces for vendors offering new and used merchandise, crafts, produce, collectibles, and ranch, and farm items. Snack bar, rest rooms, h/a, ample parking. Space from $17.50 per 10×10 inside and $15 per 10×10 outside. *Contact* Harvey Peters, Box 592, French Camp, 95231 (209) 462-2513.

TORRANCE

Roadium Open-Air Market
2500 Redondo Beach Blvd.
Between the San Diego and Harbor Freeways

Daily, 6 a.m.–3 p.m. Admission 50 cents. Average weekend attendance of 15,000 per day with approximately 500 dealers. Opened in 1955, this is one of California's oldest and finest outdoor commercial markets. It is a real trendsetter in vendors and facilities. Market has special days, antiques and collectibles during the week, and new merchandise on weekends. This market is one of my personal favorites. Highly promoted in the metropolitan Los Angeles area. Good food, rest rooms, h/a, ample parking. Space from $13. *Contact* Roadium Open-Air Market, 2500 Redondo Beach Blvd., 90504 (323) 321-3709, or (800) 833-0304, fax (213) 321-0114. E-mail: roadium@earthlink.net.

Alpine Village Swap Meet
833 W. Torrance Blvd.
(323) 770-1961 or (310) 327-4384

Saturday, Sunday, 6 a.m.–3 p.m. Admission charge. Approximately 200 dealers show in this indoor/outdoor market. New and used merchandise, jewelry, sportswear, and housewares are available. Two restaurants on premises, rest rooms, h/a, ample parking. Space from $10. No food sales allowed. Reservations recommended.

TULARE

Open Country Flea Market
23090 Rd. 152
Freeway 99, Tulare Central Exit,
east to Rd. 152

Sundays only, 6 a.m.–3 p.m. Admission charge 50 cents. Approximately 400 vendors show in this outdoor market with some covered areas. New merchandise, secondhand items, produce, lots of new clothing, some antiques, and collectibles are available. Snack bar, rest rooms, h/a, ample parking. *Contact* Rick Bateman, 23090 Rd. 152, 93274 (209) 686-9588 or 685-8424.

Tulare County Fairgrounds Swap Meet
215 E. Alpine Ave.

Tuesday, Wednesday, 6:30 a.m.–3 p.m. Outdoor market with some covered spaces. Approximately 100 dealers. Antiques, collectibles. New and used merchandise. Crafts, furniture, livestock, produce. Space from $5 on Tuesdays and $10 on Wednesdays. Wednesdays are the good day here, not much happening on Tuesdays. Rest rooms, snack bar, h/a. Ample parking. *Contact* Clifton Williams (559) 686-4707, fax (559) 686-7238.

UKIAH

Ukiah Flea Market
Fairgrounds
1055 N. State St.

Saturday, Sunday, 8 a.m.–4 p.m. Indoor market with approximately 50 dealers. Snack bar, rest room, h/a. Ample parking. *Contact* Bob Bazzano (707) 468-4626.

VALLEJO

Napa Valley Flea Market
303 Kelly Rd.
Hwy. 29

Sundays only, 6 a.m.–5 p.m. Approximately 500 dealers offer a wide range of merchandise at this market. New and used merchandise, collectibles, antiques, new and used furniture, tools, toys, silver, glassware, and produce are available. Snack bars, rest rooms, h/a, parking charge $1. This market is an endless sea of booths with miles of walking. Inside and outside space available from $15. *Contact* Nelson Hardin, 303 Kelly Rd., 94590 (707) 226-8862.

Shopper's Carnival
Corner of Redwood Ave. and Hwy. 29,
off I-80

Saturday, Sunday, 10 a.m.–5 p.m. Indoor market with approximately 75 dealers. Primarily new and used merchandise. Space from $15 per day. Snack bar, rest rooms, h/a. Ample free parking. *Contact* Dan Heckerman, 1074 Reed Ave., #69, Sunnyvale, CA 94086 (707) 274-8114, fax (707) 247-0984.

VAN NUYS

Indoor Swap Meet
8345 Haven Hurst Pl.
(818) 891-0983

Saturday, Sunday. Lots of new, trendy, and designer items, gifts, collectibles, jewelry, silver, and sports cards available. Rest rooms, snack bar, ample parking.

The Bazaar Indoor Mini Mall
6841 Lennox Ave.
(618) 994-3585

Daily. A nice indoor market with bric-a-brac and typical swap meet fare, expecially new and like-new goods.

VENICE

Fox Indoor Swap Meet
620 Lincoln Blvd.
(213) 392-3477

Friday, Saturday, 10 a.m.–8 p.m., Sunday–Thursday, 10 a.m.–7 p.m. New merchandise, imports, gifts, souvenirs, used merchandise, and lots of junk available.

VENTURA

Ventura Flea Market and Swap Meet
County Fairgrounds

Saturday, Sunday, 9 a.m.–3 p.m. Admission fee. Average attendance 10,000 with over 800 vendors. This market is an even mix of antiques, garage sale items, and new merchandise. This is a clean, well-managed market with a large number of quality professional dealers with well-stocked booths, along with many garage sale people where the treasures are found. Snack bars, rest rooms, h/a, ample parking. *Contact* R. G. Canning, Box 400, Maywood, 90270 (213) 588-2727 or 587-5100, fax (213) 560-5924.

101 Drive-In Swap Meet
101 Drive-In Theater
4826 Telephone Rd.
(805) 644-5043

Saturday, Sunday, 6 a.m.–2 p.m. New merchandise, sportswear, housewares, electronics, jewelry, used merchandise, garage sale items, crafts, collectibles, and produce are available. Snack bar, rest rooms, h/a, ample parking.

VERNALIS

Orchard Flea Market
Vernalis and Hwy. 132
(209) 835-8972

Saturday, Sunday.

VICTORVILLE

Victorville Swap Meet
14800 7th St.
San Bernardino County Fairgrounds
(800) 222-7467 or (760) 955-1167

Saturdays only, 8 a.m.–3 p.m. Admission $1. Approximately 300 dealers show in this outdoor market. New and used merchandise, gifts, imports, new and vintage clothing, crafts, produce, tools, and toys are available. Snack bars, rest rooms, h/a, ample parking. Space from $13. *Contact* Greg Hahn, 14800 7th St., 92392.

VISALIA

Visalia Sales Yard
29660 Rte. 152
1.5 miles east of town

Thursday, Sunday, 5 a.m. until dark. Approximately 350 dealers show in this outdoor market. There's a good variety here with lots of new merchandise, sports merchandise, gifts, imports, antiques, and a good selection of collector and decorator items. Toys, tools, secondhand merchandise, produce, poultry, and seafood are available. Snack bars, ample parking. Lots of walking here; dress comfortably. Space $8 per day. *Contact* Karen Green, 29660 Rte. 152, 93291 (209) 734-9092 or 733-5270.

WOODLAND

Woodland Swap Meet
611 E. State Hwy. 113

Friday, Saturday, Sunday. Approximately 100 dealers offer new merchandise, housewares, sportswear, tools, electronics, and sports items as well as used merchandise, garage sale items, and bric-a-brac. Snack bar, rest rooms, h/a, ample parking. Space $20 inside; outside space available. *Contact* Neal Pearl (916) 666-2330.

WOODLAND HILLS

Valley Indoor Swap Meet
6701 Variel Ave.

Friday, Saturday, Sunday, 10 a.m.–6 p.m. New merchandise, imports, gifts, souvenirs, used merchandise, bric-a-brac, and decorator items are available. Snack bar, rest rooms, h/a. Space rented by the month only. *Contact* Jeff Kaplan, 6320 Canoga Ave. No. 1730, 91367 (818) 340-9120 or 884-6430, fax (818) 884-9405.

Pierce College Swap Meet
Corner of Mason and Victory Sts.

Saturday, Sunday. This is an outdoor market with approximately 500 dealers. New and used merchandise, produce, garage sale items, tools, toys, and some antiques and collectibles are available. Snack bars, rest rooms, h/a, ample parking. This is a very fun and interesting market to attend. Space from $14. *Contact* Ed Saleedo, Pierce College Swap Meet, 6201 Winnetka Ave., 91303 (818) 773-3661.

DAYS, DATES, AND MARKETS ARE SUBJECT TO CHANGE!

YOUNTVILLE

Peddlers Fair
Yountville Veterans Home
Hwy. 29
(707) 944-4941

Every first Saturday. Call first before traveling to this market.

ALWAYS CALL AHEAD TO VERIFY DATES AND INFORMATION

YUCCA VALLEY

Sky Village Outdoor Marketplace
7028 Theatre Rd.

Saturday, Sunday, 5:30 a.m.–2 p.m. Outdoor market with approximately 200 dealers. Lots of new and used merchandise, produce, crafts, tools, toys, sporting goods, some collectibles, some new furniture. Space from $9 on Saturday and $8 on Sunday. Snack bars, café, rest rooms, h/a. Ample parking. *Contact* Bob Carr, Box 1808, 92286 (619) 365-9934 or 365-2104.

COLORADO

BRIGHTON

Brighton Trade Mart
5 S. Main St.
(303) 659-1985

Daily except Monday. New and used merchandise, garage sale items, collectibles, gifts, souvenirs, and decorator items are available. Rest rooms, h/a.

COLORADO SPRINGS

Flea Market Inc
3701 N. Nevada St.
Dog track
(719) 475-9439

Saturday, Sunday. New and used merchandise, garage sale items, bric-a-brac, crafts, and produce are available. Snack bar, rest rooms, h/a, ample paved parking.

City Flea Market
Kiowa and Biqou
(719) 475-9439

Every first weekend. Admission charge. Approximately 125 dealers offer antiques, collectibles, primitives, glassware, and new and used merchandise. Snack bar, rest rooms, h/a, ample parking. Spaces from $13 for the weekend.

Flea Market
5225 E. Platte Ave.

Saturday, Sunday, 7 a.m.–4 p.m. This outdoor market has approximately 125 dealers offering new and used merchandise. Stamps, coins, antiques, collectibles, books, vintage clothing, western wear, collectibles, and produce are available. Snack bar, rest rooms, h/a, ample parking. Space from $13 per day. Farmer's market Friday, June through October. *Contact* Ginger Haggard, P.O. Box 7229, 80933 (719) 380-8559 or 632-3385.

DENVER

Mile High Flea Market
I-76 and 88th Ave.

Wednesday, Saturday, Sunday. Admission charge $2. Over 1,200 seller spaces and an average attendance of 15,000 per day. New and used merchandise, lots of Indian crafts and Indian artifacts, and collectibles. Western items abound, clothes, boots, hats, etc. Overnight parking available on Friday and Saturday. Clean rest rooms, cafe, snack bars, ample parking. This is the Rocky Mountain area's premier market. Space from $17 per day. *Contact* Jim Hurrell, 7007 E. 88th Ave., Henderson, 80640 (303) 289-4656 or (800) 861-9900, fax (303) 286-1922. E-mail: jim_hfm@msn.com.

Denver Antique Market
2727 W. 27th Ave.

Saturday, Sunday. An inside market with approximately 500 dealers. Lots of quality antiques and very good collectibles at this market. Food, rest rooms, h/a, ample parking. Reservations required. *Contact* Andy Burnett, 11306 E. 7th Ave., Aurora, 80010 (303) 364-9469 or 744-7049.

Bonanza Flea Market
7175 N. York St.
1-25 east of town

Saturday, Sunday, 7 a.m.–4 p.m. Approximately 100 dealers offer new and used merchandise, crafts, art, produce, jewelry, and grocery items. Snack bar, rest rooms, h/a, ample parking. Space from $6 per day. *Contact* Marvin Hastings, 5690 N. Federal Blvd., 80221 (303) 286-7175.

Denver Collector's Fair
National Western Complex
I-70 at Brighton Bld. First exit east of I-25

Monthly. Large monthly antiques and collectibles show. Great selection of quality antiques and collectibles. Excellent market for shopkeepers, decorators and dealers to purchase stock. Food available, rest rooms, h/a. *Contact* L and S Management, 1153 Bergen Pkwy., M-475, Evergreen, CO 80439 (303) 526-7339 or (800) 333-3532.

ENGLEWOOD

Arapaho Flea Market
387 S. Santa Fe Dr.

Friday, Saturday, Sunday, 6 a.m.–4 p.m. Admission charge $1. Outdoor market with approximately 500 dealers and an average daily attendance of 5,000. Market is strong on good antiques and collectibles as well as new merchandise, cars, trucks, boats, campers, and trailers. Food, rest rooms, h/a, ample parking. Food vendors can book here. Camping available on-site. Space from $10 per day. *Contact* Manager, P.O. Box 41, 80110 (303) 789-2710.

ESTES PARK

Barter Mart Flea Market
2652 Big Thompson Canyon Rd.

Saturday, Sunday, May–October. New merchandise, souvenirs, gifts, collectibles. Space from $3. *Contact* Jan Wear (303) 586-5444.

INFORMATION IS SUBJECT TO CHANGE—ALWAYS CALL AHEAD TO AVOID DISAPPOINTMENT

FT. COLLINS

Foothills Indoor Flea Markets
6300 S. College and 6200 S. College
(Two separate markets) Hwy. 287

Daily, 10 a.m.–6 p.m. Approximately 75 dealers in each market. These indoor markets have permanent booths and offer mainly antiques, collectibles, art, crafts, and some new merchandise. Monthly space rentals only. *Contact* Ken Ludwick, 6300 S. College, 80525 (970) 223-9069.

Western Flea Mart
6012 S. College
Hwy. 287

Daily, 10 a.m.–7 p.m. Indoor market with 80 dealers offering new merchandise, western wear, booths, sportswear, electronics, housewares, and sports cards. Used merchandise, vintage clothing, glassware, and collectibles are also available. Rest rooms, snack bar, h/a, ample parking. *Contact* Keith Scott, 6012 S. College, 80525 (970) 223-6502.

LAFAYETTE

Lafayette Indoor Flea & Farmers Market
130 E. Spaulding

Daily, 10 a.m.–6 p.m. Approximately 75 dealers offer antiques, collectibles, crafts, art, and some new, consignment, and used merchandise. Snack bar, rest rooms. Monthly booth rental only. *Contact* Bill Hopkins, 130 E. Spaulding, 80026 (303) 665-0433.

LAKEWOOD

Round Up Flea Market
2800 S. Rooney Rd.
(303) 697-1023

Saturday, Sunday. Approximately 500 dealers. Antiques, western and Indian items, art, collectibles, and new merchandise. Interesting market for the collector and popular market for the traveling vendor. Rest rooms, snack bars, h/a, ample parking. Outside space from $5, inside space from $15.

LONGMONT

Front Range Flea Market
1420 Nelson Rd.

Daily. Indoor market with 60 dealers who offer new merchandise, some used merchandise, collectibles, antiques, and furniture. *Contact* Richard Schweger, 1420 Nelson Rd., 80501 (305) 776-6605.

Flea Market
S. Main St.
Longmont Furniture and Auction Co.
(303) 772-1666

Saturday. New merchandise, closeouts, surplus, new and used furniture, used merchandise, and garage sale items. Rest rooms, snack bar, h/a, ample parking.

LOVELAND

Loveland Flea Market
851 S. Lincoln St.
Hwy. 287
(303) 669-9972

Saturday, Sunday. Average daily attendance for this outdoor market with approximately 100 dealers is 2,500. New merchandise, electronics, housewares, sportswear, western wear, and western items abound. Indian jewelry, art, and artifacts, used merchandise, local and Indian crafts, and produce are also available. Rest rooms, snack bar, h/a, ample parking.

ALWAYS CALL BEFORE TRAVELING LONG DISTANCES!

NORTHGLENN

Collectors Corner
160615 Melody
(303) 450-2875

Daily. Indoor market with approximately 125 dealers.

PUEBLO

Fiesta Mart
745 Desert Flower Blvd.
The old Wal-Mart building at the Northside Mall
(719) 542-3434

Friday, Saturday, Sunday, 9:30 a.m.–5:30 p.m. New indoor market. Approximately 100 dealers. Mostly new merchandise, some crafts. Snack bar, rest rooms, h/a. Ample paved parking.

Sunset Swap Meet
Colorado State Fairgrounds
2461 I-25 North Exit 104
(719) 584-2000 or (800) 647-8368

Saturday, Sunday, 8 a.m.–4 p.m. This indoor/outdoor market with approximately 100 dealers and up to 200 during the summer months offers antiques, collectibles, new and used merchandise, crafts, art, and produce. Snack bar, rest rooms, h/a, ample parking. Space from $10 per day. *Contact* Sunset Enterprises, 2641 I-25 N., 81008.

Hilltop Flea Market & Auction
1107 Santa Fe Dr.
(719) 543-6432

Saturday, Sunday. New and used merchandise, surplus, closeouts, collectibles, and crafts. Snack bar, rest rooms, h/a, ample parking. *Contact* Manager, 1107 Santa Fe Dr.

CONNECTICUT

BETHLEHEM

Tique Market
Fairgrounds
Rte. 61
(203) 758-1571

Saturday only, April–November, 8 a.m.–4 p.m. Approximately 150 dealers in this classic New England old-fashioned flea market offer antiques and collectibles. There are a lot of decorator items and home furnishings, crafts, and art. Snack bar, rest rooms, h/a, ample parking. Space from $20 per day.

BRISTOL

Bristol Center Mall
100 North Main St., opposite City Hall

Saturday, 9 a.m.–5 p.m., Sunday, 9:30 a.m.–5 p.m. Indoor flea market, inside the mall. Oriental furniture, antiques, movies, records, stamps, coins, antique radios purchased, sales and repairs, closeouts, computers. Restaurant, rest rooms, h/a. *Contact* USA Markets Inc, Jeff Jacobs (860) 242-1849.

CANTON

The Cob-Web
Junction of Rtes. 44 and 202
West of Hartford

Sunday only, May–October, 9 a.m. until dark. This is the 28th year of operation for this outdoor market with approximately 50 dealers. Good mix of merchandise and vendors. Good market for antiques, collectibles, and decorator items. Good food, rest rooms, h/a, ample parking. Camping nearby. Space from $17 per day. *Contact* Dolly Rudder, Box 954, 06019 (860) 693-2658.

CLINTON

Clinton Village Antique and Collectible Flea Market
Clinton Village
327 E. Main St., Rte. 1
(860) 669-3839

Sundays, 10 a.m.–5 p.m. New market featuring quality collectibles, junk and antiques. Space from $15.

COVENTRY

Coventry Flea Market
44 Lake St.
Junction of Rtes. 31 and 275

Sundays only, 9 a.m.–4 p.m. This indoor/outdoor market has approximately 75 dealers offering new and used merchandise, furniture, jewelry, advertising items, antiques, collectibles, crafts, and pottery. Snack bars, rest rooms, h/a, ample parking. Clean market. Space from $12 per day and up. *Contact* Rose Fowler, 110 Wall St., 06238 (860) 742-1993 or 742-9362.

JEWETT CITY

College Flea Market
Wedgewood Dr.

Sunday only, 9 a.m.–4 p.m. This market has an average attendance of over 4,000 with approx-

---

NOTE: A Connecticut state sales tax permit is required before you can set up and sell at most Connecticut markets.

imately 150 dealers. Antique goods to miscellaneous merchandise and crafts. Snack bar, clean rest rooms, h/a, ample parking. Auction every other Friday. Space from $25 inside and outside, year-round. *Contact* Bob and Sue Leone, Wedgewood Drive, 06351 (860) 376-3935 or 672-6248.

MANSFIELD

Eastern Connecticut Flea Market
Junction of Hwys. 31 and 32
Mansfield Drive-In Theater

Saturday, Sunday, 8 a.m.–3 p.m. Average weekend attendance of 6,000 with approximately 50 dealers on Saturday and 200 on Sunday. Market has a mix of merchandise: antiques, collectibles, new and used items, toys, sportswear, and bric-a-brac. Good food here, rest rooms, h/a, ample parking. Space from $10 on Saturday and $20 for Sunday. *Contact* Michael Jungden, 228 Stafford Rd., 06250 (860) 456-2578.

MILLFORD

Flea Market
Milford Jai Alai

Saturday, Sunday, Tuesday. New merchandise, sportswear, housewares, outdoor items, sports cards, tools, toys, and collectibles are available. Snack bar, rest rooms, h/a, ample parking. Note: Market is seeking vendors with upscale merchandise. Outside space from $20 and inside space from $25. *Contact* Alan Finchley, 515 Boston Post Rd, Port Chester, NY 10573 (860) 727-1000, fax (914) 939-5046.

Antique Liquidators Flea Market
188 Past Rd.
(860) 877-3371

Sundays. Good selection antiques, furniture, collectibles, art, prints, vintage clothing, jewelry. Rest rooms, h/a, snack bar. Ample parking. Seasonal market open May–September.

NAUGATUCK

Peddlers Market
1106 New Haven Rd.

Sundays, dawn to dusk. Outdoor market with an average of 100 dealers. Antiques, collectibles, new and used merchandise, furniture, housewares, sporting goods. Snack bar, rest rooms, h/a. Clean market located in a scenic area. Space from $25 per day. Market open May–October. Ample parking. *Contact* Thomas Murray, Gunntown Rd., 06770 (203) 729-6339 or 729-7762.

NEW HAVEN

Boulevard Flea Market
500 E. T. Grasso Blvd.
I-95 Exit 44 or 45

Saturday, Sunday, 7 a.m.–4 p.m. Outdoor market with approximately 100 dealers. Market is strong on new merchandise at severely discounted prices. Some collectibles, used merchandise, closeout goods. Space from $25 per day. Snack bar, rest rooms, h/a. Paid parking. *Contact* Manager, 500 E. T. Grasso Blvd., 06519 (203) 772-1447 or (877) 228-7554.

NEW MILFORD

Elephant's Trunk Flea Market
Rte. 7, I-84 Exit 7

Sunday only. Admission $1. Approximately 300 dealers offer antiques, collectibles, jewelry, new and used merchandise, sportswear, electronics, and housewares. Food, rest rooms, h/a, ample parking. One of the area's older and better markets. Space from $25. *Contact* Greg Baecker, 23 Deerwood Lane Woodbury, CT 06798 (860) 355-1448.

INFORMATION IS SUBJECT TO CHANGE—ALWAYS CALL FIRST!

Maplewood Indoor Flea Market
Danbury Rd., Rte. 7, I-84, Exit 7, 4 miles north

Saturday, Sunday, 8:30 a.m.–4 p.m. Approximately 75 dealers. Antiques, collectibles, new and used merchandise. Some very nice collectibles here. Space from $30. Snack bars, rest rooms, h/a, game room for kids. One of the area's largest indoor markets. Ample parking. *Contact* Manager, 458 Danbury Rd., 06776 (806) 350-0454.

NIANTIC

Niantic Flea Market
65 Pennsylvania Ave.
I-95, Exit 74, right 2.5 miles

Daily except Wednesday, 10 a.m.–5 p.m. Approximately 50 vendors offer a great selection of quality items, especially glassware, figurines, and other smalls. No new merchandise and no crafts. Snack bar, ample parking. Indoor market with some outside space in good weather. Space from $25 per week. *Contact* Diane Deer, 06357 (860) 691-0170.

NORWICH

Norwich Flea Market
790 W. Thames St.

Sunday. Approximately 50 dealers offer new and used merchandise, antiques, collectibles, sports items, garage sale items, and decorator items. Snack bar, rest rooms, h/a, ample parking. Inside and outside space from $10. Reservations required. *Contact* Alan Delfiner, 50 Carrol Ave., 06360 (203) 889-7408.

OLD MYSTIC

Old Mystic Outdoor Antique Flea Market
Rte. 27 and I-95

Sunday, March–December, 8 a.m.–5 p.m. Approximately 40 dealers offer a good selection here, crafts, art, antiques, collectibles, jewelry, and glassware. This market is located in one of America's most interesting towns. Snack bar, rest rooms, h/a, ample parking. Outside space available on blacktop, approximately 20 feet long from $20. *Contact* Sonny Hendel, Hendel Bldg., 06372 (860) 536-0646.

TERRYVILLE

Plymouth Flea Market
Corner of Rte. 6 and Seymour Rd.

Friday, Saturday, Sunday, April–November. Antiques, collectibles, vintage clothing, silver, used merchandise, garage sale items, and crafts. Food available, rest rooms, h/a, ample parking. Highly traveled and visible spot; 30 outdoor spaces from $18 per day, $30 for the weekend. *Contact* Manny Bharara, Plymouth Flea Market, P.O. Box 327, Terryville, 06786 (860) 582-3097 or 585-1970.

TORRINGTON

Wrights Flea Market
Rte. 4

Saturday, Sunday, 10 a.m.–4:30 p.m. This indoor market has approximately 40 dealers. The market is mainly antiques and collectibles, some secondhand items, and some bric-a-brac. Nice place to find good-quality smalls at very attractive prices. Rest rooms, snack bar, h/a, ample parking. Space from $25. *Contact* Millie Wright, 149 Wright Rd., 06790 (860) 482-1186.

WALLINGFORD

Redwood Country Flea Market
170 Hartford Tpke.
I-91, Exit 13

Saturday, Sunday, 8 a.m.–4 p.m. Open holidays. Approximately 75 dealers. Antiques, collectibles, new items, sports items, and produce. Flea market has a restaurant, a used furniture store, and 1,000 feet of frontage on the Hartford Tpke. Outdoor market with space from $10. *Contact* Ken Dubar, 170 Hartford Tpke., 06492 (203) 269-3500.

WATERBURY

Flea Market
Corner of Aurora St. and Huntington Ave.
(203) 756-1761

Saturday, Sunday. New and used merchandise, lots of garage sale items, bric-a-brac, junk, crafts, collectibles, and produce. Snack bar, rest rooms, h/a, ample parking.

DAYS, DATES, AND MARKETS ARE SUBJECT TO CHANGE!

WOODBURY

Woodbury Antiques and Flea Market
Rte. 6
I-84, Exit 15

Saturdays only, 7 a.m.–2 p.m. Outdoor market with approximately 75 dealers who offer collectibles, antiques, bric-a-brac, tools, jewelry, and some new and used merchandise. Excellent market for antiques and collectibles. Very enjoyable market to shop at—friendly dealers and well-stocked booths, plus Woodbury is loaded with interesting antique and specialty shops. Snack bar, rest rooms, h/a, ample parking. Space from $30 per day. *Contact* Don Heavens, P.O. Box 184, 06798 (203) 263-2841.

DELAWARE

DOVER

Spence's Auction & Flea Market
550 S. New St.

Tuesday, Friday, 8 a.m. until dark. Approximately 100 dealers offer new and used merchandise, antiques, collectibles, and crafts. Snack bar, rest rooms, h/a, ample parking. Auctions held. Space from $15 for three tables. *Contact* Gregory Spence, Box 338, 19901 (302) 734-3441.

LAUREL

Bargain Bill's Flea Market
U.S. 13 Dual Hwy. and 9

Saturday, Sunday, 6 a.m.–5 p.m. Average daily attendance 8,000. Approximately 200 dealers. Wide range of merchandise. Antiques, collectibles, new and used merchandise, tools, secondhand items. Nice restaurant, camping. Rest rooms, h/a. This is one of the area's more interesting markets. Space from $15. Indoor market open all year and outdoors when weather permits. Ample parking for buses and RVs. *Contact* Leslie Brown, Rte. 4, Box 547, 19956 (302) 875-9958 or 875-2478, fax (302) 875-1830. E-mail: fleamarket@magpage.com.

Outlet Market
Rtes. 13 and 462

Friday, Sunday, 9 a.m.–7 p.m. Indoor market, 74,000-square-foot building with approximately 100 dealers and average daily attendance of 8,000. Market is primarily new merchandise that is severely discounted. Great stock-up market on all types of personal and household goods, along with a lot of business supplies and equipment. Good restaurants on the premises. Rest rooms, h/a, ample parking. Space from $50 per weekend. *Contact* R. J. Shingleton, Box 32, 19956 (302) 875-4800.

NEW CASTLE

New Castle Farmers Flea Market
Hares Corner at Rtes. 13 and 273
I-95, Exit 5

Friday, Saturday, Sunday, 10 a.m.–6 p.m. Outside flea market is closed from Thanksgiving until spring. Inside store is open daily during the winter. Average daily attendance 15,000. Indoor and outdoor market with approximately 100 dealers. Convenience store on premises. Camping nearby. Market is restricted to used and secondhand merchandise. One of the East Coast's better and more interesting markets. Good selection of quality country and Pennsylvania Dutch food and merchandise here. Space from $12 to $15. *Contact* Manager, 110 N. Dupont Hwy., 19720 (302) 328-4102, fax (302) 328-9525.

DISTRICT OF COLUMBIA

CAPITOL HILL

The Flea Market at Eastern Market
7th St. between Pennsylvania and North Carolina Ave. SE

Sunday only, 10 a.m.–5 p.m. Outdoor and covered market, one of the oldest markets in the country, dating from 1873. Approximately 150 dealers feature antiques, arts, collectibles, crafts, and imports. Plenty of restaurants nearby, rest rooms in area, h/a. Parking can be a disaster. Best way is to take the Metro. The Eastern Market station is on the orange and blue lines and is located only a block away. Very pleasant, safe area. *Contact* Tom Rall, 1101 N. Kentucky St., Arlington, VA 22205 (703) 534-7612 or (202) 546-2698, fax (703) 534-0285. E-mail: marketflea@aol.com.

GEORGETOWN

Antique Market Place
3407 K St.
(202) 337-3620 or (301) 299-8253

Daily. Flea market on weekends, 35 permanent shops open during the week. Good selection of quality antiques, collectibles, silver, decorator items, jewelry, and vintage clothing at the shops. Rest rooms, h/a, parking is difficult. Commercial vendors welcome.

Georgetown Antique Fair and Flea Market
Wisconsin Ave. and Q St. NW

Sundays only, March–November, 9 a.m.–5 p.m. Antiques, nice furniture, jewelry, collectibles, silver, and vintage clothing are available in this outdoor market. Parking is difficult. Parking lot at the Hardy Middle School. Space from $15 up. *Contact* Michael Sussman, 2109 N St. NW, 20037 (202) 223-0289 or 296-4989.

WASHINGTON

Flea Market
7th and North Carolina SE

Sundays only, March–December, 10 a.m.–5 p.m. Approximately 60 vendors offer antiques, collectibles, new merchandise, imports, gifts, vintage clothing, produce, crafts, and art—some rare and unusual pieces at this indoor and outdoor market. Snack bar. Space starts at $25. *Contact* Tom Rall, 1101 N. Kentucky St., Arlington, VA 22205 (703) 534-7612.

Flea Market
1055 Thomas Jefferson St.

Saturdays only. This flea market offers the typical flea market fare, some new, some near new, some quite secondhand goods.

FLORIDA

APOPKA

Three Star Flea Market
2390 S. Orange Blossom Trail, Hwy. 441

Saturday, Sunday, dawn to dark. Outdoor market with approximately 50 vendors. Antiques, collectibles, new and used merchandise, coins, crafts, produce and lots of general flea market goods. Space from $10 per day. Snack bars, rest rooms, h/a. Ample parking. *Contact* Mary Anderson, 2390 S. Orange Blossom Trail, 32703-1870 (407) 293-2722.

AUBURNDALE

International Market World
1052 Hwy. 92 West
(941) 665-0062
Fax (941) 666-5726

Friday, Saturday, Sunday, 8 a.m.–5 p.m. Average weekend attendance of 10,000 with approximately 500 dealers. New merchandise, imports, gifts, souvenirs, some antiques and collectibles, lots of decorator items, crafts, and art are available. Mountains of used and garage sale items. Plenty of food, rest rooms, h/a, ample parking. Inside and outside space available from $40. This is an excellent market for the commercial vendor. *Contact* International Market World, 1052 Hwy. 92 West, 33823.

NOTE: Before selling in Florida be sure to acquaint yourself with current Florida Department of Motor Vehicles transient auto/truck license requirements. Also, don't forget to check out local ordinances. Severe fines are levied for violations of these ordinances. Florida tax certificates are required at many markets.

BELLEVIEW

The Market of Marion
12888 S.E. U.S. Hwy. 441
(904) 245-6766

Friday, Saturday, Sunday, 8 a.m.–4 p.m. Average daily attendance of 15,000 to see over 700 booths under cover and another 100 booths inside. This is a large wide-open commercial market with everything from new trendy merchandise to quality collector items. Food, rest rooms, h/a, ample parking, entertainment. This is a nice, clean, well-managed market that is a pleasure to visit. Camping nearby. Space from $7 on Friday to $13 on weekends. *Contact* Manager, 12888 S.E. U.S. Hwy. 441, 32620.

Flea City USA
12180 Hwy. 441, one mile south of town
(352) 245-3532

Saturday, Sunday.

BONITA SPRINGS

Flamingo Island Flea Market
11902 Bonita Beach Rd. and I-75

Saturday, Sunday, 8 a.m.–4 p.m. New market. Indoor market with approximately 200 dealers. Antiques, collectibles, new merchandise, crafts, furniture, lots of jewelry, sportswear. Space by the month. Restaurants, rest rooms, h/a. *Contact* Glenda Farrow, 11902 Bonita Beach Rd., 34135 (941) 948-7799 or 495-9500, fax (941) 947-7882.

ALWAYS CALL AHEAD TO VERIFY DATES AND INFORMATION

BRADENTON

Red Barn Flea Market
1707 1st St. East
Rtes. 301 and 41
(941) 747-3794 or (800) 274-FLEA
Fax (941) 747-6539

Wednesday, Thursday, Sunday, 8 a.m.–4 p.m. Approximately 500 booths for vendors who offer new and used merchandise, gifts, souvenirs, imports, tools, clothing, toys, collectibles, crafts, and country and farm items. Snack bar, rest rooms, ample parking. Inside and covered booths. Shops at market are open daily.

Roma Flea Market
5715 15th St. East. Hwy. 301
(941) 756-9036

Saturday, Sunday, 8 a.m.–4 p.m. Indoor/outdoor market with approximately 50 dealers. Snack bar, rest rooms, h/a.

BROOKSVILLE

Airport Mart Flea Market
Six miles south of Brooksville at
Spring Hill Dr.

Saturday, Sunday, 8 a.m.–4 p.m. Approximately 300 dealers offer antiques, collectibles, decorator items, new and used merchandise, produce, crafts, and a good selection of country and farm collectibles. Snack bars, rest rooms, h/a, ample parking. Inside and outside booths, some covered. Most space rented by the month. Reservations required during winter months. *Contact* Judy Jones, 17375 Spring Hill Dr., 34609 (352) 796-0268.

CHIEFLAND

McCormack Flea Market, Inc.
Hwy. 19 North (98 and 27A)

Friday, Saturday, Sunday, 7:30 a.m.–4 p.m. Average attendance 2,000 daily with approximately 50 dealers. New merchandise, used items, crafts, art, produce, antiques, collectibles, and bric-a-brac. Market also has several individual specialty shops, bakery, leather, carpets, etc. Restaurant and snack bars. Rest rooms, h/a, ample parking. Camping available. This is a terrific market that always has a lot of interesting booths. There are 200 spaces, electricity, and water. Space from $6. *Contact* Jack McCormack, Box 1970, 32626 (352) 493-1493 or 493-1491, fax (352) 493-9907.

CLEARWATER

Forty-Niner Flea Market
10525 49th St. North
(813) 473-3367

Saturday, Sunday.

CRESTVIEW

Crestview Flea Market. Hwy. 85 and I-10, at Exit 12
(850) 638-1117

Saturday, Sunday, 7 a.m.–4 p.m. Indoor market with approximately 500 dealers. Lots of new merchandise, some collectibles, lots of new collector lines, sportswear, jewelry, housewares, gifts, imports, used merchandise, crafts, and produce. Snack bars, rest rooms, h/a. Ample free parking.

CRYSTAL RIVER

Stokes Flea Market
Hwy. 44, four miles east of town

Wednesday, Thursday, 7 a.m.–3 p.m. Average daily attendance 5,000. Wide range of merchandise here, lots of well-stocked booths, new and used merchandise, country and farm collectibles, crafts, produce. Snack bar, clean rest rooms, h/a, ample parking. Over 300 covered spaces. Space from $5 to $12 per day. Overnight camping available. *Contact* Stokes, Box 281, 32623 (352) 746-7200 or 746-6566.

DADE CITY

Old Timers Flea Market
Hwy. 301
South of Hwy. 98, five miles north of town
(352) 567-5085

Friday, Saturday, Sunday. Approximately 100 vendors offer new and used merchandise, housewares, electronics, sportswear, collectibles, country and farm items, crafts, and produce. Snack bar, clean rest rooms, h/a, ample parking, for RVs as well. Inside and outside space available from $3. Camping and showers available.

DAYTONA BEACH

Daytona Flea Market and Antique Showplace
1425 Tomka Farms Rd.
Southwest corner of U.S. Hwy. 92 and I-95

Friday, Saturday, Sunday, 8 a.m.–5 p.m. Over 800 vendors and an air-conditioned Antique Showplace with 100 galleries attract a strong attendance. Market is located on 40 acres. Highly recommended for the traveling dealer. During Speed Week and spring break this is the place to be. Outside you will find new, imports, gifts, used, produce, crafts, art, some really nice pieces and inside an excellent assortment of quality items. Good food available here, clean rest rooms, h/a, ample paved parking, and miles of walking. I could live right here at this market and be a very happy camper. Covered space available from $8. *Contact* Robin Ruenheck, P.O. Drawer 2140, 32115.

DE FUNIAK SPRINGS

De Funiak Springs Flea Market
Rte. 90
(850) 892-3668

Friday, Saturday, Sunday. Indoor/outdoor market. Ample parking.

DELAND

Volusia County Farmers Market
3000 E. New York

Wednesday. Approximately 450 dealers. Never-ending variety of goods at this market; pure junk to absolute treasures are here if you can spend the day poking in the hundreds of booths. Commercial vendors, note that this is one of the best weekday markets in Florida. Food available, rest rooms, h/a, ample paved parking, and miles of walking required to see this market. Indoor and outdoor space available. *Contact* Harley Cultip (561) 734-1614.

DELRAY BEACH

Hi-Way Airport Swap Meet
1930 Federal Hwy.
(561) 524-0308

Saturday, Sunday. Approximately 700 dealers show at this large classic commercial market. Mountains of new merchandise and truckloads of garage sale items are available. This market features a little bit of everything and has literally untold rows of booths stocked with goodies. Food available, rest rooms, h/a, ample parking, and miles of walking.

Delray Swap Shop
2001 N. Federal Hwy.

Wednesday–Sunday, 8 a.m.–2 p.m. Approximately 400 dealers show goods. The inside market has a special antique section with a lot of quality items; outside there is new merchandise, housewares, imports, electronics, sportswear, jewelry, and produce. Space from $5 Friday and $25 to $100 for Saturday and Sunday. Reservations required. Snack bars, rest rooms, h/a, ample parking. *Contact* Loretta Shaw, 2001 N. Federal Hwy., 33444 (561) 276-4012.

Antique Market
2399 U.S. Hwy. 1 North

Saturday, Sunday. Good selection of quality smalls, furniture, collectibles, lots of nice collector items, as well as linens, jewelry, silver, vintage clothing. Snack bar, rest rooms, h/a, ample parking.

Delray Indoor Flea Market
5283 W. Atlantic Ave.
I-95, Exit 42, west three miles

Thursday–Sunday, 9 a.m.–5 p.m. Approximately 125 exhibitors offer new merchandise, gifts, souvenirs, imports. This market has lots of designer clothes and sportswear; selection is as good as any factory outlet mall with much better prices. Market is restricted to new merchandise. Snack bar, rest rooms, h/a, ample parking. Contact Edina Frankel, 5283 W. Atlantic Ave., 33484 (561) 499-9935.

DORA

Florida Twin Markets
Hwy. 441

Saturday, Sunday. This indoor/outdoor market has approximately 400 dealers offering a good selection of antiques from furniture to smalls, as well as new merchandise. Great selection for the collector or decorator. Snack bar, clean rest rooms, h/a, ample parking, and miles of walking. Inside and outside space from $28. *Contact* Twin Markets, Box 939, Zellwood, 32798 (904) 383-8393.

EUSTIS

Lake County Farmers Market
Fairgrounds
2101 Hwy. 452-A
(352) 357-9692

Thursday only. Excellent market offers produce, new merchandise, and some collectibles. Wide range of dealers each week at this market. Excellent midweek market for commercial vendors. Food available, rest rooms, h/a, ample parking.

FT. LAUDERDALE

Thunderbird Swap-Shop
121 W. Sunrise Blvd.

Wednesday–Sunday, 7 a.m.–6 p.m. Admission charged. With approximately 1,500 dealers, this is one of the great markets of the South. Entertainment, live music, auctions, food, and bingo are all a part of this market, with every conceivable type of merchandise sold here. Tremendous selection of food, 15–17 restaurants/cafes. This market is a fun vacation within itself. *Contact* Thunderbird Swap Meet, 3121 W. Sunrise Blvd., 33311 (954) 791-7927 or (800) 345-SWAP, fax (954) 792-7962.

Oakland Park Boulevard Flea Market
3161 W. Oakland Park Blvd.
I-95, exit Oakland Park Blvd.

Wednesday–Sunday, 10 a.m.–7 p.m. Indoor market with approximately 200 dealers. Tremendous selection of new merchandise. Everything that you would find at a discount store but at much better prices. Space rented by month only. Snack bars, rest rooms, h/a. Ample parking. *Contact* Leonard Bennis, 3161 W. Oakland Park Blvd., 33311 (954) 949-7959.

FT. MYERS

Fleamasters Fleamarket
4135 Anderson Ave. on State Rte. 82
I-75, Exit 23, one mile west

Friday, Saturday, Sunday, 8 a.m.–4 p.m. Average attendance 30,000 with approximately 500 dealers. An open market with good selection, antiques, collectibles, decorator items, lots of new merchandise, imports and gifts, crafts, art, produce, glassware, toys, tools, jewelry (fine and costume), and new clothing. Great selection of food here. Clean rest rooms, h/a, ample parking. Indoor/outdoor market with over 800 booths. Electricity available. *Contact* Donna Matthews, 4135 Martin Luther King, Jr. Blvd., 33916 (941) 334-7001 or 719-7000, fax (941) 334-2087. E-mail: fleakeeper@aol.com.

Ortiz Avenue Flea Market
Ortiz Ave. and State Rte. 80B
Exit off I-75 at mile marker #24

Saturday, Sunday. One of the oldest flea markets in southwest Florida offers new merchandise, housewares, tools, electronics, sports items, used merchandise, collectibles, farm and ranch items, and glassware. Snack bar, clean rest rooms, h/a, ample parking. Credit cards accepted. This is a clean, friendly, well-managed market that is a pleasure to visit. Electricity available. *Contact* Barbara Collins (941) 694-5019.

FT. PIERCE

Biz-E-Flea Market
3252 N. US Rte. 1, between Vero Beach and Ft. Pierce

Saturday, Sunday. Antiques, collectibles, new merchandise, lots of used merchandise and fleat market goods. Space from $8. Snack bars, rest rooms, h/a. Ample parking. *Contact* Irma Partridge, 3252 N. U.S. Rte. 1, 34951 (561) 466-3063.

FRONTENAC

Frontenac Flea Market
U.S. Hwy. 1

Friday, Saturday, Sunday, 8 a.m.–4 p.m. One of the better markets in Florida—has an attendance 15–20,000 daily. Approximately 1,000 dealer spaces with approximately 400 dealers on a given day. Good selection of new merchandise, especially clothing and sportswear, and sports-related merchandise. Great vacation area. Plenty of food, clean rest rooms, h/a, ample parking. Popular stop for the traveling dealer. I have made some good buys here over the years. Space from $13 per day outside. Camping available and several campgrounds nearby. *Contact* Mike Christian, Box 10, Sharpes, 32959 (407) 631-0241 fax 631-0246.

FRUITLAND PARK

North Lake Flea Market
Hwy. 441 and 27 East
(904) 326-9335

Saturday, Sunday. This outdoor market has an average daily attendance of 2,500 with approximately 150 dealers. New merchandise, sportswear, imports, housewares, tools, electronics, outdoor and sporting goods, used merchandise, garage sale items, collectibles, farm and ranch items, crafts, and produce are available. Rest rooms, snack bar with breakfast, h/a, ample parking.

GULF BREEZE

The Flea Market
5760 Gulf Breeze Pkwy., Hwy. 98, 15 miles east of Pensacola

Saturday, Sunday. Outdoor market, antiques, collectibles, crafts, lots of new and used merchandise, produce. Approximately 300 dealers. Space from $15 per day. Snack bars, hot meals, rest rooms, h/a. Ample parking. *Contact* Audrey Thompson, 5760 Gulf Breeze Pkwy., 32561.

HALLENDALE

Hallendale Flea Market
Hollywood Dog Track
U.S. Hwy. 1 and Pembroke Rd.

Saturday, Sunday, 8 a.m.–3 p.m. Admission charge. Indoor/outdoor market with approximately 400 vendors. Good selection here, lots of new, sportswear, sports, and electronics. Some antiques, collectibles, decorator items, crafts, and art. Plenty of food, rest rooms, h/a, ample parking with lots of walking. Season varies with racing schedule; 600 booths with space starting at $13. *Contact* Daniel Adkins, 831 N. Federal Hwy., 33009 (954) 454-8666.

HOMOSASSA SPRINGS

Homosassa Springs Flea Market
6373 S. Suncoast Blvd.
Three miles south of town on Hwy. 19
(352) 628-4656

Saturday, Sunday, 6:30 a.m. until dark. Average daily attendance 8,000. Approximately 600 dealer spaces. Crafts, collectibles, jewelry, shoes, clothing, antiques, baseball cards, and lots of miscellaneous. Food concessions with good menu. Rest rooms, h/a, ample parking. Good market for the traveling vendor and a very pleasant, friendly market for shoppers. Food vendors welcome. Space starts at $8; overnight camping available. *Contact* Tom Cushman.

HUDSON

Sunshine Flea Market
2815 Sunset Blvd.

Saturday, Sunday. Market averages 250 dealers each weekend who offer new and used merchandise, imports, souvenirs, collectibles, crafts, and produce. Snack bar, rest rooms, h/a, ample parking. Inside and outside spaces. *Contact* Charles Stumm (813) 863-1805.

JACKSONVILLE

Playtime Drive-In Flea Market
6300 Blanding Blvd.
Playtime Drive-In Theater

Wednesday–Sunday, 7 a.m.–4 p.m. Average daily attendance 5,000 with approximately 350 dealers. Large commercial Florida market with a wide range of dealers who sell all types of new and used merchandise, collectibles, crafts, and produce. Snack bar, rest rooms, h/a, ample parking, and lots of walking. Space from $3 per day. *Contact* Jack Hagerty, 6300 Blanding Blvd., 33210 (904) 771-9939.

The Market Place
6839 Ramona Blvd.

Saturday, Sunday, 8 a.m.–5 p.m. Admission charge. Average attendance 20,000 per weekend with approximately 1,000 dealers. Great selection of new merchandise, imports, sportswear, sports merchandise, antiques, furniture, silver, coins, collectibles, glassware, jewelry (both fine and costume), produce, crafts, and fine art. A full day's stop, with a lot of walking required. Full-service restaurant on premises. Rest rooms and a wonderful beer garden, h/a, ample parking. Space starts at $6. Overnight camping. *Contact* Richard Waller (904) 786-1153 or 786-FLEA.

The Jacksonville Market Place
614 Pecan Park Rd.
(904) 751-6770

Saturday, Sunday. Average daily attendance 10,000 with approximately 700 dealers. Large wide-open commercial market with a great selection of dealers and booths. If it's new, if it's collected, it's sold here. Food available, rest rooms, h/a, ample parking, and lots of walking. Spaces under cover. Space from $14 per day.

The Bargain House of Fleas
6016 Blanding Blvd.

Saturday, Sunday. Indoor and outdoor market. Approximately 250 dealers. Antiques, collectibles, furniture, produce, crafts, new and used merchandise, lots of general flea market goods. Space from $7. Snack bar, rest rooms, h/a. Ample parking. *Contact* Matthew Skenes, 6016 Blanding Blvd., 32244 (904) 772-8008.

Beach Boulevard Flea Market
11041 Beach Blvd.

Saturday, Sunday, 8 a.m.–5 p.m. Outdoor market with lots of covered spaces. Some antiques, collectibles, furniture, crafts, jewelry, produce, lots of new and used merchandise. Space from $10. Restaurant, snack bars, rest rooms, h/a. Ample parking. *Contact* Charles Burchette, 11041 Beach Blvd., 32246 (904) 645-5961.

KEY LARGO

Key Largo Flea Market
103530 Overseas Hwy., Rte. 1, just north of Pennekamp State Park
(305) 451-0677

Saturday, Sunday, 7 a.m.–4 p.m. Indoor market with approximately 50 dealers. Snack bar, rest rooms, h/a. Ample parking.

KISSIMMEE

Osceola Flea & Farmers Market
2801 Earl Bronson Memorial Hwy.
U.S. Hwy. 192

Saturday, Sunday, May–September; Friday, Saturday, Sunday, October–April; 8 a.m.–5 p.m. There are 900 booths all under an insulated roof. Lots of new and secondhand merchandise here, souvenirs, produce, and some antiques and collectibles. One of the largest markets in the area. Restaurant, snack bars, h/a, ample paved parking. All dealers park at their booth. Storage sheds available. Electricity in booths. Fenced for security. A lot of walking here. Monthly rate available. *Contact* Frank Bauonauro, Jr., 2801 Earl Bronson Memorial Hwy., 34744 (407) 846-2811.

192 Flea Market
4301 W. Vine St.
Junction of Hwy. 192 and Vine St.
(407) 396-4555

Daily, 9 a.m.–6 p.m. Approximately 400 spaces. Wide variety of goods: new merchandise, imports, gifts, souvenirs, decorator items, some collectibles, bric-a-brac, produce, crafts, and jewelry. Food court, rest rooms, h/a, ample parking. New market. *Contact* Manager, 4301 W. Vine St., 34746.

LAKE CITY

Jeanett's I-10 Flea Market
U.S. Hwy. 41, N. I-10, Exit 43
(904) 755-6482 or 754-0056

Friday, Saturday, Sunday, 7 a.m. until dark. New outdoor market with some covered spaces. Approximately 100 dealers. Space from $7. Snack bars, rest rooms, h/a. Ample free parking.

Lake City Flea Market
Columbia County Fairgrounds
East of I-75 on U.S. Hwy. 90 at State Rte. 247 (Branford Hwy.)
(904) 752-1999 or 755-2816

Saturday, Sunday, 7 a.m.–4 p.m. Average daily attendance 2,000. Over 100 dealers. Antiques, collectibles, jewelry, toys, and tools. Snack bar, rest rooms, h/a, ample parking. Market has a general consignment/retail auction on Saturday. Space from $9 outside. Reservations required for inside space. Camping available. *Contact* Gateway Auction Service, Box 3331, 32056.

LAKELAND

Lakeland Farmers Market
2701 Swindell Rd.
(941) 682-4809

Thursday–Sunday, 6 a.m.–5 p.m. Approximately 250 dealers offer crafts, collectibles, new merchandise, produce, and secondhand merchandise. This is a clean, well-managed, friendly market. Snack bars, restaurant, h/a, ample parking. Inside, outside, and covered space from $14 on Saturday and $14 on Sunday. No overnight parking. *Contact* Jim Wilbanks, 2701 Swindell Rd., 33805.

International Market World
Hwy. 92 East

Friday, Saturday, Sunday. Excellent variety of new merchandise, hot new trendy items, and necessary personal and household items at much better prices than at the discount houses. An excellent market for commercial vendors. This is a clean, well-managed, and friendly market that is always a pleasure to stop at. Snack bars, rest rooms, h/a, ample parking.

LAKE WORTH

Trail Drive-In Theater Swap Meet
Trail Drive-In Theater
Lake Worth Rd., between Congress Ave. and Military Trail
(561) 965-4318

Saturday, Sunday. Approximately 250 dealers. New merchandise, sports and fishing items, housewares, tools, sportswear, electronics, gifts, souvenirs, and imports. Used merchandise, garage sale items, collectibles, crafts, and produce. Snack bar, rest rooms, h/a, ample parking.

Lake Worth High School Flea Market
1701 Lake Worth Rd., high school parking lot. Under the I-95 overpass between 6th Ave. and 10th Ave. exits. Next to the Tri-Rail Station.

Saturday, Sunday. Market is under cover. Approximate attendance 3,000 per day. Antiques, collectibles, produce, furniture, lots of locally made crafts, new and used merchandise, bric-a-brac. Space from $10 per day. Snack bars, rest rooms, h/a. This market is operated by the high school and proceeds are used for scholarships for needy students. Ample parking. *Contact* Betty Milone, Box 6592, 33466 (561) 439-1539.

MAITLAND

Maitland Flea Market
1941 Hwy. 17-92
(561) 339-2970

Saturday, Sunday, daylight until dark. New merchandise, jewelry, coins, electronics, souvenirs, gifts, and collectibles are available. Good all-around market. When the Oklahoma Sooners were winning and playing in the Orange Bowl, this market was on my route to replenish the ol' cash sock. Now that Nebraska is an Orange Bowl loser and Miami is not on my approved travel list, I have scratched this market from my list. Snack bar, rest rooms, h/a, ample parking. Some covered spaces, but the majority of space is outside.

Ole Red Barn Flea Market
8750 South 17-92

Saturday, Sunday, 8 a.m.–4 p.m. Outdoor market with some covered spaces and approximately 25 dealers. Produce market is open daily. Rest room, h/a. Ample parking. *Contact* Betty Smith (561) 789-3945.

MARGATE

Margate Swap Shop
1000 N. State Rd. 7
Hwy. 441
(954) 971-7927

Saturday–Tuesday, 5 a.m.–2 p.m. Indoor/outdoor market with over 350 dealers. Antiques, collectibles, new merchandise, sportswear, gifts, imports. Produce, crafts, art. Good all-around market. Space from $8. Snack bar, rest rooms, h/a. *Contact* Sharon Earls.

MELBOURNE

Super Flea and Farmers Market
4835 W. Eau Gallie Blvd.

Friday, Saturday, Sunday, 9 a.m.–4 p.m. Approximately 250 dealers offering a good selection of antiques, collectibles, silver, jewelry, new merchandise, sportswear, imports, electronics, crafts, art, produce, and secondhand items. Clean rest rooms, good food, h/a, ample parking; 700 covered spaces with rent from $20 per day. *Contact* Kim Clark, 4835 W. Eau Gallie Blvd., 32934 (407) 242-9124.

MIAMI

Travel advisory: When traveling in the Miami area, always be sure that the gas tank is full and *that the car is in good mechanical condition. Be extremely careful of the areas that you travel into* and *stay on the main thoroughfares. Leave well before dark.*

The No. 1 Market
11000 N.W. 7th Ave.
(305) 751-8664

Wednesday, 12 p.m.–7 p.m., Thursday–Saturday, 10 a.m.–9 p.m., Sunday, 10 a.m.–7 p.m. New and used merchandise, fishing and marine items, housewares, tools, electronics, sportswear, and lots of imports available. Snack bar, rest rooms, h/a, ample parking.

Flagler Flea Market
N.W. 37th Ave. and 7th St.
Flagler Dog Track
(305) 649-3000

Saturday, Sunday, 8 a.m.–4 p.m. Admission 50 cents. This is one of the leading markets in this area and it offers lots of new merchandise, sportswear, sports-related merchandise, electronics, housewares, and outdoor items. Food available, snack bar, rest rooms, h/a, ample parking. Clean, friendly, well-managed market that does heavy media advertising in the Greater Miami press. Indoor and outdoor spaces with daily and monthly rates. State sales tax laws enforced. *Contact* Armando Prats, P.O. Box 350940, 33135 (305) 649-3022, fax (305) 631-4529.

Flea Market USA
3015 N.W. 79th St.
(305) 836-3677

Wednesday, 12 p.m.–7 p.m., Saturday, 10 a.m.–9 p.m., Sunday, 10 a.m.–7 p.m. New merchandise, gifts, souvenirs, imports, sportswear, electronics, housewares, tools, and toys are available. Used merchandise, crafts, collectibles, and produce. Snack bar, rest rooms, h/a, ample parking.

Hialeah Opa-Locka Flea Market
12705 N.W. 42nd Ave.

Saturday, Sunday, 5 a.m.–7 p.m. New and used merchandise, crafts, collectibles, and produce are available. Snack bar, restaurants, rest rooms, h/a, ample paid parking. Space from $60 for the weekend. *Contact* Scott Miller, 12705 N.W. 42nd Ave., 33054 (305) 688-0500 or 688-0525, fax (305) 687-8312.

183rd Street Flea Market
18200 N.W. 27th Ave.

Wednesday, Sunday, 10 a.m.–7 p.m., Thursday–Saturday, 10 a.m.–6 p.m. New merchandise, lots of sportswear, electronics, imports, and gifts. Great selection of fine jewelry. Lots of specialty shops. Indoor market with approximately 400 booths. Snack bars, rest rooms, h/a, ample parking. Market does not rent to the traveling dealer. *Contact* Stanley Gaines, 18200 N.W. 27th Ave., 33056 (305) 624-1756.

7th Avenue Flea Markets
14135 N.W. 7th Ave. North and
13995 N.W. 7th Ave. North
(305) 685-7721

Thursday–Sunday. These sister indoor markets are operated by one of the leading market promotion companies in the U.S. Mainly permanent leases. New merchandise, sportswear, housewares, electronics, toys, imports, and gifts are available. Market also has strong jewelry sections, rivaled only by Cartier's in N.Y. Snack bars, restaurant, rest rooms, h/a. *Contact* IBS Flea Markets, 19920 N.W. 2nd Ave., 33169.

Jai-Alai Flea Market
3500 N.W. 37th Ave.

Sundays only, 9 a.m.–5 p.m. Approximately 250 dealers offer new merchandise, trendy Florida items, sportswear, electronics, housewares, fishing and marine items, used merchandise, crafts, produce, and collectibles. Food available, rest rooms, h/a, ample parking. *Contact* Lily Rodriguez.

MIAMI BEACH

World's Largest Indoor Flea Market
Convention Center

Quarterly. Admission $3.50. One of the premier events in the U.S. Uncommonly large attendance, excellent market for new, crafts, and high-quality items. There are quite a few new-product launches at this market. Plan to spend all day. Call for schedule. *Contact* Louis Shelley, 190 N.E. 199th St., No. 203, 33179 (305) 651-9530, fax (305) 652-2568.

MILTON

I-10 Flea market
I-10, Exit 8, one-half mile south
(850) 623-6349

Friday, Saturday, Sunday. Indoor market with approximately 125 dealers. Snack bar, rest rooms, h/a. Ample parking.

MT. DORA

Renninger's Florida Twin Markets
Hwy. 441, half mile north of Rte. 46

Saturday, Sunday, 8 a.m.–4 p.m. Admission charge. Approximately 400 exhibitors offer quality antiques and collectibles. One of the best sources for quality items in Florida. Market also holds some special events that are unusually large antique shows. Call for dates. food available, rest rooms, h/a, ample parking. *Contact* Robert Lynch, Box 1699, 32757 (352) 383-8393 or 383-3141.

NAPLES

Naples Drive-In Theater Flea Market
7700 E. Davis Blvd.
Hwy. 84 East

Wednesday, Saturday, Sunday, 7 a.m.–3 p.m. Approximately 200 dealers offer lots of new merchandise, electronics, gifts, imports, sports-related merchandise, and souvenirs. Some collectibles, bric-a-brac, secondhand items, and large farmers' market here. Snack bars, restaurant, rest rooms, h/a, ample parking. Outdoor market space from $6. *Contact* Jack Naples, 7700 E. Davis Blvd., 33942 (941) 774-2900 phone and fax.

NEW PORT RICHEY

Indoor Fleas Flea Market
3621 U.S. Hwy. 19

Friday, Saturday, Sunday, 9 a.m.–5 p.m. Indoor market, approximately 150 dealers. New and used merchandise, crafts, antiques, collectibles, electronics, imports. Space from $25 per weekend. Snack bar, rest rooms, h/a. Ample parking. *Contact* Marie, 3621 U.S. Hwy. 19, 34621 (727) 842-3665, fax (727) 842-3665.

OAK HILL

Oak Hill Flea Market
351 N. Hwy. 1

Tuesday, Friday, Saturday, Sunday, 8 a.m.–4 p.m. Indoor market with approximately 100 dealers. Snack bar, rest rooms, h/a. Ample parking. *Contact* Sue Perry (904) 345-3570 or 428-9544.

OCALA

Ocala Drive-In Flea
4850 S. Pine Ave.
Ocala Drive-In Theater

Saturday, Sunday, 7 a.m.–4 p.m. Approximately 350–400 dealers offer a wide variety of merchandise including pets, exotic birds, and a pawn shop. This is always a very interesting market, lots of colorful dealers with interesting booths. Snack bars, clean rest rooms, h/a, ample parking. Space from $10 covered and $8 outside. *Contact* Lou Williams, 4850 S. Pine Ave., 32671 (352) 629-1325.

I-75 Super Flea Market
4121 N.W. 44th Ave., I-75, Exit 70 or 71

Friday, Saturday, Sunday, 9 a.m.–4 p.m. Indoor/outdoor market. Average weekend attendance 25,000, with approximately 1,000 dealers. Large wide-open commercial Florida market, ideal for the commercial seller. Wide range of merchandise, both new and used, antique and collectible spreads here. Fun market for both the buyer and seller. Space from $10 outside, reservations recommended. Snack bars, rest rooms, h/a. Ample parking. *Contact* Sue Hogue, Box 3656, 34478 (352) 351-9220, fax (352) 401-1905.

ODESSA

Bargain Mart
200 Old Gunn Hwy.
Intersection of State Rd. 54 and Gunn Hwy.

Friday, Saturday, Sunday, 8 a.m.–4 p.m. Wide range of merchandise and dealers at this market. Complete selection of new lines, used merchandise, collectibles, country and ranch items, outdoor, sporting, and fishing items, crafts, and produce. Food available, rest rooms, h/a, ample parking. Dealers, if you are planning on selling here, you will need to make reservations in advance as this is a very popular local market; 600 booths. *Contact* Barbara Moore, 2317 Gunn Hwy., 33556 (729) 920-3181.

OKEECHOBEE

The Market Place
3600 Hwy. 441 South
(941) 467-6803

Saturday, Sunday, 7 a.m.–4 p.m. Approximately 300 dealers offer new merchandise, tools, electronics, housewares, sportswear, sports-related cards and items, fishing and marine items, country collectibles, crafts, and produce. Rest rooms, snack bar, h/a, ample parking. Space from $15 per weekend. Camping next door. *Contact* Mindy Schoppmeyer, 34974.

Trading Post & Farmers Market
3100 Hwy. 441 South
(941) 763-4114

Saturday, Sunday, 8 a.m.–3 p.m. Approximately 150 dealers offer new merchandise, electronics, tools, housewares, outdoor items, sporting and fishing items, used merchandise, collectibles, crafts, decorator items, and produce. Lighted driving range, snack bars, clean rest rooms, h/a, ample parking. Space from $13 per day. Outside market with all covered spaces.

Cypress Hut Flea Market
4701 Hwy. 441 South
(863) 357-6556

Saturday, Sunday, 8 a.m.–4 p.m. Indoor/outdoor market with approximately 200 dealers. snack bars, rest rooms, h/a.

OLDSMAR

Oldsmar Flea Market
180 N. Racetrack Rd.
(813) 855-5306 or 855-2587
Fax (813) 855-1263

Friday, Saturday, Sunday. Good, established, well-attended market with approximately 1,250 dealers who offer antiques, collectibles, and new and used merchandise. Many dealers with volume discounts on new merchandise as well as a discount grocery store. This market is almost an endless sea of booths; if you can think of it, it is here. Restaurant with beer, fortunately. Snack bars, rest rooms, h/a, ample parking, and miles of walking. Inside and outside space from $11. *Contact* Oldsmar Flea Market, Box 439, 34657.

ORLANDO

Orlando Flea Market
5022 S. Orange Blossom Trail
Two miles south of I-4 on Hwy. 441
(407) 293-5357

Saturday, Sunday. Approximately 300 exhibitors in this large commercial market with lots of new merchandise, used merchandise, crafts, produce, and collectibles. Snack bar, rest rooms, h/a, ample parking. Space from $8.60. Local license required. *Contact* Curtis Adams, 2831 Marquise Ct., 32805 (407) 857-0048.

Flea World
Hwy. 17-92
Between Orlando and Sanford
(407) 330-1792

Friday, Saturday, Sunday. Average weekend attendance is 75,000 and there are approximately 1,200 booths. Indoor and outdoor market with air-conditioned indoor shopping area that includes 96 mini stores, 11 food concessions with seating, bingo parlor, rest rooms, h/a, and ample parking with lots of walking. Market has many special promotions and is one of the largest attended attractions in Florida. This is an all-day stop; for the flea market aficionado, this market is more fun than Disney World. I have been to both and like Flea World better. Space from $10 per day. Monthly rates available. Dealer parking at booth. *Contact* Flea World, Hwy. 17-92, Sanford, 32771.

Central Florida Farmers Market
4603 W. Colonial Dr.

Saturday, Sunday, 5 a.m. until dark. Outdoor market with approximately 300 dealers. Antiques, collectibles, crafts, produce, furniture, new and used merchandise, lots of bric-a-brac here. Space from $10 per day. Free parking. *Contact* John Wild, 1552 Daly St., 32808 (407) 295-9448 or 296-3868.

Flea Market
1552 Daly St.
Central Florida Fairgrounds
(407) 295-9448

Saturday, Sunday. Approximately 300 dealers with quality antiques, collectibles, silver, coins, linen, glassware, primitives. Some very nice-quality items here. Food available, snack bar, h/a, ample parking.

PALMETTO

The Country Market
10816 N. U.S. Hwy. 41
Junction of Hwys. 301 and 41
(941) 723-6000

Saturday, Sunday, 8 a.m.–4 p.m. Large market with approximately 1,000 dealers. Lots of stuff here. New merchandise, clothing, sportswear, furniture, great selection of fishing and boating items, crafts, and art. Restaurants, snack bars, clean rest rooms, h/a, ample parking, and miles of walking. Fun upbeat family atmosphere. Clean, well-managed friendly market. Front section of the market is open daily. Inside spaces and covered booths. Covered booth $11 per day, inside $19.50 per day. *Contact* Joseph Kucej, 10816 N. U.S. Hwy. 41, 34221.

PANAMA CITY

15th Street Flea Market
2233 E. 15th St.
(850) 769-0137 or 769-7401

Thursday, 9 a.m.–3 p.m., Friday, 9 a.m.–4 p.m., Saturday and Sunday, 8 a.m.–5 p.m. Approximately 150 vendors offer new merchandise, electronics, fishing and marine items, outdoor items, sportswear, tools, used merchandise, crafts, collectibles, and produce. Snack bars, rest rooms, h/a, ample parking. Indoor/outdoor market. Food vendors may apply for space. Camping available. *Contact* Leo Adkins, 32405.

PENSACOLA

T&W Flea Market
1717 N. T St.

Wednesday, Saturday, Sunday, 6 a.m.–5 p.m. Approximately 300 dealers offer a wide variety of merchandise. New and used merchandise, collectibles, housewares, and produce galore. This market also operates a large wholesale produce market, open daily. Snack bars, camping, air conditioning, rest rooms, h/a, ample parking. Inside and outside space available from $10 per day. *Contact* Red Cotton, 1717 N. T St., 32505 (850) 433-4315.

INFORMATION IS SUBJECT TO CHANGE—ALWAYS CALL AHEAD TO AVOID DISAPPOINTMENT

PINELLAS PARK

Wagon Wheel Flea Market
7801 Park Blvd.

Saturday, Sunday, 8 a.m.–4 p.m. Average daily attendance 20,000. Approximately 1,100 dealers. Excellent market for all lines. One of the country's largest markets, with an excellent mix of merchandise from antiques to produce, arts to new merchandise. Market is so big that it has a tram that you can ride around in. International food court. Special bargain section with several hundred booths with probably the best prices in the entire country. Clean rest rooms, h/a and lots of walking. A flea market fan could make an entire vacation right here and probably never visit the same booth twice. Space from $9.50 per day. Some covered space. Ample parking. *Contact* Misty Lynch, 7801 Park Blvd., 34665 (727) 544-5319, fax (727) 541-4005.

Mustang Flea Market
7301 Park Blvd.

Wednesday, Saturday, Sunday, 6 a.m. until dark. Outdoor market. Approximately 200 vendors. Antiques, collectibles, produce, crafts, furniture, new and used merchandise. Lots of low-priced garage sale merchandise here. Space from $2.50 on Wednesday and Friday and $6 on Saturday or Sunday. Snack bars, rest rooms, h/a. Free parking. *Contact* Betty Guinn, 7301 Park Blvd., 34665 (727) 544-3066.

PLANT CITY

Country Village Flea Market
3301 Hwy. 39 North
State Rte. 39 and Sam Allen Rd.
(813) 752-4670 or 752-7088

Wednesday, Saturday, Sunday. Approximately 200 dealers offer new trendy merchandise, sportswear, jewelry, sports, fishing, and marine items, tools, silver, used merchandise, locally made crafts, and collectibles. One of the largest Wednesday markets in the Tampa area. Space from $5. *Contact* Ferris Waller, 3301 N. Hwy. 39, 33566.

POMPANO BEACH

Festival Flea Market Hall
2900 W. Sample Rd.

Daily, 9:30 a.m.–5 p.m. Closed Mondays. Indoor market. Approximately 800 dealers. Antiques, collectibles, new and used merchandise, electronics, sportswear, great selection and prices for new merchandise here. Space by the month, traveling dealers not accepted. Food court, arcade, theater—this place is almost like going to a new shopping mall. Rest rooms, h/a. Free parking. *Contact* Fran Folix, 2900 W. Sample Rd., 33073, (800) 353-2627 or (305) 979-4555, fax (305) 968-3980.

PORT CHARLOTTE

Rainbow Flea Market
4628 Tamiami Trail. Junction of Kings Hwy. and Rte. 41. Charlotte Harbor

Friday, Saturday, Sunday. Contact Loretta Meegan (941) 629-1223.

Sun Flea Market
18505 Paulson Dr., junction of U.S. Hwy. 41 and 776

Friday, Saturday, Sunday. Contact Ken Levy (941) 255-3532.

PORT RICHEY

USA Fleamarket
11721 U.S. Hwy. 19
On U.S. 19 at Hwy. 52

Friday, Saturday, Sunday, 8 a.m.–4 p.m. Average weekend attendance is 30,000, with 400 dealers. Live entertainment each weekend. Lots of variety here, tremendous selection of dealers. Restaurant, snack bars, clean rest rooms, h/a, ample parking, and lots of walking; 800 booths. Very clean, friendly, well-managed flea market that does lots of special events. Credit cards accepted. Space $10 and up. Camping with electricity available. *Contact* Marie Bruno, 11721 U.S. Hwy. 19, 34568 (727) 862-3583, fax (727) 862-5724.

RIVIERA BEACH

Beach Drive-In Theater Swap Meet
1301 Old Dixie Hwy.
Beach Drive-In Theater

Wednesday–Sunday, 6 a.m.–2 p.m. Outdoor market with approximately 400 dealers. Market is primarily new merchandise and secondhand items. Lots of low-dollar new and used merchandise here. Great market to make some real good cash deals. Snack bar, rest rooms, h/a, ample parking. *Contact* Rubin Rodriguea, 1301 Old Dixie Hwy., 33404 (561) 844-5836.

SANFORD

Flea World
See Orlando listing

Friday, Saturday, Sunday.

ST. AUGUSTINE

St. Johns Market Place
Intersection of I-95, Exit 94, and Hwy. 207

Saturday, Sunday, 8 a.m.–5 p.m. This is the area's leading market, approximately 400 dealers with antiques, collectibles, crafts, lots of new merchandise, some used merchandise. Snack bars, restaurant, rest rooms, h/a, ample parking. This is a clean, well-managed, friendly market that is always a pleasure to visit. Covered spaces and some indoor spaces. Camping available. Space from $11 per day, reservations recommended. *Contact* St. Johns Market Place, Box 1284, 32085 (904) 824-4210, fax (904) 829-5784.

STUART

B&A Flea Market
2201 S.E. Indian St.
Across street from Martin Square Mall

Saturday, Sunday, 8 a.m.–3 p.m. Average daily attendance 5,000. Approximately 325 dealers with new merchandise, electronics, tools, housewares, sportswear, collectibles, art, crafts, produce, and secondhand items. Restaurant, snack bars, rest rooms, h/a, free parking, and free shuttle to and from distant parking areas. Inside and outside space available from $12. Regular dealers need store license to comply with state law. *Contact* Arlene Rigsby, 2201 S.E. Indian St., 34997 (561) 288-4915 or 283-7015, fax (561) 288-2140.

Lucky's Flea Market
1905 S.E. Luckhardt St.

Saturday, Sunday, 8 a.m.–3 p.m. Outdoor market with approximately 150 dealers. Some antiques, collectibles, new and used merchandise, produce, crafts, sporting goods, surplus. Space from $13. Snack bars, rest rooms, h/a. Nice clean and very friendly market that is a real pleasure to shop at. Free parking. *Contact* Alice Luckhardt, Box 1185, 34995 (561) 288-4879.

TALLAHASSEE

Flea Market Tallahassee
Three miles east of Municipal Airport
(850) 877-3811
Fax (850) 656-3137

Saturday, Sunday, 9 a.m.–5 p.m. Average daily attendance 10–15,000, with approximately 350 dealers. Lots of hot new Florida merchandise, sportswear, jewelry, fishing and marine items, sports items, used merchandise, garage sale items, crafts, collectibles, sometimes good antiques, and produce. Food available, rest rooms, h/a, ample parking. Reservations recommended. Outside space only. Camping with showers $5. Electricity available. No food sales by vendors allowed. *Contact* Fleamarket, 200 Capital Circle SE

Uncle Bob's Flea Market
1501 Capital Circle NW

Saturday, Sunday, 9 a.m.–5 p.m. Outdoor market with approximately 50 dealers. New and used merchandise, garage sale items, and bric-a-brac. Space from $7 per day. No food, rest rooms. Free ample parking. *Contact* (850) 576-2949.

TAMPA

Top Value Flea Market
8120 Anderson Rd.
Corner of Waters Ave. and Anderson Rd.
(813) 884-7810

Saturday, Sunday. Twenty-fifth year of operation with approximately 1,000 dealers offering produce, plants, local artwork, and mountains of general flea market merchandise with limited new merchandise. Snack bars, beer, rest rooms, h/a, ample parking. Indoor and outdoor market with some covered booths. *Contact* John Gardner, 8120 Anderson Rd., 33614.

Big Top Flea Market
9250 E. Fowler Ave.
State Rte. 582 just east of I-75

Saturday, Sunday, 8 a.m.–5 p.m. 145,000-square-foot shopping area with 550 booths indoor, covered, and enclosed, Special antique/collectible area. Each market day, 5,000 cars can be accommodated. Market maintains an upbeat festival atmosphere and is a very pleasant shopping experience. Large crowds and one of the leading markets in the country. Antiques, crafts, plants, clothing, tools, artwork, and collectibles. Good food, rest rooms, h/a, ample parking. This is my very favorite market in the entire bay area. Daily/weekend/monthly rates. *Contact* Ross Ozimek, 9250 E. Fowler Ave., 33592 (813) 986-4004, fax (813) 986-6296.

Floriland Flea* and *Farmers Market
9309 N. Florida Ave., I-275, Exit 33
Two miles from Busch Gardens

Saturday, Sunday, 9 a.m.–5 p.m. Indoor market with approximately 250-300 dealers. Antique market, collectibles, new and used merchandise, produce, locally made crafts. Space from $27. One of the area's better markets. Features lots of live entertainment. A very fun place to shop. Restaurant, snack bars, rest rooms, h/a. Ample parking. *Contact* Harold Holden, 9309 N. Florida Ave., 33612 (813) 932-4319, fax (813) 935-5558.

Fun-Lan Swap Shop Flea Market
2302 E. Hillsboro Ave., Fun-Lan Drive-In Theater
Intersection of 22nd St. and Hillsboro Ave., one mile east of Rte. 275

Wednesday–Sunday, 6 a.m.–2 p.m. Outdoor market and some covered booths. Antiques, collectibles, produce, new and used merchandise. Locally made crafts, sporting goods, fishing and golf equipment. Snack bars, rest rooms, h/a. Ample parking. *Contact* Lauren Duren, Box 11188, 33680 (813) 237-0886.

Golden Nugget Flea Market
8504 Adamo Dr. East, Hwy. 60
(813) 621-0045

Saturday, Sunday.

THONOTOSASSA

North 301 Flea Market
11802 Hwy. 301 North
(813) 986-1023

Saturday, Sunday

WALDO

Waldo Farmers & Flea Market
Hwy. 301 North, one mile north of town
(352) 468-2255

Saturday, Sunday, 7:30 a.m.–5 p.m. Average weekend attendance 15,000. Approximately 700 dealers. Good variety of antiques, collectibles, clothing, new and vintage jewelry, glassware, new and used merchandise, and produce available. Market features a new antique mall that is open daily. Mall features a nice general line of antiques and collectibles. Snack bars, clean rest rooms, h/a, ample parking. Indoor/outdoor market with spaces from $6 per day. Camping nearby. *Contact* Manager, 2373 S.W. Archer Rd., Gainesville, FL 32608.

WEBSTER

Farmer's Flea Market
Hwy. 47 North
Center of town at the county fairgrounds

Monday only, 8 a.m.–3 p.m. Average attendance of 10,000 with 1,300 vendors. This is one of the better wholesale markets in the country with a separate section for new merchandise. If you're looking for a good source of goods to resell, bring a big truck and plenty of green money for if money talks, cash "screams." This market is a truly unique happening; it covers the entire county fairgrounds. Lots of food here because food vendors are welcome. Crowds are so big you may have to park quite a distance from the market. Miles of walking here and a don't-miss stop. Rest rooms. Covered spaces from $7. City and county license required. *Contact* Larry Story, Box 62, 33597 (352) 793-2021 or 793-3551.

Webster Westside Flea Market
N.W. Third St. and Rte. 478

Mondays only, 6 a.m. until dark. Parking $2. Outdoor market with some covered spaces and approximately 500 dealers. Antiques, collectibles, crafts, furniture, electronics, new and used merchandise, produce. Space from $15 per day. Restaurants, snack bars, rest rooms, h/a, lots of walking. *Contact* Manager 516 N.W. 3rd St., 33597 (800) 438-8559 or (800) 832-7396.

WEST PALM BEACH

Dr. Flea's International Flea Market
1200 S. Congress Ave.
One mile south of the airport

Thursday–Sunday, 10 a.m.–6 p.m. Indoor market with approximately 100 dealers. Antiques, collectibles, new and used merchandise, butterfly ballots, new furniture. Mostly monthly rentals, some weekend space occasionally available. Snack bar, café, rest rooms, h/a. Ample parking. *Contact* Dwight Hanners, 1200 S. Congress Ave, 33406 (561) 965-1500.

Uptown-Downtown Flea Market
5700 Okeechobee Rd.

Saturday, Sunday. Contact Beverly Koplowitz (561) 640-7283.

ZEPHYRHILLS

Zephyrhills Flea Market
39336 Chancey Rd.

Friday, Saturday, Sunday, 8 a.m.–3 p.m. Indoor market with approximately 300 dealers. Antiques, collectibles, coins, furniture, crafts, produce, new and used merchandise. Space from $10 per day. Snack bars, rest rooms, h/a. Free parking. *Contact* Grace Strope, 39336 Chancey Rd., 33540 (813) 782-1483.

GEORGIA

ACWORTH

Lake Acworth Antique Flea Market
4375 Cobb Pkwy.
Junction of Hwy. 41 and Rte. 92
I-75, Exit 121

Friday, 9 a.m.–5 p.m., Saturday, Sunday, 6 a.m.–6 p.m. Open holidays. Approximately 400 dealers offer antiques, collectibles, and primitives. This market has it all: produce and new merchandise sold along with livestock and pets. Snack bars, rest rooms, h/a, ample parking, parking charge $1, lots of walking. Space starts at $5, reservations recommended. *Contact* Wendell Tummlin, 4375 Cobb Pkwy., 30101 (770) 974-5896.

Great American Bargain Mart
3355 Cobb Pkwy.

Saturday, Sunday. Average attendance 6,000 per day. Approximately 125 vendors. Spaces cost $5 to $10. Inside space available. Reservations recommended. Overnight camping available. Monday wholesale vendors auction. *Contact* Rebel, 3355 Cobb Pkwy. N.W. (770) 974-9660.

Yesteryear Flea Market
43337 Hwy. 92
Junction of Hwys. 92 and 41
(770) 974-6259

Saturday, Sunday, 8 a.m.–5 p.m. Admission charge. Average weekend attendance 6,000. Approximately 250 dealers offer antiques, a good selection of collectibles, decorator items, primitives, and crafts. Good cafe, snack bars, clean rest rooms, h/a, ample parking, camping nearby. One of the area's better markets. Indoor/outdoor market with space from $6 per day. *Contact* Bill Abernathy, 4337 Acworth-Dallas Rd., 30101.

ALBANY

America's Flea Market
1030 Gordon

Friday, Saturday, Sunday. One of Georgia's largest indoor markets offers approximately 125 dealers with collectibles, silver, coins, linens, farm items, new merchandise, sportswear, jewelry, electronics, and housewares. Snack bar, rest rooms, h/a, ample parking. Indoor market, air-conditioned and heated. Spaces from $18 per weekend. *Contact* William Shockey, 1030 Gordon, 31701 (912) 435-6231.

Kitty's Flea Market
3229 Sylvester Rd.
Hwy. 82
Three miles east of town

Friday, Saturday, Sunday, 7 a.m.–4 p.m. This outdoor market with covered spaces averages 300 dealers. New and used merchandise, lots of garage sale merchandise, tools, toys, jewelry, and furniture. Food available, rest rooms, h/a, ample parking. *Contact* Jim Andrews, Box 51324, 31705 (912) 432-0007.

ASHBURN

The Friendship Store
Hwy. I-75
(912) 567-4592 or 859-2315

Friday, Saturday, Sunday. This new indoor market features antiques, collectibles, crafts, and flea market items. An antique auction is conducted the first Tuesday evening each month. Snack bar, rest rooms, h/a, ample parking.

ATHENS

J and J Flea Market
3000 Commerce Rd., Hwy. 441, 4 miles north of town

Friday, Saturday, Sunday, 8 a.m.–5 p.m. Indoor/outdoor market with an average daily attendance of 10,000. Approximately 700 dealers. Well-stocked booths, antiques, collectibles, new and used merchandise, produce, crafts. Space from $8 per day indoors and $5 outdoors. Lots of food here, rest rooms, h/a. Free parking. *Contact* Jimmy Farmer, 11661 Commerce Rd., 30607 (706) 613-2410.

The Village Market
I-85, Exit 50
One-quarter mile from the highway
(706) 693-4466

Friday, Saturday, Sunday. This new market features new merchandise, souvenirs, novelties, sportswear, electronics, and housewares. Rest rooms, h/a, ample parking, food available. Food vendors welcome.

The Market Place
Brookwood Dr.
(706) 546-1032

Saturday, Sunday. Collectibles, primitives, country and farm items, crafts, glassware, and secondhand merchandise are available in this indoor market. Snack bar, rest rooms, h/a, ample parking. Booths start at $40 per weekend.

Country Flea Market
Hardman Rd. and U.S. Hwy. 78
(706) 354-8996

Friday, Saturday, Sunday. Flea market merchandise, new and used items, crafts, produce, and collectibles are available. Snack bar, rest rooms, h/a, ample parking.

ATLANTA

Georgia Antique Center & Flea Market
6624 I-84 Access Rd.
(404) 446-9292

Friday, 12 p.m.–7 p.m., Saturday, 10 a.m.–8 p.m., Sunday, 12 p.m.–7 p.m. Antiques, furniture, collectibles, silver, coins, jewelry, linens, quilts, glassware, and primitives are available. Snack bar, rest rooms, h/a, ample parking.

Atlanta Flea Market
2424 Piedmont Rd.
North 85 Drive-In Theater

Saturday, Sunday. Approximately 300 dealers offer new merchandise, new collectibles, electronics, souvenirs, novelties, housewares, and outdoor items. Snack bar, rest rooms, h/a, ample parking. Mainly permanent booths. *Contact* Jack Hodgkins, 2424 Piedmont Rd. N.E., 30324 (404) 266-2495.

Drive-In Theater Flea Market
3265 N.E. Expressway Rd.

Sunday only. Approximately 100 dealers offer new merchandise, sportswear, electronics, housewares, sporting goods, used merchandise, tools, bicycles, toys, clothing, crafts, collectibles, and produce. Snack bar, rest rooms, h/a, ample parking. Spaces from $10. *Contact* Ken Campbell (404) 451-4570 or 233-3889.

Flea Market USA
1919 Stewart Ave.
(404) 763-3078

Thursday–Sunday, 9 a.m.–7 p.m. New merchandise, sportswear, sporting goods, toys, housewares, tools, souvenirs, novelties, used merchandise, crafts, produce, and collectibles are available. Snack bar, rest rooms, h/a, ample parking. *Contact* Manager, 1919 Metropolitan Pkwy. SW

Stewart/Lakewood Flea Market
1959 Stewart Ave.
Old Woolco Building
(404) 233-9998

Saturday, Sunday. New merchandise, housewares, sporting goods, sportswear, electronics, gifts, and imports are available. Snack bar, rest rooms, h/a, ample parking.

Atlanta Flea Market
5360 Peachtree Industrial Blvd. (Chamblee)

Friday, 12 p.m.–8 p.m., Saturday, Sunday, 12 p.m.–7 p.m. Average atendance 8,000 with approximately 200 dealers. Indoor market, permanent booths only. This market is very strong on antiques and good collectibles with a good selection of smalls, fine jewelry, and lots of quality collectibles. Monthly rentals only. Food available, rest rooms, h/a, ample parking. *Contact* W. S. Malone, 5360 Peachtree Industrial Blvd., 30341 (404) 458-0456.

Forest Square Flea Market
4855 Jonesboro Rd. (Forest Park)

Friday, Saturday, Sunday. Indoor market with approximately 150 dealers. This market is heavy on new merchandise, imports, gifts, housewares, electronics, and personal items. Snack bar, rest rooms, h/a, ample parking. Space from $30. *Contact* Joan Brown, Box 1382, 30050 (404) 361-1221.

Historic Lakewood Antiques Market
I-75 and I-85, Exit 88
East to Lakewood Freeway, follow signs
(404) 622-4488 or 627-2299
Fax (404) 627-2999

Every second weekend, 9 a.m.–6 p.m. Approximately 2,000 spaces, averages 900 dealers. Excellent selection of antiques from furniture to an extensive array of smalls and high-quality collectibles. Great market for the serious collector, investor, shopkeeper, or decorator. If you are looking for high-quality items, this is a market for you. Full-service restaurant, bar and grill, fully h/a. Security, 8,000 parking spaces. All 117 acres fenced and lighted. Inside space from $95 for 8×10. Outside space from $70 for 15×14. *Contact* Lakewood Antiques Market, Box 6826, 30315.

Antiques & Collectibles Market
Exposition Center
I-285, Exit 40 at Jonesboro Rd.

Every second weekend, 9 a.m.–5 p.m. Approximately 1,500 high-quality dealers offer antiques and collectibles only. Great selection of quality collector items and smalls. Snack bar, rest rooms, h/a, ample parking. Inside space from $65, outside from $45. *Contact* Don Scott, Box 60, Bremen, OH 43107 (740) 569-4912 or 569-4112, fax (740) 569-7595.

Pride of Dixie Antique Market
North Atlanta Trade Center
I-85 to Indian Trail, Exit 101. East on Indian Trail, right on Oakbrook Pkwy., right on Jeurgens Ct.
(404) 279-9853

Every fourth weekend. Admission $4. A very quality-oriented market with antiques, collectibles, silver, glassware, coins, jewelry, and watches. Food available, rest rooms, h/a, ample parking. *Contact* Antique Market, P.O. Box 567, Frankfort, OH 45628.

AUGUSTA

Augusta Antique & Craft Market
Fairgrounds
(404) 724-8301

Every first weekend. Admission charge. Average daily attendance 10,000 with approximately 500 dealers. Antiques, great selection of furniture, collectibles, glassware, silver, coins, jewelry (fine and estate), and vintage clothing are available. A quality-oriented market with great overall selection of items. Food available, rest rooms, h/a, ample parking. Space from $35. Overnight camping available.

South Augusta Flea Market
1531 Doug Barnard Pkwy.
(Airport Rd.)

Saturday, Sunday, 6 a.m. until dark. Outdoor market with spaces for over 500 dealers has over 200 permanent dealers. Well-established flea market, in operation for over 22 years. Excellent attendance. Largest market within a 100-mile radius. Spaces from $5 per day with tables available for $1 per day. Rest rooms, snack bars, h/a, ample parking. *Contact* Ronald Rhodes, 30906 (706) 798-5500.

BARNESVILLE

M&M Flea Market
341 Industrial Dr.
Hwy. 341

Saturday, Sunday. This new indoor/outdoor market has approximately 25 dealers. Collectibles, new and used merchandise, lots of secondhand and garage sale merchandise available. Snack bar, ample parking. Space from $3 per day. *Contact* J. B. Moss, 210 Hwy. 341, 30204 (404) 358-1724.

BRUNSWICK

Brunswick Flea Market
132 Old Jessup Rd.
I-95, Exit 7
(912) 267-6787

Saturday, Sunday. New and used merchandise, antiques, collectibles, crafts, quilts, and secondhand items are available. Eighteen-acre grounds with 45,000-square-foot building. Food available, rest rooms, h/a, ample parking. Camping available.

BUFORD

Buford Highway Flea Market
5000 Buford Hwy.
(404) 452-7140

Friday, Saturday, 11 a.m.–9:30 p.m. Indoor market with approximately 250 dealers. Primarily new merchandise at severely discounted prices. Everything you would find at a discount store and more. Snack bar, rest rooms, h/a, ample parking. Space rented on a monthly basis only. *Contact* Grace Creta, 5000 Buford Hwy., 30341.

CALHOUN

New Town Flea Market
I-75, Red Bud exit to New Town Rd.

Saturday, Sunday, 7 a.m.–7 p.m. Approximately 50 dealers offer collectibles, primitives, crafts, used merchandise, and lots of secondhand items. Snack bar, rest rooms. Outdoor market with space from $5. *Contact* Earl Abernathy, Rte. 1, 30701 (706) 625-1157.

CARROLLTON

West Georgia Flea & Farmers Market
Hwy. 27, two miles south of I-20
(770) 832-6551

Saturday, Sunday, 8 a.m.–5 p.m. Large animal/livestock section at this market along with lots of secondhand merchandise, nice collectibles, and locally made crafts. Food, rest rooms, and camping available.

Peddler's Pavilion Flea Market
I-20, Exit 5, south eight miles
(770) 830-9304

Friday, Saturday, Sunday. New open-air market with some covered spaces. Crafts, baseball cards, ceramics, woodworking, photography, jewelry, and secondhand merchandise are available. Food concessions, rest rooms, h/a. Spaces start at $3.

CHAMBLEE

Buford Highway Flea Market
Buford
(770) 452-7140

Friday, Saturday, 8 a.m.–4 p.m. Indoor market with approximately 250 dealers. Lots of new merchandise severely discounted. Gifts, imports, crafts, used merchandise. Snack bar, rest rooms, h/a. Ample parking.

CLAYTON

Appalachian Trader Flea Market
Hwy. 441 South
(404) 872-2486

Saturday, Sunday, May–August. Antiques, collectibles, primitives, farm and country collectibles, new and used merchandise, crafts, and produce are available. Food available, rest rooms, h/a, ample parking.

CLEVELAND

Henry's Mountain Flea Market
Hwy. 129 South

Friday, Saturday, Sunday, 8 a.m.–5 p.m. Approximately 100 dealers offer collectibles, country items, primitives, advertising items, crafts, and used merchandise. Snack bar, rest rooms, h/a, ample parking. RV hookups, showers, electricity available. Indoor and covered spaces from $20. *Contact* Jim Tallent (706) 865-1716.

CUMMING

Dixie 400 Flea Market
4755 Setting Down Circle
Off Hwy. 400, 8 miles north of town

Saturday, Sunday, 9 a.m.–6 p.m. Indoor and outdoor market with approximately 75 dealers. Market mainly consists of used and garage sale merchandise with some new merchandise. Space from $5 per day. Snack bar, rest room. *Contact* Manager, 4755 Setting Down Circle, 30040 (770) 889-5895.

DECATUR

Columbia Drive-In Flea Market
1395 Columbia Dr.
Columbia Drive-In Theater
(404) 288-2935

Wednesday, Saturday, Sunday. New merchandise, used and flea market merchandise, crafts, collectibles, produce, and lots of county collectibles are available. Snack bar, rest rooms, h/a, ample parking.

Kudzu Antiques Flea Market
2874 W. Ponce De Leon Ave.

Friday, Saturday, 10:30 a.m.–5:30 p.m., Sunday, 12:30 p.m.–5:30 p.m.. About 25 dealers in a 27,000-square-foot old barn. Antiques, collectibles, primitives, advertising items, and furniture are available. This is one of those places where treasures can be found if you have the patience to poke through the mountains of junk. This is a truly one-of-a-kind stop. Rest rooms, ample parking. *Contact* Emily Campbell, 178 Lamond Dr., 30030 (404) 373-6498.

DEKALB

Dekalb Flea Market
Glenwood Drive-In Theater
(404) 289-6011

Sunday. Antiques, collectibles, crafts, new and used merchandise, and garage sale items are available. Snack bar, rest rooms, h/a, ample parking.

DOUGLASVILLE

Red Barn Antique Village
Hwy. 78

Saturday, Sunday. Outdoor antique and collectible market. Good selection of country and farm items, primitives, advertising items, jewelry, watches, books, and prints. Food available, rest rooms, h/a, ample parking. Space from $3. *Contact* Bill Wilson (404) 942-3598.

DUNWOODY

Dunwood Flea Market
2490 Mt. Vernon Rd.
(404) 457-2330

Friday, Saturday, Sunday. General flea market merchandise, crafts, collectibles, and produce are available. Snack bar, rest rooms, h/a, ample parking.

EAST POINT

Greenbriar Flea Market
2925 Headland Dr.
Hwy. 285 West

Wednesday–Sunday, 12 p.m.–9 p.m. Average weekend attendance of 10–15,000 with approximately 150 dealers. New merchandise, sportswear, furniture, electronics, jewelry, and housewares are available. Several very nice specialty shops. Market does not allow used merchandise. Great market for the bargain-conscious shopper. Snack bars, rest rooms, h/a, ample parking. *Contact* Michael Mahkosi, 2925 Headland Dr., 30344 (404) 349-3994.

ELLIJAY

Holden's Triangle Flea Market
165 N. Main St.
(706) 635-5003

Thursday–Sunday. Collectibles, antiques, furniture, primitives, farm items, used merchandise, and lots of bric-a-brac are available. Clean rest rooms, snack bar, ample parking. Outdoor market with some covered spaces from $5 per day.

FOREST PARK

South Atlanta Flea Market
4140 Jonesboro Rd.
I-285, Exit 40, one-half mile south

Friday, Saturday, Sunday, 10 a.m.–9 p.m. Good selection of small antiques, collectibles, vintage clothing, primitives, crafts, and new merchandise. Snack bar, rest rooms, h/a, ample parking. Space from $25 per day. *Contact* Betty Ratledge (404) 363-6694.

GAINESVILLE

Mule Camp Trade Days
Hwy. 13 South
I-985, Exit 4
Fairgrounds
(770) 536-8068 or 534-9157

Every first weekend, 9 a.m.–5 p.m. Average weekend attendance of 6–7,000 with approximately 70 dealers in this indoor/outdoor market. Antiques, collectibles, primitives, crafts, decorator items, new and used merchandise, quilts, and fine and costume jewelry are available. Snack bar, rest rooms, h/a, ample parking. Space from $30 per weekend. *Contact* Johnny Benefield, Box 224, Oakwood, 30566.

GRANTVILLE

Good Times Flea Market
Hwy. 29, I-85, Exit 7
(404) 583-3442

Saturday, Sunday, 7 a.m.–6 p.m. Admission charge 50 cents. This new market has approximately 100 dealers offering new merchandise, novelties, gift items, imports, housewares, electronics, sportswear, and collectibles. Food, clean rest rooms, h/a, ample parking. Camping available. Market holds many special events; call for their schedule.

HAMPTON

Sweetie's Flea Market Mall
2316 Hwys. 19 and 41
Two miles south of the Atlanta Motor Speedway. I-75, Exit 77, twelve miles to the right
(770) 946-4721

Friday, Saturday, Sunday, 8 a.m.–5:30 p.m. Antiques, collectibles, farm and country collectibles, primitives, advertising items, used merchandise, and new items. Snack bar, rest rooms, ample parking. *Contact* Pat Martin, Box 181, 30228.

KINGSTON

Ruby's Trade Day
Hwy. 411 and Hardin Bridge Rd.

Thursday only. New and used merchandise, lots of garage sale items, collectibles, farm items, produce, livestock, and crafts are available. Food available, rest rooms, h/a, ample parking.

LAFAYETTE

M&J Flea Market
Hwy. 27, six miles north of town

Friday, Saturday, Sunday, 7 a.m.–3 p.m. Approximately 75 dealers offer antiques, crafts, produce, and new merchandise. Snack bar, rest rooms. Inside and outside space available from $2. Camping available. *Contact* Melvin Smith, 30728 (404) 764-2022.

LA GRANGE

Lee's Crossing Flea Market
1854 West Point Rd.
(404) 882-5780

Wednesday–Sunday. New and used merchandise, general flea market lines, lots of good secondhand items, crafts, collectibles, and produce are available. Snack bar, rest rooms, h/a, ample parking.

LAKE PARK

Bargainville Flea-Esta
Frontage Rd., I-75, Exit 2

Saturday, Sunday, 9 a.m.–5 p.m. Approximately 150 vendors offer collectibles, vintage clothing, fine and costume jewelry, antiques, livestock, new and used merchandise, housewares, primitives, and junk. Snack bar, rest rooms, h/a, ample parking. Covered and inside booths with space from $12 per day. Reservations recommended. Camping available for $8 per night. New market. *Contact* Terry or Debbie, Rte. 3, Box 1050, 31636 (912) 559-5192 or 559-0141.

MACON

Macon Jockey Lot
6717 Hawkinsville Hwy.
Located halfway between Macon and Warner Robbins on Hwy. 129

Friday, Saturday, Sunday, daylight to dark. New and used merchandise, mountains of good secondhand items, collectibles, glassware, linens, quilts, crafts, produce, and livestock are available. Food available, rest rooms, h/a, ample parking, and lots of walking. Inside and outside spaces available from $5. Electricity and camping available. *Contact* Cletus Smith (912) 788-3700.

Smiley's Flea Market & Antique Mall
U.S. Hwys. 247 and 129
Four miles south of town

Flea market, Saturday and Sunday only, 7 a.m.–5 p.m; Mall, 10 a.m.–5 p.m. daily. Average weekend attendance is 10,000 with approximately 300 dealers and 50 antique dealers in the antique mall, which has a nice selection of merchandise. Outside on the weekends, you'll find a good selection of country crafts, primitives, collectibles, advertising items, both large and small antiques, and much more. Snack bar, clean rest rooms, h/a, ample parking. Space from $10 per day. Camping available. *Contact* George Kulcsar, 6717 Hawkinsville Rd., 31206 (912) 788-3700 or (352) 331-2999, fax (912) 788-5344.

Sama's Flea Market
Hwy. 245
Glendale Ave., Exit 49 from I-75

Friday, Saturday, Sunday. Approximately 100 dealers offer new merchandise, surplus, closeouts, imports, tools, clothing, toys, used merchandise, and some collectibles. Snack bar, rest rooms, h/a, ample parking. Overnight parking and hookups available. Auctions on Saturday night. *Contact* Henry Sama, 4156 Pionono Ave., 31206 (912) 781-1104.

MARIETTA

Antique Fair & Flea Market
Fairgrounds
(404) 428-8165

Every first weekend. Popular regional event. Good selection of antiques, collectibles, furniture, silver, linens, coins, primitives, vintage clothing, and jewelry. Food available, rest rooms, h/a, ample parking.

McDONOUGH

Peachtree Peddlers Flea Market
155 Mill Rd.
Thirty miles south of Atlanta
(770) 914-2269 or (888) 661-3532

Saturday, Sunday, 9 a.m.–6 p.m. Large 70,000-square-foot indoor flea market. Approximately 300 individual shops here with a wide variety of merchandise, including new merchandise, crafts, antiques, and memorabilia. Heated and air-conditioned space from $150 per week for 10×13. Rest rooms, ample parking, bus parking, h/a. *Contact* Peachtree Peddlers, 155 Mill Rd., 30253.

NORCROSS

Georgia Antique Center & Flea Market
6624 N.E. Expwy.
I-85, Exit 36
(770) 446-9292

Friday, 12 p.m.–7 p.m., Saturday, 10 a.m.–8 p.m., Sunday, 12 p.m.–7 p.m. Average weekend attendance of 20,000 with approximately 250 dealers. Great selection of quality antiques and collectibles, new merchandise, primitives, advertising and decorator items available. Snack bar, rest rooms, h/a, ample parking. Inside and outside spaces from $20. New market. *Contact* Pat Chastain. Several antique shops located on the premises open daily.

MILLEDGEVILLE

Bargain & Auction Center
Hwy. 441 South, N. Columbia St. 31061
(912) 451-2977

Saturday, Sunday

Swinnet Drive-In Flea Market
5785 Jimmy Carter Blvd.
Swinnet Drive-In Theater

Wednesday and Thursday, 12 p.m.–7 p.m., Friday and Saturday, 11 a.m.–8:30 p.m., Sunday, 12 p.m.–6 p.m. Collectibles, antiques, primitives, country items, crafts, fine art, silver, glassware, and jewelry are available. Snack bar, rest rooms. Monthly space rentals only. *Contact* Anne Osmerg, 5675 Jimmy Carter Blvd., 30071 (770) 449-8189.

Pride of Dixie Antiques Market
North Atlanta Trade Center
1700 Jeurgens Ct.

Every fourth weekend, Friday and Saturday, 9 a.m.–6 p.m.; Sunday, 11 a.m.–5 p.m. Admission $4. Indoor market with quality antiques and collectibles. Approximately 300 dealers. Lots of great booths here that are well stocked with quality smalls. Space from $125 for the weekend. Snack bars, rest rooms, h/a. *Contact* Rhonda Perkins, 1700 Jeurgens Ct., (770) 279-9853, fax (770) 279-0019.

PENDERGRASS

Pendergrass Flea Market
I-85, Exit 50 and junction of Rte. 129

Saturday, Sunday, 9 a.m.–6 p.m. Large commercial market with approximately 350 dealers. Wide variety and selection here. Antiques, collectibles, furniture, produce, livestock, new and used merchandise. Plenty of food, rest rooms, h/a. Space from $16. Outdoor market, ample parking. *Contact* Reed Smith, 5641 U.S. Hwy. 129 N, 30567 (706) 693-4466 or (770) 945-1900.

PERRY

Southeastern Antiques & Collectibles Market
Georgia National Fairgrounds
(912) 742-8614

Monthly, call for dates. Antiques, collectibles, and crafts. This is a very nice, clean, friendly, and well-managed market located on one of the nation's newest and prettiest fairgrounds. Good food, rest rooms, h/a, ample parking. Inside space from $65 and outside space from $60. *Contact* Southeastern Antiques, Box 730, Macon, 31202.

PORTERDALE

Porterdale by the River Antique Mall & Flea Market
Hwy. 81 at Yellow River
I-20, Exit 44, South to Hwy. 81
(404) 786-1100

Friday, Saturday, Sunday. Antiques, collectibles, silver, linens, glassware, primitives, and a great selection of locally made country crafts are available. Food available, rest rooms, h/a, ample parking. Market holds a first-weekend auction and a craft show on the third weekend. Market is located in a very scenic setting.

RINGOLD

Flea Market
Battlefield Pkwy.
West of I-75
(706) 937-2303

Friday, Saturday, Sunday; also open the first Tuesday of each month. New and used merchandise, collectibles, country and farm collectibles, crafts, produce. Food available, rest rooms, h/a, ample parking.

RIVERDALE

Antique & Flea Market
7471 Hwy. 85
(404) 478-9084

Saturday, Sunday. Antiques, collectibles, furniture, glassware, silver, coins, jewelry, primitives, and used merchandise are available. Food available, rest rooms, h/a, ample parking.

ROME

Rome Trade Days
Across from the sale barn

Wednesday, 6 a.m.–2 p.m. Wide-open country market with lots of new and used merchandise, collectibles, primitives, glassware, and sometimes nice antiques available. Food available, rest rooms, ample parking.

ROSWELL

Antique Center & Flea Market of Roswell
39th and Hill Sts.
(404) 642-2267

Friday, Saturday, Sunday. Approximately 150 dealers show in this indoor market with 43,000-square-foot of space. Antiques, good selection of furniture, collectibles, glassware, silver, linens, quilts, coins, jewelry, new and used merchandise, gift items, and imports are available. Snack bar, rest rooms, h/a, ample parking.

SAVANNAH

Coastal Empire Flea Market
Montgomery Street Drive-In Theater

Friday, Saturday, Sunday. Approximately 100 dealers offer new merchandise, housewares, tools, imports, electronics, sportswear, used merchandise, lots of garage sale and bric-a-brac items, collectibles, crafts, and produce. Snack bar, rest rooms, h/a, ample parking. Space from $2 per day.

Keller's Flea Market
Hwy. 17 South
I-95, Exit 16

Friday, Saturday, Sunday, 8 a.m.–6 p.m. Average daily attendance 5,000. Approximately 400 dealers offer antiques, collectibles, primitives, advertising items, paper goods, glassware, silver, crafts, and fine art. Cafe with excellent barbecue. Rest rooms, h/a, ample parking. Outdoor and indoor spaces, some covered, starting at $10. Camping available. *Contact* Cheri Keller, 5901 Ogeechee Rd., 31419 (912) 927-4848, fax (912) 925-2638.

SUMMERVILLE

Ye Old Trading Grounds
Hwy. 27
One mile north of town

Tuesday, Saturday, Sunday. Approximately 350 dealers on Tuesday, about 100 dealers on weekends. Tuesday is the big day at this market. On Tuesdays, shoppers will find a classic, wide-open country market with a good, upbeat, everything-goes atmosphere. Antiques, collectibles, crafts, and new and used merchandise are available. Weekends have pretty much the same merchandise mix, just not as much of it. Food available, rest rooms, h/a, ample parking, and lots of walking. *Contact* Jane Schlachter, Rte. 2, Box 32, 30745 (706) 857-1433 or 862-2442.

THOMASVILLE

Rose City Flea Market
2069 County Line Rd.

Friday, Sturday, Sunday, 7 a.m.–4 p.m. Outdoor market with some covered booths. Approximately 10 dealers. Rest room. Ample parking. *Contact* Virginia Bossier (912) 377-3000.

THOMPSON

The Market Place
Corner of Whiteoak and Harrison Sts.

Friday, Saturday, Sunday, 8 a.m.–5 p.m. Average daily attendance 2,000. Approximately 100 dealers. Wide range of merchandise here—an everything-goes market. Good selection of new merchandise and lots of used garage sale items. Cafe, rest rooms, h/a, ample parking. Inside and outside market. *Contact* H. M. Smith, P.O. Box 352, Warrenton, 30878 (404) 465-3397 or 595-9875.

TIFTON

Tifton Flea Market
201 W. 7th St.
(912) 386-1734 or 388-9313
Fax (912) 388-9809
E-mail: louie@surfsouth.com

Friday, Saturday, Sunday. Approximately 150 dealers offer new merchandise, tools, housewares, outdoor items, sportswear, jewelry, cards, coins, used merchandise, garage sale items, collectibles, crafts, and produce. Snack bar, rest rooms, h/a, ample parking. Spaces from $6 per day. Electricity available. Camping nearby. *Contact* Helen Barr, 44 Old Brookfield Rd., 31794.

New River Market
Hwy. 82 East
(912) 387-0016 or 388-9313

Friday, Saturday, Sunday. Outdoor market with some covered spaces. Approximately 125 dealers.

WAYCROSS

Crystal's Flea Market
1631 Genoa St.
(912) 283-9808

Saturday, Sunday, 8 a.m.–5 p.m. New and used merchandise, collectibles, crafts, and produce are available. Snack bar, rest rooms, ample parking.

HAWAII

AIEA

Kam Super Swap Meet
98850 Moanalua Rd.
Kam Drive-In Theater

Wednesday, Saturday, Sunday, 5:30 a.m.–1 p.m. Admission 25 cents. Outdoor market, with approximately 600 dealers. Wednesday is the market's big day. All types of items sold here, including a great selection of Polynesian crafts, collectibles, decorator items, food, and produce. This is a very nice, clean market that's lots of fun to attend. Great selection of food, rest rooms, h/a, ample parking. Space from $6 per day on weekends and $8 on Wednesday. *Contact* Manager, 99-500 Salt Lake Blvd., 96701 (808) 483-5535, fax (808) 847-9270.

BERETANIA

Flea Market
1290 Aala St.

Monday only. New and used merchandise, Polynesian crafts and produce, and gifts and souvenirs are available. Food available, rest rooms, ample parking.

HONOLULU

Aloha Flea Market
Aloha Stadium
(808) 486-1529 or 732-9611
Fax (808) 737-7764

Wednesday, Saturday, Sunday, 6 a.m.–3 p.m. Admission charge 50 cents. Hawaii's largest market with approximately 1,200 dealers offering sportswear, fishing, diving, and boating equipment, decorator items, gifts, souvenirs, imports, crafts, and some collectibles. Space starts at $10 per day. Rest rooms, food, h/a, ample parking. *Contact* Edward Medeiros, 3478 Waialae Ave., 96816.

KAILUA

Kailua Super Swap Meet
Junction of Pali Hwy. and Quarry Rd.
Kailua Drive-In Theater

Sunday only. New merchandise, housewares, electronics, sportswear, souvenirs, novelties, secondhand merchandise, and garage sale items are available as well as native Hawaiian crafts and produce. If that's not enough, you're likely to find: collectibles, fishing, marine, and swimming items. Snack bar, rest rooms, h/a, ample parking.

KILEI

Kilei Swap Meet
St. Theresa Catholic Church
(808) 879-2649

Saturday only. Lots of secondhand and garage sale items; bric-a-brac abounds from mostly local exhibitors. Shoppers will also find locally made crafts and food items, produce, and occasionally collectibles. Food available, rest rooms, h/a, ample parking.

IDAHO

BOISE

Treasure Valley Flea Market
Western Idaho Fairgrounds
5610 Glenwood
(208) 376-3247

Monthly, call for dates. Antiques, collectibles, Indian jewelry and art, lots of western wear, and western collectibles are available. Food available, rest rooms, h/a, ample parking.

CASCADE

Cascade Farmers and Flea Market
1455 Main St., Hwy. 55

Friday, Saturday, Sunday, 9 a.m.–6 p.m. Seasonal market open mid-May through Labor Day weekend. Indoor/outdoor market with approximately 15 dealers. Some collectibles, mostly used and garage sale items. Space from $25 for the weekend. This is a most pleasant mountain country flea market. Snack bar, rest room. Free parking. *Contact* Glenna Young, Box 399, 83611 (208) 382-3600.

DONNELLY

Donnelly Flea Market & Swap Meet
Hwy. 55
(208) 325-8604

Friday, Saturday, Sunday, Opens at daylight and runs until dark. May–September. This is a postcard-beautiful western outdoor market. Western and Native American items abound. Lots of collectibles, primitives, ranch items, and tack are available. Food available, rest rooms. Space from $10. Camping available. Located in one of the country's most scenic areas. *Contact* Jerry Livingston, Box 399, 83615.

FRUITLAND

Open Air Flea Market
1011 N.W. 16th St.
Hwy. 95N to junction, west one block

Saturday, Sunday. Outdoor market only. New and used merchandise, crafts, western and Indian items, collectibles. Food available, rest rooms. Shaded spaces from $4.50. Reservations recommended. Overnight camping on premises. Electricity available. *Contact* Paul Baker, 1355 Anderson, Parma, 83660 (208) 278-1015 or 452-5335.

IDAHO FALLS

Northway Flea Market
2070 N. Woodruff Ave.

Friday, Saturday, Sunday, April–September. Average weekend attendance 3–4,000. New and used merchandise, lots of western wear, tack, Indian jewelry, art and artifacts, collectibles, and primitives are available. Snack bar, rest rooms, food vendors welcome. Inside and outside spaces from $5. *Contact* Al Kaiser, 2070 N. Woodruff Ave., 83401 (208) 522-5368.

POST FALLS

Indoor Flea Market
710 Seltice West
(208) 772-5055

Saturday, Sunday. Approximately 50 dealers offer new merchandise, souvenirs, electronics, sportswear, western wear, jewelry, used merchandise, collectibles, and farm and ranch items. Snack bar, rest rooms. Spaces from $5.

SAGLE

Sagle Flea Market
130 Algoma Rd., Hwy. 95
(208) 263-2244

Saturday, Sunday. Seasonal market May through September.

SAND POINT

Flea Market
Hwy. 95 North
(208) 265-4304

Friday, Saturday, Sunday. New and used merchandise, secondhand merchandise, collectibles, primitives, advertising items, western and Indian jewelry, art, and artifacts are available. Snack bar, rest rooms.

TWIN FALLS

Twin Falls Flea Market
Twin Falls County Fair Grounds
Merchants Building, Filer, Idaho
Located 7 miles west of the Hwy. 30-93 junction, Jackpot, Nevada

Monthly, Saturday, 9 a.m.–5 p.m.; Sunday, 10 a.m.–4 p.m. New merchandise, antiques, crafts. Rest rooms, h/a. Ample parking. *Contact* Dana Jo Cameron (208) 532-4439 or 532-4565. E-mail: camcam@pmt.org.

ALWAYS CALL BEFORE TRAVELING LONG DISTANCES!

ILLINOIS

ALSIP

Tri-State Swap-O-Rama
4350 W. 129th St.
I-294 to Rte. 50, east one mile

Wednesday, Saturday, Sunday, 7 a.m.–4 p.m. Admission 75 cents. The average attendance is 12,000. Over 700 dealers show in inside and outside spaces. Lots of new merchandise, sportswear, sports-related merchandise, collectibles, glassware, crafts, art, and used merchandise are available. Snack bar, rest rooms, h/a, ample parking. Space from $20. Reservations required. Electricity available. No overnight camping. *Contact* Jim Pierski, 4600 W. Lake St., Melrose Park, 60160 (708) 344-7300 or 721-8864.

AMBOY

Antique Show & Flea Market
4-H Fairgrounds
Rte. 30

Every third Sunday, 8 a.m.–4 p.m. Admission $1. Approximately 80 dealers. Market consists of antiques, collectibles, primitives, jewelry, furniture, and crafts with some new merchandise. Excellent market. Snack bar, rest rooms, h/a, ample parking. Space from $35. Camping available. This market conducts many special events; call for schedule. *Contact* Bill Edwards, Box 99, 61310 (815) 626-7601.

BELLEVILLE

Belleville Flea Market
200 South Belt East, St. Clair County Fairgrounds
(618) 235-0666 or 233-3377

Every third weekend, Saturday, 6 a.m.–4 p.m., Sunday, 7 a.m.–4 p.m. Inside and outside spaces. Excellent market. One of the country's better antique markets. For the collector or person interested in quality antiques this will be an all-day stop you won't want to miss. New merchandise, sportswear, electronics, jewelry fine, estate, and costume. Space from $13. Food available, rest rooms, h/a, ample parking.

BLOOMINGTON

Third Sunday Market
Interstate Center. I-55, Exit 160B

Every third Sunday, 8 a.m.–4 p.m. Admission $4.50. Large indoor/outdoor quality-oriented antique market. Approximately 300 dealers. Lots of great booths here with some real quality spreads. Very professional dealers. Space from $75 outside. Ample free parking. *Contact* Market, Box 396, 61702 (309) 662-1978 or 452-7926.

CENTRALIA

Don's Flea Market
Junction of Rtes. 161 and I-57

Friday–Monday, 9 a.m.–5 p.m. Indoor/outdoor market. Ample parking. *Contact* Don Mercer (618) 533-2778.

CHICAGO

Ashland Avenue Swap-O-Rama
4100 S. Ashland Ave.
One mile west of I-94 (near the new White Sox ballpark)

Thursday, Saturday, Sunday, 7 a.m.–4 p.m. Admission charge. Large new indoor/outdoor market with approximately 500 dealers offering a wide selection of new and used merchandise, electronics, clothing, jewelry, and furniture. Space from $18 inside and $8 outside. Rest rooms, snack bars, restaurants, h/a, ample parking. *Contact* Jim Pierski, 4600 W. Lake St., Melrose Park, 60160 (708) 344-7300 or (773) 376-6993.

Brighton Park Swap-O-Rama
3429 W. 47th St.
Near 47th and Archer

Saturday, Sunday. Admission charge. Average daily attendance of 5,000. Inside and outside spaces year-round with approximately 300 dealers who offer mountains of new merchandise, imports, gifts, decorator items, sportswear, electronics, sports merchandise, used merchandise, and collectibles. Food available, snack bars, rest rooms. Space from $14 to $18. Good market for commercial vendors. Reservations recommended. Electricity available. No overnight camping. *Contact* Jim Pierski, 4600 W. Lake St., Melrose Park, 60160 (708) 344-7300.

Double Drive-In Flea Market
2800 W. Columbus Ave.
Double Drive-In Theater

Saturday, Sunday, 6 a.m.–5 p.m. Approximately 600 dealers offer a wide variety of new merchandise, some used merchandise, and lots of garage sale items at this large commercial market. This is the market for the thrifty shopper—lots of great buys on new merchandise. Snack bar, rest rooms, ample parking, and lots of walking. *Contact* Ron Swislow, 2750 W. Columbus Ave. (312) 925-9602.

International Amphitheater Swap-O-Rama
4200 S. Halstead

Saturday, Sunday. New merchandise, upscale and trendy items, fine jewelry, sportswear, electronics, sports merchandise, and collectibles are available. Snack bar, rest rooms, h/a, ample parking. *Contact* Jim Pierski, 4600 W. Lake St., Melrose Park, 60160 (708) 344-7300.

The Buyers Market
4545 W. Division St.

Saturday, Sunday, 7 a.m.–4 p.m. Admission charge. The average attendance is 8–10,000 with approximately 300 sellers. This indoor market offers lots of new merchandise, some collectibles, and used items. This is one of the area's most popular markets because of the great deals available on new merchandise, especially for hot, new trendy items. Snack bar, rest rooms, h/a, ample parking. Space from $12. *Contact* Lenny Kraut, 4545 W. Division St., 60651 (773) 227-1889 or 342-4546.

Regency Flea Market
4001 W. Grand Ave.

Saturday, Sunday, 9 a.m.–5 p.m. The average attendance is 3,000. Approximately 125 sellers offering new merchandise, sportswear, tools, electronics, jewelry, outdoor items, toys, used merchandise, crafts, collectibles, and produce. Food available, rest rooms, h/a. *Contact* Andre, 4001 W. Grand Ave., 60659 (312) 772-6685.

Great American Flea Market
1400 S. Cicero Ave.

Saturday, Sunday, 8 a.m.–5 p.m. The average attendance is 10,000. Approximately 250 dealers offer a great selection of new merchandise, used merchandise, crafts, and collectibles. Food available, rest rooms, h/a. Space from $13. *Contact* Don Horwitcz, 1400 S. Cicero Ave., 60650 (312) 780-1600.

Maxwell Street Market
Canal St., between Taylor and 15th Sts.

Sunday, 7 a.m.–3 p.m. Parking $3. Outdoor market with approximately 400 dealers. Wide variety, lots of flea market and garage sale items, some new merchandise and collectibles. Very interesting and colorful market with lots of different ethnic vendors and ethnic food. Space from $15. Rest rooms, food available. *Contact* Manager, 548 W. Roosevelt Rd., 60607 (312) 922-3100

CICERO

Cicero Swap-O-Rama
1333 S. Cicero Ave.

Saturday, Sunday, 7 a.m.–4 p.m. This indoor and outdoor market has an average attendance of 3,000 with approximately 125 dealers. Lots of new merchandise, sports-related items, housewares, electronics, and used merchandise are available. Snack bar, rest rooms, h/a, ample parking. Electricity available. No overnight camping. Space from $15. Reservations recommended. *Contact* Jim Pierski, 4600 W. Lake St., Melrose Park, 60160 (708) 344-7300 or (773) 376-6993.

DECATUR

Giant Flea Market
Civic Center

Every second Sunday, 8:30 a.m.–4:30 p.m. Admission charge. This indoor market with approximately 75 dealers offers antiques, crafts, collectibles, and used and new merchandise. Food available, rest rooms, h/a, ample parking. Space from $15 per table. Reservations required. *Contact* John Crouch, Box 5058, Springfield, 62705 (217) 529-6939.

DUQUOIN

Giant Flea Market
Fairgrounds

Every first Sunday, 8:30 a.m.–4:30 p.m. Admission charge. Approximately 100 dealers offer antiques, collectibles, primitives, country items, glassware, jewelry, silver, new and used merchandise, and crafts. Snack bar, rest rooms, h/a, ample parking. Space from $12 per table. *Contact* John Crouch, Box 5058, Springfield, 62705 (217) 529-6939.

EAST DUNDEE

Dundee Drive-In Flea Market
Dundee Drive-In Theater
Junction of Hwys. 72 and 25
(312) 426-6736

Sunday. Antiques, collectibles, glassware, country collectibles, crafts, glassware, primitives, and new and used merchandise available. Food available, rest rooms, ample parking.

ELMHURST

Flea Market
310 W. Butterfield Rd.
American Legion Hall
(312) 393-1795

Every second Sunday. This market shows primarily antiques and collectibles. Glassware, vintage clothing, coins, silver, jewelry, linens, advertising items, primitives, and some quality secondhand merchandise are also available. Food available, rest rooms, h/a, ample parking.

FAIRMONT

Fairmont City Flea Market
Junction of Rtes. 40 and 111
(618) 271-9885

Saturday, Sunday. Indoor/outdoor market with approximately 50 dealers.

GLENDALE

World Bazaar Giant Indoor/Outdoor Flea Market
500 E. North Ave.
One mile west of I-355
(630) 858-6410

Saturday, Sunday. Lots of new merchandise, some used merchandise, and collectibles. Great market for the thrifty shopper looking for new merchandise, both personal and household. Food available, rest rooms, h/a, ample parking.

GRAFTON

Riverside Flea Market
400 Front St.

Every fourth weekend. Market is located in a historic boatworks building right on the banks of the Mississippi River. Great selection of quality collectibles here along with antiques, uniques, and new merchandise. This is a very cutesy and fun market, located in an interesting little river town. Great riverside restaurant and bar here. Ample parking, rest rooms, h/a although parking and walking to the building can be difficult. *Contact* Trudi Allen, Box 705, Alton, 62002 (618) 462-8210.

GRAYSLAKE

Flea Market
Lake County Fairgrounds
Intersection of State Rte. 20 and U.S. Rte. 45
(708) 223-1433 or 356-7499
Fax (847) 356-1362

Every second Sunday, 8 a.m.–3 p.m. Approximately 75 dealers. Lots of antiques and good quality collectibles to be found at this market. Primitives, advertising items, silver, fine and estate jewelry, coins, linens, and furniture are available. This is a good market to shop for those who are looking for quality items. Food available, rest rooms, h/a, ample parking. Space from $90.

Grays Lake Swap-O-Rama
Junction of Hwys. 120 and 83

Sunday, April–October. New merchandise, used merchandise, garage sale items, crafts, collectibles, and produce are available. Snack bar, rest rooms, h/a, ample parking. *Contact* Manager, Box 461, 60030 (847) 223-9890.

GRIFFITH

Swap-O-Rama Flea Market
Ridge Road Drive-In Theater
(312) 774-3900

Sunday only. New and used merchandise, flea market fare from bric-a-brac, crafts, and collectibles to produce available. Rest rooms, food available, h/a, ample parking.

HIGHLAND

Highland Flea Market
Linden Dale Park
(618) 654-3573

Every second Sunday. Indoor market held during the fall and winter months. Antiques, collectibles, lots of glassware. New and used merchandise, garage sale items, bric-a-brac, crafts, and produce are available. Food available, rest rooms, h/a, ample parking.

JOLIET

Derald's Indoor Flea Market
219 Maple St.
(815) 722-9232

Saturday, Sunday. Offerings at this market include: new merchandise, housewares, tools, sportswear, electronics, sports memorabilia, used merchandise, jewelry, clothing, collectibles, crafts, and more. Rest rooms, food available, ample parking.

KANKAKEE

Giant Flea Market
Fairgrounds

Every second Sunday. Admission charge. Approximately 50 sellers in this indoor market. Antiques, collectibles, crafts, primitives, advertising items, paper goods, and coins are available. Rest rooms, snack bar, h/a, ample parking. Space from $12 per table. *Contact* John Crouch, Box 5058, Springfield, 62705 (217) 529-6939.

Court Street Flea Market
1933 E. Court St.
I-57, Exit 312
(708) 755-4931

Saturday, Sunday. Admission charge. A small indoor market with an average daily attendance of 200 with approximately 25 dealers. New and secondhand items, collectibles, crafts, gifts, and decorator items are available. Rest rooms, snack bar, ample parking.

LA GRANGE

Antique Flea Market
900 S. La Grange Rd.
American Legion Hall

Every second Sunday. Antiques (smalls), collectibles, primitives, glassware, silver, coins, linens, vintage clothing. Food available, rest rooms, h/a, ample parking.

LAURA

Outdoor/Indoor Flea Market
Millbrook Township Center, Rte. 78

Every third Sunday, 7 a.m.–4 p.m. Note: Seasonal market, April through November. Approximately 50 dealers. Snack bar, rest rooms, h/a. *Contact* Karen Megan (309) 446-3619.

MARION

Flea Market
Fairgrounds
(618) 933-3764

Saturday only. Lots of garage sale and used merchandise, new merchandise, collectibles, crafts, and produce. Snack bar, rest rooms, h/a, ample parking.

MELROSE PARK

Melrose Park Swap-O-Rama
4600 W. Lake St.
Lake St. at Mannheim Rd.

Saturday, Sunday, 7 a.m.–4 p.m. Admission 50 cents. The average attendance is 6,000. Approximately 300 dealers offer new merchandise, sports-related items, sportswear, new collectibles, electronics, crafts, and some used and garage sale merchandise. Snack bar, rest rooms, h/a, ample parking. Space from $17 to $19 inside, $11 outside. Reservations required. Electricity available. No overnight camping. Good market for commercial vendors and an excellent market to shop for those looking for bargain prices on new merchandise. *Contact* Jim Pierski, 4600 W. Lake St., 60160 (708) 344-7300 or 681-4335.

A. M. Bargain Bazaar Flea Market
1945 Cornell St. at North Ave.

Thursday, Saturday, Sunday. New and used merchandise, garage sale and bric-a-brac items, lots of good secondhand merchandise, collectibles, gifts, and decorator items are available. Snack bar, rest rooms, h/a, ample parking. *Contact* Mary Gowenlock, 1945 Cornell St., 60160 (708) 450-0277.

Ashland Avenue Swap-O-Rama
4100 S. Ashland Ave.
(708) 344-7300

Friday, Saturday, Sunday, 7 a.m.–4 p.m. Indoor/outdoor market with approximately 450 dealers offers lots of sports merchandise and memorabilia, new merchandise, imports, collectibles, crafts, and used desirables. Snack bar, rest rooms, ample parking. Space from $17.

Wolff's Flea Market
2031 N. Mannheim
On Mannheim just north of North Ave.
Minutes from O'Hare Airport

Saturday, Sunday. Indoor market with approximately 400 vendors and an average daily attendance of 4,500. Space from $45 for the weekend. Approximately 60 percent new merchandise, 30 percent antique and collectible and 105 used items. Ample parking, food available, rest rooms, h/a. *Contact* David Wolf, 970 Arkansas, Elk Grove Village, IL (847) 524-9590.

MENDOTA

Fourth Sunday Flea Market
810 Main St.
(815) 539-7595

Every fourth Sunday, May–September. Antiques, collectibles, primitives, country collectibles, farm items, new and used merchandise, crafts, and produce are available. Snack bar, rest rooms, h/a, ample parking.

MONEE

County Line Swap-O-Rama
Rte. 50 to Cicero Ave. at Steger Rd.

Sunday only, April–November. Average attendance is 2,500. Approximately 130 dealers offer new merchandise, electronics, tools, housewares, sports items, outdoor wares, sportswear, used merchandise, garage sale items, crafts, collectibles, and produce. Food available, rest rooms, h/a, ample parking. Outside space only. Space from $5 to $8. Electricity available. No overnight camping. *Contact* Jim Pierski, 4600 W. Lake St., Melrose Park, 60160 (708) 344-7300.

NAUVOO

Flea Market & Crafts Show
(319) 524-7611

Every first Sunday. Approximately 30 dealers offer collectibles, farm items, religious items, and used merchandise. Snack bar. Market is located in a very historical city with lots of interesting shops and sightseeing opportunities. Inside and outside space available from $5.

NORMAL

Giant Flea Market
Illinois State University Ballroom

Every first Sunday, May–October. Admission charge. Approximately 50 dealers offer antiques, collectibles, primitives, coins, silver, new merchandise, gift items, decorator items, used merchandise, and crafts. Snack bar, rest rooms, h/a, ample parking. Space from $11 per table. *Contact* John Crouch, Box 5058, Springfield, 62705 (217) 529-6939. I would sure like to live in a town called Normal.

OREGON

Trading Fair
Fairgrounds
(815) 239-1188

Every third Sunday. Admission charge. Antiques, collectibles, primitives, country collectibles, housewares, linens, quilts, and crafts are available. Food available, rest rooms, h/a, ample parking.

PANA

Dutch Mill Flea Market
Dutch Mill Bldg.
E. Rtes. 16 and 51

Friday, Saturday, Sunday, 9 a.m.–4:30 p.m. Approximately 50 dealers inside and 25 outside offer antiques, collectibles, memorabilia, advertising items, primitives, country items, crafts, used merchandise, and produce. Snack bar, rest rooms, h/a, ample parking. Tables and electricity available. Space from $10 daily or $25 all three days. Self-contained camping okay. *Contact* Carl Spalding, Rte. 2, Box 268, 62557 (217) 562-4825 or 423-4591.

PEORIA

Giant Flea Market
Fairgrounds, Expo Gardens

Every fourth Sunday, 8:30 a.m.–4:30 p.m. Admission charge. Approximately 100 sellers in this indoor market offer new merchandise, tools, collectibles, used goods, crafts, art, and more. Snack bar, rest rooms, h/a, ample parking. Space from $13 per table. *Contact* John Crouch, Box 9500, Springfield, 62791 (217) 529-6939.

PEOTONE

Antique Show & Flea Market
Will County Fairgrounds
One mile east of I-57

Every fourth Sunday. Admission charge $2. Approximately 60–70 dealers offer a wide variety of antiques and collectibles. Space from $25. Space for 700 sellers. *Contact* Robert Mitchell, Jr., 223 E. Main St., Amboy, 61310 (815) 857-2253 or 284-9216.

PRAIRIE VIEW

Country Boy Flea Market
193 Milwaukee Ave.
(847) 541-1952

Wednesday, Saturday, Sunday. New and used merchandise, lots of garage sale and bric-a-brac items, crafts, collectibles, and produce are available. Snack bar, rest rooms, h/a, ample parking.

PRINCETON

Second Sunday Flea Market
Fairgrounds
Junction of Rte. 6 and 34
(815) 872-1601

Every second Sunday. Antiques, collectibles, vintage clothing, silver, coins, linens, and quilts available. Food available, rest rooms, h/a, ample parking. *Contact* Tony Martin.

ROCKFORD

Greater Rockford Indoor/Outdoor Antique & Flea Market
3913 Sandy Hollow Rd.
Rte. 20, Exit Alpine St.

Saturday, Sunday, 8 a.m.–5 p.m. Approximately 200 outside spaces and 50 inside spaces. Good selection of collectibles, small antiques, primitives, country and advertising items, paper goods, coins, silver, glassware, new merchandise, crafts, and used merchandise. Snack bar, rest rooms, h/a, ample parking. Space from $25 for the weekend. Reservations required. *Contact* Carol Fritsch, 6350 Canyon Wood Dr., 61109 (815) 397-6683 or 874-6020.

Rockford Flea Market
Forest Hills Lodge, Rte. 173

Saturday, Sunday. Outdoor market with admission charge. New and used merchandise, garage sale items, crafts, collectibles, and produce are available. Food available, rest rooms, h/a, ample parking. *Contact* Paul Arduini (815) 633-5328.

ROSEMONT

Wolff's Flea Market
Rosemont Horizon parking lot
I-90 west to Lee St. Exit near intersection of I-90 and I-294

Sunday, spring–summer, 7 a.m.–3 p.m. Admission charge of $1 for adults, 50 cents children 6–12 and seniors. This outdoor market with approximately 450 dealers offers antiques, collectibles, crafts, used and new merchandise, and furniture. Space from $23. Rest rooms, snack bars, h/a, ample parking. *Contact* David Wolff, 970 Arkansas, Elk Grove, 60007 (847) 524-9590 or (630) 833-7469.

ST. CHARLES

Kane County Flea Market
Kane County Fairgrounds
Randall Rd., between Rtes. 64 and 38

Every first weekend, Saturday, 12 p.m.–5 p.m., Sunday, 7 a.m.–4 p.m. Admission charge $4. Approximately 1,000 dealers offer quality antiques (both furniture and smalls) and a great selection of collectibles, lots of fine jewelry, and quality junk. Good market for antique dealers, serious collectors, investors, and decorators to make some great buys. This is one of America's greatest antique markets. Good home-cooked meals served. Rest rooms, h/a, ample parking. Inside and outside space available from $125 indoors and $115 outside. *Contact* Helen Robinson, Box 549, 60174 (630) 377-2252.

SANDWICH

Sandwich Antiques Market
Fairgrounds
State Rte. 34

Monthly, call for dates, 8 a.m.–4 p.m. Admission charge $5. Approximately 500 exhibitors. Quality antique market, lots of furniture. Excellent market for antique dealers, serious collectors, shopkeepers, and decorators. Great selection of collectibles, glassware, silver, and fine jewelry. Snack bar, rest rooms, h/a, ample parking. *Contact* Robert Lawler, 1510 N. Hoyne, Chicago, 60622 (773) 227-4464 or (815) 786-3337, fax (773) 227-6322.

SPARTA

The Olde Hotel Flea Market & Auction
(618) 295-2440

Saturday, Sunday. A typical flea market in every sense. Even a bride-to-be could find what she needed at this market: something old, something new, something blue, and much more. Market also runs an auction service.

SPRINGFIELD

Giant Flea Market
Fairgrounds, Illinois Bldg.

Monthly, call for dates, 8:30 a.m.–4:30 p.m. Admission charge. Indoor market with approximately 100 exhibitors. Market heavy on antiques and collectibles. Some new and used merchandise. Snack bar, rest rooms, h/a, ample parking. Space from $13. *Contact* John Crouch, Box 9500, 62791 (217) 529-6939.

Frank's Gigantic Flea Market
Corner of Dirksen and Clearlake at the entrance of Kmart Shopping Center
Clearlake Exit off I-55, one mile

Saturday, Sunday, 6 a.m. until dark. New and used merchandise, flea market finds, including: crafts, collectibles, and produce. Food available, rest rooms, h/a, ample parking. Outside space for 150 dealers from $1. *Contact* Frank Reynolds, 3208 E. Clearlake, 62703 (217) 544-3142.

Giant Flea Market
Holiday Inn East

Every third Sunday. Admission charge. Approximately 50 dealers offer antiques, collectibles, silver, coins, linens, glassware, and vintage clothing. Food available, rest rooms, h/a, ample parking. Indoor market with space from $12 per table. *Contact* John Crouch, Box 5058, 62705 (217) 529-6939.

Flea Market
Springfield Drive-In
(217) 496-2088

Sundays only, April–November. New merchandise, electronics, tools, housewares, toys, sportswear, sports merchandise, used merchandise, garage sale items, crafts, collectibles, and produce. Snack bar, rest rooms, h/a, ample parking.

TINLEY PARK

I-80 Collectibles & Flea Market
Rte. 191 and Oak Park Ave.

Saturday, Sunday, 6 a.m. until dark. New and used merchandise, crafts, collectibles, antiques, and produce are available. Food available, rest rooms, h/a, ample parking. Indoor and outside space available. *Contact* Ralph Bruno, 60477 (708) 532-8238.

WARREN

Flea Market, Antiques & Crafts
Fairgrounds
(608) 759-3493

Every second Sunday. Antiques, collectibles, glassware, primitives, quilts, vintage clothing, jewelry, watches, plus a good selection of locally made crafts. Food available, rest rooms, h/a, ample parking.

WAUKEGAN

Waukegan Swap 'N Shop Flea Market
Belvedere Mall
Rte. 120 and Lewis Ave.

Friday, Saturday, Sunday, 9 a.m.–6 p.m. This large indoor market offers new and used merchandise, housewares, tools, sports items, sportswear, electronics, outdoor items, collectibles, and jewelry. Snack bar, rest rooms, h/a, ample parking. *Contact* Larry Lemer (847) 263-0160.

WHEATON

"All Night Flea Market"
2015 Manchester Rd.
I-88 west to Naperville Rd., north to Rte. 38, west to County Farm Rd., north to Manchester

The weekend of August 25–26, 2001. Always the weekend of the third Sunday in August, 5 p.m.–9 a.m. The original overnight flea market. Hundreds of dealers, both old and new merchandise. Space from $90. Rest rooms, lots of food, h/a. "Come for dinner, shop until breakfast." *Contact* Faith Sugarman, Box 32, Itasca, IL 60143 (847) 455-6090. E-mail: lovesoldstuff@prodigy.net.

Du Page Antique & Flea Market
Du Page County Fairgrounds

Every third Sunday. Admission charge. Large indoor/outdoor antique and collectible market. Great selection of antiques, furniture, many quality collector lines, silver, coins, glassware, farm items, advertising items, vintage clothing, and jewelry. Food available, rest rooms, h/a, ample paved parking. *Contact* Marilyn Sugarman (847) 455-6090 or 668-6636.

WHEELING

Twin Flea Market
1010 S. Milwaukee Ave., 60090

Saturday, Sunday, 6 a.m.–4 p.m. Approximately 300 dealers. Large outdoor market with lots of new merchandise, hot new items for the fashion conscious, secondhand items and some collectibles. Snack bar, rest rooms, h/a. Ample parking. *Contact* Ron Swislow (847) 229-0909.

INFORMATION IS SUBJECT TO CHANGE—ALWAYS CALL FIRST!

INDIANA

ANDERSON

Olympia Expo Center Flea Market
1312 W. 29th St.
Olympia Expo Center
(765) 642-0550

Saturday, Sunday. New merchandise, housewares, sportswear, electronics, sports merchandise, collectibles, glassware, primitives, and country collectibles are available. Snack bar, rest rooms, h/a, ample parking. Inside and outside space available.

AURORA

Aurora Flea Market
Rte. 50
(812) 423-3231

Friday, Saturday, Sunday. New merchandise, electronics, tools, housewares, toys, used merchandise, garage sale items, crafts, collectibles, and sportswear. Snack bar, rest rooms, ample parking.

BIRDSEYE

Flea Market
Birdseye Auction Barn

Every second and fourth Sunday. New merchandise, surplus, closeouts, clothing, housewares, country collectibles, used merchandise, and garage sale items are available. Snack bar, rest rooms, ample parking.

BLOOMINGTON

Starlite Drive-In Theater Flea Market
Old Hwy. 37 South

Saturday, Sunday. New merchandise, electronics, tools, sportswear, housewares, outdoor items, toys, used merchandise, garage sale items, crafts, collectibles, and produce are available. Snack bar, rest rooms, h/a, ample parking. *Contact* Carl Stewart (812) 824-7911.

Bloomington Antique Show & Flea Market
Fairgrounds

Every fourth weekend, 8 a.m.–4 p.m. Antiques, furniture, collectibles, glassware, advertising items, farm and ranch collectibles, coins, and silver are available. Food available, rest rooms, h/a, ample parking.

BORDEN

Borden Flea Market
Hwy. 60, west of town

Saturday, Sunday. A seasonal market. Approximately 150 dealers offer new and used merchandise, garage sale items, country collectibles, crafts, and produce. Rest rooms, snack bar, ample parking. Space from $2. Camping available. *Contact* Norma Wright (812) 967-3033.

BROOKVILLE

White Farmers Market
152nd at White Livestock Auction Grounds

Wednesday only, daylight until early afternoon. Approximately 300 dealers offer new and used merchandise, collectibles, crafts, and produce. Market conducts several special events during

---

NOTE: Indiana has state legislation requiring a transient vendor's license, and the city of Indianapolis also requires a transient vendor's license. Requirements are actively enforced.

the year. It is located on a 160-acre farm in Amish country. One of the most interesting tourist markets in the country. Market conducts livestock auction at 1 p.m. on Wednesday. Snack bar, rest rooms, h/a. Inside and outside space available from $8. *Contact* Dave White, 6119 Little Cedar Rd., 47012 (765) 647-3574 or 647-5360, fax (765) 647-6396.

BUNKER HILL

North Drive-In Flea Market
North Drive-In Theater, Hwy. 31

Saturday, Sunday, 7 a.m.–4 p.m. Indoor and outdoor market with approximately 200 dealers. Ample parking. *Contact* Dennis Miller (765) 689-9432 or (219) 699-7760.

CEDAR LAKE

Barn & Field Flea Market
9600 W. 151st Ave. 151st and Parish Ave.
One mile east of Rte. 41

Saturday, Sunday, 9 a.m.–5 p.m. Approximately 100 dealers offer fine antiques and quality collectibles, toys dolls, jewelry, and clothes. It has companion antique shops with many fine antiques and collectibles. Snack bar, rest rooms, h/a. Inside and outside space available from $2 per day. Electricity available and camping on-site. *Contact* Larry Toomey, Box 411, 46303 (219) 696-7368.

Uncle John's Flea Market
15205 Wicker Ave., Rte. 41
Eleven miles south of Rte. 30 on Rte. 41 (Wicker Ave.)

Saturday, Sunday, 7 a.m.–4 p.m. Ten buildings with over 200 indoor spaces open year-round; 200 outdoor spaces available. Attendance averages 2,000 plus per day. Average number of vendors 400 during summer and 150 during the winter months. Space from $10. Inside space on monthly rental. New, used merchandise, antiques, collectibles, fresh produce, plants and flowers in season. Homemade, hot food available in diner. Rest rooms, h/a. Ample parking. *Contact* Kathy Antosch, 15205 Wicker Ave., 46303 (219) 696-7911, fax (219) 374-5605.

CENTERVILLE

Big Bear Flea Market
Centerville Rd. and I-70, Exit 145

Saturday, Sunday, 7 a.m.–5 p.m. Approximately 100 dealers show in this outdoor open-air and covered market. Antiques, collectibles, new and used merchandise, and crafts are available. Good food available here. Campground with hookups. *Contact* Ed Newman (765) 855-3912.

CLARKSVILLE

Trading Fair
520 Marriott Dr.
(812) 288-0600

Saturday, Sunday. In this indoor market new merchandise, electronics, tools, housewares, sports merchandise, jewelry, used merchandise, collectibles, glassware, and advertising items are available. Snack bar, rest rooms, h/a, ample parking.

EVANSVILLE

Diamond Flea Market
1250 E. Diamond Ave., Hwy. 66 West

Saturday, Sunday, 9 a.m.–5 p.m. Average daily attendance 750. Approximately 75 dealers offer collectibles, country items, primitives, some antiques, new and used merchandise, crafts, and produce. Snack bar, clean rest rooms, ample parking. Overnight camping nearby. Space from $20 for the weekend. *Contact* Barbara Staub, 1250 E. Diamond Ave., 47711 (812) 464-2675.

Evansville Flea Market
1800 Mesker Park Dr.
(812) 422-2559 or 867-3425

Saturday, Sunday. Approximately 70 dealers offer new and used merchandise, garage sale items, collectibles, farm and ranch items, crafts, and produce. Snack bar, rest rooms, ample parking. Space from $5. Market is located in an old amusement park. No alcohol allowed.

FT. WAYNE

Ft. Wayne Flea Market
6901 S. Hanna and U.S. Hwy. 27 South

Saturday, Sunday. Primarily indoor market with approximately 100 dealers, limited outside space. New merchandise, imports, gifts, sportswear, electronics. Snack bar, rest rooms, h/a. *Contact* Kap Lee, 6901 S. Hanna St., 46816 (219) 447-0081.

Ft. Wayne Antique & Collectors Market
Memorial Coliseum

Call for dates; usually last weekend of month. Friday, 12 p.m.–7 p.m., Saturday, 10 a.m.–7 p.m., Sunday, 11 a.m.–5 p.m. Admission fee $1. This is a new market. Antiques, collectibles, crafts, and new merchandise; market has a special antique section. Snack bar, rest rooms, h/a, ample parking. *Contact* Stewart Promotions, 2950 Breckenridge Lane, No. 4A, Louisville, KY 40220 (502) 456-2244 or www.stewartpromotions.com.

FOUNTAINTOWN

Moonlite Flea Market & Crafts Show

Saturday, Sunday, May–October. Approximately 50 vendors. Used and secondhand items, garage sale items, country collectibles, farm and ranch items, lots of locally made crafts, and produce are available. Food available, rest rooms, ample parking. Space from $6 per day. Camping available. *Contact* Donny Wyss, Box 104, 46150 (317) 861-9775.

Fountaintown Emporium
Old Greenfield Rd.
Located at the old schoolhouse

Every first weekend. Antiques, collectibles, silver, glassware, primitives, advertising items, and new and used merchandise are available. Food available, rest rooms, h/a, ample parking. Space from $5. Inside and outside spaces available. *Contact* Art Goodblood (317) 861-7989 or 862-2187.

FRANKLIN

Franklin Antique Show & Flea Market
Fairgrounds

Every third weekend, 9 a.m.–5 p.m. Approximately 50 dealers. Inside market. Excellent market for antiques and quality collectibles. Some new merchandise. Snack bar, rest rooms, h/a, ample parking. Space from $28 for the weekend. *Contact* Elmer Judkings, 122 Woodland Dr., New Whiteland, 46184 (317) 535-5084.

FRIENDSHIP

Friendship Flea Market
Hwy. 62, west of Dillsboro
(606) 341-1400
Fax (606) 363-8184

Spring and fall. Dawn until late in evening. Excellent market, strong attendance usually in excess of 100,000 for the spring show with approximately 500 dealers. One of the most fun markets to sell at or to attend. Great place to see living American heritage in action. Indian and frontier encampments and reenactment, national black powder shoot. The very finest in Indian memorabilia and frontier collectibles are available at this event. Space from $150 for the entire show or $20 per day. Camping permitted at selling space. *Contact* Tom Kerr, 654 Wayskin Dr., Covington, KY 41015 (606) 356-7114.

GARY

Market City Flea Market
4121 Cleveland St.
(219) 887-3522

Saturday, Sunday, 9 a.m.–5 p.m. Indoor/outdoor market with over 200 dealers. Crafts, art, memorabilia, decorator items. New merchandise, secondhand items, and garage sale junk. Some antiques and collectibles, but most of market is discounted new merchandise. Snack bar, rest rooms, h/a, ample parking. Space from $30. *Contact* Manager, 4121 Cleveland St., 46408.

Village Flea Market
1845 W. Ridge Rd.

Friday, Saturday, Sunday, 9 a.m.–5 p.m. Indoor market with approximately 75 dealers. Antiques, collectibles, lots of locally made crafts, new and used merchandise, furniture. Space from $25 for weekend. Rest rooms, snack bar, h/a. Ample parking. *Contact* Joseph Harkin, 5719 Hohman Ave., Hammond, IN 46320 (219) 933-6622 or (219) 980-1111.

GOSHEN

Peddlers Flea Market
2626 Peddlers Village Rd.
(219) 533-9723

Tuesday–Saturday, 10 a.m.–8 p.m. New merchandise, gifts, imports, sportswear, used merchandise, garage sale items, collectibles are offered. Rest rooms, snack bar, ample parking.

HAMMOND

41 Swap-O-Rama
2500 Calumet
(312) 774-3900

Sunday only, April–October. New merchandise, used merchandise, garage sale items, collectibles, produce, and crafts are available. Snack bar, rest rooms, ample parking.

HOBART

Holiday's Barn Market
I-65 and Rte. 6

Saturday, Sunday. Approximately 100 dealers offer new and used merchandise, antiques, glassware, country collectibles, and crafts. Food available, rest rooms, ample parking. Spaces $10. *Contact* Robbie Robinson, 2785 Eleanor St., Portage, 46368 (219) 942-6682.

INDIANAPOLIS

Big Red Flea Market
11777 Lafayette Ave.
(317) 769-3266

Friday, Saturday, Sunday. Antiques, collectibles, linens, quilts, glassware, primitives, advertising items, decorator items. This is an interesting market to poke around in. Snack bar, rest rooms, h/a, ample parking. Inside and outside spaces available. Camping available. Auction held on Saturday night. Fun auction to attend.

Twin Drive-In Theater Flea Market
3000 Southeastern Ave.

Saturday, Sunday, 9 a.m.–5 p.m. Approximately 200 dealers. Good commercial market with lots of new merchandise, sportswear, electronics, jewelry, watches, housewares, sports merchandise, used merchandise, garage sale items, produce, and crafts. Snack bar, rest rooms, h/a, ample parking with lots of walking. This market is on my approved "good sales" market list. Space from $5. *Contact* Don Ross, Twin Drive-In, 3000 Southeastern Ave., 46201 (317) 631-8494 or www.stewartpromotions.com.

Indiana Flea Market
State Fairgrounds, Expo Hall

Usually held midmonth, Friday, 12 p.m.–7 p.m., Saturday, 10 a.m.–8 p.m., Sunday, 11 a.m.–5 p.m. Admission charge. All indoors, averages over 500 booths. One of the better antique and collectible markets in the U.S.A. Collector's paradise, some very high-quality dealers here with great setups of very high-grade merchandise. If you're looking for a great source market, this is it. This market will have you singing the old song "Back Home in

Indiana." Snack bars, rest rooms, h/a, good security, ample paved parking. *Contact* Stewart Promotions, 2950 Breckenridge Lane, No. 4A, Louisville, KY 40220 (502) 456-2244 or (317) 927-7500.

Liberty Bell Flea Market
8949 E. Washington St.
(317) 898-3180 or 898-3181

Friday, 12 p.m.–8 p.m., Saturday, 10 a.m.–7 p.m., Sunday, 10 a.m.–6 p.m. Approximately 200 dealers offer a wide range of merchandise. Antiques, collectibles, coins, paper, vintage clothing, country items, primitives, advertising items, new and used merchandise, electronics, and crafts are available. This market is a very worthwhile stop. Snack bar, clean rest rooms, h/a, ample parking. Space from $45. Inside and outside space available. *Contact* Noble Hall, 8949 E. Washington St., 46219.

Lafayette Road Flea Market
2366 Lafayette Rd.

Friday, Saturday, Sunday. New and used merchandise, garage sale items, crafts, collectibles, and produce are available. Snack bar, rest rooms, h/a, ample parking. Inside and outside spaces available from $21. *Contact* Jerry Williams (317) 639-4292.

West Washington Flea Market
6445 W. Washington St.

Friday 1 p.m.–9 p.m., Saturday 11 a.m.–7 p.m., Sunday 11 a.m.–6 p.m. Approximately 100 dealers offer new merchandise, sportswear, housewares, electronics, tools, sports merchandise, toys, used merchandise, garage sale items, crafts, farm collectibles, and produce. Snack bar, rest rooms, h/a, ample parking. Space from $48 for the weekend. *Contact* Mr. Baig (317) 244-0941.

JEFFERSONVILLE

Antiques Center & Flea Market
(812) 288-4251

Saturday, Sunday. A typical flea market with some great antiques, some nice collector items amidst the booths of new and nearly new junk of all descriptions.

KENDALLVILLE

Connie's Corner Flea Market
1551 S. Main St.

Monday–Saturday, 9 a.m.–5:30 p.m. Indoor market with antiques, collectibles, glassware, and gifts. Market is primarily permanent booths. Rest rooms, h/a, ample parking.

KINGMAN

Festival Flea Market
Junction of Hwy. 41 and State Rte. 234
(317) 397-8352

Friday, Saturday, Sunday, May–October, 9 a.m.–5 p.m. This outdoor market with 300 spaces offers antiques, collectibles, glassware, linen, silver, primitives, and country collectibles. Ample parking, snack bar, rest rooms. Overnight camping available. Market has many special holiday promotions. It is open for 10 days straight during the mid-October Covered Bridge Festival, one of Indiana's better special events. *Contact* Festival Flea Market, Rte. 1, Box 21, 47952.

KINGSLAND

Flea Market
State Rte. 1 and U.S. Hwy. 224
(219) 597-7375

Every second weekend. Antiques, collectibles, glassware, silver, vintage clothing, primitives, decorator items, used merchandise, crafts, and produce are available. Food available, rest rooms, ample parking. Inside and outside spaces available.

KOKOMO

Flea Market
Kokomo Home Center
1940 S. Elizabeth St.
(317) 453-7000

Friday, Saturday, Sunday. Approximately 75 dealers offer new merchandise, electronics, sportswear, tools, jewelry, sports merchandise, and toys, as well as used merchandise and garage sale items. Snack bar, rest rooms, h/a, ample parking. Space from $28 for weekend.

The Merchants Market
211 E. Morgan
Farm Co-op Bldg.

Saturday, Sunday. New and used merchandise, jewelry, gifts, imports, used merchandise, garage sale items, and collectibles are available. Snack bar, rest rooms, h/a, ample parking. Indoor and outdoor spaces. *Contact* Nan Statler (314) 452-9800.

LAFAYETTE

East Drive-In Flea Market
3500 State Rte. 26

Sunday, 8 a.m.–4 p.m. Average attendance is 1,000. Approximately 35 sellers offer used merchandise, garage sale items, collectibles, farm items, crafts, and produce. Snack bar, rest rooms, ample parking. Space from $5. *Contact* Glenda Hart (317) 447-2771 or 463-3111.

LAKE STATION

Central Avenue Flea Market
2750 Central Ave.
I-94 to Reapel St.

Saturday, Sunday, 9 a.m.–5 p.m. Approximately 75 dealers offer new and used merchandise, antiques, collectibles, crafts, and produce. Snack bar, rest rooms. Inside and outside space available. Overnight parking available. *Contact* Delbert Miller, 2750 Central Ave., 46405 (219) 962-5524.

Dunes Swap-O-Rama
1227 Ripley St.
Dunes Drive-In Theater
(312) 774-3900

Sunday only. New and used merchandise, antiques, collectibles, crafts, and produce are available. Snack bar, rest rooms, h/a, ample parking.

LAPORTE

Wildwood Park Farm & Flea Market
4938 W. Hwy. 20
(219) 879-5660

Friday, Saturday, Sunday. Average weekend attendance is 3,500. Approximately 100 dealers offer new and used merchandise, garage sale items, collectibles, primitives, jewelry, produce, and crafts. Snack bar, rest rooms, h/a, ample parking. Inside and outside space available from $4. Camping available.

LAWRENCEBURG

Tri-State Antique Market
Rte. 50, off I-275, Exit 16

Every first Sunday, May–November, 7 a.m.–3 p.m. Admission fee. Approximately 175 dealers at this indoor/outdoor market, which features fine antiques and collectibles. Market is strong on antique furniture. No new merchandise or crafts allowed. Food available, rest rooms, h/a. Space from $20. *Contact* Bruce Metzger, Box 35, Shandon, OH 45063 (513) 738-7256.

LEBANON

Old Canyon Works Flea Market
(317) 482-6180

Saturday, Sunday. Bargain hunters will enjoy the array of diverse merchandise to poke through at this typical Indiana flea market.

LOGANSPORT

Peddlers Acre
Rural Rte. 6
Four miles west of Logansport on State Rd. 24
(219) 722-2031

Friday, Saturday, Sunday, 12 p.m.–7 p.m. Approximately 15 dealers offer used merchandise, garage sale items, clothing, collectibles, and bric-a-brac. Snack bar, rest rooms, ample parking. Overnight parking available.

LOWELL

Livery Stable Antique Mart
Rte. 45 East
(219) 696-9395

Saturday, Sunday. Antiques, furniture, collectibles, glassware, primitives, advertising items, silver, coins, jewelry, and watches are available. Food available, rest rooms, ample parking.

LYNN

Parkers Flea Market
U.S. Hwy. 27 South

Saturday, Sunday. Approximately 100 dealers offer new merchandise, sportswear, tools, electronics, jewelry, watches, decorator items, used merchandise, garage sale items, crafts, collectibles, and produce. Snack bar, rest rooms, ample parking. Space from $2. *Contact* Tom Ward (317) 861-1015.

MADISON

Rivertown Flea Market
2670 Michigan Rd.
(812) 276-1616

Friday, Saturday, Sunday. This indoor market offers new merchandise, sportswear, electronics, tools, jewelry, housewares, toys, used merchandise, collectibles, gifts, and decorator items. Snack bar, rest rooms, h/a, ample parking.

MANSFIELD PARK

Mansfield Park Monthly Flea Market
Mansfield Park, Hwy. 59
(765) 569-6847

Every first weekend. Admission $1. Covered spaces. Rest rooms, snack bar, h/a. Overnight camping.

MARION

Open Air Flea Market
On bypass between 30th and 31st Sts.
State Rtes. 9 and 15

Friday, Saturday, Sunday. Seasonal market. New and used merchandise, collectibles, crafts, and produce are available. Snack bar, rest rooms, ample parking. Outside space from $5. Free overnight camping. Approximately 65 acres. *Contact* Fred Emmons, 3703 S. Western Ave., 46953 (317) 674-4408 or 674-2613.

Marion Flea Market and Antiques
26th St. and bypass
(765) 674-2613 or 674-9258

Friday, Saturday, Sunday. Antiques, collectibles, new and used merchandise, gifts, crafts, glassware, coins, silver, jewelry, and primitives are available. Snack bar, rest rooms, h/a, ample parking.

MARTINSVILLE

The Collector's Fair
Hwys. 37 and 252
(317) 342-6833

Saturday, Sunday. Antiques, collectibles, glassware, jewelry, coins, silver, primitives, advertising items, and used merchandise are available. Snack bar, rest rooms, h/a, ample parking. Inside and outside spaces available.

MEMPHIS

Burtons Farmers & Collectors Flea Market
I-65 and Memphis Rd. Exit
(812) 294-4685

Friday, Saturday, Sunday. Approximately 25 dealers offer used merchandise, collectibles, farm and ranch items, produce, and livestock. Snack bar, rest rooms, ample parking.

MERRILLVILLE

Hoosier Swap-O-Rama
2821 E. Lincoln
Hwy. 30
(219) 774-3900

Sunday only. New and used merchandise, collectibles, glassware, decorator items, coins, jewelry, and bric-a-brac are available. Snack bar, rest rooms, h/a, ample parking.

Y&W Drive-In Flea Market
6600 Broadway
(219) 769-2203

Sunday only. New and used merchandise, garage sale items, crafts, produce, and collectibles are available. Snack bar, rest rooms, h/a, ample parking.

METAMORA

Cracker Ridge Flea Market
U.S. Hwy. 52
Four miles west of Metamora

Saturday, Sunday, May–November. Used merchandise, collectibles, glassware, primitives, jewelry, crafts, and produce are available. Snack bar, rest rooms, ample parking. *Contact* Larry Mannie, Box 76, 47030 (765) 698-2311.

MICHIGAN CITY

Lilac Park Country Fair Craft & Flea Market
2612 W. 1000 North

Saturday, Sunday, April–October. Approximately 150 spaces outside for crafts, new and used merchandise, some collectibles, vintage clothing, and jewelry. Snack bar, rest rooms, ample parking. *Contact* Leona Turner (219) 874-6048.

MITCHELL

Ed's Gift Shop & Flea Market
State Rte. 60 East
(812) 849-4815

Saturday, Sunday. New merchandise, gifts, imports, decorator items, jewelry, used merchandise, and garage sale items. Rest rooms, ample parking.

MODOC

Halfway Flea Market
State Rte. 36 and Carlos St.
(317) 853-5029

Sunday only. New and used merchandise, advertising items, primitives, farm items, crafts, sports memorabilia, and produce are available. Snack bar, rest rooms, h/a, ample parking.

MONTICELLO

Norway Flea Market
309 W. Norway Rd.

Saturday, Sunday. Approximately 25 dealers offer used merchandise, garage sale items, collectibles, and crafts. Rest rooms, ample parking. *Contact* Guy Harrison (219) 583-3058.

Twin Lakes Flea Market
1617 W. Shafer Dr.

Daily, May–September, 9 a.m.–5 p.m. Small indoor/outdoor market with approximately 25 dealers. Lots of memorabilia, collectibles, books, vintage clothing, used merchandise, and some new merchandise are available. *Contact* Guy Harrison, 3016 W. Shafer Dr., 47960 (219) 583-4145.

MUNCIE

Kilgore Flea Market
2004 Kilgore Ave.

Saturday, Sunday. New and used merchandise, collectibles, jewelry, glassware, housewares, gifts, and crafts. Snack bar, rest rooms, h/a, ample parking. Inside and outside space available. *Contact* Charles Terry (317) 747-6069.

Main Street Flea Market
1710 E. Main St.
(765) 289-5394

Saturday, Sunday, 9 a.m.–5 p.m. New and used merchandise, secondhand items, gifts, imports, decorator items, crafts, and produce. Snack bar, rest rooms, h/a, ample parking. Inside and outside space available. *Contact* Leonard Lewis (765) 289-5394.

Greenwalts Flea Market
Fairgrounds, I-69, Exit 332
Seven miles to Wheeling Ave., south to fairgrounds

Monthly, 9 a.m.–5 p.m. Approximately 75 sellers offer antiques, collectibles, primitives, memorabilia, advertising items, and decorator items. Market has a wonderful traditional family atmosphere. Snack bar, rest rooms, h/a, ample parking. Space from $35 for the weekend. *Contact* Mary or Keith Greenwalt, 604 N. Kettner Dr., 47304 (765) 289-0194.

NAPOLEON

Ye Olde Central House Flea Market
Main St.

Every first weekend. Approximately 25 dealers offer used merchandise, garage sale items, and collectibles. Rest rooms, ample parking. Space $3 per day. *Contact* Richard Ramey, Rte. 2, Box 379, Osgood, 47037 (812) 689-4373.

NAPPANEE

Borkholder Dutch Village Market
(219) 773-2828

Tuesday, Friday, Saturday, 7 a.m.–6 p.m. Market restricted to antiques and collectibles. Great selection of smalls and quality hard-to-find collector items at this market. Snack bar, rest rooms, h/a, ample parking. Auction on Tuesday evening.

NASHVILLE

Old Time Flea Market
State Rte. 46

Saturday, Sunday, April–November, 9 a.m.–5 p.m. Approximately 50 dealers. New and used merchandise, garage sale items, farm and ranch items, collectibles, and glassware are available. Snack bar, rest rooms, h/a, ample parking. Outside and covered space available. Space from $5 per day. Overnight parking available. *Contact* Phyllis Thompson, Box 1167, 47448 (812) 988-0750 or 988-2346.

NEW ALBANY

Pine Ridge Flea Market
3328 Corydon Pike
Four miles west of downtown

Friday, Saturday, Sunday. Antiques, collecibles, farm items, primitives, and used merchandise are available. Snack bar, rest rooms, ample parking. Inside and outside space available from $15. *Contact* Pat Tinius, 3328 Corydon Pike, 47150 (812) 941-1111.

NORTH VERNON

Green Meadows Flea Market
Hwy. 7N

Friday, Saturday, Sunday. New and used merchandise, decorator items, gifts, imports, clothing, tools, and kitchenware are available. Snack bar, rest rooms, h/a, ample parking. Inside and outside market. Camping available. *Contact* Charles Conehan (812) 346-9945.

NORTH WEBSTER

Flea Market
Land O'Lakes Barn
(219) 834-7014

Saturday, Sunday. Antiques, collectibles, jewelry, vintage clothing, farm and ranch items, and used merchandise are available. Snack bar, rest rooms, ample parking.

OSCEOLA

Highway 20 Flea Market
10156 McKinley
(219) 674-8334

Friday, Saturday, Sunday. New and used merchandise, garage sale items, and bric-a-brac are available. Snack bar, rest rooms, h/a, ample parking.

PETERSBURG

Antiques & Collectibles Flea Market
Hwy. 57 South

Every second and fourth weekend. Antiques, collectibles, furniture, jewelry, glassware, silver, coins, primitives, advertising items, and decorator items are available. Food available, rest rooms, h/a, ample parking.

PORTLAND

Antique Show & Flea Market
Fairgrounds
U.S. Hwy. 27
(219) 726-4150

Saturday, Sunday, 8 a.m.–4 p.m. Antiques, collectibles, furniture, glassware, jewelry, watches, vintage clothing, advertising items, and primitives are available. Food available, rest rooms, h/a, ample paved parking. Lots of bargain prices on nice items at this market. A good buyer's market.

RENESSELAER

Renesselaer Antique & Flea Market
McKinley and Merrioll Sts.
(219) 866-7493

Sunday only. Antiques, collectibles, furniture, jewelry, sports cards, watches, vintage clothing, reproductions, gifts, used merchandise, and decorator items are available at this popular local market. Snack bar, rest rooms, h/a, ample parking. Inside and outside spaces available.

RICHMOND

Wayne County Flea Market
4-H Fairgrounds, Khulman Center
Salisbury Rd.
(317) 966-9074

Monthly, call for dates, 9 a.m.–5 p.m. This inside and outside market has a wide variety of merchandise. New and used, antiques, collectibles, jewelry, housewares, electronics, and glassware are available. Snack bar, rest rooms, h/a, ample parking.

Eastern Indiana Flea Market
Fairgrounds
Salisbury Rd.

Monthly, call for dates. Primarily antiques and collectibles. *Contact* John Ford, Box 68, Springport, 47386 (317) 755-3565.

Yesteryears Antique & Collectible Mall & Flea Market
Old Melody Skating Rink
1505 S. 9th St.

Thursday–Sunday. Approximately 75 dealers offer antiques, furniture, collectibles, decorator items, linen, jewelry, coins, silver, primitives, and advertising items. Snack bar, rest rooms, h/a, ample parking. *Contact* Lysle Sheeley, 1505 S. 9th St., 47374 (317) 966-0594 or 935-9865.

RUSHVILLE

Inside Flea Market
State Rd. 3 South
Behind Lloyd's Motors

Saturday, Sunday, 8 a.m.–5 p.m. Market is strong on antiques and collectibles. This is a good buyer's market with quality items at very desirable prices. Food available, rest rooms, h/a, ample parking.

SCOTTSBURG

Moonglo Treasure Chest Flea Market
U.S. Hwy. 31 South (old drive-in theater)

Saturday, Sunday. Average attendance is 2,000. Approximately 100 vendors offer new merchandise, electronics, tools, housewares, sports merchandise, toys, sportswear, jewelry, used merchandise, and lots of garage sale items. Snack bar, rest rooms, h/a, ample parking. Space $4 to $7. *Contact* Carl Spellman, Box 183, 47170 (812) 752-3551.

SHIPSHEWANA

Shipshewana Auction & Flea Market
Rte. 5, south of town
(219) 768-4129
Fax (219) 768-7041

Tuesday, Wednesday, 7 a.m. until dark. Approximately 800 dealers at this excellent antique and wholesale market. This is one of the outstanding events in America. From major wholesalers of new merchandise to beautiful Amish-made goods and food. The public can buy individual new items here at prices not available anywhere else. Over five auctions running simultaneously, including livestock auction. Have motel or bed-and-breakfast reservations early; the area is a complete sellout when the market is operating. Allow plenty of time for this market and the quaint Amish village it is located in. Great food, rest rooms, h/a, ample parking, but lots of walking. Space from $30. *Contact* Shipshewana Auction, Box 185, 46565.

SOUTH BEND

Thieves Market
2309 E. Edison at Ironwood St.

Saturday, Sunday, 10 a.m.–6 p.m. Permanent shops open daily and outside flea market on weekends with approximately 25 dealers. Nice selection of collectibles, memorabilia, primitives, and lots of vintage jewelry and older fine jewelry, along with several specialty shops. Space $5 per day. *Contact* David Ciesiolka, Box 6114, 46615 (219) 273-1352.

TERRE HAUTE

Terre Haute Flea Market
Wabash County Fairgrounds

Monthly, call for dates. Inside and outside market. Antiques, collectibles, crafts, new merchandise, and limited used items are available. Food available, rest rooms, h/a, ample parking. Space from $15 outside per day. *Contact* Stewart Promotions, 2950 Breckenridge Lane, No. 4A, Louisville, KY 40220 (502) 456-2244 or www.stewartpromotions.com.

TRAFALGAR

Trafalgar Antique Market
Hwys. 135 and 252
(317) 933-3402

Saturday, Sunday. Quality-oriented indoor market with antiques, good selection of furniture, collectibles, primitives, jewelry fine and estate, watches, coins, silver, linens, and vintage clothing available. Snack bar, rest rooms, h/a, ample parking.

WORTHINGTON

Green County Hill Flea Market
Four miles north of Worthington on Rte. 57

Every first and third weekend. Antiques, collectibles, primitives, coins, glassware, new and used merchandise, crafts, and produce are available. Food available, rest rooms, h/a, ample parking. Spaces from $25 for the weekend. *Contact* Lynn McGarnsney, Rte. 4, Box 150, Franklin, 46131 (317) 736-4564.

ZANESVILLE

Flea Market
17727 Indianapolis Rd.
(219) 638-4767

Every second and fourth Sunday. Antiques, collectibles, primitives, glassware, new and used merchandise, garage sale items, crafts, and produce are available. Snack bar, rest rooms, h/a, ample parking.

IOWA

BENTONSPORT

Flea Market and Craft Show
Greef General Store
(319) 592-3579

Periodically. Outdoor event weather permitting. Call for current schedule.

BOONE

Original Hillbilly Flea Market & Auction
Six miles outside of town

Saturday, Sunday, May–October. Lots of used merchandise, farm collectibles, glassware, vintage clothing, and primitives are available. Snack bar, rest rooms, ample parking.

COUNCIL BLUFFS

Tomes Flea Market

Every third Sunday. Average daily attendance 500 with approximately 25 vendors. New and used merchandise, bric-a-brac, garage sale items, and farm and ranch collectibles are available. Rest rooms, snack bar, ample parking. Space from $10. *Contact* Bud Tomes (912) 366-0363.

DAVENPORT

Giant Flea Market
Holiday Inn
5202 N. Brady St.

Every third Sunday. Admission charge. Approximately 50 dealers offer antiques, collectibles, crafts, and new merchandise in this indoor market. Food available, rest rooms, h/a, ample parking. Space from $12 per table. *Contact* John Crouch, Box 5058, Springfield, IL 62705 (217) 529-6939.

Mississippi Valley Flea Market
Fairgrounds. 2815 W. Locust

Every last Sunday, 8 a.m.–4 p.m. Admission $1.50. Indoor/outdoor market with antiques, collectibles, new and used merchandise, crafts. Snack bar, rest rooms, h/a. Ample parking. *Contact* Robett Balzer (319) 323-2319 or 326-5338.

DES MOINES

Flea Market
State Fairgrounds
E. 30th St. and University Ave.

Monthly. This indoor market offers antiques, collectibles, glassware, vintage clothing, jewelry, coins, silver, sports memorabilia, and advertising items. Food available, rest rooms, h/a, ample paved parking. Space from $16. The area's leading market. Reservations recommended. *Contact* Evelyn Jennings, 1601 Capitol Ave., 50317 (515) 262-4282 or 262-3111.

DUBUQUE

Flea Market
Fairgrounds
Five miles west of town on Hwy. 20

Sunday only. Admission charge. Approximately 100 dealers offer good-quality antiques and collectibles here at very attractive prices. A good market for the serious shopper or casual browser. Inside and outside space available from $6. *Contact* Norma Koppen, 1887 Carter Rd., 52001 (319) 583-7940.

IOWA CITY

Sharpless Flea Market
5049 Hoover Hwy. NE, I-80, Exit 249

Every second Sunday, 8 a.m.–4 p.m. Admission $2. Antiques, collectibles, furniture, lots of primitives and quality smalls here. Toys, new and vintage clothing. Space from $20 per table. Snack bar, rest rooms, h/a. *Contact* Karen Dunlap, 5049 Hoover Hwy. NE, 52240 (319) 351-8888 or 338-1714.

KEOKUK

Bryants Flea Market
River Rd.
Six miles north of city
(319) 463-7727

Every third Sunday. Approximately 200 dealers offer antiques, collectibles, primitives, furniture, jewelry, coins, silver, and advertising items. This is a good source market for the shopkeeper, dealer, serious collector, or decorator. Food available, snack bar, rest rooms, h/a. Space from $6.

MARSHALLTOWN

Central Iowa Flea Market
Fairgrounds

Monthly. Approximately 50 dealers. Lots of different items carried at this market including pets, birds, chickens, and other live animals. Inside and outside space available from $5. *Contact* Arnold Klaas (515) 483-2781 or 753-3671.

MUSCATINE

King's Flea Market
1700 Grandview
(319) 264-8190

Monthly, April–October, call for dates. Admission charge. Approximately 100 dealers under cover offer used merchandise, collectibles, antiques, furniture, glassware, clothing, jewelry, and housewares. Market is held in an old lumberyard. Space from $20 for the weekend. Snack bar, clean rest rooms, ample parking. Overnight camping available.

OTTUMWA

Collectors Fair
Coliseum basement
Hwys. 34 and 63

Saturday, Sunday, 9 a.m.–4 p.m. Admission charge 50 cents. Indoor market with approximately 40 dealers offering collectibles, used merchandise, tools, toys, and lots of secondhand items. Snack bar, rest rooms, ample parking. Space from $12.50 *Contact* Frosti Chicchelly, 3636 Clark Rd. SE, Cedar Rapids, 52403 (515) 582-0071.

SIOUX CITY

Flea Market
City Auditorium

Every first weekend. Approximately 200 dealers offer antiques, collectibles, jewelry, sports cards, coins, silver, linens, primitives, advertising items, and new and used merchandise. Food available, rest rooms, h/a, ample parking. Space from $13. *Contact* Ed Benson, Box 286, 57101 (712) 279-4850.

WATERLOO

Kozy Corner Flea Market
7023 Osage Rd.

Saturday, Sunday. Used merchandise, bric-a-brac, imports, gifts, collectibles, and crafts are available. Rest rooms.

WHAT CHEER

Collectors Paradise Flea Market
Keokuk County Fairgrounds
I-80, Exit 201, south 20 miles

Monthly, call for dates, 7 a.m.–5 p.m. Admission charge $1. This indoor/outdoor market has approximately 400 dealers. Antique and collectible market with many quality items, fine jewelry, toys, coins, primitives, and furniture available. Excellent source market for dealers who want to buy for resale. Space from $35 per weekend outside. Food available, rest rooms, h/a, ample parking. *Contact* Larry Nicholson, Box 413, 50268 (515) 634-2109.

KANSAS

ARKANSAS CITY

Arkansas City Flea Market
712 W. Washington St.
Seven blocks west on Washington,
off Hwy. 77

Every first Sunday. Seasonal market. Approximately 80 dealers offer new merchandise, electronics, housewares, tools, jewelry, toys, sportswear, used merchandise, antiques, collectibles, glassware, primitives, and farm and ranch collectibles in this indoor market. Snack bar, rest rooms, h/a, ample parking. Space $10. Camping available. Reservations recommended. *Contact* Don Jackson, Box 290, 67005 (316) 442-0848 or 442-9566.

CONCORDIA

Concordia Flea Market
One mile north of town

Saturday, Sunday. New and used merchandise, collectibles, decorator items, farm items. Market does special promotions and has a great selection of locally made crafts. *Contact* Charles Chartier, Box 98, Clyde, 66938 (913) 446-3411.

HUTCHINSON

Hutchinson Flea Market (Known also as the Mid-America Flea Market)
Kansas State Fairgrounds
20th and Main Sts.

Every first Sunday, 9 a.m.–4 p.m. Admission charge 50 cents. Approximately 200 dealers specializing in antiques and collectibles, good selection of memorabilia, primitives, and advertising items. Indoor market. Snack bar, rest rooms, h/a, ample parking. Space from $17. *Contact* Schartz Enterprises, Box 1585, 67504 (316) 663-5626.

KANSAS CITY

Boulevard Drive-In Swap Shop
1051 Merriam Lane

Saturday, Sunday, 7 a.m. until dark. Admission charge. Average attendance 1,200 with approximately 150 dealers. New merchandise, electronics, tools, housewares, sports merchandise, toys, and sportswear are available. Also used flea market finds, garage-sale-type items, crafts, collectibles, and produce. Snack bar, rest rooms, ample parking. Space from $3. *Contact* Wes Neal (913) 262-2414.

LAWRENCE

Quantrill's Flea Market
811 New Hampshire St., downtown
(913) 842-6616

Friday, Saturday, Sunday, 10 a.m.–5 p.m. New and used merchandise, collectibles, primitives, glassware, crafts. The market has 10,000 square feet, three rooms, 45 booths. Snack bar, rest rooms, ample parking. Company also operates an antique mall on the premises with a good selection of antiques and collectibles.

MANHATTAN

Airport Flea Market
Junction of Hwys. 171 and 57 at the Missouri state line

Saturday, Sunday, 9 a.m.–5 p.m. Approximately 15 dealers. Market is heavy on antiques, and collectibles. Snack bar, rest rooms, ample parking. Inside and outside space available from $8. *Contact* Market Manager, 723 Moro St., 66502 (913) 776-6906.

OPOLIS

Opolis Flea Market
At the junction of Hwys. 171 and 57, at the Missouri state line

Saturday, Sunday, 9 a.m.–5 p.m. Approximately 15 dealers. Market is heavy on an-tiques, collectibles and antique auto parts. Auto enthusiasts will find some really nice and very unusual antique auto items and accessories at this market. Lots of old Volkswagen stuff. Snack bar, rest rooms. Inside and outside space available from $8. Ample parking. *Contact* Norma Kukovich, Box 42, 66760 (316) 231-2543.

OSWEGO

Oswego Flea Market
Junction of Hwys. 59 and 96
(316) 795-4415

Saturday. Country market with used merchandise, bric-a-brac, housewares, clothing, crafts, collectibles, and produce available. Food available, rest rooms, ample parking.

SPARKS

Sparks Flea Market
290th Rd. and K-7 Hwy.

Every first Sunday. Seasonal market, first Sunday in May and the three preceding days. Also held in mid-July, Labor Day weekend, and a five-day show late in fall. Call for specific dates. Approximately 400–500 dealers. Indoor and outdoor market. Market is strong on quality antiques, collectibles, and antique furniture. Lots of great collectible/smalls spreads here along with many high-grade quality dealers that set excellent booths. Space from $45 outdoors and $55 inside. Great source market for the serious collector, investor, or shopkeeper. Lots of food here, rest rooms, h/a and lots of walking. Ample parking. *Contact* Ray Tackett, Box 223, Troy, KS 66087 (785) 985-2411

TOPEKA

Flea Market
Fairgrounds
(785) 233-4444

Every third Sunday. Antiques, collectibles, coins, linens, silver, quilts, primitives, advertising items, and farm collectibles. Food available, rest rooms, h/a, ample parking. Regularly scheduled events. One of the better markets in the area.

Topeka Flea Market
5247 S.W. 28th Ct.
(785) 273-2969

Tuesday–Sunday, 9 a.m.–5 p.m. New merchandise, gifts, decorator items, sportswear, tools, housewares, electronics, toys, used desirables, collectibles, and crafts are available in this indoor market. Space from $11 per day. Snack bar, rest rooms, food vendors allowed.

WICHITA

The Market
Wichita Greyhound Park
(316) 755-2440

Saturday, Sunday. Admission charge. New merchandise, electronics, housewares, tools, sportswear, coins, sports items, used merchandise, and flea market merchandise are available in this new market. Rest rooms, snack bar, h/a,

ALWAYS CALL BEFORE TRAVELING LONG DISTANCES!

ample parking. Space from $10. *Contact* The Market, P.O. Box 277, Valley Center, 67147.

Village Flea Market
2301 S. Meridian

Friday, Saturday, Sunday, 9 a.m.–6 p.m. Approximately 100 dealers offer antiques, collectibles, primitives, crafts, produce, and lots of secondhand and garage sale merchandise. Snack bar, rest rooms, h/a, ample parking. Inside and outside space available from $30 per weekend. *Contact* Dale Cooper, 2301 S. Meridian, 67213 (316) 942-8263 or 942-8264.

Wichita Flea Market
Kansas Coliseum
North 85th St. & I-135

Every fourth Sunday, 9 a.m.–4 p.m. Market also known as Mid-America Flea Market. Admission charge 50 cents. Average attendance 5,000 with approximately 700 dealers. Wide range of merchandise carried at this large indoor market, lots of good-quality small antiques, collectibles, memorabilia, antique toys, and advertising items. Snack bars, clean rest rooms, h/a, ample parking. Space from $15. Reservations required. *Contact* Schartz Enterprises, Box 1585, Hutchinson, 67504 (316) 663-5626. Call first to confirm dates.

Treasure Plaza Flea Market
4201 S. Seneca

Daily. New merchandise, antiques, collectibles, giftware, crafts. Rest rooms, snack bar, h/a, ample parking. Indoor market with mainly permanent spaces. Space $44 weekly or $125 monthly. Market has retail consignment auction on Sunday. *Contact* James Smith (316) 522-9480.

The New Ponderosa Flea Market
2427 W. Pawnee St.

Friday, Saturday, Sunday. New merchandise, gifts, imports, used desirables, and collectibles. Snack bar, rest rooms, h/a, ample parking. Indoor and outdoor space available. *Contact* Carroll Ghan, 67213 (316) 941-9953.

KENTUCKY

ASHLAND

Hillbilly Flea Market
U.S. Hwy. 23 North

Friday, Saturday, Sunday, 7 a.m.–5 p.m. Average daily attendance 5,000 with approximately 150 dealers. This indoor/outdoor market is air-conditioned and heated. New and used merchandise, imports, souvenirs, some antiques, collectibles, primitives, memorabilia, books, jewelry, coins, and advertising items are available. Clean rest rooms. Restaurant, h/a, ample parking. Camping available. *Contact* Elwood Gibbs, 100 Main St., Greenup, KY 41144 (606) 329-1058 or 473-9018.

AB&D Flea Market
635 Winchester Ave.
(606) 324-2429

Thursday, Friday. Inside and outside spaces with approximately 200 dealers. New and used merchandise, great selection of decorator items and bric-a-brac, country and farm collectibles, jewelry, coins, sportswear, and crafts are available. Snack bar, rest rooms, h/a, ample parking.

AURORA

Hillbilly Peddlers Flea Market
Junction of Rtes. 68 and 80, Kentucky Lake

Saturday, Sunday. Seasonal market. Used merchandise, garage sale items, crafts, and produce are available. Rest rooms, snack bar, ample parking. Space from $5. *Contact* Bobby Morris, Box 5, Benton, 42025 (502) 527-0836.

DAYS, DATES, AND MARKETS ARE SUBJECT TO CHANGE!

BEAVER DAM

Kay's Flea Market
Hwy. 231 South

Thursday. Country and farm collectibles, used merchandise, crafts, produce. Outdoor market. Clean rest rooms, ample parking. Camping available. Electricity available. No alcohol. *Contact* Kay's, Rte. 4, No. 256, 42320.

BEREA

Robbie's Antique & Flea Market
Hwy. 25 South

Saturday, Sunday. Antiques, collectibles, furniture, silver, glassware, and lots of country collectibles are available. Food available, rest rooms, ample parking.

Berea Mini Mall
Hwy. 25 South
Thirty minutes south of Lexington
(606) 986-1719

Daily. Indoor, 56,000 sq.-ft. facility.

BOONVILLE

Boonville Flea Market
Rte. 3

Wednesday only. Used merchandise, flea market merchandise, farm collectibles, crafts, and produce are available. Food available, rest rooms, ample parking.

BOW'LING GREEN

Flea Land of Bowling Green
1100 Three Springs Rd.

Saturday, Sunday. Contact Grant Lewis (502) 843-1978.

BURLINGTON

Burlington Antique Flea Market
Fairgrounds
(606) 311-7394 or 341-1400

Monthly, call for dates. Approximately 50 dealers offer a wide range of quality collectibles and small antiques. Market is a collector's paradise. Food available, rest rooms, h/a, ample parking.

CAMP NELSON

Camp Nelson Flea Market
Old U.S. Hwy. 27
(606) 885-9304

Saturday, Sunday. Secondhand and flea market merchandise, some new items, collectibles, crafts, and produce are available. Snack bar, rest rooms, ample parking.

CARROLLTON

Carroll County Flea Market
Hwy. 42
(502) 732-5851

Saturday, Sunday. Used merchandise, garage sale items, country collectibles, and crafts. Rest rooms, snack bar, ample parking.

CENTRAL CITY

Flea Market
Hwy. 70

Wednesday only. Farm items, used merchandise, country collectibles, crafts, produce, and livestock are available. Food available, rest rooms, ample parking.

CORBIN

Cumberland Gap Flea Market
Cumberland Gap Pkwy. and I-75, Exit 29

Saturday, Sunday, 8 a.m.–4 p.m. Indoor market, 80,000 sq.-ft. facility. Snack bar, rest rooms, h/a. *Contact* Bill Hamblin (606) 526-9712, fax (606) 526-1629.

Sammy's Flea Market & Auction
25 C St.

Saturday, Sunday. Approximately 75 dealers offer new merchandise, surplus, closeouts, housewares, sports merchandise, sportswear, used merchandise, collectibles, and crafts. Snack bar, rest rooms, ample parking. Inside and outside spaces. *Contact* Sammy Issao, 704 Vine St., 40701 (606) 528-5260.

COVINGTON

American Legion Flea Market
Hwy. 68-80
Five miles east of Elkton, 10 miles west of Russelville

Saturday, 9 a.m.–9 p.m., Sunday, 9 a.m.–6 p.m. New and used merchandise, country and farm collectibles, advertising items, primitives, glassware, crafts, and produce are available. Inside and outside spaces available. Live entertainment. Food available, rest rooms, h/a, ample parking. Overnight parking on-site. *Contact* Kathy Walker (502) 265-2630 weekends or 265-2338 weekdays and nights.

DAYSVILLE

Old Southern Flea Market
Hwy. 68-80
Five miles east of Elkton, 10 miles west of Russelville

Saturday, 9 a.m.–9 p.m., Sunday, 9 a.m.–6 p.m. New and used merchandise, great selection of country and farm collectibles, advertising items, primitives, glassware, crafts, produce. Inside and outside spaces available. Live entertainment. Food available, rest rooms, h/a. Overnight parking on-site. *Contact* Kathy Walker (502) 265-2630 weekends or 265-2338 weekdays and nights.

ELIZABETHTOWN

Bowling Lanes Flea Market
4547 N. Dixie
Hwy. 31 West

Saturday, Sunday, 8 a.m.–6 p.m. New merchandise, electronics, housewares, sportswear, used merchandise, collectibles, crafts, and produce are available. Approximately 100 dealers. Rest rooms, food available, h/a. Market open all year, inside and outside space available, electricity available, showers. *Contact* Dean Taylor (502) 737-5755, fax (502) 737-8300.

Starlite Drive-In Theater Flea Market
Hwy. 31 West

Sunday only. Approximately 250 dealers offer a wide variety of new merchandise, used desirables, antiques, collectibles, glassware, primitives, advertising items, lots of farm and ranch collectibles, crafts, and produce. A good market to poke around in for treasures or bargains. Snack bar, rest rooms, h/a, ample parking. Space from $3. *Contact* Don Ford, Lake Shore Dr., Hardinsburg, 40143 (502) 769-3937.

Flea Market Mall
Hwy. 31 West
(502) 769-5374

Friday, Saturday, Sunday. New and used merchandise, antiques, collectibles, furniture, vintage clothing, silver, linens, and glassware are available. Snack bar, rest rooms, h/a, ample parking.

FLORENCE

Flea Market
Boone/Kenton Warehouse
8471 Hwy. 42

Saturday, Sunday. Approximately 250 dealers offer new and used merchandise, garage sale items, antiques, collectibles, glassware, primitives, silver, linens, advertising items, and a good selection of tobacco collectibles. Snack bar, rest rooms, h/a, ample parking. *Contact* Shirlie Elliott, Box 834, 41042 (606) 525-7066.

FRANKFORT

Flea for All Flea Market
Hwy. 60
(502) 340-7579

Friday, Saturday, Sunday. Used merchandise, garage sale items, bric-a-brac, new merchandise, gifts, imports, collectibles, country crafts, and produce are available. Snack bar, rest rooms, h/a, ample parking.

FRANKLIN

South Central Kentucky Flea Market
210 Cherry St.
(502) 586-9058

Saturday, Sunday. New and used merchandise, rest rooms, ample parking.

GEORGETOWN

Country World Flea Market
Hwy. 460 and I-75, Exit 125
Off the Georgetown interchange
(502) 867-0831

Friday, Saturday, Sunday, 7 a.m. Friday and continuously until Sunday evening, April through November. Approximately 100 dealers offer lots of new and good used merchandise, including crafts, country collectibles, and produce. Snack bars, rest rooms, h/a, ample parking. Space from $8 per day. *Contact* Glenn Juett, 111 Montgomery Ave., 40324.

GILBERTSVILLE

Welk's Flea Market
Hwy. 641
(502) 362-8514

Friday, Saturday, Sunday. New and used merchandise, garage sale items, bric-a-brac, crafts, collectibles, and produce are offered. Snack bar, rest rooms, ample parking.

GLASGOW

Antique Flea Market
31 E. South St.
(502) 678-4620

Saturday, Sunday. Antiques, collectibles, furniture, silver, glassware, advertising items, tobacco items, country and farm collectibles, toys, and primitives are available. Snack bar, rest rooms, ample parking.

GREENVILLE

Town & Country Flea Market
Hwy. 62
One mile west of town

Monday, Tuesday, 8 a.m. until dark. Approximately 2–300 sellers offer antiques, collectibles, livestock, poultry, crafts, produce, new merchandise, and furniture both new and used. No alcohol. Very nice outdoor market to attend as a buyer or a seller. Scenic area with lakes and motels, neighboring antique and specialty shops. This market provides a great backdrop for a most enjoyable early-week adventure. Snack bar, rest rooms, ample parking, camping available. Space from $3. *Contact* Judy Rice, 2006 Hwy. 62 West, 42345 (270) 338-4920 or 338-6284.

GUTHRIE

Southern Kentucky Flea Market
52 Waste Water Rd. Hwy. 41, I-24, Exit 4
(270) 483-2166

Wednesday–Sunday. Indoor market with approximately 100 dealers. Snack bar, rest rooms, h/a.

HENDERSON

Flea Market
3199 Hwy. 41 North

Sunday. New and used merchandise, farm and sports collectibles, crafts, and produce. Snack bar, rest rooms, ample parking.

Flea Market
2100 S. Green St.
(502) 826-6263

Thursday, Friday, Saturday. New and used merchandise, lots of used housewares, tools, clothing, outdoor items, crafts, collectibles, and produce. Snack bar, rest rooms, h/a, ample parking. Outside and inside space available. Auctions on Friday evening.

Ellis Park Flea Market
Ellis Park Race Track

Monthly, call for dates. Approximately 300 dealers offer new merchandise, antiques, quality collectibles, primitives, and advertising items. Inside and outside spaces available. *Contact* Stewart Promotions, 2950 Breckenridge Lane, No. 4A, Louisville, 40220 (502) 456-2244.

INDEPENDENCE

North Kentucky Flea Market
5209 Madison Pike

Friday, Saturday, Sunday. New and used merchandise, garage sale items, crafts, collectibles, and produce are available. Snack bar, rest rooms, ample parking. *Contact* Dick Young, 1602 Crossridge Lane, Louisville, 40222 (606) 356-9602.

IRVINGTON

Drive-In Theater Flea Market
U.S. Hwy. 60
(502) 769-3937

Saturday, Sunday. New merchandise, electronics, tools, sportswear, jewelry, housewares, used merchandise, garage sale fare, crafts, produce, and collectibles are available. Snack bar, rest rooms, h/a, ample parking.

LEITCHFIELD

Bratcher's Flea Market
Hwy. 62 East
One mile east of town

Wednesday, Saturday, from sunup. This outdoor market with approximately 100 dealers offers antiques, collectibles, crafts, new merchandise, produce, and used items. Rest rooms, ample parking. Space from $6. *Contact* Carol Heffley, Box 396, 47254 (502) 259-5948.

LEXINGTON

Lexington Antique & Flea Market
Lexington Civic Center, downtown

Monthly; Friday, Saturday, 11 a.m.–8 p.m., Sunday, 11 a.m.–5 p.m., call for dates Usually held midmonth. Lots of high-quality antiques and collectibles at this market along with some new merchandise. Snack bar, rest rooms, ample paid parking, although you may have to park a good distance from the building. *Contact* Stewart Promotions, 2950 Breckenridge Lane, No. 4A, Louisville, 40220 (502) 456-2244 or www.stewartpromotions.com.

Lexington Flea Mall and Antique Center
1230 Eastland Center

Friday, Saturday, Sunday, 10 a.m.–6 p.m. Indoor/outdoor market with indoor mall area open daily. Approximately 175 dealers. Antiques, collectibles, lots of collector and decorator items here. Space from $10 per day outside. Rest rooms, cafe, h/a. Ample parking. *Contact* Manager, 1230 Eastland Center, 40505 (606) 252-1076.

Show & Sell Flea Market
2592 Palumbo Dr.
(800) 442-1324 or (606) 269-8141

Friday, Saturday, Sunday. Average daily attendance is 4,000. This indoor market offers new merchandise, housewares, outdoor items, sportswear, novelties, jewelry, used merchandise, collectibles, crafts, and sports merchandise. Snack bar, rest rooms, h/a, ample parking.

LONDON

Dean Tobacco Warehouse Flea Market
I-75, Exit 41
Dean Tobacco Warehouse

Friday, Saturday, Sunday. Approximately 50 dealers offer new and used merchandise, farm and ranch collectibles, and tobacco collectibles. Snack bar, rest rooms, h/a, ample parking. *Contact* Carl Tuttle, Rte. 2, Box 333, 40741 (606) 864-2185 or 878-7726.

Flea World Flea Market
192 Bypass and Hwy. 229
Two miles east of I-75, Exit 38

Saturday, Sunday, 9 a.m.–5 p.m. Approximately 100 spaces outside and 250 spaces inside. Large commercial market offers lots of new merchandise, general flea market merchandise, country collectibles, advertising items, primitives, glassware, silver, coins, sports merchandise, crafts, and produce. Snack bar, rest rooms, h/a, ample parking. *Contact* Brenda Hail, Box 862, 40741 (606) 864-3532.

LOUISVILLE

Derby Park Traders Circle Flea Market
2900 S. 7th St. Rd.
One-half mile from Churchill Downs (look for the huge green-and-white billboards)

Friday, Saturday, Sunday, 8 a.m.–6 p.m. Approximately 60 dealers offer antiques, collectibles, primitives, memorabilia, country items, antique toys, new and used merchandise, crafts, and art. Snack bar, rest rooms, h/a, ample parking. Inside and outside spaces from $29 for the weekend. RV parking, electrical hookups, and showers. *Contact* Art Henoch, 2900 7th St., 40216 (502) 636-3532 or 636-5817.

Country Fair & Flea Market
3502 7th St.
(502) 368-6186

Saturday, Sunday. New and used merchandise, garage-sale-type items, and produce are available. Good market and excellent selection of locally made crafts. Snack bar, rest rooms, h/a, ample parking.

INFORMATION IS SUBJECT TO CHANGE—ALWAYS CALL FIRST!

Kentucky Flea Market
Fairgrounds

Monthly, call for exact dates, Friday, 12 p.m.–8 p.m., Saturday, 10 a.m.–8 p.m., Sunday, 11 a.m.–6 p.m. Admission fee. One of America's greatest markets; it is an excellent market for both the wholesale buyer and the retail shopper and decorator. It has a large section devoted solely to quality antique dealers. It also hosts one of the most popular events over New Year's holiday, with 1–2,000 dealers. Attendance at the monthly Louisville market is 30–50,000. Over 100,000 shoppers attend the special promotions and holiday event. Large motel at entrance to fairgrounds; reserve room here early for New Year's event, and you can shuttle back and forth to the market. Space from $60. *Contact* Stewart Promotions, 2950 Breckenridge Lane, No. 4A, 40220 (502) 456-2244.

High Grove Antiques & Flea Market
Junction of Hwys. 31E and 48
Twenty-two miles south of town
(502) 895-7585

Tuesday–Sunday, 10 a.m.–5 p.m. Antiques, collectibles, farm and ranch items, tobacco items, new and used merchandise, country crafts, and produce are available. Food available, rest rooms, ample parking. Country store next door.

Flea Market
National Tpke. and Outer Loop

Saturday, Sunday. Approximately 50 dealers offer new and used merchandise, lots of farm and ranch items, collectibles, crafts, and produce. Snack bar, rest rooms, h/a, ample parking. Space from $3 per day. *Contact* Maxine Moran, 4021 Crittenden Dr., 40209 (502) 367-1397.

MAYFIELD

Mayfield-Graves County Park Flea Market
Fairgrounds
(502) 247-0049

Every second and third Monday. Approximately 150 dealers offer antiques, furniture, collectibles, farm and ranch items, glassware, silver, jewelry, tobacco collectibles, primitives, books, and art. Food available, rest rooms, h/a, ample parking.

MONTICELLO

Kay's Fleaground
Kelley Lane Rd.

Friday, Saturday, Sunday. New and used merchandise, garage sale items, bric-a-brac, crafts, produce, and collectibles. Snack bar, rest rooms, h/a, ample parking.

MURRAY

Murray Drive-In Theater Flea Market
South 4th St.

First and fourth Monday. Average daily attendance is 2,000. Approximately 100 dealers offer new and used merchandise, typical flea market treasures: antiques, collectibles, glassware, silver, farm and ranch items, crafts, and produce. Snack bar, rest rooms, h/a, ample parking. Space from $2. *Contact* Tommy Brown, Box 229, 42071 (502) 753-8084.

NEW LONDON

New London Flea Market
Tobacco Rd.
Tobacco Warehouse 4

Friday, Saturday, Sunday, 7 a.m. until dark. This indoor market offers new and used merchandise, garage sale items, souvenirs, novelties, sportswear, country collectibles, glassware, jewelry, and tobacco collectibles. Food available, rest rooms, h/a, ample parking. *Contact* Graham Cole, 40741 (606) 878-9000.

NICHOLSVILLE

Windmill Flea Market
Hwy. 27 South
Windmill Restaurant parking lot

Saturday, Sunday. New and used merchandise, garage sale items, collectibles, crafts, and produce are available. Rest rooms, food available, h/a, ample parking. *Contact* Charles Curtis (606) 498-4722.

OWENSBORO

Flea Market
Consumers Mall
2930 E. 4th St.
(502) 685-3592

Friday, Saturday, Sunday. New merchandise, electronics, sportswear, housewares, sports memorabilia, tools, used merchandise, garage-sale-type treasures, as well as crafts, collectibles, and produce are available. Snack bar, rest rooms, h/a, ample parking.

Hog Heaven Flea Market
8424 Hwy. 60 East
Seven miles from Owensboro
(502) 246-4420

Saturday, Sunday. New merchandise, used merchandise, lots of farm and country collectibles, advertising items, glassware, primitives, country crafts, produce, and livestock are available. Food available, rest rooms, h/a, ample parking. A new indoor/outdoor market with approximately 200 spaces.

PADUCAH

Great American Flea Market
Bluegrass Downs Racetrack
32nd and Park Ave.
(502) 443-5800

Every third weekend.

Traders Mall Flea Market
6900 Benton Rd., I-24, Exit 16

Saturday, Sunday, 10 a.m.–6 p.m. Antiques, collectibles, new and used merchandise, lots of new sportswear and new toys. Space from $25 per weekend. One of the area's better markets and one of the largest indoor markets in the state. Restaurant, rest rooms, h/a. Located in a very nice tourist area and close to one of the Kentucky casinos. Ample parking. *Contact* Manager, 6900 Benton Rd., 42003 (502) 898-3144.

PAINTSVILLE

Flea Market
Hwy. 172
(606) 297-3991

Friday, Saturday, Sunday. New and used merchandise, garage sale items, collectibles, crafts, and produce are available. Snack bar, rest rooms, ample parking.

RADCLIFF

Hardin County Flea Market
Knox Blvd. and Wilson Rd. at Redmar Plaza

Friday, Saturday, Sunday. Indoor market. Air-conditioned and heated. Nice market located next to Ft. Knox with a wide range of merchandise. Plenty of parking, snack bar, rest rooms, h/a. *Contact* B. J. Dozier, 1487 W. Elm Rd., 60160 (502) 351-0200 or 351-1118.

RICHMOND

Flea Mart USA
I-75, Exit 97, Clays Ferry Exit
(606) 625-0463

Saturday, Sunday.

RICHWOOD

Richwood Flea Market
10915 Dixie Hwy.
U.S. Hwy. 25, I-175, Exit 175
Four miles south of Florence, 13 miles south of Cincinnati, Ohio

Saturday, Sunday, 9 a.m.–5 p.m., Tuesday, daylight until dark, outdoors only. Admission $1. Average attendance of 6,000 per weekend with approximately 320 dealers. This market is heavy on new merchandise, sportswear, electronics, housewares, and collectibles. Good snack bar/cafe, rest rooms, h/a, ample parking. Space from $65 per weekend. Inside and outside space available. Camping available. Good market for commercial vendors. *Contact* Mike Stallings, Box 153, 41022 (606) 371-5800. E-mail: richflea10@aol.com.

ROCHESTER

Rochester Flea Market
Rochester Ball Park

Friday only. Approximately 25 dealers offer used merchandise, garage sale items, bric-a-brac, crafts, and produce. Snack bar, rest rooms, ample parking. *Contact* Steve Rubuno (502) 934-4024.

RUSSELL

Hillbilly Flea Market
Rte. 23 North
(606) 329-9821

Saturday, Sunday. Used merchandise, garage sale items, country and advertising collectibles, primitives, crafts, and produce are available. Rest rooms, ample parking.

RUSSELL SPRINGS

Russell Springs Flea Market
Hwy. 80
(502) 866-6366

Friday, Saturday, Sunday, February–November. New and used merchandise, bric-a-brac, collectibles, crafts, and produce are available. Snack bar, rest rooms, ample parking.

SHELBYVILLE

Shelbyville Flea Market
Hwy. 60 East
At the Big Top Warehouse
(502) 633-1244

Every first weekend, March–October. Approximately 50 dealers offer antiques, glassware, primitives, advertising and tobacco items, silver, and jewelry. Also, lots of used merchandise, garage-sale-type items, and crafts are available. Food available, rest rooms, h/a, ample parking. Space $15 for the weekend.

SHEPHARDSVILLE

Bullett County Flea Market
I-65 and Hwy. 24
South at the fairgrounds

Every second weekend. Approximately 100 dealers offer antiques, glassware, linens, silver, jewelry, watches, farm and country collectibles, new and used merchandise, and crafts. Food available, rest rooms, h/a, ample parking. *Contact* Claude Lundy, Box 915, Knob Creek Rd., Brooks, 40109 (502) 955-8967.

SIMPSONVILLE

Shelby County Flea Market
I-64, Exit 28
(502) 722-8883
Fax (502) 722-8883

Saturday, Sunday, 9 a.m.–5 p.m. New and used merchandise, flea market merchandise, collectibles, decorator items, giftware, crafts, and produce are available. Snack bar, rest rooms, h/a, ample parking.

SOMERSET

Lake Cumberland Flea Market
95 Super Service Dr.

Saturday, Sunday, 7 a.m.–6 p.m. Approximately 75 dealers. Market is heavy on new merchandise, electronics, imports, toys, sportswear, furniture, gifts, and crafts. Some collectibles. Space from $34 per weekend. Restaurant, rest rooms, h/a. Ample parking. *Contact* Anna Gutting, 95 Super Service Dr., 42501 (606) 678-0250.

SOUTHGATE

Beverly Flea Market
601 Alexandria Pike
(502) 356-5622

Saturday, Sunday. New and used merchandise, garage sale items, bric-a-brac, crafts, collectibles, and produce are available. Snack bar, rest rooms, h/a, ample parking.

UNION CITY

Union City Flea Market
Fairgrounds
(502) 469-5663

Every second weekend. Antiques, collectibles, jewelry, silver, glassware, advertising items, primitives, farm and country items, new and used merchandise, and crafts are available. Food available, rest rooms, h/a, ample parking.

WALTON

Lakewide Flea Market
Hwy. 27
(606) 356-9473

Tuesday only. Approximately 100 dealers offer a large selection of new and used merchandise, good secondhand items, farm and ranch items, country collectibles, glassware, jewelry, silver, primitives, crafts, produce, and livestock. Food available, rest rooms, h/a, ample parking. Space from $4.

WAYNE

Flea Market
3420 Sullivan Dr.
(502) 443-8706

Friday, Saturday, Sunday. Used merchandise, garage sale items, collectibles, crafts, and produce are available. Rest rooms, snack bar, h/a, ample parking.

WILLIAMSBURG

Helping Hand Flea Market
Old Hwy. 25 West
Nine miles south of town
(606) 549-2337

Daily. Approximately 10 dealers offer used merchandise, lots of junk, some good collectibles, glassware, primitives. Rest rooms, ample parking.

WINCHESTER

Winchester Flea Market
4400 Oliver Rd.
I-64, Exit 94

Saturday, Sunday, 8 a.m.–5 p.m. Average daily attendance is 1,000. Approximately 60 dealers offer new and used merchandise, collectibles, glassware, silver, jewelry, and antiques. Snack bar, rest rooms, h/a, ample parking. Inside space from $10 daily, tables furnished, outside space from $5 daily. Sales tax required. Camping and electricity available. *Contact* Raymond Huls, 202 Boone, 40391 (606) 744-1179 or 745-4332.

Winchester Flea Market
1465 W. Lexington Ave.
(606) 744-4510

Saturday, Sunday. Seasonal market. Approximately 75 dealers offer new and used merchandise, collectibles, jewelry, crafts, decorator items, and advertising items in this indoor market. Rest rooms, ample parking.

Winchester Flea Market
5000 W. Lexington Ave.

Friday, Saturday, Sunday. New and used merchandise, garage sale treasures, bric-a-brac, crafts, country and new collectibles, and produce are available. Snack bar, rest rooms, h/a, ample parking. *Contact* Raymond Huls, 202 Boone, 40391 (606) 745-4332.

ALWAYS CALL AHEAD TO VERIFY DATES AND INFORMATION

LOUISIANA

ARCADIA

Bonnie & Clyde Third Monday Trade Days
I-20, Exit 69
3.3 miles south on Hwy. 9
(318) 263-2437 or (888) 835-6112
Fax (318) 263-9803

Friday, Saturday, Sunday, usually third weekend. Monthly, dawn until dark, call for dates. Art, crafts, antiques, and collectibles are available. Market is located on 130 acres with lakes for fishing. Plan to spend the day or weekend here. Approximately 700 spaces. RV hookups, dump station, electricity, and water. Space from $30. *Contact* Ed Jones, Box 243, 71001.

BATON ROUGE

Joor Road Flea Market
4206 Joor Rd.
(225) 928-0287

Friday, Saturday, Sunday. Approximately 25 dealers offer new and used merchandise, garage sale items, souvenirs, novelties, and gifts. Food available, rest rooms, h/a, ample parking. Inside and outside spaces available. Camping available.

Deep South Flea Market
5905 Florida Blvd.

Friday, Saturday, Sunday, 10 a.m.–6 p.m. This indoor market with approximately 250 dealers has a wide variety of goods. Lots of new merchandise, good selection of used merchandise, collector items, country collectibles, lots of Cajun merchandise, and both new and used desirables are available. Food available, rest rooms, h/a, ample parking. Space from $50. Reservations required. *Contact* Bill Valley, 5905 Florida Blvd., 70807 (504) 923-0333 or 923-0142.

Catfish Town Flea Market
1606 Nicholson Dr.
One mile from the State University

Friday, Saturday, Sunday. Approximately 200 dealers of new and used merchandise, electronics, tools, housewares, sportswear, toys, sports merchandise, garage sale items, crafts, collectibles, jewelry, and produce. Snack bar, rest rooms, h/a, ample parking. Inside and outside space from $25 for three days. Camping nearby. *Contact* Joel Atheyeh, 1606 Nicholson Dr., 70782 (225) 389-9678 or 387-3372.

Greater Baton Rouge Flea Market
15545 Airline Hwy.
(225) 673-2682

9 a.m. to 5 p.m. New and used merchandise, all under one roof. Over 400 vendors. Great food, good family environment, rest rooms, ample parking, entertainment.

Merchants Landing Flea Market
9800 Florida Blvd.
Broadmoor Shopping Center

Saturday, Sunday, 10 a.m.–7 p.m. 40,000-square-foot facility. Antiques, collectibles, glassware, silver, linens, vintage clothing, housewares, souvenirs, secondhand items. Food available, rest rooms, h/a, ample parking. *Contact* Rosemary Gilbert, 70815 (504) 925-1664.

BREAUX BRIDGE

Pioneer Flea Market
I-10, Exit 109
(318) 235-2752

Saturday, Sunday. Approximately 20 dealers offer new and used merchandise, collectibles, gifts, decorator items. Plenty of crafts, collectibles, and produce. Snack bar, rest rooms, h/a. Inside and outside space from $2.50.

GREENWOOD

Greenwood Flea Market
9249 Jefferson Paige Rd.
I-20, Exit 5

Saturday, Sunday, 10 a.m.–6 p.m. Indoor/outdoor market with approximately 100 exhibitors offering antiques, collectibles, crafts, vintage clothing, jewelry, lots of new and used merchandise, and produce. Interesting market with dealers set up in old railroad boxcars. Snack bar, rest rooms, ample parking. Space from $30 for the weekend. *Contact* Larry Millican, 9249 Jefferson Paige Rd., 71033 (318) 938-7201.

HAMMOND

Southeast Louisiana Flea Market
101 E. Coleman St.
Two miles north of I-12, Exit 40 onto Highway 51

Friday, Saturday, Sunday. Market is held in an old railroad depot dating back to Civil War days. Good selection of collectibles, glassware, and historical items. Gifts, souvenirs, and new merchandise also available. Food available, rest rooms, h/a, ample parking. Inside space from $8, reservations required. Outside space $5. *Contact* Linda Walden, 601 E. Robert St., 70401 (504) 345-2381 or 345-4800.

HOUMA

Louisiana Flea Market
2316 Westpark
(504) 876-0696

Friday, Saturday, Sunday. Approximately 100 dealers offer new and used merchandise, electronics, tools, sportswear, housewares, toys, sports merchandise, garage sale goodies, collectibles, and lots of country items. Snack bar, rest rooms, h/a, ample parking. Inside and outside space available. Camping available.

LACOMBE

The New Midway Flea Market & Antique Mall
31204 Hwy. 190

Thursday–Sunday, 9 a.m.–5 p.m. New indoor market with 24 booths offering new and used furniture, vintage clothing, and Beanie Babies. Snack bar, clean rest rooms, h/a, ample parking. *Contact* Midway Flea Market, 31204 Hwy. 190, 70445 (504) 882-3111 or 882-3285.

190 Trading Post Flea Market
31184 Hwy. 190
Four miles east of town

Friday, Saturday, Sunday, 9 a.m. until dark. Approximately 25 dealers offer lots of used and secondhand items, farm items, new merchandise, some antiques and collectibles, primitives, furniture, and crafts in one of the oldest markets in the state. Inside and outside space available from $6. *Contact* Mary Fayard, 743 W. Hall Ave., Slidell, 70460 (504) 882-6442.

LAFAYETTE

Cajun Country Flea Market
123 Carmel Ave.
(318) 235-2141

Saturday, Sunday. Approximately 50 dealers offer new and used merchandise, jewelry, sportswear, tools, housewares, electronics, decorator items, collectibles, glassware, kitchen collectibles, and primitives. Snack bar, rest rooms, h/a, ample parking. Indoor and outdoor market with space from $50 per weekend. *Contact* Stanford Ballard, 123 Carmel St., 70501 (318) 235-2141.

LAKE CHARLES

Cornerstone Flea Market
2001 Ryan St.
Corner of Ryan and Sallier (or 12th) Sts. in the big brown building with the green trim

Monday, 12 noon–6 p.m.; Tuesday–Saturday, 9 a.m.–6 p.m. Forty plus dealers at all times with shops overflowing with variety of antiques, collectibles. Good selection of Depression glassware, furniture, and accessories. Gift shop and florals. Unique clothing, primitives, Avon products, gold, silver and costume jewelry, old clocks, and so much more! Clean family environment.

NEW ORLEANS

French Market Community Flea Market
1235 N. Peters St.

Daily 7 a.m.–7 p.m. This outdoor market with approximately 250 dealers offer antiques, collectibles, country items, primitives, farm items, antique toys, crafts, art, new and used merchandise, sportswear, and sports-related memorabilia. Snack bar, difficult parking. Space from $7 per day. Local licenses required. *Contact* Sunny Davidson, 1235 N. Peters St., 70116 (504) 596-3420, fax (504) 596-3427.

Jeff Indoor Flea Market
5501 Jefferson Hwy.

Friday, Saturday, Sunday, 10 a.m.–6 p.m. Antiques, collectibles, country items, primitives, advertising items, crafts, art, some new and used merchandise including furniture, household items, and souvenirs are available. Snack bar, rest rooms, h/a, ample parking. Indoor market with some outside covered spaces. 70,000-square-foot facility. Space from $15. *Contact* Jim Russell, P.O. Box 23223, Harahan, 70183 (504) 734-0087, fax (504) 734-0304.

New Orleans Market Place
8700 Lake Forest Blvd.

Friday, Saturday, Sunday. Collectibles, jewelry, used merchandise, crafts, decorator items, and trendy gifts are available. Rest rooms, snack bar, h/a, ample parking. Inside and outside space available. *Contact* Betty Washington, 70127 (504) 244-6558.

River Road Flea Market
3908 River Rd.
I-10, Causeway Exit South

Saturday, Sunday, 10 a.m.–6 p.m. In this indoor market, antiques, collectibles, vintage clothing, memorabilia, and lots of used merchandise are available. Snack bar, rest rooms, h/a, ample parking. *Contact* Bill Black, 3908 River Rd., 70121 (504) 833-6766.

PRAIRIEVILLE

The Greater Baton Rouge Flea Market
See Baton Rouge listing

Saturday, Sunday.

RAYNE

Rayne Antique Flea Market
Downtown
(318) 334-9847

Every first and third weekend. Approximately 60 exhibitors offer antiques, furniture, silver, coins, glassware, advertising items, jewelry, watches, books, art, Civil War items, and farm and ranch collectibles. Rayne is also the home of one of America's great festivals, The Rayne Frog Festival. *Contact* Connie Menard, Box 552, 70578.

SHREVEPORT

Ark-La-Tex Trade Fair & Flea Market
North of I-20, one block east of Monkhouse Dr.

Friday, Saturday, Sunday. Admission charge $1. Average attendance 1,500 daily; 50,000-square-foot air-conditioned facility. Wide-open Cajun market with lots of new and used merchandise, good selection of collectibles of all types, glassware, primitives, kitchen collectibles, and many other interesting booths here. Clean, friendly, well-managed market. Good food on the premises, rest rooms, h/a, ample parking. Inside space from $25 for the weekend or $10 daily. Outside space from $5 per day. Self-contained camping only, no charge. *Contact* Frank or Vickie Lollar, 4725 Greenwood Rd., 71109 (318) 631-1165 or 425-8768.

Antique Fair & Trade Show
Fairgrounds, Expo Hall
(318) 856-7990

Every fourth weekend. Admission charge. Large antique and collector event with a great selection, from furniture to jewelry, buttons to glassware—great variety and selection of booths here. Food available, rest rooms, h/a, ample paved parking.

Greenwood Flea Market
I-20, Exit 5
(318) 938-7201

Saturday, Sunday. Approximately 150 dealers offer new merchandise, electronics, tools, housewares, souvenirs, sports merchandise, jewelry, sportswear, used merchandise, collectibles, silver, coins, sports cards, crafts, gifts, and decorator items in this indoor market. Restaurant, snack bar, rest rooms, h/a, ample parking. Camping available.

WEST MONROE

Trade Center Flea Market
5223 Cypress St.
Wells Rd. Exit to Hwy. 80, right one block on right

Friday, Saturday, Sunday. Approximately 20 vendors offer new and used merchandise, garage sale items, crafts, some collectibles, and produce. Rest rooms, ample parking. Space from $35 for weekend. No alcohol allowed. *Contact* David Ashcraft, 5223 Cypress St. (318) 396-5133.

MAINE

BRUNSWICK

Waterfront Flea Market
14 Main St.
I-95, Exit 24A to Main St.

Saturday, Sunday. Indoor market with approximately 75 dealers. Antiques, collectibles, new and used merchandise. Good food here, rest rooms, h/a. Ample parking. *Contact* Arthur Young, 14 Main St., 04011 (207) 729-0378.

EAST LEBANON

202 Flea Market
Rte. 202
Approximately six miles west of Sanford

Friday, Saturday, Sunday, May–October. Approximately 25 exhibitors offer new and used merchandise, antiques, collectibles, jewelry, vintage clothing, and primitives. Space from $5. Camping available for $2 per night. *Contact* Lester Martell, Box 280, Acton, 04001 (207) 457-1459.

FREEPORT

Red Wheel Antiques & Flea Market
U.S. Hwy. 1 and I-95 at Yarmouth Rd.
Fifteen miles north of Portland

Saturday, Sunday, May–October, 9 a.m.–5 p.m. Approximately 100 dealers offer lots of quality antiques and collectibles here. Good selection of primitives and advertising items. New merchandise and crafts also available. Snack bar, rest rooms, h/a, ample parking. Space from $7. Overnight parking. Inside and outside space available. *Contact* Ed Collett, Rte. 2, Box 299, 04032 (207) 865-6492.

GORHAM

Gorham Flea Market
19 State St.

Thursday–Sunday, 10 a.m.–5 p.m. Average attendance 2–300 per day. Collectibles, glassware, jewelry, sportswear, crafts, and produce are available here. Snack bar, rest rooms, h/a, ample parking. Space from $5 per day. *Contact* Walter Libby, 19 State St., 04038 (207) 389-3153.

LEEDS

Red Roof Flea Market
Rte. 202, behind the Red Roof Store

Saturday, Sunday. Seasonal market during warm weather. Outdoor market with approximately 12–15 dealers. *Contact* Ed Frost (207) 933-4533.

NEWCASTLE

Foster's Flea Market and Antique Hall
Rte. 1

Saturday, Sunday. Seasonal market May through October. Indoor/outdoor market weather permitting. Approximately 25 dealers. *Contact* Robert Foster (207) 529-5422.

OXFORD

Undercover Antique Mall and Flea Market
Rte. 26, about one mile north of the Oxford Plains Speedway

Daily, 7 a.m.–5 p.m. Indoor and outdoor market with approximately 50 dealers. Antiques, collectibles, lots of good small collectibles, primitives, and quality decorator items here. Space from $5 per day outdoors and $60 per month inside. Snack bar, rest rooms, h/a. Ample parking. *Contact* Bert Morin, 960 Main St., 04270 (207) 539-4149.

PORTLAND

Portland Expo Flea Market
Portland Exposition Bldg.
239 Park Ave.

Sunday only, March–October, 9 a.m.–4 p.m. Approximately 150 dealers offer a good selection of antiques, collectibles, primitives, antique toys, country items, crafts, art, and new merchandise. Indoor flea market, with space from $20. *Contact* Manager, 239 Park Ave., 04102 (207) 874-8200, fax (207) 874-8130. E-mail: dennis@ci.portland.me.us.

SACO

Cascade Flea Market
Corner of Rte. 1 and Cascade Rd.

Saturday, Sunday, 8 a.m.–6 p.m. Approximately 100 dealers offer new merchandise, used merchandise, antiques, collectibles, country crafts, art, jewelry, decorator items, and farm collectibles. Snack bar, rest rooms, h/a, ample parking. Space from $4. *Contact* Betty O'Donnell, 885 Portland Rd., 04072 (207) 282-1800 or 284-8875, fax (207) 883-9033.

SCARBOROUGH

Scarborough Fair Open-Air Market
Scarborough Downs
U.S. Hwy. 1, Exit 6 off Maine Tpke.

Saturday, Sunday, 8 a.m.–4 p.m. The outdoor market has approximately 100 dealers during the summer. Indoor market operates year-round. New and used merchandise; limited amounts of antiques and collectibles are available. Snack bar, clean rest rooms, h/a, ample parking. This is a clean, friendly, well-managed market. Space from $15 per day. *Contact* Audrey Gerry, 423 South St., 04038 (207) 883-4331 or 839-3035.

SEARSPORT

Searsport Flea Market
Rte. 1

Friday, Saturday, Sunday. Approximately 100 dealers offer new merchandise, electronics, tools, housewares, jewelry, sportswear, used merchandise, garage sale items, collectibles, farm collectibles, crafts, and produce. Snack bar, rest rooms, h/a, ample parking. Space from $4. *Contact* William Banks, Box 328, 04974 (207) 526-4249.

Searsport Hobby Horse Flea Market
Rte. 1
Three miles north of town

Daily, May–October, 8 a.m.–5 p.m. This indoor/outdoor market with approximately 30 exhibitors offers antiques, collectibles, new and used merchandise, crafts, jewelry, and sportswear. Snack bar, rest rooms, h/a, ample parking. Space from $5. *Contact* Philip Harrimon, Box 215, Stockton Springs, 04981 (207) 548-2981.

WOOLWICH

Nequasset Flea Market
Rte. 1 North
Five miles north of Bath

Saturday, Sunday, 6:30 a.m.–4 p.m. Seasonal market early May through mid-October. Approximately 50 dealers offer antiques, collectibles, glassware, jewelry, new and used merchandise, and crafts. Snack bar, rest rooms, h/a, ample parking. Space from $7 for a table.

Reservations required. *Contact* Norma Scopino, Box 252, 04579 (207) 443-2809.

Montsweag Flea Market
Corner of State Rte. 1 and Mountain Rd.

Wednesday, Friday, Saturday, Sunday, June–September, 6:30 a.m.–5 p.m. Average daily attendance 2,500 with approximately 100 dealers. Wednesday is restricted to antiques and collectibles. Good range of merchandise here with plenty of new and used merchandise as well as a good selection of quality items. Very clean market, fun and most enjoyable whether you are a seller or a buyer. Good food here, rest rooms, h/a, ample parking. No martial arts items or live-animal sales allowed. Space from $5. Camping available. *Contact* Norma Thompson, Box 252, 04579 (207) 443-2809.

MARYLAND

BALTIMORE

Edmondson Drive-In Flea Market
8000 Baltimore National Pike
(410) 747-5425

Saturday, Sunday. New merchandise, electronics, tools, sportswear, jewelry, toys, housewares, sports merchandise, outdoor items, used merchandise, collectibles, crafts, and produce. Snack bar, rest rooms, h/a, ample parking.

Pataspco Flea Market
1402 W. Pataspco Ave.
(410) 354-3041 or 354-5262
Fax (410) 254-3876

Saturday, Sunday, 7 a.m.–4 p.m. There are over 300 dealers at this indoor/outdoor market who offer new and used merchandise, collectibles, and crafts. Snack bar, rest rooms, h/a, ample parking. Space from $10 *Contact* Bob Lomonico, 21230.

Antiques, Collectibles, Crafts & Flea Market
I-695, Exit 34
(410) 679-2288

Saturday, Sunday. Open during summer months. Antiques, collector items, farm and sports memorabilia, tools, vintage clothing, glassware, jewelry, new and used merchandise, and lots of locally made crafts are available. Food available, rest rooms, h/a, ample parking.

North Point Drive-In Flea Market
4001 North Point Blvd.

Saturday, Sunday. Admission fee. This indoor and outdoor market has approximately 100 dealers who offer a wide variety of merchandise including lots of flea market items and new merchandise. Snack bar, rest rooms, ample parking. Space from $10. *Contact* Frank Durkee, 7721 Old Battlegrove Rd., 21222 (410) 477-1337.

BETHESDA

Farmers Flea Market
7155 Wisconsin Ave.
(202) 966-3303 or (301) 968-1593

Saturday, Sunday, 8 a.m.–5 p.m. Seasonal market open first Sunday in March through mid-December. This outside market has approximately 50 dealers offering antiques, collectibles, furniture, primitives, country items, books, and coins. Snack bar, rest rooms, h/a, ample parking. Space from $20. *Contact* James Bonfis, Box 39034, Washington, DC 20016.

COLUMBIA

Columbia Flea Market
Columbia Mall
I-95, Exit 175

Sunday only, April–October. Approximately 250 dealers offer antiques, collectibles, primitives, memorabilia, silver, glassware, and crafts. Snack bar, rest rooms, h/a, ample parking. Lots of interesting shops located in the mall here. Inside and outside spaces. Space from $55. *Contact* Bellman Promotions, 11959 Philadelphia Rd., Bradshaw, 21021 (410) 329-2188 or 679-2288.

NOTE: Maryland has a new area code, 410, which replaces a portion of the 301 telephone calling area.

EDGEWOOD

Bonnie Brae Flea Market
1301 Pulaski Hwy.

Saturday, Sunday, 7 a.m.–until dark. Inside and outside space with approximately 50 dealers who offer collectibles, primitives, books, memorabilia, crafts, art, glassware (lots of quality collectible glassware here), and new and used merchandise. Snack bar, ample parking. Space from $10. *Contact* Juanita Merritt, 1003 Magnolia Rd., Joppa, 21085 (410) 679-6895 or 679-2210.

GAITHERSBURG

Flea Market
Fairgrounds
I-270, Exit 11

Every fourth weekend. Indoor market has approximately 75 dealers. New merchandise, imports, gifts, antiques, collectibles, primitives, handmade crafts, and used merchandise are available. This is an excellent market with many quality booths of collectible treasures. An additional note: Nice shops in Gaithersburg for a side trip. The city is also the site of one of the largest and finest craft shows, held at the fairgrounds. Snack bar, rest rooms, h/a, ample parking. *Contact* Brad Thomas, Box 39068, Birmingham, AL 35208 (205) 786-3532 or (800) 362-7538.

GOLDEN RING

Golden Ring Sunday Market
Golden Ring Mall
I-695, Exit 34

Sunday only, April–October. This inside/outside market has approximately 40 dealers offering antiques, art, crafts, collectibles, and much more. Space from $25. *Contact* Bellman Promotions, 11959 Philadelphia Rd., Bradshaw, 21021 (410) 679-2288.

HUGHESVILLE

Hughesville Bargain Barn
Rte. 5
(301) 934-8580

Saturday, Sunday. New and used merchandise, collectibles, silver, jewelry, sports merchandise, and housewares are available. Snack bar, rest rooms, h/a, ample parking. Indoor market. Space from $30 per weekend. Market open to food vendors.

INDIAN HEAD

Village Green Flea Market
1107 Strauss Ave.
Village Green

Saturday, Sunday, April–October. Outdoor market with approximately 20–25 dealers. Secondhand items, garage sale merchandise, crafts—mainly local residents doing a community yard sale weekly. This is the type of place where the great treasures are found. Space from $5. Food available, rest rooms, ample parking. *Contact* Town Hall, 4195 Strauss Ave., 20640 (301) 753-6633.

LAUREL

Laurel Drive-In Theater Flea Market
Rte. 1
(301) 423-3768

Sunday only. Antiques, collectibles, glassware, silver, coins, new and used merchandise, crafts, and produce are available. Snack bar, rest rooms, h/a, ample parking.

NORTHEAST

Northeast Auction Gallery & Flea Market
U.S. Rte. 40 and Mechanics Valley Rd.

Daily 8 a.m.–5 p.m. Average attendance 2,000. Approximately 125 dealers. Wide variety of antiques and collectibles. Lots of traditional

Amish country crafts, new merchandise, used desirables, and produce. Snack bar, rest rooms, h/a, ample parking. This market conducts a large retail consignment auction on Tuesday. Space from $10 to $15 per day. Reservations recommended. Camping available. *Contact* R. C. Burkheimer, Box 551, 21901 (410) 287-5588, fax (410) 287-2029.

Barb's Flea Market
Rte. 40
(301) 287-8560

Friday, Saturday, Sunday. The flea market features: new merchandise, jewelry, housewares, sportswear, electronics, tools, sports merchandise, also used goodies, garage sale items, souvenirs, and decorator items. Snack bar, rest rooms, h/a. Inside and outside market.

OCEAN CITY

Flea Market
Convention Hall parking lot
4001 Coastal Hwy.

Saturday, Sunday, May–October, 9 a.m.–5 p.m. Approximately 35 dealers offer antiques, collectibles, some furniture, and secondhand merchandise. No new merchandise. Covered space available, space from $40 per day. Food available, rest rooms, h/a, ample parking. *Contact* Dot Robinson, Convention Center, 4001 Coastal Hwy., 21842 (410) 835-3687 or 289-8313.

OXON HILL

Super Flea Market
Rosecroft Raceway
Capital Beltway, Exit 4-A
(301) 567-4220 or 567-5815

Sunday only. New and used merchandise as well as lots of general flea market lines here such as collectibles, clocks, watches, coins, glassware, vintage clothing, and jewelry. Snack bar, rest rooms, ample parking.

PASADENA

Dutch Treat Flea Market
8370 Jumpers Hole Rd.
(410) 647-3545

Saturday, Sunday. This is a typical flea market with rows of booths with all types of used merchandise, collectibles, farm items, housewares, clothing, and jewelry. Also a good selection of locally made crafts and produce. Food available, rest rooms.

REGISTERTOWN

Flea Market
218 Main St.
(301) 883-3212

Sunday only. Buyers will find a variety of great flea market merchandise from collectibles to crafts, from toys to produce. Food available, rest rooms, h/a, ample parking.

RISING SUN

Hunter's Sale Barn
Rte. 276; I-95, Exit 93

Monday only, 3 p.m.–9 p.m. Approximately 100 dealers offer new merchandise, sportswear, imports, collectibles, jewelry, bric-a-brac, and used merchandise. Indoors, heated, rest rooms, h/a, ample parking. Auctions year-round in this 18,000-square-foot facility. Indoor and outdoor space available from $20. *Contact* Norman Hunter, Box 427, 21911 (410) 658-6400, fax (410) 658-3864.

ST. LEONARD

Chesapeake Flea Market & Specialty Shops

Friday 5 a.m.–9 p.m., Saturday 9 a.m.–5 p.m., Sunday 10 a.m.–5 p.m. Sixty dealers with shelves and tables full of antiques, collectibles, new and used furniture, ceramics, dolls, books, jewelry, glassware, brass, crafts, sports cards, and much more. Market has many regularly scheduled auctions. *Contact* Larry Forman (800) 286-0033 or (410) 586-1161.

SALISBURY

Salisbury Flea Market
805 E. Main St.
(443) 749-0095

Friday, Saturday, Sunday. A treasure hunter's paradise. Expect the unexpected at this market with a good variety of new merchandise, used desirables, garage sale items, handmade crafts, collectibles, produce. Snack bar.

SILVER SPRING

International Flea Market
Blair Mill Rd.
(301) 585-1717

Saturday, Sunday. New merchandise, flea market finds of all kinds including collectibles, jewelry, clothing, crafts, produce. Snack bar.

MASSACHUSETTS

ASHLAND

Ashland Craft & Flea Market
250 Elliot St.
(508) 481-4918

Sunday only, 7 a.m.–4 p.m. Antiques, collectibles, farm collectibles, used merchandise, good selection of locally made crafts. Food available, rest rooms, ample parking.

AUBURN

Auburn Antique & Flea Market
773 Southbridge St.
Rte. 12; I-290, Exit 8 or Exit 7 off I-395
(508) 832-2763

Saturday, Sunday, 9 a.m.–5 p.m. Admission charge 50 cents. Market is heavy on antiques and good collectibles, memorabilia, primitives, country items, collectible glassware, and silver. Saturday market is outside only. Sunday inside and outside. This is an excellent market, clean, friendly, well managed. Snack bar, rest rooms, h/a, ample parking. Inside and outside spaces. Approximately 100 booths inside. Space from $10. *Contact* Manager, Box 33, 01501.

AVON

Rainbow Flea Market
44 Bodwell St.
Avon Industrial Park
Route 24, Exit 19A

Saturday, Sunday, 9 a.m.–5 p.m. Admission charge 50 cents. This indoor market has approximately 50 dealers who offer collectibles, small antiques, coins, silver, jewelry, glassware, and lots of new and used merchandise. Market conducts a public auction on Wednesday starting at 6:30 p.m. Snack bar, rest rooms, ample parking. Space from $30 inside and $10 outside. *Contact* Gary Montgomery, 44 Bodwell St., 02322 (617) 583-3781.

BEDFORD

The Great Road Indoor Antique and Flea Market
Rtes. 4 and 225
(781) 275-2559

Sunday only. Antiques, nice furniture, glassware, country and farm collectibles, jewelry, watches, Civil War items, books, art, linens, primitives, and advertising items are available. Plenty of decorator items at this market. Snack bar, rest rooms, h/a, ample parking.

BOSTON

Boston Flea Market
Bayside Expo Center
Route 93, Exit 15
(800) 759-7469

October–December, every third weekend. Antiques, collectibles, new merchandise in a large indoor setting. Paid admission and parking. Rest rooms, snack bars, h/a. Reservations required.

Country Place Antique Flea Market
Corner of Judson and South St. Rayne

Saturday, Sunday.

Todd Farms Flea Market
Rte. 1A North
(617) 948-2217

Indoor market open throughout the year; outdoor market open April–October.

BRIMFIELD

Antique & Collectibles Shows
Antique Acres
Rte. 20

Periodically. For the year 2001, the dates are May 11–12, July 13–14 and September 7–8. Usually three times per year. One of the largest and finest of all antique and collector shows in the U.S. Eight hundred to 1,000 dealers set up outside selling quality wares. Over 20 farm fields of merchandise from tableware to fine art to furniture. If you are a serious buyer or collector/investor, this is a show that you do not want to miss. Plan to spend a couple of days. Good food available, rest rooms, parking is difficult, plan on a lot of walking. For dates and more information, *Contact* Jill Lukesh, J&J Promotions, P.O. Box 385, 01010 (413) 245-3436 or (978) 597-8155. E-mail: jnjbrimfld@hey.net.

Gordon Reids Original Brimfield Antique Flea Market
Rte. 20
(413) 245-3733

Monthly, call for dates. Quality antiques, furniture, collectibles, wide spectrum of fine collector items here. Food available, rest rooms, lots of walking.

BROOKFIELD

Ye Olde Brookfield Mill Flea Market
Mass. Tpke. and Sturbridge Exit on Rte. 148

Sunday only. Approximately 200 dealers offer a large antique and collectibles market with a great variety of booths and many fine lines of collector items. Inside space. Food available, rest rooms, ample parking. *Contact* David Quinn, Box 246, 01506 (617) 867-8793.

BURLINGTON

Jolly Jim's Flea Market
Northeast Trade Center

Monthly. Indoor market also held occasionally at the Bayside Expo Center. One of New England's better markets. Promotion company does several other fine events in New England. *Contact* Marvin Getman, Box 873, 01803.

BYFIELD

Olde Byfield Antiques Flea Market
I-95 and Exit 55

Sundays, 7:30 a.m.–2 p.m. Admission charge. Outdoor antique market. Indoor antique mall located here is open daily. Approximately 150 dealers. Large and excellent variety of quality antiques, antique furniture, and quality smalls and collectibles. Space from $30. Great food here, rest rooms, h/a. Free parking. *Contact* Rick Hurst, 12 Kent Way, 01922 (781) 272-2899 or (978) 463-0655, fax (978) 463-0653. E-mail: rickhur@prodigy.net.

CHELMSFORD

Flea Market
Rte. 10
Chelmsford Drive-In Theater
(617) 256-6393 or 978-6393

Sunday only. Antiques, collectibles, jewelry, glassware, coins, sports cards, used merchandise, clothing, household items, outdoor items, crafts, and produce. Snack bar, rest rooms, h/a, ample parking.

CHILMARK

Community Church Flea Market
Chilmark Community Church
Menemsha Crossroads

Saturdays, 8:30 a.m.–3 p.m. Seasonal market, late spring to fall. Outdoor market with approximately 50 dealers. Furniture, new and lots of new closeouts. Used merchandise, some antiques and collectibles. Lots of bric-a-brac. Space from $20 per day. Good food, rest rooms, h/a. *Contact* Phyllis Conway, Box 16 RFD, 15 Moses West Rd., 02535 (508) 645-5216.

DENNISPORT

Dennisport Flea & Antique Market
Route 28, downtown
(508) 394-6752

Thursday–Sunday.

DOUGLAS

Douglas Flea Market
N.E. Main St. Rtes. 16 and 146

Saturday 10 a.m.–2 p.m., Sunday 8 a.m.–4 p.m. This indoor/outdoor market offers antiques, collectibles, farm collectibles, new and used merchandise, handmade crafts, and produce. Market is located in a historic dairy barn. Food available, rest rooms, h/a, ample parking. Space from $2 outside. *Contact* Marlene Bosma, Box 634, 01516 (508) 476-3298 or 278-6027.

FALL RIVER

Big Top Flea Market

Saturday, Sunday. Approximately 100 dealers offer new merchandise, electronics, housewares, sportswear, jewelry, used desirables, collectibles, and crafts at this indoor market. Snack bar, rest rooms, ample parking. *Contact* Dave Bernado (508) 672-2274.

Cook Pond Flea Market
394 Kilburn St.
(508) 677-2244

Saturday, Sunday. New, used, and antique merchandise, collectibles, glassware, silver, linens, jewelry, and watches are available. Indoor and outdoor restaurant, rest rooms. Approximately 210 dealer spaces, 8×10.

FRAMINGHAM

Framingham Carousel Flea Market
Rte. 9
(508) 872-4470 or 872-8426

Sundays only, April–October. Antiques, collectibles, sports memorabilia, vintage clothing, used merchandise, crafts, and new merchandise are available. Food available, rest rooms.

GRAFTON

Grafton Flea Market
Rte. 140
Grafton-Upton town line

Sunday only, March–December, 6 a.m.–5 p.m. Admission charge. Approximately 200 dealers offer a wide variety of antiques and collectibles, some crafts, new merchandise, and produce. This market has a special collector section, coins, stamps, cards, etc. Snack bar, rest rooms, h/a, ample parking. Indoor/outdoor market. Space from $25. *Contact* Harry Peters, Box 206, 01519 (508) 839-2217.

HADLEY

Olde Hadley Farm Market
Rte. 47, north of town

Sunday only, April–October, 7 a.m.–5 p.m. Outdoor market with over 100 dealers who offer antiques, farm items, primitives, crafts, coins, collectibles, and used merchandise. Snack bar, rest rooms, h/a, ample parking. Space from $15. *Contact* Raymond Szala, 45 Lawrence Plain Rd., Rte. 47S, 01035 (413) 586-0352.

Hadley Antique Center Market
Rte. 9
(413) 588-4093

Saturday only. Antiques, furniture, collectibles, jewelry, silver, decorator items, glassware, linens, art, books, and prints are available. Food available, rest rooms, h/a, ample parking.

HUBBARDSTOWN

Rietta Flea Market
Rte. 68 183 Gardner Road

Sunday only, 6 a.m. until dark. Approximately 500 dealers offer antiques, collectibles, and decorator items. Clean, well-run market with good family atmosphere. Good variety of food here, rest rooms, h/a, ample parking. Space from $10. *Contact* Ronald Levesque, Box 35, 02048 (978) 632-0559.

KINGSTON

Kingston 106 Antique Flea Market
20 Wapping Rd.
Rte. 106

Sunday only, 9 a.m.–4 p.m. This indoor market has approximately 50 dealers who offer antiques, antique furniture, collector items, silver, collectibles, glassware, military items, and crafts. Ample parking. Monthly rentals only. *Contact* Barbara Stevens, Church St., Duxbury, 02332 (617) 934-6711.

LAWRENCE

The Jolly Flea
Plaza 114, I-495, Exit 42B, quarter mile on left

Saturday, Sunday, 10 a.m.–5 p.m. Admission charge. Market has only been open 2 to 3 years. Indoor market with approximately 150 dealers. Heavy on new merchandise, electronics, toys, jewelry, sportswear, tools, gifts, and imports. Locally made crafts. Space from $45 per weekend. Snack bar, rest rooms, h/a. Ample free parking. *Contact* Manager, 73 Winthrop Ave., 01843 (978) 682-2020.

Pacific Mills Flea Market
300 Canal St.

Saturday, Sunday, 9 a.m.–4 p.m. About 250 dealers offer new and used merchandise, electronics, housewares, sportswear, antiques, collectibles, and crafts. Snack bar, rest rooms, h/a, ample parking. Space from $25. Market is located in a historic old woolen textile mill. *Contact* Vince Michaels (508) 683-7107.

LENOX

Flea Market
Rtes. 7 and 20
(413) 440-2893

Saturday, Sunday. New and used merchandise, general flea market fare including crafts, collectibles, giftware, and produce are available. Snack bar, rest rooms, ample parking. Inside and outside space from $8.

LUDLOW

Ludlow Flea Market
1099 Center St., Rte. 21 North
Massachusetts Turnpike, Exit 7

Sundays. Outdoor market. *Contact* Grace Machado (413) 589-0419.

LYNN

Lynnway Antique & Flea Market
Loew's Drive-In Theater
Rte. 1A

Sunday, April–October. Approximately 100 dealers offer antiques, furniture, collectibles, Civil War items, books, art prints, silver, jewelry, glassware, and farm collectibles. Snack bar, rest rooms, h/a, ample parking. Space from $15. Reservations recommended. *Contact* Costos Mavros, 159 Washington St., 01902 (781) 595-5904.

Massachusetts Merchandise Mart
810 Lynnway
(781) 598-5450

Wednesday, Saturday, Sunday, 10 a.m.–6 p.m., Thursday, Friday, 10 a.m.–9 p.m. New merchandise, electronics, housewares, jewelry, tools, sportswear, sports merchandise, toys, decorator items, gifts, and imports are available. Snack bar, rest rooms, h/a, ample parking. Good market for the budget-conscious shopper to stock up on new household and personal items.

MALDEN

Malden Flea Market
42 Ferry St. Junction of Rte. 60 and Ferry St.

Saturday, Sunday. Indoor market. *Contact* Stanley Krigman (781) 324-0113.

MASHPEE

Dick & Elle's Flea Market
Rte. 28

Tuesday, Saturday, Sunday, April–September, 6 a.m. until dark. Average weekly attendance 2,500 and approximately 200 dealers. Large classic New England market. Antiques, collectibles, crafts, glassware, linens, silver, furniture, and farm and country collectibles are available. Restaurant, rest rooms, h/a, ample parking. This market is located in a beautiful tourist area. Space from $10. *Contact* Dick or Elle Wasil (508) 477-3550.

MECHANICSVILLE

Amish Farmers Market
Route 5
(301) 494-3966

Wednesday, Saturday. Used merchandise, collectibles, antiques, furniture, farm items, lots of Amish crafts, produce and products. Food available.

MERRIMACK

Merrimack Antique & Flea Market
Broad St.

Sundays only. Antiques, collectibles, glassware, farm and country collectibles, sports memorabilia, china, linens, primitives, advertising items, used merchandise, crafts, and produce are available. Snack bar, rest rooms, h/a, ample parking. Indoor market.

METHUEN

Fanny's Flea Market
Methuen Mall
Rte. 113

Sunday only. Approximately 200 dealers show at this indoor market full of typical flea market finds, including: new merchandise, sportswear, tools, sports cards, housewares, electronics, sports merchandise, outdoor items, decorator items, gifts, used merchandise, crafts, and produce. Snack bar, rest rooms, h/a, ample parking. *Contact* Chuck Romanow, 187 N. Woodstock Rd., Southbridge, 01550 (800) 759-SHOW or (617) 765-9343.

MIDDLETON

Flea Mart
263 Galvin Blvd.
Rte. 114
(617) 922-8212

Saturday, Sunday. The bargain-conscious shopper will enjoy this market with its rows of new and used merchandise, garage sale items, bric-a-brac, crafts, produce, and collectibles. Snack bar, rest rooms, ample parking.

MILLIS

The Millis Antiques & Collectible Market
813 Main St.
(508) 376-4774

Saturday, Sunday. A nostalgia lover's market with antiques, furniture, collectibles, glassware, silver, coins, jewelry, clocks, and quality decorator items. Snack bar, rest rooms, ample parking.

NAUGATUCK

Flea Market
173 Church St.
(508) 723-2845

Sunday only, 10 a.m.–4 p.m. Antiques, collectibles, used merchandise, bric-a-brac, decorator items, crafts, and produce are available. Food available, rest rooms.

NEPONSET

Neponset Swap 'N Shop
775 Galivan Blvd.
(617) 282-3500

Sunday only. New and used merchandise, collectibles, antiques, furniture, glassware, silver, jewelry, vintage clothing, and housewares are available. Approximately 350 dealers. Snack bar, rest rooms, h/a, ample parking. Space from $7.

NEW BEDFORD

Country Fair Flea Market
Coggeshall St.
(617) 994-4644

Saturday, Sunday, Monday. Approximately 200 dealers offer antiques, furniture, collectibles, vintage clothing, glassware, kitchen collectibles, jewelry, books, art, and prints. Snack bar, rest rooms, h/a. Indoor market. Space from $8.

The Whaling City Flea Market
1145 Kempton St.
Rtes. 6 and 140
(508) 999-5127

Sunday only, 9 a.m.–5 p.m. Antiques, collectibles, glassware, linens, silver, toys, farm collectibles, decorator items, and crafts are available. Food available.

NORTH ATTLEBORO

Witchi's Giant Flea Market
Junction of Rtes. 1 and 295
(508) 699-4712

Sunday only, April–November. Approximately 100 dealers offer new and used merchandise, garage sale items, antiques, collectibles, jewelry, glassware, farm collectibles, handmade trinkets and treasures, and produce. Snack bar, rest rooms, h/a, ample parking. Space from $6.

NORTH OXFORD

North Oxford Flea Market
Rtes. 20 and 56
(508) 987-5098

Saturday, Sunday. Outdoor market.

NORTH QUINCY

Naponset Flea Market
2 Hancock St.

Saturday, Sunday, 9 a.m.–5 p.m. Admission charge 50 cents. New and used merchandise, garage sale items, collector items, giftware, handicrafts, and produce are available. Food available, rest rooms, ample parking, h/a. Space from $35. *Contact* David Stanton, 2 Hancock St., 02171 (617) 472-3558 or 471-8387.

NORTH READING

Antique Flea Market
Main St.
Rte. 28

Sunday only. Admission charge. Approximately 300 dealers offer fine jewelry, art, collectibles, crafts, and antiques. Indoor and outdoor market. Space from $25. Reservations required. *Contact* Marilyn Paul, 4 Longstreet Rd., Peabody, 01960 (617) 532-0606 or 664-8623.

Macsonny's Antique & Flea Market
Atlantic Plaza
Rte. 28
(617) 922-6391

Sunday only. Antiques, furniture, collectibles, decorator items, china, silver, glassware, kitchen collectibles, Civil War items, and farm collectibles. Food available, rest rooms, h/a, ample parking.

NORTHFIELD

Flea Market
Warwick Ave.
I-91, Exit 28N

Sunday, May–October. Outdoor market with approximately 50 dealers who offer new and used merchandise, antiques, collectibles, crafts, and produce. Food available, rest rooms, ample parking. Space from $6. *Contact* Ken Miller, Box 163, 01360 (413) 498-2749.

NORTON

Norton Flea Market & Antique Sale
Mansfield Ave.
Rte. 140

Sunday only, third Sunday in April through last Sunday in October. Admission charge. One of the largest weekly flea markets in New England. It offers new and used merchandise, antiques, collectibles, a full range of collector items, and crafts. Food available, rest rooms, ample parking. Space from $15. *Contact* Richard Pino or George Bemheimer, P.O. Box A1, Rte. 140, 02766 (617) 285-6765.

ORANGE

Bailey's Antique Flea Market
West River St.
Rte. 2, W. River St. Exit

Saturday, Sunday. Approximately 300 vendors offer a large selection of quality antiques and furniture, collectibles, silver, coins, linens, glassware, housewares, toys, and vintage clothing. Food available, rest rooms, h/a, ample parking and lots of walking. Space from $10 outside and $25 inside. *Contact* Ronald Paoletti, Box 6, 01364 (508) 456-8593.

RAYNHAM

Country Place Flea Market
Rtes. 24 and 44 on South St.

Sundays, 8 a.m.–6 p.m. Admission charge. Market is also open on Saturdays from Thanksgiving to Christmas. Approximately 300 dealers. New merchandise, sportswear, jewelry, silver, glassware, vintage clothing and jewelry, antiques, books, collectibles, coins. Used merchandise, bric-a-brac and housewares. Inside and outside space available form $20. Full-service restaurant. Snack bar, rest rooms, h/a. Ample parking. *Contact* Jeff Mann, Judson and South Sts., 02767 (508) 584-4432 or 823-8923, fax (508) 824-2339. E-mail: raynhamflea@aol.com.

READING

Country Fair Antique & Flea Market
Rtes. 129 and 128, Exit 34

Sundays. Antiques, furniture, collectibles, silver, glassware, primitives, advertising items, Civil War items, books, art, prints. Snack bar, rest rooms, h/a. Indoor market. Ample parking. *Contact* Ron Letch (617) 944-7882.

REHOBOTH

All Antique Flea Market
Rte. 44

Sunday only. Large selection of antiques, furniture, and quality collectibles, plus nice decorator items, silver, glassware, toys, vintage clothing, kitchen collectibles, and primitives available. Food available. *Contact* Rick Verdi (617) 252-4353.

REVERE

Revere Swap 'N Shop
Showcase Cinema, 565 Squire Rd.

Saturday, Sunday, 7 a.m.–4 p.m. Admission $1 per person. Seasonal market open March through December. Outdoor market with approximately 250 dealers. New and used merchandise, lots of flea market and garage sale merchandise. Crafts, imports, gifts, some antiques and collectibles. Space from $30 per day. Snack bar, rest rooms. Ample free parking. *Contact* John Nerich, 565 Squire Rd., 02151 (781) 289-7100.

SALEM

Antique Market Place
29 Congress St.
(978) 745-9343 or 774-6677

Sunday only. Antiques, collectibles, furniture, silver, coins, jewelry, watches, primitives, advertising items, and decorator items are available. Food available.

SHREWSBURY

Flea Market & Farmers Market
Edgemere Drive-In Theater
Rte. 20

Saturday, Sunday. New and used merchandise, lots of household items, some antiques and collectibles and crafts are available. Snack bar, rest rooms, h/a, ample parking. *Contact* Jeff Saletin (508) 831-3696.

SOMERSET

Condesa Antique & Flea Market
3129 County St.
Rte. 138

Sunday only, 9 a.m.–5 p.m. Antiques, furniture, collectibles, glassware, primitives, vintage clothing, linens, jewelry, silver, coins, Civil War items, art, books, and prints, as well as more traditional flea market wares. Approximately 200 dealers. Snack bar, rest rooms, h/a, ample parking. Indoor market. *Contact* Richard Mansueto (617) 676-3519.

SOUTHBRIDGE

Fanny's Flea Market
Main St.
Rte. 131 at the Polish Club

Saturday, Sunday. New and used merchandise, collectibles, crafts, art, books, housewares, and jewelry are available. Food available, rest rooms, ample parking. *Contact* Donna Frances (617) 764-6307.

SPENCER

Spencer Flea Market
411 E. Main St.
Rte. 9

Saturday, Sunday, Monday. Approximately 100 dealers offer new and used merchandise, garage sale items, antiques, collectibles, furniture, decorator items, crafts, and produce. Snack bar, rest rooms, h/a, ample parking. Outdoor market with space from $5. *Contact* Jim Devereux, 411 E. Main St., 01562 (508) 885-3558.

SWANSEA

Oceangrove Antique & Flea Market
458 Oceangrove Ave.
(617) 678-9598

Saturday, Sunday. Antiques, collectibles, glassware, silver, primitives, coins, jewelry, watches, books, art, prints, farm and country collectibles, used merchandise, and good secondhand items are available. Food available.

The Swansea Flea Market
1046 GAR Hwy.
Rte. 6
(800) 679-9466

Saturday, Sunday, Monday, 9 a.m.–5 p.m. New and used merchandise, prints, collectibles, crafts, decorator items, gifts, imports, art, and books are available. Food available.

TAUNTON

The Pavilion Market Place
Taunton Expo Center
Rte. 44
(508) 880-3800
Fax (508) 880-5100

Saturday, Sunday, 8 a.m.–5 p.m. Approximately 800 vendors are accommodated indoors, over 2,000 outdoors. The Pavilion Market Place is held at the fourth largest exhibition facility in New England. It is strong on high-quality antiques and collectibles. Literally hundreds of quality booths here, an endless variety of collector items. Food available, rest rooms, h/a, ample parking with miles of walking. *Contact* Market Place, P.O. Box 68, 02780.

UXBRIDGE

Douglas Flea Market
N.E. Main St.

Sunday only, 9 a.m.–4 p.m. Approximately 250 daily attendance. New merchandise, baseball cards, collectibles, antiques, bake shop and caterer on premises. Good market for the dealer, collector, or decorator to shop. Clean rest rooms, ample parking. Country atmosphere. Indoor/outdoor market. *Contact* Marlene Alsop, Bosma 01516 (508) 278-6027.

WALPOLE

Country Time Antique & Flea Market
Rte. 1
(508) 668-7672

Saturday, Sunday. Nostalgia buffs' haven with antiques, furniture, collectibles, jewelry, silver, linens, vintage clothing, primitives, military items, books, art, prints, farm and country collectibles, used merchandise, housewares, and sports merchandise available. Food, rest rooms.

WAREHAM

Wellfleet Drive-In Flea Market
Rte. 6
(508) 349-2520 or 255-0619

Saturday, Sunday, April–October; also open Wednesday, June 24–Sept. 9 and all Monday holidays. New and used merchandise, garage sale items, collectibles, handicrafts, and produce are available. Approximately 200 dealers. Snack bar, rest rooms, h/a, playground, ample parking. Space from $5.

WEARHAM

Antique Fair & Flea Market
Rte. 28
(508) 295-2702

Sundays. Antiques, collectibles, furniture, sports memorabilia, coins, linens, primitives, Military items, art, prints, books, farm and country collectibles. Food available, rest rooms, h/a. Ample parking.

WELLFLEET

Wellfleet Flea Market
Rte. 6
Wellfleet Drive-In Theater

Saturday, Sunday, 8 a.m.–4 p.m. Admission charge. The number of sellers depends on the season and runs from 50 to 300. Antiques, new merchandise, lots of crafts. Garage sale items, bric-a-brac, housewares. Outdoor market. Market open April through October. Ample parking. *Contact* Eleanor Hazen, Box 811, 02667 (508) 349-2520, fax (508) 349-2902.

WESTBORO

Westboro Homestead Flea Market & Antique Show
Rte. 9 Westboro Speedway
(508) 872-0085

Saturday, Sunday, April–October. Antiques, collectibles, china, glassware, coins, vintage clothing, jewelry, linens, farm and country collectibles, and furniture are available. Food available.

WEST FALMOUTH

Saconesset Homestead Flea Market & Antique Show
Rte. 9
(617) 548-8540

Saturday, Sunday. Antiques, collectibles, china, glassware, coins, vintage clothing, jewelry, linens, farm and country collectibles, furniture. Food available. Market open April through October.

WEYMOUTH

Weymouth Flea Market Discount Weekend Marketplace
Corner of Rte. 53 and Middle St.
Shaw's Plaza

Saturday, Sunday. Approximately 200 dealers offer new merchandise, electronics, housewares, toys, jewelry, watches, silver, sporting merchandise, tools, and sportswear. Air-conditioned, refreshments, rest rooms, ample parking. Good market for the budget-conscious to shop for new household and personal items. *Contact* Tony Abbott (617) 783-3040.

Weymouth Antique Flea Market
Rte. 53
(781) 475-3112

Sundays only. Antiques, collectibles, glassware, furniture, lamps, silver, art, prints, decorator items. Lots of quality items here. Food available.

INFORMATION IS SUBJECT TO CHANGE—ALWAYS CALL AHEAD TO AVOID DISAPPOINTMENT

Weymouth Mini Mall & Antique Market
555 Washington St.
(617) 335-2373

Saturday, Sunday. Antiques, collectibles, furniture, decorator items, gifts, imports, glassware, and jewelry are available. Snack bar, rest rooms, h/a, ample parking.

WOBURN

Jolly Jim's Flea Market
Northeast Trade Center

Monthly. Average attendance 25–30,000 with approximately 300 dealers. Quality show with professional dealers setting excellent booths. Like a great home show with all the builders' clutter out of the way. One of the Northeast's largest indoor shows. Promotion company conducts other fine shows in New England; call for schedule. *Contact* Marvin and Carol Getman, Box 873, Burlington, 01803 (800) 759-7469 or (781) 686-1010.

YARMOUTH

Cape Cod Bazaar
Hwy. 28
Yarmouth Drive-In Theater

Saturday, Sunday.

MICHIGAN

ALLEGAN

Allegan Antique Market
Allegan County Fairgrounds.
Rte. 94, Exit 34, 131 Expressway,
Allegan Exit

Every last Sunday, 7:30 a.m.–4 p.m. Admission $3. Seasonal market April through September. Indoor and outdoor market with approximately 300 dealers. Strong on quality antiques, collectibles, and antique furniture. Lots of professional dealers here who set very high-quality booths of collectibles and smalls. Space from $55 outside. Reservations recommended. Snack bars, rest rooms, h/a, lots of walking. This is an excellent source market for serious collectors, investors, decorators, and shopkeepers. Free parking. *Contact* Larry Wood, 2030 Blueberry Dr. NW, Grand Rapids, MI 49504 (616) 453-8780 or 735-3333.

ANN ARBOR

Ann Arbor Antiques Market
5055 Saline Rd.

Every third Sunday, April–November. Admission $4. Approximately 350 dealers. This market is strong on memorabilia and collectibles with lots of fine antiques. A very quality-oriented market. Great attendance. This is one of the finest antique markets in the entire country. Many, many fine investment-quality pieces here. Fun, friendly, well-managed market. A collector's paradise. Food available, rest rooms, h/a, ample parking, and lots of walking. *Contact* Margaret Brusher, P.O. Box 1512, 48106 (313) 429-9838.

ARMADA

Armada Outdoor Flea Market
25381 Ridge Rd. M-97
(810) 784-9604

Tuesday, Sunday, May–October, 6 a.m.–3 p.m. Average daily attendance of over 1,000 with approximately 250 dealers who offer antiques, collectibles, country and farm collectibles, glassware, silver, and vintage clothing. Shoppers will find a good selection and wide range of merchandise. Farmers' market here also. Good food available on premises. Space from $10.

CENTERVILLE

Caravan Antiques Market
Fairgrounds
Hwy. M-86

Periodically, call for dates. Admission charge. Large indoor/outdoor antique market with approximately 600 dealers who offer antiques, fine art, and high-caliber collectibles. Food available, rest rooms, h/a, ample parking. Market is usually held five times a year during the spring and summer. *Contact* Robert Lawler, 1510 N. Hoyne St., Chicago, IL 60622 (312) 227-4464.

COPEMISH

Copemish Flea Market
Rte. 115

Saturday, Sunday, May–October, 8 a.m.–6 p.m. Approximately 100 dealers offer new merchandise, lots of flea market items, crafts, collectibles, glassware, silver, primitives, farm and ranch collectibles, and produce. Snack bar, rest rooms, ample parking. Space from $4.50. *Contact* Jerry Dillingham, Box 116, 49625 (616) 378-2430 or 929-4317.

DAVIDSON

Midway Flea Market
205 Davison Rd.

Saturday, Sunday. New and used merchandise, jewelry, clothing, housewares, sports merchandise, handmade gifts, collectibles, and produce are available. Snack bar. Inside and outside space from $18 for both days. *Contact* Ken Lamson, 504 N. Dayton, 48423 (313) 653-8766.

DETROIT

Penn-Huron Flea Market
17076 Huron Dr.

Saturday, Sunday. Inside and outside market with approximately 150 dealers. Wide range of merchandise. Especially heavy on new merchandise. Much like shopping at a severely discounted discount store. Rest rooms, snack bar, h/a, ample parking. Space from $7. *Contact* Richard Slater, 8100 Longworth, 48209 (313) 841-2196 or 753-4133.

Metro Flea Market
6665 W. Vernor

Friday, Saturday, Sunday, 8 a.m.–4 p.m. Indoor/outdoor market with approximately 75 dealers. Snack bar, rest rooms, h/a. Ample parking. *Contact* Ralph Najor (313) 841-4890.

FLINT

Giant Trade Center Flea Market
4204 Davison Rd.

Friday, Saturday, Sunday, 10 a.m.–7 p.m. Average attendance 5–6,000 with approximately eighty dealers. Large selection of new merchandise at severely discounted prices. Great market for bargains on personal, household, and recreational items. Better prices than any discount store on many things. Space from $45 for three days. *Contact* Jerry Keeley, 4204 Davison Rd., 48509 (313) 742-5371.

GRAND RAPIDS

Jack Loek's Studio 28 Flea Market
1400 W. 28th St. Southwest
Movie theater parking lot

Saturday, Sunday, May–September. Average attendance 5,000 with approximately 350 dealers. Large commercial market with great selection of new merchandise. Lots of good secondhand items and garage sale merchandise, some antiques, collectibles, glassware, silver, coins, primitives, farm and ranch collectibles, and produce are available. Snack bar, rest rooms, h/a, ample parking. Come dressed for a great deal of walking. *Contact* Bruce Johns (616) 532-6301 or 532-8218.

GRASS LAKE

Grasslake Mini Mall Flea Market
Burtch Rd.

Saturday, Sunday, 10 a.m.–6 p.m. Average attendance 200 with approximately 40 dealers offering new merchandise, used desirables, country collectibles, gifts, imports, crafts, and produce. Food available. Space from $2.50. Overnight parking. *Contact* E. C. Caler, 242 Burtch Rd., 49240 (517) 522-8810.

GREENVILLE

Clay Street Flea Market
913 Clay St.
Take Hwy. 56 from Grand Rapids, go past Main St. and right on Clay about three blocks. Big green sign.

Friday, Saturday, 10 a.m.–5 p.m. Approximately 10–12 vendors, space from $10 per day. New and used merchandise. Reservations recommended. Seller's permit recommended. *Contact* Judy Nowakowski, P.O. Box 143, 48838 (616) 225-8426.

HATTIESBURG

The Flea Market
Hwy. 98
Three miles west of town

Saturday, Sunday, 8 a.m.–6 p.m. Average attendance 1,000. Approximately 50 dealers. New and used merchandise, garage sale items. Lots of country collectibles, farm and ranch items, antiques, glassware, decorator items, crafts, produce. Food available, rest rooms, h/a. Space from $10. Ample parking. *Contact* Tommy Curtis, Box 514, 39401 (601) 268-3667 or 264-7823.

HILLSDALE

Andy Adams Sale Barn Flea & Farmers Market
Fairgrounds
(517) 437-7230

Saturday only. Average daily attendance 2,000. Approximately 25 dealers offer new and used merchandise, antiques, collectibles, produce, and livestock. Food available, rest rooms, ample parking. Indoor/outdoor market. Space from $10. Camping and electricity available. Market has been at the same location for over 80 years. Market conducts livestock and consignment auctions Saturday morning.

HOMER

Thurstons Flea Market
Five miles east of I-69 on M-60
(517) 568-3851

Sundays only. Average attendance 1,000. Approximately 30 dealers offer antiques, collectibles, jewelry, coins, linens, vintage clothing, primitives, advertising items, used merchandise, crafts, decorator items, and produce. Food available. Space from $5. Camping available.

HOWARD CITY HEIGHTS

Burley Park Swap Meet
Hwy. 131 North, Exit 120

Saturday, Sunday, Holidays, Memorial Day–October. Primarily antiques and collectibles in this popular market. Great selection of offerings for collectors of just about everything. Lots of quality items, including furniture. Clean, friendly, and well managed. Approximately 600 dealer spaces from $10. Camping available. *Contact* Judy Rogers, 4540 Bailey Rd., Coral, 49322 (231) 354-6354.

HOWELL

Howell Flea & Farmers Market
2300 E. Grand River
Auction Barn

Wednesday only, 8 a.m.–5 p.m. Approximately 40 dealers. New and used merchandise, housewares, jewelry, collectibles, clothing, kitchen items, lots of farm items. Also large farmers' market here. Snack bar, rest rooms, h/a, ample parking. Space from $6. *Contact* David Anderson, 2205 Oak Grove Rd., 48843 (517) 546-0136 or 548-3300.

IONIA

Ionia Antique & Collectible Market
Fairgrounds

Sunday only. Great antique and collectible market with excellent selection and wide range of booths. This is an excellent market for those looking for quality items. Food available, rest rooms, h/a, ample parking, and lots of walking. Indoor, outdoor spaces from $30. Tables available. Reservations recommended. Overnight camping on your rented space outside. Electricity charge $5. *Contact* Judith Kramer, 496 S. State St., P.O. Box 3, Pewamo, 48873 (616) 527-2724.

KALAMAZOO

Bank Street Market
Kalamazoo City Market
1205 Bank St.

Wednesday and Friday. Seasonal market from May through September. Approximately 125 dealers. Outdoor market with some covered spaces.

Fairgrounds Flea Market
Fairgrounds
(616) 383-8778

Seasonal market, April through November, also some Tuesdays and Wednesdays, call for current schedule.

LAMBERTVILLE

Lambertville Antique Market
River Rd.
Rte. 29
(609) 397-0456

Saturday, Sunday. Market features a bit of Americana, from the offbeat to the highly collectible. For the serious collector, shopkeeper, dealer, or decorator this market is a most interesting stop. Food available, snack bar, rest rooms.

Jo's Ceramic Art & Flea Market
8177 Sector Rd.
Three miles north of Toledo, Ohio

Friday, Saturday, Sunday. Approximately 20 dealers offer used merchandise, collectibles, decorator items, gifts, imports, crafts, and produce. Snack bar. Space from $25 for the weekend. *Contact* Jo Peart, Box 387, 48144 (313) 856-8000.

LANSING

Lansing Flea Market
3215 S. Pennsylvania Ave.

Friday, Saturday, Sunday, 9 a.m.–6 p.m. Approximately 35 dealers offer general flea market lines, new and used, collectibles, crafts, and produce. Snack bar, rest rooms, h/a, ample parking. *Contact* Joe Scrattan, 4240 Love Joy Rd., Perry, 48872 (517) 394-7047 or 625-7262.

LAPEER

Lions Club Flea Market
County Center Bldg.

Sundays only, May–September. Antiques, collectibles, fine jewelry, vintage clothing, glassware, country collectibles, kitchen collectibles, silver, and toys. Snack bar, rest rooms, h/a, ample parking.

LEXINGTON

Lexington Harbor Bazaar
5590 Main St.
(810) 359-5333

Saturday, Sunday, 10 a.m.–5 p.m. Approximately 50 dealers offer new merchandise, gifts, jewelry, souvenirs, novelties, sportswear, clothing, lots of trendy new items in the boutique section, used merchandise, garage sale items, collectibles, glassware, antiques, silver, and vintage clothing. Boutiques open daily. Food available, rest rooms, h/a, ample parking. Space from $25 per weekend or $40 per week. Reservations required. *Contact* Bazaar, 5590 Main St., 48450.

MARSHALL

Marshall Antiques Market
Fairgrounds
Intersection of I-94 and I-69

Saturday only, 8 a.m.–5 p.m. Admission $3. Large covered market, primarily antiques and quality collector lines. Quality-oriented antique market. Food available, rest rooms, h/a, ample parking. *Contact* Ted or Donna Tear (616) 789-0990, fax (616) 781-7868.

MASON

Antique Flea Market
Mason St.

Wednesday, Saturday, Sunday, 10 a.m.–6 p.m. Approximately 60 dealers offer lots of quality antiques, furniture, collectibles, fine jewelry, vintage clothing, art, prints, books, military items, memorabilia, and quality decorator pieces. Food available, rest rooms. Space from $8. *Contact* David Fincock (517) 676-9753.

MERRILL

Tillie's Treasures Flea Market
Hwy. M-46
(517) 643-7516

Saturday, Sunday, 10 a.m.–5 p.m. This indoor market offers new and used merchandise, sportswear, decorator items, souvenirs, collectibles, gifts, and imports. Snack bar, rest rooms, h/a, ample parking. Open year-round.

MONROE

Dallas Corner Flea Market
15300 S. Dixie Hwy.

Friday, Saturday, Sunday. New and used merchandise, lots of garage sale items, collectibles, imports, crafts, and produce are available. Snack bar. *Contact* Norman Sayer (313) 242-6284.

MT. CLEMENS

Old Timers Flea Market
36000 Grosbeck Rd.

Friday, Saturday, Sunday, 10 a.m.–6 p.m. Average daily attendance 2–4,000. Approximately 100 dealers offer antiques, collectibles, silver, jewelry, vintage clothing, primitives, advertising items, memorabilia, plenty of new and used merchandise, garage sale items, crafts, gifts, imports, decorator items, and produce. Food available on premises, rest rooms, h/a. Space from $30. *Contact* Dora Pet, 36000 Grosbeck Rd., 48043 (810) 792-1612.

Gibralter Trade Center
I-94 and 237 N. River Rd.
Exit 237 from I-94

Friday, 12 p.m.–9 p.m., Saturday, 9 a.m.–9 p.m., Sunday, 9 a.m.–6 p.m. Admission charge. Large indoor market with mostly permanent booths. Gibralter is known mainly for its massive array of new merchandise, discount-house-type sweats, cookware, etc. Some collectibles. Limited outdoor space available. Market also conducts many special events. Snack bars, rest rooms, h/a, ample parking. Market management not very friendly to traveling commercial dealers. *Contact* Jan Sullivan, 237 N. River Rd., 48043 (810) 465-6440, fax (810) 465-0458.

MUSKEGON

Gold Token Flea Market
1300 E. Laketon Ave.

Saturday, 6 a.m.–2 p.m. Indoor/outdoor market with approximately 75 dealers who offer lots of secondhand and garage sale items, new imports, antiques, and collectibles. Space from $5 per table. Snack bar, rest rooms, ample parking. *Contact* Gold Token, 1300 E. Laketon Ave. (616) 773-1137, fax 722-4646.

Muskegon Flea Market
Junction of Seaway Dr. and Eastern Ave.
One-half mile north of downtown

Wednesday, May–October. Large outdoor market with approximately 300 dealers who offer antiques, collectibles, clothing, used and new merchandise, produce, and crafts. Space from $7. Snack bars, rest rooms, h/a. *Contact* Cheri Burdick, City of Muskegon, 933 Terrace St., 49443 (616) 722-3251.

Select Auditorium Flea Market
1445 Laketon Ave.
U.S. Hwy. 31 and Laketon Ave.

Saturday, 6 a.m.–6 p.m. New and used merchandise, collectibles, art, crafts, gifts, decorator items, and produce are available. Rest rooms, snack bar, h/a. Space from $4. *Contact* Terry Durham, 1445 E. Laketon Ave., 49442 (616) 726-5707.

MUSKEGON HEIGHTS

Farmers Market Flea Market
700 Yuba St.

Wednesday, May–October, 6 a.m.–6 p.m. Average attendance 3,000. Approximately 250 dealers at this large wide-open market offer lots of merchandise new and used, antiques, collectibles, housewares, farm items, clothing, produce, livestock, and crafts. Food available, snack bar, rest rooms, h/a, ample parking, and lots of walking. Space from $5. *Contact* John Albertie (616) 722-3251 or 728-6433.

NILES

Great Bazaar Flea Market
2021 Oak St.
Eastgate Shopping Center

Friday, Saturday, Sunday, 9 a.m.–6 p.m., indoor market hours. Outside market is open Saturday, Sunday, and holidays. Outside market opens April 15. Indoor market has 52,000 sq. ft. and 170 spaces. Approximately 1,500 spaces outside. Spaces are 22 ft. long by 20 ft. deep and are $9 per day. Electricity is available outside. Monthly and seasonal rates available. Snack bar, rest rooms, h/a. Ample parking with special parking for buses. *Contact* Phil or Terri Odle (616) 687-6666.

NEW BALTIMORE

Penn-Huron Flea Market
17076 Huron River Dr.
(313) 753-4133

Saturday, Sunday. Approximately 150 dealers. New merchandise, electronics, housewares, sportswear, outdoor items, jewelry, gifts. Used merchandise, garage sale items, collectibles, glassware, decorator pieces, coins, sports cards. Crafts, produce. Snack bar, rest rooms, h/a. Ample parking.

PAW PAW

LaRue's Flea Market
37908 Red Arrow Hwy.
One mile west of Paw Paw, via I-94

Saturday, Sunday, 9 a.m.–6 p.m. Average daily attendance 1,000. Approximately 75 dealers outside and 100 inside. Wide selection of new and used merchandise, antiques, collectibles, jewelry, gifts, decorator items, and crafts. Snack bars, rest rooms, h/a, ample parking. Space from $3. Camping available. Market conducts retail consignment auction on Sunday. *Contact* Donald LaRue, Jr. (616) 657-3533.

Reits Flea Market
One-half mile north of I-94, Exit 56

Saturday, Sunday, May–October, 8 a.m.–4 p.m. Average attendance 10,000. Approximately 450 dealers offer lots of new merchandise, collectibles, antiques, glassware, used merchandise, crafts, art, and more. Plenty of good food here. Good restaurant, rest rooms, h/a, ample parking. This is a good market for commercial vendors. Clean, friendly, and well managed. It is always a pleasure to sell or to shop here. Space from $8 daily, no inside space. Camping from $3. Electricity available. Space charge $1 without Michigan sales tax license. Fireworks, martial arts, and alcohol prohibited. *Contact* Bill Reits, 45293 Red Arrow Hwy., 49079 (616) 657-3428 or (219) 259-8292.

PONTIAC

Dixieland Flea Market
2045 Dixie Hwy.
End of Telegraph Rd.
(616) 338-3220

Friday, Saturday, Sunday. Average daily attendance 8,000. Approximately 400 dealers offer a wide range of new merchandise, from hot new trendy to necessaries. Used merchandise, lots of antiques, collectibles, silver, coins, glassware, primitives, crafts, produce, and decorator items. Food available, rest rooms, ample parking, and acres of walking. Inside and outside space available at this large commercial market. Overnight parking available. Good security. Reservations recommended. Good market for antiques and collectibles.

PORT HURON

Wurzel Flea Market Inc.
Rte. 136 north of Port Huron
(313) 385-4283

Saturday, Sunday. Average attendance 2,500. Approximately 90 dealers offer new and used merchandise, crafts, collectibles, and produce. Space from $7 outside and $12 inside. Electricity available. *Contact* Anna Weeks, 6575 Fredmoore Hwy., St. Clair, 48079.

RAVENNA

Ravenna Flea Market
Folcum Road 2 miles north of the Livestock Sales Grounds
I-96, Coopersville Exit, north 13 miles

Monday, 7 a.m. until dark. Average attendance 4,000. Approximately 200 dealers offer lots of country stuff and country collectibles here; primitives, auctions, and advertising items abound. This is a market designed for the collector or decorator. Space from $5. Auctions on Monday. *Contact* Jim Lund, 1685-19 Mile Rd., Cedar Springs, 49319 (616) 696-1247 or 853-2952.

ROMULUS

Green Line Road Flea Market
16447 Middlebelt Rd.

Saturday, Sunday, 7 a.m.–4 p.m. Approximately 250 exhibitors offer primarily new and used merchandise, some crafts, limited antiques, and collectibles. Snack bar, rest rooms, h/a, ample parking. Space from $12. *Contact* William Pai (313) 941-6930.

ROYAL OAK

Flea & Farmers Market
316 E. 11 Mile Rd.

Sunday only. Approximately 120 dealers offer antiques, collectibles, decorator items, country treasures, new and used merchandise, jewelry, sportswear, housewares, crafts, produce, and livestock. Food available. Inside and outside space available from $12. *Contact* Steve Sendek, 316 E. 11 Mile Rd., 48067 (313) 548-8822.

SAGINAW

Giant Public Market
3435 Sheridan
Corner of Sheridan and Williamson

Friday, Saturday, 10 a.m.–7 p.m., Sunday, 10 a.m.–6 p.m. Average attendance 5,000. Approximately 100 dealers offer new merchandise, imports, sportswear, gifts, collectibles, decorator items, crafts, art, coins, jewelry, and glassware. Clean, well-managed market in modern building. Snack bar, rest rooms, h/a. Space $15 and up. *Contact* Bob Reiss (517) 754-9090, fax (517) 754-7465.

Saginaw Flea Market
Fairgrounds

Thursday. Average attendance 4,000. Approximately 100 dealers offer antiques, collectibles, silver, jewelry, new and used merchandise, crafts, and produce. Food available, rest rooms, h/a, ample parking. *Contact* Deloris Holtrop, 420 Fisher, 48604 (517) 754-6004 or 753-4408.

SAUGATUCK

Saugatuck Flea Market
3604 64th St.

Saturday, Sunday, 8 a.m.–5 p.m. Approximately 20 dealers offer used merchandise, collectibles, gifts, and imports. Space from $5. *Contact* Everett Slendz, 3604 64th St., 49419 (616) 857-2726.

SIX LAKES

Flea Market
303 N. Railroad St.
Junction of Rtes. M-46 and M-66
(517) 365-9057

Saturday, Sunday, April–October. Average daily attendance 300. Approximately 50 dealers offer new and used merchandise, garage sale items, gifts, imports, decorator pieces, country collectibles, outdoor items, and produce. Outdoor, open-air market. Food and rest rooms. Camping available.

TRUFANT

Trufant Auction & Flea Market
303 North C St.

Thursdays, April–September, Dawn to 4 p.m. Auctions at 10 a.m. Approximately 250 dealers. Large, wide-open market: antiques to imports, used merchandise to fine jewelry. This is an excellent one-day market with a wide variety of booths. Snack bar, rest rooms, h/a, ample parking, and lots of walking. Space from $5. *Contact* Maurice Peterson, 13670 Dickerson Lake Rd., 49347 (616) 984-2168 or 984-2573.

UTICA

Country Fair Flea Market
45300 Mound Rd. at Rte. M-59

Friday, Saturday, Sunday. Indoor market with approximately 150 dealers who offer a good mixture of merchandise with lots of antiques and collectibles. Snack bar, rest rooms, ample parking. Space from $30. *Contact* Country Fair, 45300 Mound Rd., 48087 (313) 254-7110.

ALWAYS CALL BEFORE TRAVELING LONG DISTANCES!

WARREN

Country Fair Antique Flea Market
20900 De Quindre Blvd.
One block north of Eight Mile Rd.
(810) 757-3740 or 757-3741

Friday, 4 a.m.–9 p.m., Saturday, Sunday, 10 a.m.–6 p.m. Indoor market with approximately 350 dealers who offer new and used merchandise, and market has well-publicized area known as "Famous Antique Village." Over-night parking available. Good security. Snack bars, rest rooms, h/a, ample parking. Space from $50. *Contact* Country Fair, 20900 De Quindre Blvd., 48034.

Michigan Flea Market
24100 Groesback Hwy.

Thursday, Friday, 4 a.m.–9 p.m. Indoor market with approximately 30 dealers. Antiques, collectibles, new and used merchandise, crafts, jewelry, new collector lines, sportswear. Snack bar, rest rooms, h/a. Ample free parking. *Contact* Manager, 24100 Groesbeck Hwy., 48089 (810) 771-3535.

WATERFORD

Dixie Land Antique Flea Market
2045 Dixie Hwy.
Corner of Hwy. 10 and Telegraph Rd., at Hwy. 24.

Friday, 4 p.m.–9 p.m., Saturday, Sunday, 10 a.m.–6 p.m. Average daily attendance 8,000. Approximately 250 dealers offer new and used merchandise, lots of secondhand garage sale items, antiques, and some nice spreads of collectibles. Four snack bars, rest rooms, h/a, ample parking, and camping nearby. Space from $45. Inside and outside space available. *Contact* Barbara Kemen, 2045 Dixie Hwy., 48328 (810) 338-3220, fax (248) 338-3221.

WYOMING

Beltline Flea Market
28th St. SW

Saturday, Sunday. Admission charge. Outdoor market with approximately 300 dealers. Lots of antiques and collectibles. Some new merchandise. Good range of collector items here. Market open May–October. Space from $8. Ample parking. *Contact* Don Moinet, 1400 28th St. SW, 49509 (616) 532-6302.

YPSILANTI

Bunky's Flea Market
822 Michigan Ave.
(313) 483-8336

Friday, Saturday, Sunday. Used and garage sale merchandise, crafts, collectibles, produce, new merchandise, and much more to attract collectors and bargain-conscious shoppers. Snack bar, rest rooms, h/a.

Huron Trade Center & Flea Market
210 E Michigan, corner of Michigan at Park

Friday, Saturday, Sunday. Average attendance 3–5,000 and over 150 dealers. Mainly antiques, collectibles, jewelry, and lots of classic flea market items available. Great market for pleasurable shopping. Interesting booths and friendly people. Inside and outside space available from $35 per weekend. Camping nearby. *Contact* James White, 214 E. Michigan, 48198 (313) 480-1539, fax (734) 480-9043.

MINNESOTA

ANNANDALE

Wright County Swap Meet
13594 100th St. NW Rte. 3, two miles west of city
(320) 274-9005

Saturday, Sunday, April–October. Collectibles, used merchandise, country treasures, handcrafts, and produce are available. Snack bar, rest rooms. *Contact* Gladys Miller, 55382.

BATTLE CREEK

Rainbow Bait Flea Market
Hwy. 78
(218) 864-5569

Saturday, Sunday. Used merchandise, gifts, all sorts of classic flea market bric-a-brac, souvenirs, and collectibles are available.

BLAINE

Blaine Flea Market
Hwy. 65, downtown
(612) 757-9906

Friday, Saturday, Sunday, 10 a.m.–6 p.m. Large indoor flea market offers used and new merchandise, furniture, lots of secondhand and garage sale items, plenty of bric-a-brac, and gift items. Snack bar, rest rooms, h/a, ample parking.

BRAINERD

Searcy Flea Market
Hwy. 210, six miles west of city

Friday, Saturday, Sunday. Used merchandise, country and farm collectibles, crafts, and produce available. Food available, rest rooms. Pleasant country market.

BRECKENRIDGE

Auctions Unlimited Flea Market

Every third weekend. Antiques, collector items, housewares, clothing, secondhand desirables, farm collectibles, and jewelry are available. Snack bar, rest rooms, h/a, ample parking.

DETROIT LAKES

Shady Hollow Flea Market
Hwy. 59, five miles south of town

Sunday only, May–October, 7 a.m.–5 p.m. Approximately 100 dealers offer antiques, collectibles, silver, glassware, toys, new and used merchandise, and crafts. Food available, rest rooms, ample parking. *Contact* Ardis Hanson, 1760 E. Shore Dr., 56501 (218) 847-9488 or 847-5706.

ELKO

Traders Market
I-35 and Country Rd.
(612) 461-2400

Saturday, Sunday, May–October. New and used merchandise, antiques, collectibles, crafts, and produce. Snack bar, rest rooms.

FAIRBAULT

Flea Market
(507) 334-5159

Saturday, Sunday. A typical weekend market with a little of everything from baseballs to clocks, electronics to T-shirts.

HACKENSACK

Flea Market
Catholic Church on Hwy. 371

Monthly, call for dates. Approximately 50 dealers offer new and used merchandise, antiques, collectibles, jewelry, and crafts. Food available, rest rooms. *Contact* Chamber of Commerce (218) 675-6135.

HINCKLEY

Hinckley Flea Market
Hwy. 48; I-35, Exit 183

Thursday–Sunday, April–October, 9 a.m.–6 p.m. Average daily attendance over 500. Approximately 125 dealers. Indoor/outdoor market, some covered spaces, new merchandise, sportswear, imports, handmade crafts, art, collectibles, antiques, advertising items, antique toys, and more. Snack bar, rest rooms, h/a, ample parking. Camping available. Space from $30. *Contact* Gus Atrooz, 803 Hwy. 48, 55037 (612) 384-9911, fax (612) 384-6589.

JENKINS

Flea Market
Hwy. 371

Thursday–Sunday, May–September, call for dates. Used merchandise, garage sale items, crafts, and farmers' market. Food available. *Contact* Tillman Rude (218) 947-3313.

INFORMATION IS SUBJECT TO CHANGE—ALWAYS CALL FIRST!

LITCHFIELD

Meeker County Swap Area

Saturday, Sunday. New and used merchandise, crafts, collectibles, and produce are available. Snack bar. *Contact* Jerry Krambler, 501 Pleasant Ave., 55355 (612) 693-7698.

MANKATO

Smitty's Flea Market
Hwy. 371, 1.5 miles south of Nisswa

Saturday, May–September, dawn until dark. Outdoor market with approximately 100 dealers who offer antiques, collectibles, books, vintage clothing, advertising items, farm items, antique toys, primitives, and lots of fishing collectibles. Snack bar, rest rooms, h/a. Space from $15 per day. *Contact* Jim Schmidt, P.O. Box 585, 56002 (507) 931-2449.

MINNEAPOLIS

Flea Market
Lyndale and Glenwood Sts.

Saturday only. New and used merchandise, tools, garage sale items, crafts, housewares, and produce are available. Food available.

Flea Market
Midway Shopping Center
Snelling and Hwy. 36

Saturdays. Used merchandise, garage sale items, crafts, collectibles, produce. Food available.

Blaine's Flea Market
10980 Central Ave. Northeast
(612) 757-9906

Saturday, Sunday, 10 a.m.–8 p.m. Good selection of collectibles, glassware, silver, crafts, art, new and used merchandise, gifts, and imports available. Snack bar. Monthly rental only.

MONTICELLO

Orchard Fun Market
Orchard Rd.
Three miles west of stoplight in Monticello
Turn left after power plant.
(612) 295-2121

Saturday, Sunday. Indoor/outdoor market with approximately 500 dealers who offer antiques, collectibles, crafts, used merchandise, and new merchandise. Market has entertainment and kids' rides. Good food available on site. Rest rooms, h/a, ample parking. Space from $10. *Contact* Orchard Fun Market, 127 St. NW, 55362.

MOORHEAD

Bud's Flea Market
Hwys. 10 and 75

Saturday, Sunday. Approximately 50 dealers offer new and used merchandise, jewelry, housewares, clothing, sports items, gifts, and decorator items. Indoor market. Snack bar, rest rooms, h/a. Space from $23 for the weekend. *Contact* Bud Granfor, Perley, 56574 (218) 861-6635.

NEW MARKET

Traders Market
County Rd. 2
I-35 South, Elko/New Market Exit
(612) 461-2400 or 435-7327

Saturday, Sunday. One of the area's better antique and collectible markets. Food available, rest rooms, ample parking. Market produces many special events—call for current schedule of upcoming events.

NISSWA

Flea Market
Hwy. 371 North
(218) 963-2844

Friday, Saturday. Used merchandise, garage sale items, crafts, collectibles, and produce are available. Snack bar.

OMEGA

Wild Cat Swap Meet

Saturday, Sunday. Approximately 100 dealers offer new merchandise, tools, electronics, sportswear, toys, housewares, sports merchandise, used merchandise, garage sale items, crafts, produce, collectibles, and sometimes antiques. Snack bar, rest rooms, ample parking. *Contact* Dave Mertens (218) 983-3325.

OTTERTAIL

Carol's Flea Market
Hwy. 78
(218) 367-2742

Saturday, Sunday. Indoor market. New merchandise, jewelry, sportswear, electronics, housewares, used merchandise, collectibles, glassware, silver, vintage clothing, art, and books are available. Snack bar, rest rooms, h/a, ample parking.

PINE CITY

Flea Market
805 6th St.
Gibsons parking lot
(320) 629-5828

Sunday only. Antiques, collectibles, country and farm items, new and used merchandise, crafts, and produce are available. Food available.

REDWING

Flea Market
Gibson's Parking Lot

Sundays. Antiques, collectibles, country and farm items, new and used merchandise, crafts, produce. Food available.

ROCHESTER

Olmstead County Gold Rush Antique Show & Flea Market
Fairgrounds
(507) 288-0320 or 346-7530

Semiannual, second weekend of May and third weekend of August. Admission charge. Fifty-acre facility with 12–14 buildings in use for this combination show and flea market. Indoor/outdoor with antiques only. Strong attendance with over 1,000 vendors selling high-quality antiques. Plenty of good food at this event. Ample rest rooms, lots of parking, and miles of walking. Space from $40 indoors and $30 outdoors. Reservations necessary. *Contact* Joyce Fuchs, Rte. 2, Box 2X, Pine Island, 55963. This is a don't-miss event if you are looking for quality items.

ST. CLOUD

Flea Market
Armory
8th St.
(612) 251-9189

One weekend monthly, call for dates.

ST. PAUL

Flea Market
Armory
1530 E. Maryland
(612) 457-4999

Saturday, Sunday, three weekends per month. Antiques, collectibles, jewelry, silver, linens, and new and used merchandise. Food available, rest rooms, h/a, ample parking.

LAKE ELMO (TWIN CITIES)

Flea Market
Washington County Fairgrounds

Every fourth weekend. Ample parking. Antiques, collectibles, jewelry, silver, vintage clothing, art, farm items, glassware. Food available. Rest rooms, h/a. Seasonal market. Inside and outside space available. *Contact* Ron Johnstone (612) 439-3183.

WABASHA

Wabasha Indoor/Outdoor Flea Market
Hwy. 61 and Industrial Ct.

Saturday, Sunday, 9 a.m.–5 p.m. New and used merchandise, furniture, lots of garage sale items, and small newer collectibles. Food available, rest rooms, h/a. Space from $8 per table. *Contact* Don Carlson, Box 230, 55981 (612) 565-4767.

WINONA

Flea Market
Levee Plaza Mall

Saturday only. Used merchandise, lots of garage sale items, bric-a-brac, crafts, and produce are available. Food, rest rooms, h/a, ample parking.

MISSISSIPPI

AMORY

Bigbee Waterway Trade Days
30211 Hwy. 371, three miles north of town

Every first Monday. Approximately 100 dealers offer new and used merchandise, sportswear, electronics, housewares, some antiques and collectibles, crafts, and lots of secondhand items here. Snack bars, rest rooms, h/a, ample parking. Space from $15 for the weekend outside and $30 for inside space. Camping and electricity available. Market open to food vendors. *Contact* Jim Roby, Rte. 2, Box 159B (601) 256-1226.

CHARLESTON

Flo-Mart Flea Market
Hwy. 35, three miles south of town
(601) 647-5995 or 647-8832

Every second weekend. Antiques, collectibles, farm and ranch items, primitives, advertising items, jewelry, glassware, vintage clothing, and garage sale merchandise are available here. This is an open-air, outdoor market with some covered spaces. Food available, rest rooms, h/a, ample parking, and lots of walking. Camping and electricity also available.

COLUMBUS

Traders Village Flea Market
2608 Hwy. 82 East
(601) 328-6750

Friday, 10 a.m.–6 p.m., Saturday, 9 a.m.–6 p.m., Sunday, 12 p.m.–6 p.m. New and used merchandise, antiques, collectibles, gifts, crafts, and produce are available. Food available.

CORINTH

Corinth Flea Market
Corinth Square Shopping Center
1224 Hwy. 72 East
One mile east of Hwys. 45 and 72 intersection

Wednesday, Thursday, 10 a.m.–6 p.m., Friday, Saturday, 10 a.m.–7 p.m., Sunday, 1 p.m.–6 p.m. Approximately 120 dealers. Average attendance 3,000. Building is heated and air-conditioned. New merchandise, sportswear, used merchandise, antiques, collectibles, and crafts. Cafe in flea market. Rest rooms, h/a, ample parking. Space from $25 per weekend. Reservations recommended. Camping with showers on premises. Electricity available. *Contact* Ray King, 1224 Hwy. 72E, 38834 (601) 287-9110 or 287-1387.

GAUTIER

Flea Market City (formerly Deep South Flea Market)
3813 Hwy. 90
(601) 497-9401

Daily. New and used merchandise, antiques, collectibles, jewelry, silver, clothing, and housewares are available. Indoor, outdoor, and covered space available. Approximately 25 dealers. Space from $5 per day.

GULFPORT

A-1 Trade World
I-10 and Menge Ave. at Exit 24
(228) 452-0590

Saturday, Sunday, 8 a.m.–5 p.m. Covered market with approximately 200 dealers. Space from $10 per day. Electricity available and new RV park. Snack bars, rest rooms, h/a. Ample free parking.

HATTIESBURG

Calico Mall Antique Flea Market & Crafts Show
801 Mississippi St.
(601) 582-4351 or 583-2971

Saturday, 8 a.m.–5 p.m., Sunday, 10 a.m.–5 p.m. Everything from antiques, collectibles, crafts, and produce to new merchandise is allowed at this antique market. Excellent antique market with some very quality displays. Snack bar, rest rooms, h/a, ample parking.

JACKSON

Antique Flea Market
State Fairgrounds
801 Mississippi St.

Saturday, 8 a.m.–5 p.m., Sunday, 10 a.m.–5 p.m. Admission $1. Average weekend attendance 2,000. Indoor market with approximately 200 dealers. Everything from antiques, collectibles, crafts, produce, and new merchandise is allowed at this antique market. Excellent antique market with some very quality displays. Space from $35 for the weekend. Snack bar, rest rooms, h/a. Ample free parking. *Contact* Frank Barnett, Box 23579, 39225 (601) 353-5327, fax (601) 353-5367.

PASCAGOULA

The Super Flea Market
4502 Chico Rd.

Thursday–Tuesday, 9 a.m.–6 p.m. Inside and outside market. Approximately 75 dealers offer collectibles, crafts, new merchandise, used and garage sale items, and electronics. Market conducts several special events. Snack bar, rest rooms, h/a, ample parking. Chapel with religious services on Sunday. Market is operated by the Bible Way Ministries. *Contact* Bill Day (601) 769-8714 or 826-5651.

PASS CHRISTIAN

A-1 Trade World
Menge Ave. I-10, Exit 24
(228) 452-0590

Saturday, Sunday. Large commercial outdoor market with some covered spaces.

RIPLEY

First Monday Trade Days
Hwy. 15 South

Weekend of first Monday, dawn until dark. Admission charge. Approximately 600 dealers with everything imaginable. Outdoor market. One of the oldest markets in America. One of the better markets in the South for all types of merchandise. This is a tremendous source market for shops, dealers, and decorators. Restaurant, convenience store, gas station, ample rest rooms. Sellers should be sure to make reservations early. Parking can be difficult due to the tremendous crowds, and you will do a lot of walking here. Camping available. Space from $25. *Contact* Wayne Windom, 10590 Hwy. 15 South, 38663 (601) 837-7442 or 837-4051, fax (601) 837-7080. E-mail: hww@dixie-net.com.

TUPELO

Gigantic Flea Market
Tupelo Furniture Market Building
18799 N. Coley Rd.

Friday, 6 p.m.–9 p.m., Saturday, 9 a.m.–7 p.m., Sunday, 10 a.m.–5 p.m. Large commercial indoor/outdoor market with approximately 800 dealers. Lots of antiques and collectibles along with mountains of new merchandise at great prices. Space from $65 for the weekend. Snack bars, rest rooms, h/a. *Contact* Debbie Griffin (601) 842-4442, fax (601) 844-3664.

MISSOURI

ASBURY

Stateline Trade Center & Flea Market
Hwy. 171, ten miles southeast of Pittsburg, Kansas
(417) 642-5850

Friday and Saturday, 10 a.m.–8 p.m., Sunday, 1 p.m.–6 p.m., Monday, 10 a.m.–6 p.m. Used merchandise, country and farm collectibles, decorator items, advertising items, and primitives are available. *Contact* Donna Lair.

AURORA

Highway 39 Merchants Flea Market
4.5 miles south of Wal-Mart
(417) 678-6314

Tuesday–Sunday, 9 a.m.–6 p.m. Used merchandise, garage sale items, country collectibles, crafts, and produce are available. Food available, rest rooms.

AVA

Granny's Attic Flea Market
412 N.W. 12th Ave.
One block north of town square
Business Rte. 5 and Hwy. 14
Close to Branson

Monday–Thursday, 9 a.m.–5 p.m., Friday, Saturday, 9 a.m.–7 p.m., Sunday, 10 a.m.–5 p.m. More than 150 indoor booths, with approximately 100 outdoor exhibitors on the weekend. Antiques, collectibles, memorabilia, nice reproduction furniture, souvenirs, glassware, gifts, imports, new merchandise, and sportswear. Snack bar, rest rooms, ample parking. Space from $4 outdoors. *Contact* Ronald Hammer (417) 683-5776 or 683-3395.

BARNHART

Barnhart Flea Market
6850 Hwy. 61-67

Saturday, Sunday, 6 a.m.–5 p.m.. Approximately 250 indoor spaces and 300 outdoor spaces. Mostly new merchandise and a lot of great junk. A local market not recommended for the traveling commercial vendor. Dealer setup 8 a.m.–8 p.m. Thursday and Friday. Space from $12 daily. Quantity rates available. Food concessions by prior approval only. No alcohol sales permitted. Snack bar, rest rooms, h/a, seven acres of parking. *Contact* Ed Samnee or Joyce Suermann, 6850 Hwy. 61-67, Imperial, 63052 (636) 464-5503.

BRANSON

Coffelt Country Crossroads
State Hwy. 165
One-quarter mile south of Hwy. 76

Friday, Saturday, Sunday. Average daily attendance 300. Dealers range 20–100. There are 13 permanent shops. Ice cream shop, candle shop, quilts, wood signs, etc. Very interesting and enjoyable country market. All types of merchandise. Market is located in the heart of country music's new "Nashville." Branson is packed with tourists during the summer months. Rest rooms and snack bar, h/a. Space from $5 daily. Tables and electricity available. *Contact* Sandra Smith, HCR, Box 1829 (417) 334-7611 or 334-1282.

NOTE: Missouri has a new area code, 573, which covers most of southeast Missouri and the boot heel.

CABOOL

Lloyd's Flea Market
Hwy. 63

Saturday, Sunday. Average attendance of 1,000. Approximately 30 dealers. Country and farm collectibles, glassware, clothing, jewelry, used merchandise, garage sale items. Outside market. Snack bar, rest rooms. Space from $3. *Contact* Lloyd Ayers, State Rte. 1, Box 211, Houston, 65483 (417) 967-4473.

CAPE GIRARDEAU

Antique Flea Market
Southeast Missouri Fairgrounds
(573) 334-2451

Monthly, call for dates. Nice country market with crafts, collectibles, antiques, and new merchandise. Snack bar, rest rooms, h/a, ample parking.

CARTHAGE

71 Flea Market
Hwy. 71
(417) 358-1988 or 358-FLEA

Friday, Saturday, Sunday. Used merchandise, garage sale items, crafts, sports memorabilia, new merchandise, souvenirs, produce. Snack bar.

Flea Market
Old Furniture Bldg.
(417) 358-1901

Daily, 10 a.m.–5 p.m. Collectibles, furniture, glassware, silver, jewelry, lots of secondhand merchandise, trash and treasures.

Carthage Route 66 Antique Mall & Flea Market
1221 Oak St.
(417) 359-7240

Daily. More than 100 dealers. New and used items, antiques, collectibles, crafts, and lots of good Route 66 collectibles. Air-conditioned and heated facility. Rest rooms, ample parking.

Deants Antique Mall & Flea Market
1200 Oak St.
(417) 358-6104

Daily. Indoor market with over 100 booths; lots of good collectibles and secondhand merchandise here.

CASSVILLE

De Ole Garage Antique Mall & Flea Market
Hwy. 112 South 65625
(417) 847-5919

Daily, Monday–Saturday, 10 a.m.–5 p.m., Sunday, 12:30 p.m.–5 p.m. Antiques, collectibles, primitives, glassware, jewelry, tools, linens. Lots of secondhand merchandise. New market.

E&E Flea Market
Five miles north of town on Hwy. 37

Daily, 9 a.m.–5 p.m. Used merchandise, garage sale items, collectibles, and decorator items are available. *Contact* Elizabeth Schaar, Rte. 1, Box 1567, 65625 (417) 847-3888.

COLE CAMP

Flea Market
Hwy. 65

Saturday, Sunday, May–November. Used merchandise, garage sale items, bric-a-brac, crafts, produce, and country collectibles are available. Food available, rest rooms, ample parking.

COLUMBIA

Stop 'N Scratch Flea Market & Antiques
1907 N. Providence Plaza
(314) 443-8275

Monday–Friday, 9 a.m.–7 p.m., Saturday, 9 a.m.–6 p.m., Sunday 11 a.m.–6 p.m. Antiques, sports memorabilia, glassware, primitives, advertising items, toys, linens, and collectibles available.

Morton's Flea Market
Hwy. 63 South
(314) 449-6306

Saturday, Sunday. Approximately 25 dealers. New and used merchandise, souvenirs, and collectibles available. Indoor market.

Midway Flea Market
Hwy. 40
(314) 445-6717

Saturday, Sunday. Used merchandise, garage sale items, collectibles, crafts, and produce available. Food available.

CROCKER

Bear Ridge Antique & Collectible Flea Market
Hwy. 17, seven miles north of Waynesville
(417) 736-5858

Monday–Saturday, 9 a.m.–5 p.m., Sunday, 1 p.m.–4 p.m. Glass, jewelry, crafts, paper items, Americana, and dolls.

DEXTER

Old Timers Flea Market
Hwy. 60 West
(314) 624-8288

Daily. Collectibles, farm and ranch items, used merchandise, garage sale items, and bric-a-brac.

DOOLITTLE

Indoor Flea Market
I-44 Frontage Rd. & Hwy. MM 179

Saturday, Sunday. New and used merchandise, gifts, souvenirs, jewelry, glassware, silver, and crafts available. Snack bar. *Contact* Alice Jones (314) 762-2065.

EAGLE ROCK

Antiques & Uniques Flea Market
Hwy. 86
(314) 271-4509

Daily. Lots of secondhand merchandise and some good junk treasures are here. Building covers two floors.

ELDON

Eldon Flea Market
Hwy. 54
(573) 392-7113

Saturday, Sunday, April–October. Used merchandise, garage sale items, bric-a-brac, crafts, and produce. Food available. Outdoor market, space from $3 per day. Camping available.

FAIR GROVE

Old Mill Flea Market
Main St.
(417) 759-2040

Monday–Saturday, 10 a.m.–5 p.m., Sunday, 12 p.m.–5 p.m. This market covers 6,000 square feet. Kitchenware, antiques, collectibles, glass, furniture, quilts, and toys available.

FARMINGTON

Farmington Flea Market
4602 Hwy. 67, one mile north of town

Saturday, Sunday, 9 a.m.–4 p.m. Approximately 60–80 vendors. Outdoor market. Antiques, collectibles, memorabilia, primitives, country, sports items, brewery items, crafts, art, etc. Also, new and used merchandise. Very nice antique mall next door to this market. Snack bar, rest rooms, h/a. Space from $5. Ample free parking. *Contact* Manager, 4602 Hwy. 67, 63640 (573) 756-1691.

GOODMAN

Kelly Springs Antique Mall & Flea Market
Hwy. 71 South
(417) 364-7799

Thursday–Sunday. Collectibles, Coca-Cola memorabilia, cast iron, quilts, dolls, jewelry, and glassware are available.

GRANBY

Granby Flea Market
Four miles east of Alternate Hwy. 71 on Hwy. 60
(417) 472-3532

Daily, 9 a.m.–5 p.m. Forty inside dealers offer collectibles, flea market items, and antiques. Outdoor setups available on weekend, weather permitting. Camping with electricity available.

GREENVILLE

Hillbilly Park Flea Market
Hwy. 67, eight miles south of Greenville
(314) 297-3522

Friday, Saturday, Sunday. New merchandise, used merchandise, crafts, collectibles, furniture, and produce are available. Food available. New market. Space from $8.

HANNIBAL

Bonanza Flea Market
110 Church St.
(314) 248-1505

Saturday, Sunday. Used desirables, new merchandise, collectibles, crafts, and produce are available. Snack bar. Inside and outside spaces. Many neighboring antique and specialty shops here.

HOLDEN

Iron Kettle Antiques & Flea Market
South of Hwy. 50 on Hwy. 131
Nine miles from Holden, east on Hwy. 58, three miles
(816) 732-4031

Saturday, 1 p.m.–5 p.m., Sunday, 1 p.m.–6 p.m. Glassware, furniture, collectibles, baseball cards, and jewelry available.

HOUSTON

Lloyd's Flea Market
Hwy. 17, east of town

Friday, Saturday, Sunday. Outdoor market with approximately 50 dealers who offer new and used merchandise, some small antiques, good selection of collectibles, and memorabilia. Snack bar, rest rooms, h/a. Space from $3. *Contact* Lloyd Ayers, State Rte. 1, Box 211, 65483 (417) 932-6656.

JOPLIN

Joplin Flea Market
1200 Virginia Ave.

Saturday, Sunday. Approximately 150 dealers. This market has 40,000 square feet of exhibit space. Heavy on used and flea market items, some antiques and collectibles. Inside and outside space available. Cafe, snack bar, rest rooms; parking can be difficult here. Space from $5. *Contact* LaVerne Miller, 2572 Markwardt Ave., 64801 (417) 623-6328 or 623-3743.

Rusty Nail Flea Market
3004 Silver Creek Dr.
Two blocks south of I-44 on Hwy. 71, Exit 8A
(417) 624-7157

Thursday–Monday, 9 a.m.–5 p.m. Antiques, collectibles, dolls, furniture, crafts, jewelry, and primitives are available.

North Main Street Antique/Craft Mall & Flea Market
Five miles north of I-44 on Hwy. 43 (Main St.)
Behind Lumberjack Carpet Store
(417) 781-9700

Monday–Saturday, 9 a.m.–5 p.m., Sunday, 12 p.m.–5 p.m. New market. Air-conditioned.

Outside space available on weekends, weather permitting.

KAHOKA

Hickory Hills Flea Market
Hwy. 136, between Kahoka and Wayland
Fifteen miles east of Keokuk, Iowa

Monthly. Antiques, collectibles, and used merchandise available. Food available. Space from $4 daily outside. Camping available. *Contact* Gloria Johnsierken, Rte. 3, Box 65, (816) 727-3769.

KANSAS CITY

Jeff Williams Original Kansas City Flea Market
Governor's Bldg., American Royal Center
I-435 and Front St., next to Kemper Arena

Monthly, 8 a.m.–4 p.m. Approximately 500 dealers. Market is wide-open for all types of items. Antiques, collectibles, coins, jewelry, silver, glassware, new merchandise, sportswear, imports, electronics, and used merchandise available. Snack bar, rest rooms, h/a, ample parking. Space from $30. For schedule *contact* Jeff Williams, Box 543, Blue Springs, 64013 (816) 228-5811.

The Kansas City Flea Market
1775 Universal St.
North Kansas City
Market Center
(303) 526-5494 or (888) 333-3532
Fax (303) 526-7339

Monthly. Admission charge $1. Large indoor one-day show with lots of new merchandise at severely discounted prices. Snack bar, rest rooms, h/a, ample parking. Space from $58. *Contact* Manager, 1153 Bergen Parkway, Evergreen, CO 80439.

DAYS, DATES, AND MARKETS ARE SUBJECT TO CHANGE!

Heart Swap Meet
6403 E. Hwy. 40
(816) 923-3366

Saturday, Sunday. Admission charge. Average daily attendance 4,000. Approximately 500 dealers. New merchandise, electronics, jewelry, sportswear, tools, housewares, sports merchandise, toys, decorator items, gifts, used merchandise, lots of garage sale items, crafts, produce, and collectibles available. Outdoor market. Space from $3 to $25. Camping available.

Nate's 63rd Street Swap Meet
Drive-In Theater
Hwy. 50 East and I-435
(816) 353-1627

Saturday, Sunday. New and used merchandise, crafts, collectibles, and produce available. Snack bar.

Things Unlimited (formerly Westport Flea Market)
817 Westport Rd.
(816) 931-1986

Saturday, Sunday. Approximately 75 dealers. New merchandise, sportswear, tools, jewelry, watches, sports merchandise, housewares, electronics, used merchandise, glassware, primitives, kitchen collectibles, and crafts. Snack bar, rest rooms, h/a. Indoor market. One of the oldest markets in the area. Great restaurant next door.

Waldo's Flea Market
224 W. 75th St.
(816) 363-9938

Saturday, Sunday. East of Broadway. Used merchandise, garage sale items, collectibles, decorator items, gifts, imports. Snack bar, rest rooms. Ample parking.

KNOB NOSTER

B&B Flea Market
600 E. Allen St.
(816) 563-9766

Saturday, Sunday. Used merchandise, collectibles, primitives, silver, glassware, and a little bit of everything you might expect to find at a flea market.

Knob Noster Flea Market
585 N. Jefferson St.
(417) 588-7430

Saturday, Sunday. Souvenirs, gifts, jewelry, used merchandise, and collectibles available.

LAMAR

Treasure Seekers Antique Mall & Flea Market
West side of town square
(417) 682-2900

Monday–Saturday, 9 a.m.–5 p.m., Sunday, 1 p.m.–5 p.m. This new market has antiques, collectibles, furniture, jewelry, silver, coins, glassware, primitives, advertising items, art, prints, and books available.

LEBANON

Remember When Flea Market
577 N. Jefferson St.
(417) 588-1029

Daily. Antiques, collectibles, furniture, used merchandise, and primitives. Dealers welcome.

The Country Corner Flea Market and Antiques
585 N. Jefferson, just off I-44

Monday–Saturday, 9 a.m.–6 p.m., Sunday, 12 p.m.–6 p.m. Indoor market with approximately 40 dealers, 7,500 sq. ft. Mostly permanent booths with lots of flea market goods and tourist items. Space from $5. *Contact* Marilyn Allen, 585 Jefferson St., 65536 (417) 588-1430.

ALWAYS CALL AHEAD TO VERIFY DATES AND INFORMATION

LINN CREEK

Hillbilly Al's Flea Market
Junction of Hwy. 54 and A-Rd.
(314) 346-5890

Saturday, Sunday. New and used merchandise, crafts, collectibles, and produce available.

LOWRY CITY

J&L Flea Market
Hwy. 13 South
(417) 644-2929

Monday–Saturday, 9 a.m.–6 p.m., Sunday, 1 p.m.–6 p.m. Antiques, collectibles, and used merchandise available.

MACON

Flea Market
903 Hwy. 63 South
(660) 385-1333

Saturday, Sunday. Used merchandise, garage sale items, bric-a-brac, crafts, produce, and plenty of hidden flea market treasures. Snack bar.

MARIONVILLE

Kountry Korner Flea Market
Junction Hwys. 60 and 265
(417) 463-2923

Monday–Saturday, 10 a.m.–5 p.m., Sunday, 1 p.m.–5 p.m. Railroad items, antiques, primitives, furniture, glass, Indian artifacts, western items, and books. RV and bus parking.

MARSHFIELD

Bobbie's Wishing Well Flea Market
222 S. Crittenden
I-44, Exit 100

Monday–Saturday, 9:30 a.m.–5 p.m., Sunday, 12:30 p.m.–5 p.m. Antiques, junk, and collectibles. Lots of interesting shops in Marshfield make this a great stop. *Contact* Bobbie Reed (417) 468-6380.

Hidden Treasures Antiques & Flea Market
301 S. Clay St.
I-44, Exit 100

Monday–Saturday, 9 a.m.–5 p.m., Sunday, 10 a.m.–4 p.m. Antiques, furniture, glass, advertising items, crocks, collectibles, toys, tools, clocks, baskets, teddy bears, primitives, and books available. *Contact* Donna Arehart (417) 468-6088 or 468-4165.

MOUNTAIN VIEW

Weavers Auction & Flea Market
Nine miles west of Mountain View

Daily. Flea market, animal swap meet, auction on Saturday night, campfires and country music on the weekend. Camping available. RV hookups from $7.50 nightly. *Contact* Wayne Weaver, Rte. 3, Box 102, 65546 (417) 934-2160 or 469-3351.

MT. VERNON

Mt. Vernon Flea Market
Rte. 1
(417) 466-2422

Daily except Wednesday. Used merchandise, new merchandise, gifts, souvenirs, and collectibles available. Inside and outside space available.

NEOSHO

Verns Flea Market
One mile south of junction 60 and 71A
(417) 451-9565

Monday–Friday, 9 a.m.–6 p.m., Saturday, Sunday, 6 a.m.–6 p.m. Collectibles, new and used merchandise, dinnerware, glassware, depression glass, antiques, tools, and jewelry available. Outdoor setups available on the weekend, weather permitting.

71 Craft & Flea
Rte. 8, 1.5 miles north of town on Hwy. 71
(417) 451-9575

Tuesday–Saturday, 9 a.m.–5 p.m., Sunday, 11 a.m.–5 p.m. Closed Monday. Air-conditioned. Furniture, primitives, ceramics, collectibles, wood crafts, gifts, books, antiques, and secondhand items.

South Elwood Flea Market
Alternate Hwy. 71 South
(417) 451-5140

Saturday, Sunday, 8 a.m. until dark. Memorial Day through Labor Day weekend. Outdoor market with lots of covered sheds. New merchandise, gifts, lots of secondhand and used merchandise. Excellent selection of tools, both new and used. Wide variety of in-season produce. Snack bars, rest rooms, ample parking, difficult terrain for the handicapped. *Contact* Manager, 17895 Kentucky Rd., 64850.

Neosho Gallery & Flea Market
900 N. College
Business Rte. 60
(417) 451-4675

Tuesday–Sunday, 9 a.m.–5 p.m. There are 100 indoor shops here. Antiques, furniture, collectibles, glassware, and toys.

Chea's Place
523 N. College St.
(417) 451-2511

Tuesday–Saturday, 10 a.m.–5 p.m., Sunday, Monday, 1 p.m.–5 p.m. Antiques and collectibles here.

NIXA

Camel Back Antiques & Flea Market
Junction of Hwy. 160 and Northview Rd.
(417) 725-5125

Monday–Saturday, 10 a.m.–5 p.m., Sunday, 11 a.m.–5 p.m. Antiques, primitives, collectibles, and glassware available.

Red Barn Flea Market & Antiques
One mile west of Hwy. 160
(417) 725-3338

Thursday–Monday. This market has a little bit of everything from antiques to dishes, collectibles, furniture, memorabilia, and concrete yard ornaments.

OAK GROVE

Inge's Oak Grove Flea Market
1120 Broadway
(816) 625-8885

Monday–Saturday, 10 a.m.–6 p.m., Sunday, 1 p.m.–6 p.m. Antiques, collectibles, furniture, and tools available. Credit cards accepted.

OLD MINES

Starlite Flea Market
Five miles north of Potosi on Hwy. 21

Friday–Monday. Average weekly attendance of 2,500. Used merchandise, garage sale items, bric-a-brac, and junk. Snack bar. Space from $4. Camping available with electricity. *Contact* Terry Mercille, Rte. 2, Box 123, Cadet, 63630 (314) 438-4975.

OSCEOLA

Wisner's Flea Market & Antiques
Hwy. 13
(417) 646-8555

Daily. Collectibles, jewelry, glassware, primitives, memorabilia, souvenirs, and used merchandise available.

Trade Fair Market
Trade Fair Mall
Hwy. 13
(417) 647-8085

Wednesday–Monday. New merchandise, used merchandise, crafts, and produce available. Snack bar.

INFORMATION IS SUBJECT TO CHANGE—ALWAYS CALL AHEAD TO AVOID DISAPPOINTMENT

OZARK

Country Junction Flea Market & Baird's Antiques
Junction of Hwys. 14 and 65 South
(417) 485-8116

Monday–Saturday, 9:30 a.m.–5 p.m., Sunday, 1:30 p.m.–5 p.m. Large selection of antique furniture, glass, jewelry, linens, and housewares available.

Ozark Flea Market
519 S. Town Center
East Hwy. 14
(417) 581-8544

Daily. Antiques, furniture, Coke items, quilts, toys, tools, primitives, and advertising signs available.

PARK HILLS

Jose's Flea Market
233 W. Main St.

Monday–Saturday, 9:30 a.m.–5:30 p.m. New merchandise, new and secondhand furniture, bric-a-brac, and garage sale items available.

The Little Red School House Flea Market
Vo-Tech Rd., south of Bonne Terre
(636) 358-0570

Thursday–Sunday, 10 a.m.–6 p.m. Antiques, collectibles, secondhand items, tools, bric-a-brac, and new merchandise available.

PEVELY

Pevely Flea Market
Hwy. 61 South Drive-In Theater
I-55, Exit 180
(636) 479-5400
Fax (636) 479-7680
E-mail: pevelyfleamkt@jenl.com

Saturday, Sunday, 6 a.m.–5 p.m. Approximately 500 dealers. Excellent market year-round. Indoor, outdoor, and covered spaces.

Good mix of quality booths with collectibles, lots of secondhand items, garage sale items, new merchandise, imports, sportswear, and produce. Food available, h/a, restrooms, ample parking. *Contact* Lee Douglas, Box 419, 63070.

POPLAR BLUFF

Flea Market
Next to livestock market

Thursday–Sunday. Used merchandise, garage sale items, farm and ranch items, housewares, clothing, and produce. Food available, rest rooms, ample parking.

POTOSI

Mainstreet Market
207 E. High St.
(636) 438-7731

Daily. Antiques, glassware, collectibles, period furniture, toys, books, quilts, Indian articles, western memorabilia, and coins.

REPUBLIC

West County Flea Market
336 N. Hwy. 60, 65738
(417) 732-8415

Monday–Saturday, 10 a.m.–5 p.m., Sunday, 1 p.m.–5 p.m. Antiques, collector items, dolls, Precious Moments collectibles.

RUTLEDGE

Dog, Gun, Hillbilly Consignment Auction & Flea Market

Monthly. Call for exact times. *Contact* Irvin Johnson (816) 883-5816 or 883-5322.

ST. GENEVIEVE

Antique Mart
305 N. Main St.
(636) 883-7333

Daily. Indoor market. Primarily antiques and collectibles with lots of primitives, kitchenware, and advertising items. Many neighboring antique and specialty shops nearby in this historic old French town.

ST. LOUIS

Frison Flea Market
7025 St. Charles Rock Rd.

Friday, Saturday, Sunday, 8 a.m.–5 p.m. Average attendance 1,200. Approximately 300 spaces. New merchandise, sportswear, imports, gifts, lots of new decorator and collectible items, and used and secondhand merchandise available. Snack bar, rest rooms, h/a, ample parking. Space from $10 daily, electricity available. *Contact* Jack Frison, 7025 St. Charles Rock Rd., 63133 (314) 727-0460.

ST. ROBERT

Freddy Bees Flea Market
I-44 and 160 mile marker
(636) 336-4750

Thursday–Sunday. New and used merchandise, garage sale items, bric-a-brac, crafts, and produce. Snack bar. Camping available.

SEDALIA

Sedalia Flea Market
Hwy. 65 South
(816) 827-5860

Daily. Souvenirs, used merchandise, garage sale items, glassware, dolls, toys, and jewelry.

SELIGMAN

Highway 37 Flea Market
Hwy. 37
(417) 662-3890

Daily. Used merchandise, country and farm collectibles, souvenirs, novelties, handcrafts, giftware. Indoor/outdoor market nine miles from Roaring River State Park. Great trout fishing in the area. Camping available. Market open to food vendors.

SEYMOUR

The Living Rock Sell R' Swap
226 Clinton Ave.
Old Hwy. 60

Monday–Saturday, 10 a.m.–6 p.m. Antiques, collectibles, crafts, and lots and lots of secondhand junk. *Contact* David Winter (417) 935-2743.

SIKESTON

Tradewinds Flea Market
875 Malone Ave.
Old Hwy. 60
(573) 471-3965
Fax (573) 471-8419

Friday, Saturday, Sunday, dawn to dusk. Average daily attendance 3,500. Approximately 200 dealers. Indoor, wide-open market, lots of new merchandise, sports-related merchandise, sportswear. Some good collectible booths, glassware, silver, crafts, art, and decorator items. Good market for wintertime selling. Snack bars, rest rooms, h/a, ample parking. Space from $7. *Contact* Kim Byrd, 875 W. Malone Ave., 63801.

Sikeston Trade Fair
Blodgett Rd.
330 H Hwy.
(573) 472-2683 or 472-9964

Friday, Saturday, Sunday. New and used merchandise, garage sale items, crafts, and produce available. Snack bar, rest rooms.

SPRINGFIELD

South Peer Antique Mall & Flea Market
317 South Ave.
South of town square
(417) 831-6558

Daily, 9:30 a.m.–5 p.m. Sixty dealers. Furniture, glass, china, linens, jewelry, primitives, toys, and books available.

Cherry Tree Flea Market
1459 E. Cherry St.
(417) 831-7230

Daily, Monday–Saturday, 10 a.m.–6 p.m., Sunday, 12 p.m.–5 p.m. Used furniture, collectibles, comics, clothing, jewelry, new and used electronics available.

S.T.D. East Flea Market (formerly The Variety Shop)
1820 E. Trafficway
(417) 831-6367

Daily, 10 a.m.–6 p.m. Glassware, baseball cards, toys, crafts, books, furniture, collectibles, and antiques available.

S.T.D. West Flea Market (formerly The Variety Shop)
651 S. Kansas
(417) 831-6331

Daily, 10 a.m.–7 p.m., Friday, until 9 p.m. Glassware, antiques, collectibles, furniture, books, crafts, toys, and baseball cards available.

G&W Antiques & Collectible Flea Market
400 W. Commercial
(417) 869-0061

Monday–Saturday, 10 a.m.–6 p.m. Glass, furniture, jewelry, railroad items, quilts, linens, primitives, and toys available. Credit cards accepted.

Flea Market & Swap Meet
University Plaza Trade Center

Monthly, market opens at 7:30 a.m. Approximately 200 dealers. RV hookups available. Space from $20. *Contact* Floyd Cillabough, 809 E. Hill St., 65803 (417) 833-1380.

NOTE: Springfield is the gateway to the Ozarks vacation land and springboard to Branson, home of today's country music. There are many fine shops and attractions here; plan to spend a few days exploring. Many excellent restaurants.

Viking Flea Market
626 W. Chase
(417) 869-4237

Daily, except Wednesdays. Indoor market with approximately 30 permanent dealers. *Contact* Viking Flea Market, 626 W. Chase St., 65803.

Olde Towne Flea Market
600 Booneville Ave.

Monday, Wednesday, Thursday, Friday, Saturday, 9:30 a.m.–5 p.m., Sunday, 1 p.m.–5 p.m. Approximately 100 dealers. Antiques, collectibles, and furniture available. Snack bar, rest rooms, h/a, ample parking. Monthly rentals only, from $125. *Contact* Lana Hall, Olde Towne Flea Market, 600 Booneville Ave., 65801 (417) 831-6665.

Sac River Trade & Antique Mall
Hwy. 13
(417) 756-2201

Friday, Saturday, Sunday. Antiques, furniture, collectibles, silver, coins, linens, quilts, glassware, kitchen collectibles, books, art, and prints. Snack bar, rest rooms, h/a, ample parking.

Park Central Flea Market
429 Booneville
(417) 831-7516

Monday–Saturday, 10 a.m.–5 p.m., Sunday, 12 p.m.–5 p.m. Antiques, primitives, glass, linens, toys, collectibles, china, furniture, and sports cards available. Market is located on two floors.

Northtown Flea Mart
3310 N. Glenstone

Daily. Indoor market with approximately 20 permanent dealers. Some antiques and collectibles, mostly used and flea market merchandise, and lots of bric-a-brac available. Monthly rentals only. Market closed on Wednesday. *Contact* Peggy Humbird, 3310 N. Glenstone Ave., 65801 (417) 833-3533.

I-44 Swap Meet
1724 W. Kearney
I-44 and Neergard, fronts on I-44
(417) 864-4340 or 866-7493
Fax (417) 864-6508

Saturday, Sunday, March–December, dawn to dusk. Outdoor market with over 200 dealers who offer lots of new merchandise, sportswear, electronics, imports, gifts, sports-related merchandise, farm items, and secondhand and garage sale merchandise. Snack bar, rest rooms, ample parking. Space from $6 per day. *Contact* Bob, 2743 W. Kearney, 65803.

Southtown Flea Market
2139 S. Campbell
Two blocks south of Bass Pro
(417) 882-1707

Monday–Saturday, 9:30 a.m.–5 p.m., Sunday, 12 p.m.–5 p.m. More than 35 dealers, 5,000-square-foot facility. Antique furniture, advertising items, glassware, and lots of miscellaneous items. Free coffee.

Springfield Flea Market
Fairgrounds
(417) 833-5119

Every second weekend. New market with inside and outside space available. Market is strong on antiques, collectibles, and new merchandise.

Great Discoveries Flea Market & Antique Furniture
416 W. Commercial
(417) 869-9101

Monday–Saturday. Collectibles, glass, linens, jewelry, primitives, and books. Credit cards accepted.

Kountry Korner Flea Market
1917 W. Atlantic
(417) 865-9510

Monday–Saturday, 9 a.m.–5 p.m; summer hours, 9 a.m.–6 p.m. Collectibles, crafts, new merchandise, glass, jewelry, used furniture, tools, and lots of secondhand merchandise.

Country Corner Flea Market
351 Booneville
(417) 862-1597

Monday–Saturday, 10 a.m.–5 p.m., Sunday, 12 p.m.–5 p.m. Antiques, collectibles, records, books, tapes, toys, jeans, and furniture available.

Treasure Finders Antiques & Flea Market
1722 S. Seiger
Behind Andy's
(417) 883-3373

Monday–Saturday, 9 a.m.–6 p.m., Sunday, 12 p.m.–5 p.m. Antique furniture, tools, baseball cards, glass, toys, dolls, and general secondhand merchandise.

UNION

Mason-Dixon Line Flea Market
I-44 and Hwy. 50
(636) 583-2014

Saturday, Sunday. Primarily new merchandise and secondhand junk. Inside and outside spaces. Snack bar, rest rooms, h/a, ample parking.

WARRENSBURG

B&B Swap & Shop, Flea Market & Large Variety Mall
Hwy. 50 and Southside Rd.
One-half mile east of Knob Noster

Tuesday–Sunday, 9 a.m.–5:30 p.m. Antiques, collectibles, crafts, glassware, primitives, sports cards, furniture, and new merchandise available.

WARSAW

AJ's Trade Fair
Hwy. 7 and Truman Dam
(816) 438-5707

Daily, 9 a.m.–7 p.m. Approximately 75 dealers. Indoor/outdoor market with some covered spaces. New and used merchandise, some collectibles and primitives. Restaurant and bakery. Rest rooms, ample parking. Camping with electricity available. Market is located in the center of resort area and often has live entertainment. Space from $3 per day.

WASHINGTON

Washington Flea Market
217 Elm St.
(636) 239-5386

Wednesday–Sunday. Collectibles, glassware, primitives, farm items, new merchandise, crafts, produce, snack bar.

WENTZVILLE

Wentzville Flea Market
City Park, Downtown Main St.
(314) 327-6538

Sunday. Large outdoor market with unusually large amounts of antiques and quality collectibles. Limited inside space. New and used merchandise, garage sale items, crafts. Strong attendance for this one-day event. Snack bar, rest rooms, ample parking, h/a, although there is some difficult terrain here. Space from $15. Note: This market does not take reservations and is a real madhouse to set up in. You have to get there at 3–4 a.m. For me it's not worth the stress.

WEST PLAINS

Monthly Flea Market
Fairgrounds
(417) 256-2198

Monthly. Antiques, collectibles, new and used merchandise, and crafts available. Food available, rest rooms, h/a, ample parking. Call for current schedule.

MONTANA

BEATRICE

Town & Country Flea Market
U.S. Hwy. 77

Saturday, Sunday.

BILLINGS

Great American Flea Market
1600 Main St.
North of fairgrounds

Daily. Indoor space year-round—outside space during April–November. Approximately 110 dealers. Average attendance 1,100 daily. Market is strong on antiques and good collector items. Space from $80 per month. Reservations recommended. Electricity available. *Contact* Jake Jabs, 1600 Main St., 59105 (406) 259-6490.

Big Sky Flea Market
2221 Old Hardin Rd.
I-90, Exit 452 or 455

Saturday, Sunday, 7 a.m.–5 p.m. Seasonal market open March–October. Small outdoor market with approximately 15 dealers. Snack bar, rest room. Space from $10. Free parking. *Contact* Tom Moore, Box 22732, 59104 (406) 248-2424.

ALWAYS CALL BEFORE TRAVELING LONG DISTANCES!

GLENDIVE

Flea Market

Saturday, Sunday. Overnight camping available. *Contact* Gordon Matisheck, 518 Snyder Ave., 59930.

GREAT FALLS

Big Sky Swap-O-Rama
Fairgrounds

Monthly. Average attendance 5,000. Approximately 100 vendors. Space from $20 daily. Reservations recommended. Camping from $3 to $6. No outside food concessions allowed. *Contact* Mark or Chuck, Box 7281, (406) 791-8086.

Great Falls Farmers Market
Civic Center parking lot

Saturday, Wednesday, July–October. Traditional outdoor farmers' market with crafts. Space from $25 plus 10%. Food available, rest rooms, h/a. *Contact* Michael Winters, 2406 6th St. Northwest 59401 (406) 761-3881.

Great Falls Flea Market
5700 2nd Avenue North
(406) 453-4615

Saturday, Sunday.

Kat's Swap Mart
112 Central Avenue

Daily. Indoor market. Space from $3 daily. *Contact* Kathleen Rodgers (406) 761-9401.

KALISPELL

Kalispell Flea Market
265 N. Meridan Rd.
(406) 257-7461

Saturday, Sunday.

MISSOULA

The Eldorado Weekend Market
1900 W. Broadway
(406) 721-4743

Saturday, Sunday. Indoor/outdoor market. Camping and electricity available.

NEBRASKA

GRAND ISLAND

Great Exchange Indoor Flea Market
3235 S. Locust Hwy.
Junction of Hwy. 34
I-80, Exit 312, north five miles

Monday–Saturday, 10 a.m.–5 p.m., Sunday, 12 p.m.–5 p.m. Closed on holidays. Indoor market with approximately 50 dealers. Mostly collectibles, advertising items, primitives, country items, collectibles, glassware, silver, and new and used merchandise available. Rest rooms, ample parking. Rental by month only. *Contact* Andrea Lee, 3235 S. Locust Ave., 68801 (308) 381-4075.

KEARNEY

Buffalo County Antique Fair
Fairgrounds
Corner of 34th and N St.
(308) 987-2633

Monthly. Indoor and outdoor market. Antiques, collectibles, farm items, western collectibles, quality jewelry, new and used merchandise available. Food available, rest rooms, ample parking. *Contact* Cynthia Svarvari, 403 9th St., Overton 68863. Market is seasonal, usually during spring and fall. Promoter also produces other antique and collector events in the local area; call for dates and locations.

LINCOLN

Sunrise Sunset Flea Market
State Fairgrounds
(402) 467-4836 or 466-0334

Saturday, Sunday. Large midwestern commercial market with a wide range of goods. A bit of everything including: new merchandise, used desirables and garage sale items, antiques, collectibles, farm and ranch items, western and Indian jewelry, art, decorator items, and collectibles. Food available, rest rooms, h/a, ample parking Space from $10 daily for 22×18. Approximately 600 spaces. *Contact* Manager, Box 4212, 68504.

Indoor Flea Market
Pershing Auditorium
226 Centennial Mall

Monthly, 10 a.m.–5 p.m. Admission charge. Antiques, collector items, farm-related fare, handcrafted treasures, and new and used merchandise available. Snack bar, rest rooms, h/a. Parking can be difficult. Space from $45. For dates for more information *contact* Derek Anderson, Box 81126, 68501.

Flea Market Emporium
Indian Village Shopping Center
3235 S. 13th St.

Monday–Saturday. Indoor market with approximately 50 dealers. Snack bar, rest room, h/a. Ample free parking. *Contact* Ruth Trobee (402) 423-5380.

OMAHA

CLBC Flea Market
11000 N. 72nd St.

Saturday, Sunday. Approximately 40 dealers. New and used merchandise, housewares, jewelry, sportswear, garage sale items, western wear and collectibles, T-shirts, and plenty of this-n-that. Food available. Inside and outside space available from $6. *Contact* Richard Bechtloff, 12434 Westwood Lane 68144 (402) 572-9568 or 333-4507.

36 & W Flea Market
Bingo Hall
36th and W Sts.

Every second Sunday. Approximately 50 table-top dealers. Collectibles, silver, coins, jewelry, sports-cards, vintage clothing, glassware, tools, toys, marbles, and western and Indian collectibles available. Snack bar, rest rooms, h/a. Space from $8.50 per day. *Contact* Ronald Beranek, 5215 S. 21st St., 68107 (402) 291-6280.

Soko Hall
13th and Martha Sts.
(402) 493-0133

Last Sunday. Approximately 100 dealers. New and used merchandise, collectibles, antiques, silver, glassware, tools, toys, coins, sports cards, and jewelry are available. Food available, rest rooms, h/a, ample parking. Space from $12.50.

Blue Ribbon Flea Market and Antique Mall
6606 Grove St.

Daily, 9 a.m.–6 p.m. Closed on major holidays. Indoor market with approximately 200 dealers. Antiques, collectibles, crafts, new and used merchandise, furniture. Space by the month from $42. Snack bar, rest rooms, h/a. Ample free parking. *Contact* George LaPole, 6606 Grover St., 68106 (402) 397-6811.

Flea Market
Mueller Recreation Hall

Every second Sunday. Average attendance 1,000. Approximately 100 dealers. Antiques, collectibles, western and Indian jewelry, art and collectibles, kitchen collectibles, toys, farm and ranch collectibles, glassware, jewelry, primitives, coins, silver, vintage clothing. Space from $8.50. Ample parking. *Contact* Ronald Beranek, 16606 Iske Dr., 68123 (402) 291-6280.

SOUTH SIOUX CITY

Siouxland Flea Market
2009 Dakota Ave.

Monday–Saturday, 9 a.m.–6 p.m. Indoor market with approximately 100 dealers. Antiques, collectibles, ceramics, art, memorabilia, advertising items, collectible glassware, silver, new and used merchandise, and housewares available. Snack bar. Monthly rentals only. *Contact* Roberta Gallup, 2009 Dakota Ave., 68776 (402) 494-3221.

Flea Market
Sioux Land Convention Center
Corner of 5th St. and C Ave.
(605) 361-1717

Every second weekend, Saturday, 9 a.m.–5 p.m., Sunday, 11 a.m.–4 p.m. Admission charge. Approximately 250 dealers. Good antiques, collectibles, primitives, farm items and farm toys, glassware, silver, furniture, and jewelry are available. This market is always worth attending. There are always some real fine bargains on quality items. Snack bar, rest rooms, h/a, ample street parking. Space from $16 per day. *Contact* Ed Benson, Box 236, 57101.

WALTHILL

Flea Market and Hillbilly Auction
I-75, 60 miles north of Decatur

First weekend. Seasonal market February–October. Indoor/outdoor market with approximately 50 dealers. New and used merchandise, garage sale merchandise, collectibles, some quality primitives, farm equipment, livestock. Auctions at 1 p.m. Space from $10 for the weekend. Ample free parking. *Contact* Don Nottleman, Rte. 1, 68067 (402) 846-9150 or 349-9320.

NEVADA

CARSON CITY

Carson City Flea Market
1888 Hot Springs Rd.
Corner of Hot Springs and Goni Rds.
at the west end of Carson City Airport

Saturday, Sunday, May–October. Approximately 40 vendors. New and used merchandise, garage sale items, souvenirs, and lots of western and Indian items here. Snack bar, rest rooms, h/a, ample parking. Space from $10. *Contact* Bill Reeves, Box 4069, 89702 (702) 882-4238.

Carson Flea Market
9000 E. Hwy. 50

Saturday, Sunday, 8 a.m.–5 p.m. Average daily attendance 400. Approximately 50 dealers offer used merchandise, garage sale items, farm and ranch items, jewelry, housewares, clothing, and crafts. Plenty of useful desirables for the whole family. Food on premises, rest rooms, h/a. Inside and outside exhibit space available from $4. No overnight parking. *Contact* Elmer Rickey, Box 436, 89702 (702) 246-3500.

FERNLEY

Frontier Village Flea Market
Hwy. 46 off I-80

Friday, Saturday, Sunday. New and used merchandise, sportswear, and western wear. Also jewelry, Indian trinkets, western collectibles, art, and artifacts. An array of crafts, produce, and much more. Food available, rest rooms, h/a, ample parking. Space from $4 daily. Overnight parking available. *Contact* Lew Sprankle, Box 1547, 89408 (702) 574-4445.

LAS VEGAS

Fantastic Indoor Swap Meet
1717 S. Decatur

Friday, Saturday, Sunday, 10 a.m.–6 p.m. Admission $1. Large indoor market. Mainly new merchandise and imports. Housewares, sportswear, sports items, jewelry, electronics, and lots of hot new trendy California merchandise here, including souvenirs and novelties. Snack bars, rest rooms, h/a, ample parking. *Contact* Berny Krebs, Box 26179, 89126 (702) 877-0087, fax (702) 877-3102.

Las Vegas Swap Meet
Sunset Drive-In Theater
(702) 748-7550

Saturday, Sunday. New merchandise, electronics, sportswear, housewares, jewelry, lots of western clothing, sports merchandise, souvenirs, and novelties available. Also plenty of used and garage sale items, Indian jewelry, art, and artifacts. Snack bar, rest rooms, h/a, ample parking.

Tanner's World Wide Flea Market
Convention Center

Monthly. Admission charge. Approximately 400 dealers. Inside, well-attended market. Wide range of merchandise with many fine-quality items. Lots of fine jewelry to be found here, quite often some rare pieces. Food available, rest rooms, h/a, ample parking, parking charge. Space starts at $45. Reservations recommended.

NOTE: Sellers be advised, Las Vegas requires a city license to sell at its flea markets. There is a two-week waiting period to obtain the license.

Contact Clare Tanner, 1636 E. Charleston Blvd., 89104 (702) 382-8355.

Indoor Swap Meet
3455 Boulder Hwy.

Friday, Saturday, Sunday, 10 a.m.–6 p.m. Admission charge $1. Primarily new merchandise, imports, electronics, tapes, sportswear, western wear, sports cards, souvenirs, jewelry, housewares, and gifts available. Some good bargains on new discounted merchandise. Approximately 400 booths packed with a little of everything bargain hunters are looking for. Snack bars, rest rooms, h/a, ample parking. Space by the month only. *Contact* Benny Krebs, 3455 Boulder Hwy., 89121 (702) 641-7927.

The Sampler Shoppers
6115 W. Tropicana (at Jones St.)
(702) 368-1170

Daily, 10 a.m.–6 p.m. New 40,000-square-foot indoor market with approximately 150 dealers. Antiques, collectibles, fine art, primitives, jewelry, and interior design items available. Tearoom, rest rooms, h/a, ample parking. *Contact* The Sampler Shoppers, 6115 W. Tropicana, 89103.

NORTH LAS VEGAS

Broad Acres Flea Market
2934 Las Vegas Blvd. North

Friday, Saturday, Sunday, from 6:30 a.m. Admission charge 75 cents. Outdoor market with average attendance of 20,000 for the weekend. Approximately 400 dealers. New and used merchandise, antiques, collectibles, jewelry of all types, western and Indian items, crafts, and produce available. Lots of shade, snack bars, beer and soda carts, rest rooms, h/a, ample parking. One of the oldest and best swap meets in Nevada. Great market to plan a stop. Space from $8 daily. *Contact* Jake Bowman, Box 3059, 89030 (702) 642-3777.

RENO

El Rancho Swap Meet
555 El Rancho Dr. (Sparks)

Friday, Saturday, Sunday, 6 a.m.–4 p.m. Admission charge 50 cents. Average daily attendance 3,000. Approximately 200 dealers. A classic swap meet with loads of new and used merchandise, secondhand items, collectibles, and advertising items available. Snack bar, rest rooms, h/a, ample parking. Space from $15 per weekend. *Contact* Denise Grays, 555 El Rancho Dr., 89431 (775) 331-3227, fax (775) 359-2833.

Tanner's World Wide Flea Market
Reno Convention Center

Monthly. Admission charge. Inside market with excellent attendance. Trendy and upscale items with lots of better-grade merchandise. Food available, rest rooms, h/a, ample parking. Space from $40 daily. Call for exact dates. *Contact* Clare Tanner, 1636 E. Charleston Blvd., Las Vegas, 89104 (702) 382-8355.

Bonanza Indoor Arts, Crafts & Flea Market
Western Village
(775) 329-5437

Saturday, Sunday. New and used merchandise, souvenirs, novelties, sportswear, western wear, crafts, lots of imported crafts, jewelry, and used merchandise available. Snack bar, rest rooms, h/a, ample parking.

SILVER SPRINGS

Silver Springs Flea Market
Hwy. 50
Three miles west of Junction of Hwys. 50 and 95A

Daily. Approximately 10–15 vendors. Average attendance 500. New and used merchandise, souvenirs; market is heavily loaded with garage sale items. Market has cafe, tire shop, auction, propane, water, rest rooms, and ample parking. Space $2 to $10. *Contact* Wanda Merritt, Box 21, 89429 (702) 577-2582.

NEW HAMPSHIRE

AMHERST

Outdoor Antiques Market
Rte. 122

Sunday, April–October, weather permitting. Admission charge. Indoor and outdoor market with approximately 100 dealers. Lots of antiques, antique furniture, memorabilia, advertising items, antique toys, and collectibles at this market. Good food here. Rest rooms, h/a, ample parking. This is a quaint and very classic New England market. Space from $5. Reservations recommended. *Contact* Werner Carlson, 51R Dudley St., Arlington, MA 02174 (603) 673-2093 or (781) 641-0600, fax (781) 641-0647.

DAVISVILLE

Davisville Barn Sale & Flea Market

Sundays, 8 a.m.–4 p.m. Seasonal market open May–October. Indoor market. *Contact* Toby Nickerson (800) 662-2612 or (603) 746-4000.

DERRY

Grandview Farm Flea Market
Rte. 28 at bypass

Saturday, Sunday, May–October, 7 a.m.–4 p.m. Admission charge. Inside and outside market with approximately 300 dealers. Wide range of goods at this market. Antiques, collectibles, jewelry, primitives, memorabilia, glassware, new and used merchandise, sportswear, and housewares are available. Market has live entertainment on weekends. This market sells a lot of reptiles. Strong attendance and a most interesting and enjoyable market to shop at or to sell at. Food available, rest rooms, h/a, ample parking. Space from $20. *Contact* Kathi Taylor, 34 S. Main St., 03086 (603) 432-2326.

HOLLIS

Hollis Flea Market
436 Silver Lake Rd.
Rte. 122

Sunday, April–November, 7 a.m.–4 p.m. Outdoor market. Over 200 dealers. Collectibles, memorabilia, farm items, primitives, advertising items, new and used merchandise, sportswear, housewares, and interesting secondhand items abound here. Good attendance at this market. Snack bar, rest rooms, h/a, ample parking, $1 parking charge. Space from $14. *Contact* Gil or Alice Prieto, 36 Atherton Ave., Nashua, 03060 (603) 465-7813 or 882-6134, fax (603) 882-0927. E-mail: hollisflea@aol.com.

Silver Lake Flea Market and Antique Fair
447 Silver Lake Rd. (Rte. 122)

Sundays, 5:30 a.m.–4 p.m. Outdoor market with approximately 100 dealers. Antiques, collectibles, primitives, crafts, new and used merchandise. Space from $15. Ample free parking. *Contact* Bradford Tukey, Box 100, 03049 (603) 465-7677, fax (603) 465-9898. E-mail: bhtukey@aol.com.

HUDSON

Hudson Antique Show & Flea Market
Rte. 111

Sunday, April–October. Admission charge. Lots of quality items here, antiques, furniture, silver, glassware, pottery, memorabilia, coins, vintage clothing, and a great selection of desirable collector items. Food available, rest rooms, h/a, ample parking. Indoor market. Space from $14. *Contact* Don Hold (603) 880-8149 or 883-1738. Market is restricted to antiques and is sponsored by the local Lions Club.

KEENE

Fairgrounds Antique Co-op
Fairgrounds
Rte. 12 South
(603) 352-0679

Saturday, Sunday. Antiques, collector items, furniture, silver, glassware, pottery, vintage clothing, jewelry, kitchen collectibles, primitives, and advertising items available. Good food here. Rest rooms, h/a, ample parking. Clean, friendly, well-managed market.

LONDONDERRY

Londonderry Gardens
Rte. 102
(603) 883-4196 or 880-9935

Saturday, Sunday, April–October, 8 a.m.–4 p.m. Average daily attendance 3,000. Approximately 200 dealers. Large market with a wide variety of goods; antiques, collectibles, new and used merchandise, and crafts available. Snack bars, rest rooms, h/a, ample parking with lots of walking. Space from $10. Food vendors allowed.

MERRIMACK

Merrimack Flea & Antique Market
Rte. 3

Sunday. Approximately 100 dealers. Admission charge. Antiques, furniture, quality booths of many collector lines, silver, jewelry, and vintage clothing available. Food available, rest rooms, h/a, ample parking. Inside and outside space available from $10. *Contact* Walter Lang, 175 Amherst St., Nashua, 03060 (603) 882-6962.

NORTH CONWAY

North Conway Flea Market
Mt. Washington Valley Trade Center

Saturday, Sunday. Approximately 200 dealers. New merchandise, electronics, sportswear, tools, jewelry, housewares, clothing, toys, sports cards, used merchandise, garage sale items, crafts, produce, collectibles, and decorator items available. Snack bars, rest rooms, h/a, ample parking. *Contact* Robert Tate (603) 356-3665.

SALEM

New England's Largest Flea Market
20 Hampshire Rd.
(603) 893-8888

Sunday. Antiques, furniture, complete line of collector items, kitchenware, primitives, memorabilia, vintage clothing, art, prints, books, silver, coins, jewelry, new and used merchandise, and crafts available. Food available, rest rooms, h/a, ample parking.

WEST LEBANON

Colonial Antique Market
Airport Rd.
Route 12-A. I-89, Exit 20

Sundays, 9 a.m.–5:30 p.m. Outdoor flea market on Sundays with a full-scale antique mall open daily. Lots of quality antiques and smalls here at both the antique mall and the Sunday flea market. Approximately 50 dealers. Space from $12 per day for the flea market. Good food here, rest rooms, h/a. Ample free parking. *Contact* The Andersons, 5 Airport Rd., #23, Colonial Plaza, 03784 (603) 298-8132 or 298-7712.

INFORMATION IS SUBJECT TO CHANGE—ALWAYS CALL FIRST!

NEW JERSEY

ABSECON

L'erario's Flea Market
Jim Leeds and Pitney Rds.
Rte. 561

Saturday, Sunday, April–October, 7 a.m. until dark. Over 50 dealers. New and used merchandise, antiques, collectibles, crafts, video shop, and pet shop. Restaurant, deli, and ice cream shop. Outdoor market. Space from $12 Saturday and $15 Sunday. Camping available (no charge). *Contact* J. L'erario, Box 572, 08201 (609) 652-0540.

BELVEDERE

Five Acres Flea Market
Rte. 46 South

Saturday, Sunday, 7 a.m. until dark. Indoor and outdoor market with approximately 100 vendors. New merchandise, sportswear, housewares, antiques, collectibles, crafts, art, produce, and secondhand items available. Food available, bar, rest rooms, game room, h/a, ample parking. Space from $15. *Contact* Totsy Phillips, Box 295, 07823 (908) 475-2572.

BERLIN

Berlin Farmers Market
41 Clementown Rd.
Rte. 54

Thursday–Sunday, 8 a.m.–4 p.m. Average daily attendance over 10,000. On any given day there are 4–500 dealers. Wide range of merchandise outdoors. A pure New England flea and farmers' market. Indoor mini mall with over 80 specialty shops. One of the area's largest and best markets. This one is a real pleasure for shoppers and sellers. A wide variety of food here. Rest rooms, h/a, ample parking. Approximately 7–800 spaces from $20. Reservations required. *Contact* Stan Giberson, Jr., 41 Clementown Rd., 08009 (856) 767-1246, fax 767-1284.

CINNAMINSON

House of Antiques Flea Market
Cinnaminson Mall
Rte. 130
(609) 829-9711

Friday. Antiques, furniture, collectibles, silver, coins, advertising items, primitives, kitchen collectibles, plenty of country and Victorian-era desirables, and jewelry available. Snack bar, rest rooms, h/a, ample parking.

CLIFFSIDE PARK

Flea Market
588 Anderson Ave.
(201) 941-0007

Second and fourth Sunday, May–October. Antiques, collectibles, new and used merchandise, crafts, and produce available. Food available, rest rooms, ample parking.

CLINTON

Colonial Clinton Fleatique
Rte. 31, north of city
(201) 638-8716

Saturday, Sunday, April–November. New and used merchandise, general flea market merchandise, crafts, and collectibles available. Food available, rest rooms, h/a, ample parking.

COLUMBUS

Columbus Farmers Market
2919 Rte. 206 South
New Jersey Tpke., Exit 7
Five miles south
(609) 267-0400

Thursday–Sunday, from 9 a.m. Outdoor market with approximately 1,000 dealers. Antiques, collectibles, produce, and lots of used merchandise available. This is a don't-miss market with an excellent variety of dealers selling just about everything. Some really nice booths here. Good selection of food on premises including a bakery, clean rest rooms, ample parking. Over 70 inside stores and specialty shops. Lots of walking here so dress accordingly. Space from $30. *Contact* Columbus Shopping Center, 2919 Rte. 206 South, 08022.

DORCHESTER

Campbell's Flea Market
Rte. 47
Three miles south of Hwy. 55

Saturday, Sunday, March–December, 7 a.m.–4 p.m. Indoor/outdoor market with approximately 100 dealers. Lots of collectibles, vintage clothing, crafts, jewelry, and housewares available. Snack bar. Very picturesque market located in a scenic area. *Contact* Stewart Campbell, Box 131, 08316 (609) 785-2222.

EAST BRUNSWICK

Route 18 Multi Merchandise Market Inc.
290 Rte. 18
New Jersey Tpke. Exit 9

Friday, Saturday, Sunday, 10 a.m.–6 p.m. Average attendance 20–30,000 per weekend. Approximately 250 dealers. Large selection of new merchandise. Everything you will find at Wal-Mart, except all merchandise is severely discounted. A bargain hunter's dream. Snack bar, rest rooms, h/a, ample parking. Indoor market. Monthly rentals only. *Contact* Barbara Posswaters, 08816 (908) 254-5080, fax 254-1761.

EAST ORANGE

Brick Church Flea Market
540 Main St.

Thursday–Sunday. Approximately 75 dealers. New merchandise, electronics, sportswear, jewelry, gifts, sports merchandise, housewares, used merchandise, and collectibles available. Year-round, indoor market. Snack bar, rest rooms, h/a, ample parking. Space from $45. *Contact* Tony Spina, 540 Main St., 07018 (201) 674-2226.

EAST RUTHERFORD

Meadowlands Marketplace
Giants Stadium parking lot 17
Rte. 3 West
I-80, take Rte. 46 East

Thursday, Friday, Saturday, 9 a.m.–5 p.m. Large outdoor market with approximately 500 dealers. Good selection of merchandise here and a wide variety in dealers. Lots of new items, gifts, imports, glassware, collectibles, advertising items, beer items, crafts, and art available. Good selection of food, rest rooms, h/a, ample parking. Space from $40. *Contact* Larry Fishman, Meadowlands, 07073 (888) 445-6543 or (201) 935-5474, fax (201) 935-5495.

EDISON

Flea Market
New Dover United Methodist Church
690 New Dover Rd.
(908) 381-7904

Tuesday, March–December. Approximately 100 dealers offer collectibles, produce, crafts, new and used merchandise, bric-a-brac, and lots of garage sale items. Food available, rest rooms, ample parking. Inside and outside space available from $20. *Contact* United Methodist Church, 690 New Dover Rd., 08820.

ENGLISHTOWN

Englishtown Flea Market
90 Wilson Ave.
New Jersey Tpke., Exit 9
(732) 446-9644
Fax (732) 446-1220

Saturday, 7 a.m.–5 p.m., Sunday, 9 a.m.–5 p.m. Approximately 400 dealers. Wide range of merchandise at this market. Booths are well stocked by many quality-conscious dealers. Plenty of good food. Well-attended market. A good market for commercial vendors. The Englishtown Flea Market has been in business since 1929. Very popular local attraction. Indoor and outdoor space available from $5 per day. Snack bars, rest rooms, h/a, ample parking. *Contact* English Auction Sales, 90 Wilson Ave., 07726 (732) 446-9644, fax (732) 446-1220.

FARMINGDALE

Collingswood Auction & Flea Market
Hwys. 33 and 34

Friday, Saturday, Sunday. New merchandise, closeouts, surplus, used desirables, housewares, clothing, jewelry, sports merchandise, country collectibles, antiques, and furniture are available. Food available, rest rooms, h/a, ample parking. Year-round market. Approximately 125 inside spaces, 550 outside. Space from $2 on Friday, Saturdays $6 and $9. Permit required for food. *Contact* Roland Schneider, 1350 State Hwy. 33, 07727, (732) 938-7941 or 919-9821, fax (732) 938-4652.

FLEMINGTON

Flemington Flea Market
Hwy. 31
Approximately one mile off Flemington Circle

Wednesday, Friday, April–November, 7 a.m.–3 p.m. Approximately 75 dealers. In addition to the mountains of new and used flea market goodies shoppers will find antiques, memorabilia, primitives, advertising items, paper goods, collectibles, not to mention crafts and produce. Snack bar. Indoor and outdoor space available from $6. *Contact:* Melissa Yerkes, 25 Kuhl Rd., 08822 (908) 782-7326 or 782-2413.

FRENCHTOWN

Frenchtown Merchants Market
(201) 526-4620

Saturday, Sunday. Inside and outside spaces. New and used merchandise, garage-sale-type finds, crafts, gifts, decorator items, collectibles, coins, and sports cards available. Snack bar, rest rooms, h/a, ample parking.

GILLETTE

Meyersville Grange Antique Mart
Meyersville Rd. between Rtes. 78 and 24

Sunday, April–October, 8 a.m.–3 p.m. Approximately 35 dealers. Antiques, collectibles, and nice-quality decorator and craft items available. Indoor market with space from $15 per table. *Contact* Ron Miller, 1163 Washington Valley Rd., Basking Ridge, NJ 07920.

HIGHLANDS

L'eranio's Flea Market
Jim Leeds and Phitney Rds.
(201) 595-5041

Every second Sunday. Antiques, furniture, collectibles, country and farm items, silver, vintage clothing, used merchandise, housewares, crafts. Rest rooms, h/a, food available. Market operates April–October. Ample parking.

LAKEWOOD

Route 70 Flea Market
117 Rte. 70 and Lakewood Ave.

Friday–Sunday, 7 a.m.–4 p.m. Indoor/outdoor market with approximately 400 dealers. Lots of collectibles, advertising items, jewelry, new merchandise, sportswear, and housewares available here. Snack bar, rest rooms, h/a, ample parking. Space from $7. *Contact* Yvonne

Weintraub, 117 Rte. 70, 08701 (908) 370-1837, fax (908) 840-5684.

LAMBERTVILLE

Lambertville Antique Flea Market
Rte. 29, 1.5 miles south of town

Wednesday, Saturday, Sunday, 8 a.m.–4 p.m. Market also has an indoor mini mall that is open daily, 10 a.m.–4 p.m. Indoor and outdoor market with approximately 150 dealers. Market is heavy on quality antiques and collectibles. A good stop for the serious collector/investor, shopkeeper, or decorator. Nice restaurant and clean rest rooms. Space from $12. *Contact* Heidi Cekoric, 1864 River Rd., 08530 (609) 397-0456.

Golden Nugget Antique Flea Market
Rte. 29, two miles south of town

Wednesday, Saturday, Sunday, 6 a.m.–4 p.m. Approximately 150 dealers. Antiques, antique furniture, collectibles, crafts, and produce available. Indoor shops open daily with outside weekend flea market. Space from $12. *Contact* Manager, 1850 River Rd., 08530 (609) 397-0811. Note: Market produces a great fall antique extravaganza, usually late in October.

MANAHAWKIN

Manahawkin Flea Market
629 E. Bay Ave., Garden State Pkwy.,
Exit 63

Friday, Saturday, Sunday, 8 a.m.–5 p.m. Indoor/outdoor market with approximately 100 dealers. Antiques, collectibles, locally made crafts, produce, new and used merchandise. Space from $20. Snack bars, rest rooms, h/a. Ample free parking. *Contact* Jill Petrucci, Box 885, 08050 (609) 597-1017, fax (609) 597-1017.

MANVILLE

Manville Flea Market
Washington Ave. and South 13th Ave.
(908) 526-2519

Every first Sunday. Antiques, collectibles, silver, coins, sports cards, sportswear, jewelry, memorabilia, advertising items, primitives, housewares, and used merchandise available. Food available, rest rooms, h/a, ample parking. Inside and outside market sponsored by the fire department.

MEYERSVILLE

Meyersville Grange Antique Market
Myersville Rd.

Sundays, 8 a.m.–3 p.m. Seasonal market open April through October. Indoor market with approximately 25 dealers. *Contact* Ron Miller (908) 689-5188.

MONTCLAIR

Montclair Antiques Market
Lackawana Plaza

Tuesday, Friday. Antiques, furniture, collectibles, memorabilia, jewelry, glassware, silver, vintage clothing, decorator items, kitchen collectibles, primitives, and toys available. Snack bar, rest rooms, h/a, ample parking. *Contact* Mrs. June Emrich, 574 Grove St., Upper Montclair, 07043.

MT. ARLINGTON

Hopatcong Elks Flea Market
Howard Blvd.
(201) 398-9835

Sunday. Antiques, collectibles, silver, coins, jewelry, decorator items, advertising memorabilia, as well as the typical used flea market fare. Approximately 25 spaces. Inside market.

NESHANIC STATION

Neshanic Flea Market
100 Elm St., off Hwy. 202

Sunday, March–December, 7 a.m.–2 p.m. Admission charge. Approximately 100 dealers. Varied line of merchandise here with lots of new merchandise, used items, crafts, bric-a-brac, and some collectibles. Snack bar, rest rooms, h/a, ample parking. Outdoor market with space from $12. *Contact* Mary Weiss, 100 Elm St., 08853, (201) 369-3660.

NEWARK

The Market Place
6839 Ramona Blvd.
I-10, exit at Lane Ave. South

Saturday, Sunday. Indoor/outdoor market with approximately 750 dealers. Wide range of new merchandise, antiques, collectibles, crafts, and produce available. Space from $6. *Contact* Rick Waller, 6839 Ramona Blvd., 07102 (609) 786-1153.

NEW BRUNSWICK

Brunswick Bazaar
710 Somerset Ave.
Rte. 27
(201) 846-9838

Friday, Saturday, Sunday. New and used merchandise, garage sale items, housewares, clothing, and outdoor items available. Snack bar, rest rooms, h/a, ample parking.

NEW EGYPT

New Egypt Auction & Farmers Market
Rte. 537
Between Rtes. 528 and 539
New Jersey Tpke., exit at 7 or 7A

Wednesday, Saturday, Sunday, 7 a.m. until early afternoon. Approximately 100 dealers—all types of merchandise. Many unusual shops here that you would not expect to find at a flea market but make for an interesting place to poke around. Antique and collectible auctions held on Sunday starting at 12 p.m. Space from $6. Inside space available, ample parking. Camping on-site for sellers. *Contact:* Les Heller, Rte. 537, 08533 (609) 758-2082 or (800) 660-2582.

NEWTON

Super Flea Market
Rte. 537
Newton Drive-In Theater

Wednesday, Saturday, Sunday. New merchandise, sportswear, housewares, lots of jewelry and souvenirs, electronics, tools, used merchandise, garage sale fare, collectibles, crafts, and produce available. Approximately 75 dealers. Space from $6. *Contact* Ann Carol Perry (973) 366-4955.

NORTH BERGEN

Hudson County Church Flea Market
1069 89th St.
(201) 861-9798

Sunday, June–September. Antiques, collectibles, glassware, silver, coins, linens, vintage clothing, memorabilia, and country collectibles available. Food available, rest rooms, h/a, ample parking. Indoor market.

PALMYRA

Tacony Palmyra Drive-In Flea Market
Rte. 73 South

Saturday, Sunday, 6 a.m.–3 p.m. Approximately 300 dealers, outdoor market. Lots of new merchandise, sportswear, imports, gifts, housewares, also collectibles, crafts, and fine art available. Plenty of used merchandise, and garage sale items abound. Snack bar, rest rooms, h/a, ample parking. Space from $15 on Saturday and $25 on Sunday. A good market for the commercial vendor. *Contact* Lauresia Phillips, Box 64, 08065 (609) 829-3001.

PATERSON

Paterson Flea Market
Rte. 22

Sunday, April–October. Outdoor market with approximately 50 dealers. Mostly secondhand merchandise. Mountains of trash along with some treasures. Space from $15 per day. *Contact* Paterson Flea Market (914) 878-6660.

PENNSAUKEN

Pennsauken Flea Market
Rtes. 73 and 130
(609) 662-7800

Friday, Saturday, Sunday. New and used flea market merchandise, collectibles, crafts, silver, jewelry, and produce available. Inside and outside spaces. Food available.

PERTH AMBOY

Perth Amboy Moose Lodge Flea Market
Moose Lodge
Convery Blvd.
Rte. 35
(201) 382-3680

Thursday. Antiques, country collectibles, jewelry, watches, linens, vintage clothing, memorabilia, kitchen collectibles, decorator items, and crafts available. Food available, rest rooms, h/a, ample parking.

PISCATAWAY

Arbor Fire Department Flea Market
1780 W. 7th St.
(201) 968-6386

Sunday. Antiques, collectibles, coins, silver, linens, vintage clothing, memorabilia, advertising items, used merchandise, new merchandise, and crafts available. Food available, rest rooms, h/a, ample parking.

PLEASANTVILLE

Pleasantville Flea Market
306 S. Main St.
(609) 344-5079

Friday, Saturday, Sunday, Monday, 9 a.m.–5 p.m. Approximately 50 dealers. New and used merchandise, souvenirs and novelties, jewelry both fine and costume, housewares, sportswear, collectibles, electronics, sports, fishing, and beach merchandise, and crafts available. Indoor/outdoor market. Food available, rest rooms, h/a, ample parking. Space from $10 per day. Camping nearby. Five miles from Atlantic City.

RAHWAY

Rahway Italian-American Club Flea Market
Corner of New Brunswick and Inman Aves.
(732) 574-3849

Wednesday, Friday. Approximately 75 tabletop dealers. New merchandise, sportswear, jewelry, used and secondhand items, and some collectibles available. Snack bar, rest rooms, h/a, ample parking. Space from $15 per table. *Contact* Italian-American Club, 530 New Brunswick Ave., 07065.

RANCOCAS WOODS

William Spencer's Flea Market
Creek Rd. and I-295

Every second Sunday, March–December, 9 a.m.–5 p.m. Outdoor market with approximately 150 dealers.Wide range of goods, collectibles, glassware, silver, antiques, advertising items, paper goods, coins, and primitives available. Quality-oriented market. No new merchandise allowed. Snack bar, rest rooms, h/a, ample parking. Market holds many special events during the season. Well-attended market. *Contact* Isabel Michaski, 118 Creek Rd., 08054 (609) 235-1830, fax 235-8552.

ROCKAWAY

Rockaway Flea Market
350 Rte. 46
(201) 625-9272

Saturday, Sunday. Indoor and outdoor market with approximately 100 dealers. Wide range of goods at this market. New, used, antiques, collectibles, and lots of interesting booths here. Food available, rest rooms, h/a, ample parking. *Contact* Rockaway Flea Market, 350 Rte. 46, 07866.

RUTHERFORD

Super Flea Market
Rte. 3
Drive-In Theater
Across from Meadowlands Sports Complex

Saturday, Sunday. Attendance 5–10,000. Approximately 200 dealers. Large wide-open commercial market with a broad range of goods from new, used, antiques, and collectibles to just plain interesting. Market also open on Tuesday and Thursday evenings. Food available, rest rooms, h/a, ample paved parking. Space from $15 daily, reservations recommended, no food sales allowed. *Contact* Philip LaPorta, 454 Park Ave., 07070, (201) 933-4388.

SOMERVILLE

Packards Farmer & Flea Market
135 Rte. 205 South
(908) 369-3100

Wednesday, Friday. Antiques, collectibles, silver, coins, housewares, jewelry, electronics, lots of secondhand merchandise, as well as crafts, produce, and livestock available. Food available, rest rooms, ample parking.

SPRINGDALE

Springdale Farmers Market
Rte. 206 and Stickles Pond Rd.
(201) 383-9997

Saturday, Sunday. New and used merchandise, antiques, collectibles, silver, jewelry, sportswear, housewares, clothing, country collectibles, crafts, and produce available. Food available, rest rooms, h/a, ample parking. Indoor market.

TRENTON

International Bazaar
Marine Park at the waterfront

Saturday, Sunday. New merchandise, gifts, souvenirs, novelties, imports, used merchandise, crafts, produce, and ethnic packaged food items. Food available, rest rooms, h/a, ample parking. *Contact* Mr. Franklin (609) 695-7532.

VAUXHALL

Union Market
2445 Springfield Ave.
(201) 688-6161

Friday, Saturday, 11 a.m.–9 p.m.; Sunday, 11 a.m.–6 p.m. Year-round market. Wide range of new merchandise. A treasure hunter's bonanza amid the mountains of bric-a-brac, antiques, collectibles, crafts, produce. Approximately 300 spaces. Food available, h/a, lots of walking, rest rooms. Ample parking.

VINELAND

U-Sell Flea & Farm Market
Delsea Dr. and Gant Ave.
(609) 691-1222

Friday, Saturday, Sunday. Approximately 75 dealers offer new merchandise, lots of general flea market and garage sale items, crafts, collectibles, and produce. Snack bar, rest rooms, h/a, ample parking.

Rovers Flea Market
South Delsea Dr.
(609) 691-7654

Friday, Saturday, Sunday. This market has some new merchandise but is heavily weighted with used merchandise, some collectibles, crafts, and produce. Snack bar, rest rooms, ample parking. Space from $2.

WANTAGE

Franklin/Sussex Indoor Flea Market
Junction of Rtes. 23 and 565

Saturday, Sunday. New merchandise, sportswear, jewelry, gifts, decorator items, electronics, housewares, antiques, collectibles, silver, glassware, vintage clothing, and sports cards available. Snack bar, rest rooms, h/a, ample parking.

WARREN

Washington Valley Flea Market
140 Washington Valley Rd.

Sunday, 7:30 a.m.–4 p.m. Outdoor market with approximately 150 dealers during the summer. (Market open indoors only during the winter.) Antiques, collectibles, and new merchandise available here. Market is produced by the Volunteer Fire Department. Space from $12. *Contact* Jerome Boschen, 12 Washington Valley Rd., 07060 (732) 469-2443.

WATCHUNG

Route 22 Watchung Market
1601 Rte. 22 West

Thursday–Sunday. This is a 120,000-square-foot indoor, air-conditioned market. Acres of new merchandise, all the hot, new, trendy items from TV. Personal, household, sports, outdoor merchandise available. This is a budget-conscious shopper's bonanza. Open since 1982. International food court, rest rooms, h/a, 1,500-car parking lot. *Contact* Robert A. Brumale (201) 561-4920.

Watchung Antiques Market
(201) 622-3189

Friday, Saturday, Sunday. Antiques, collectibles, nice furniture selection, lots of quality decorator pieces, silver, coins, glassware, primitives, kitchen collectibles, linens, vintage clothing, fine and estate jewelry available. Snack bar, rest rooms, h/a, ample parking.

WOODBRIDGE

Woodbridge Auction Market
Rte. 9
(908) 634-9760

Wednesday, Friday, Saturday. Approximately 100 dealers. Lots of everything from housewares, clothing, furniture, collectibles, antiques, used and garage sale items, and new merchandise to closeouts and surplus. This is a good finder's market. Food available, rest rooms, ample parking.

WOODSTOWN

Cowtown Flea Market
Rte. 40
Eight miles east of Delaware Memorial Bridge

Tuesday, Saturday. Indoor and outdoor market with approximately 400 dealers. Wide variety of items at this market. Antiques, collectibles, crafts, new and used merchandise, lots of western wear and western items here. Market conducts livestock sales on Tuesday and has a rodeo on its premises on Saturday night. One of the area's better markets. This one has always reminded me more of a big Texas flea market than an eastern market. Space from $15. *Contact* Robert Becker, 780 Rte. 40, Pilesgrove, 08098 (609) 769-3000 or 769-3202.

DAYS, DATES, AND MARKETS ARE SUBJECT TO CHANGE!

NEW MEXICO

ALAMOGORDO

Peddler's Village
900 Zuni Dr.

Saturday, Sunday, 7 a.m.–3 p.m. New market, opened in 1999. Indoor/outdoor market with approximately 50 dealers. Good food here, rest rooms, h/a. Space from $5. Ample free parking. *Contact* Art Page, 900 Zuni Dr., 88310 (505) 443-800, fax (505) 443-8045.

ALBUQUERQUE

Show & Sell Flea Market
State Fairgrounds
I-40, Louisiana St. Exit

Saturday, Sunday. Admission charge $2 plus parking. Outdoor market with approximately 6–700 dealers. This is a large commercial market with mostly new merchandise. Lots of Native American jewelry, art, and artifacts. Lots of food, rest rooms, h/a, ample paved paid parking. Space from $12. *Contact* Hugh Perry, Box 8546, 87198 (505) 265-1791, fax (505) 266-7784.

Indoor Swap Meet
2035 12th St. Northwest
I-40 and 12th St.

Friday, Saturday, Sunday, 10 a.m.–6 p.m. Admission charge. New indoor market with 200 dealers. Lots of southwestern arts and crafts, authentic Indian jewelry, great selection of western wear and cowboy merchandise. Antiques, collectibles, and new and used merchandise also available. Snack bar, rest rooms, h/a, ample parking. *Contact* Richard Westfall, 2035 12th St. NW, 87104 (505) 243-8111.

Classic Century Square Flea Market
4616 Central Southeast
(505) 285-3161 or 294-9904

Daily. Approximately 75 dealers. New and used merchandise, souvenirs, Indian art, jewelry, and artifacts, western wear, and country collectibles available. Food available, rest rooms.

Classic Century Square Market
3100 Juan Tabo Northeast
(505) 285-3161 or 294-9904

Daily. Approximately 75 dealers. New and used merchandise, souvenirs, Indian art, jewelry, and artifacts, western wear, and country collectibles available. Food available, rest rooms, ample parking.

Star Flea Market
543 Coors Blvd. SW

Saturday, Sunday, 6 a.m. until dark. Outdoor market with approximately 100 dealers. New and used merchandise, lots of Indian items and jewelry. Western wear and ranch collectibles. Space from $6 per day. Food available, rest rooms. Ample free parking. *Contact* Joe Rue, 139 Old Coors Rd., 87105 (505) 831-3106, fax (505) 836-1628.

BLOOMFIELD

Highway 64 Flea Market

Friday, Saturday, Sunday. Average daily attendance 400. New and used merchandise, garage sale items, farm and ranch items, western and Indian art, jewelry, and collectibles available. Food available, rest rooms, h/a, ample parking. Spaces 14×24, cost $3. Overnight camping welcome. *Contact* Kent Doak, Box 1235, 87413 (505) 632-2204.

BOSQUE FARMS

BJ's Flea Market
17775-A Bosque Farms Blvd.

Friday, Saturday, Sunday. Outdoor market with approximately 25 dealers. *Contact* Bennie Garcia (505) 869-6995.

CARLSBAD

The Bull Ring
4303 National Parks Hwy.

Tuesday–Sunday, 9 a.m.–5 p.m. Small market with approximately 20 dealers. Lots of secondhand desirables, some new items, collectibles, great amount of western and Indian souvenirs. Space from $5 per day. Food available, rest rooms, h/a. *Contact* Wes Reynolds (505) 887-9174.

CHAPARRAL

The Bounty Hunter Flea Market
413 Chaparral Dr.
Eight miles north of El Paso
(505) 824-4232

Tuesday–Sunday, 7 a.m. until dark. New and used merchandise, garage sale items, jewelry, western wear, housewares, farm and ranch items, produce, and locally made crafts available. Food available, rest rooms. Commercial vendors welcome.

DEMING

Discount Furniture & Variety Flea Market
Motel Dr.
Three blocks west of K-mart

Daily. Average attendance 2,000. Approximately 30–50 dealers. All types of merchandise available here: new merchandise, surplus, overruns, souvenirs, novelties, western wear, new and used furniture, and housewares. Food available, rest rooms, h/a, ample parking, and camping available. Space from $5 per day with electricity. *Contact* George Reynolds, 1316 E. Pine St., 88030 (505) 546-6652.

FARMINGTON

Farmington Flea Market
7701 E. Main St.
Hwy. 550

Friday, Saturday, Sunday, dawn to dusk. Outdoor market with approximately 200 dealers. Wide variety of merchandise here: new and used, including livestock and pets. Snack bar, rest rooms, h/a, ample parking. Space from $3 on Friday and Sunday and $6 on Saturday. *Contact* John Wright, 7701 E. Main St., 87401 (505) 325-3129.

GALLUP

Gallup Flea Market
Old Rte. 666. I-40, Exit 26

Daily, 8 a.m. until dark. Outdoor market with approximately 350 dealers. Antiques, collectibles, lots of Indian jewelry. Indian items and Indian fine art. Space from $10. Snack bar, lots of good Indian food here, rest rooms. Ample free parking. *Contact* Vi Fenley, Box 1888, 87305 (505) 722-7328.

LAS CRUCES

Big Daddy's Flea Market
7320 N. Main St.
Hwy. 70 East
(505) 382-9404 or 382-4055

Saturday, Sunday, 6 a.m.–5 p.m. Average daily attendance of 2,500. Approximately 300 dealers. Large commercial western market with lots of new merchandise, Mexican imports, jewelry, clothing, art, artifacts, western collectibles, crafts (Indian and Mexican), housewares, and produce available. Convenience store, restaurant, rest rooms, h/a, ample parking. Covered and outside spaces available. Space from $8. Camping and electricity available. Market is undergoing major construction and is converting into a large commercial shopping area.

ROSWELL

Traders Village
2200 S. Sunset

Saturday, Sunday, 7 a.m.–4 p.m. Indoor and outdoor market with approximately 50 dealers. Lots of Indian jewelry and handicrafts here. Also new and used merchandise, collectibles, crafts, housewares, and local garage salers. Snack bar, rest rooms, h/a, ample parking. Space from $4. *Contact* Dalton Ross, 2200 S. Sunset, 88201 (505) 622-7410.

SANTA FE

Trader Jack's Flea Market
Cerrillos Rd. and Truck Bypass

Friday, Saturday, Sunday, 7 a.m.–6 p.m. Outdoor market with over 200 dealers. Antiques, collectibles, new and used merchandise, crafts, and livestock available. Great selection of authentic Indian jewelry and Indian art. Good finds in tack and western items. One of the leading markets in the Southwest. Cafe with excellent food, rest rooms, h/a, ample parking. Space from $12 per day. *Contact* Jack Daniels, Box O, Pajoaque Station, 87501 (505) 455-7874.

ALWAYS CALL AHEAD TO VERIFY DATES AND INFORMATION

Pueblo Flea Market
3211 Cerrillos Rd.
(505) 983-2656 or 470-0609

Saturday, Sunday, March–December. Average daily attendance 2,500. Approximately 300 vendors. This is one of the leading markets in the country for Native American and western items of all types. Food available, rest rooms, h/a, ample parking. Space from $8. Camping, electricity, and showers available. Nice friendly family-oriented market.

SILVER CITY

Silver City Flea Market
Main St. Downtown

Daily. This is a 12,500-square-foot indoor flea market in an old 1897 adobe-style building. Antiques, collectibles, primitives, and western items available. Ample parking and rest rooms. *Contact* Patsy (505) 388-8989.

TAOS

Taos Rendezvous
Corner of Paseo Del Pueblo Sur and
Albright Rd.

Friday, Saturday, Sunday, 9 a.m.–5 p.m. (open daily during summer months). Indoor/outdoor market. Average daily attendance 1,000. Approximately 100 dealers. Market features high-quality Indian jewelry, artifacts, and art. Also collectible, new, and used merchandise available. This is a very enjoyable and definitely all-day stop. Food available, rest rooms, h/a, ample parking. Space from $10 per day. Camping available. Food vendors welcome. *Contact* Bob Gherardi, Box 804, Angel Fire, 87710 (505) 758-7511.

NEW YORK

ADDISON

Flea Market
Rte. 17, west of Corning

Sunday. Antiques, collectibles, pottery, jewelry, glassware, memorabilia, silver, vintage clothing, and a variety of the new and not-so-new typical flea market fare. Food available, rest rooms, ample parking.

AKRON

Newstead Auction and Flea Market
1311 Main Rd.

Sunday. Antiques, collectibles, furniture, glassware, kitchen collectibles, silver, vintage clothing, used merchandise, housewares, crafts, and produce. Approximately 75 dealers. Snack bar, rest rooms, h/a, ample parking.

ALEXANDRIA BAY

Ameri-Can Market
Rte. 12

Friday, Saturday, Sunday, 10 a.m.–6 p.m. Seasonal market open Memorial Day through Labor Day weekend. Indoor/outdoor market with approximately 50 dealers. Market is mainly used and garage sale merchandie, bric-a-brac, locally made crafts and some collectibles, gifts and imports. Space from $10 per day. Snack bar, rest rooms, h/a. Ample free parking. *Contact* Manager, Box 2169, Liverpool, NY 13088 (315) 482-2016.

AVON

Flea Market
Rte. 15
(716) 226-8320

Sunday, 6 a.m.–4 p.m. Antiques, collectibles, furniture, jewelry, vintage clothing, primitives, sports items, and crafts available. Snack bar, rest rooms, h/a, ample parking. *Contact* Manager 1520 Rochester Rd., 14414.

BALDWIN

Baldwin Antique Center
906 Merrick Rd.

Thursday. Large selection of American and European furniture, fine and estate jewelry, glassware, primitives, pottery, art, prints, books, silver, advertising items, and kitchenware available. Food available, rest rooms, h/a, ample parking.

BALLSTON SPA

Circle C Year-Round Flea Market
Middleline Rd.
(518) 885-6128 or 885-6640

Friday, Saturday, Sunday. New merchandise, sportswear, housewares, electronics, jewelry, sports merchandise, used merchandise, collectibles, and decorator items. Food available, rest rooms, h/a, ample parking.

NOTE: A New York State sales tax certificate is required by most markets before you are allowed to sell. Certificates can usually be purchased at the market.

BATAVIA

Kiwanis Flea Market
Fairgrounds
East Main St., one mile east of town

Sunday. Antiques, collectibles, new and used merchandise, bric-a-brac, farm items, and crafts available. Indoor and outdoor open-air market. Food available, rest rooms, h/a, ample parking. Space from $8. *Contact* Bernard Kowaiski, 24 Richmond Ave., 14020 (716) 343-1594.

BAYSHORE

U.S.A. Bayshore Trade 'N' Sell Market
Bay Shore Drive-In Theater
(516) 665-5697 or 288-0406

Sunday. Admission charge. Approximately 350 dealers. Large commercial market with a complete line of new merchandise, lots of used merchandise, garage sale items, antiques, collectibles, coins, jewelry, housewares, crafts, and produce available. Food available, rest rooms, h/a, ample parking, and acres of walking.

BELMONT

Belmont Flea Market
Belmont Racetrack

Saturday, Sunday, March–October and Christmas holiday season, 7:30 a.m.–4 p.m. Approximately 2,000 vendors. Good mix of merchandise, art, crafts, collectibles, antiques, lots of new merchandise, sportswear, housewares, electronics, and new sports-related merchandise available. One of the area's most popular markets. International food court, rest rooms, h/a, ample paved parking, and be prepared for lots of walking. Space from $35 per day. *Contact* M. Cannava, 257 Hempstead, 11003 (516) 775-2100 or 775-8774.

INFORMATION IS SUBJECT TO CHANGE—ALWAYS CALL AHEAD TO AVOID DISAPPOINTMENT

BLOOMINGBURG

Flea Market
Corner of Main St. and Burlington Rd.

Saturday, Sunday. New and used merchandise, large amounts of flea market merchandise, crafts, collectibles, and produce available. Snack bar, rest rooms, ample parking.

BLOOMINGTON

Indoor Flea Market
Main St.
(914) 773-4141

Saturday, Sunday. New merchandise, electronics, sportswear, housewares, jewelry, sports merchandise, used merchandise, decorator items, books, some antiques, art deco, and collectibles available. Snack bar, rest rooms, h/a, ample parking.

BOUCKVILLE

Bouckville Antique Pavilion
Rte. 20, downtown

Sunday, May–October, 6 a.m.–4 p.m. Approximately 200 dealers. High-quality antiques, furniture, silver, quality glassware, and collectibles available at this market. Country and Victorian-era finds, lots of good sports-related items at this market. Approximately 35 specialty shops under one roof. Snack bar, rest rooms, h/a, ample parking. Space from $10. Market conducts many special events. *Contact* Steve or Lynda Bono, Rte. 1, Box 111, 13310 (315) 893-7483 or 893-7912.

BRONX

Bronx Flea for All
(212) 409-1216

Thursday–Sunday. Prowl through the aisles of this market and find new and used merchandise of all kinds for work, home, and play. A good mixture of housewares, clothing, imports, toys, collectibles, memorabilia, crafts, and electronics available.

Fordham Plaza Flea Market
Fordham Plaza
Next door to Sears and across the street from Fordham University
Metro North station

Wednesday, Thursday, 8 a.m.–4 p.m. Outdoor market with some covered spaces. Approximately 25 dealers.

St. John's School Flea Market
3030 Godwin Terrace
(718) 543-3003

Saturdays. Seasonal market, open September through June.

BRONXVILLE

Antique Flea Market
Boy Scout Field
Bronx River Pkwy, Bronxville Exit

Monthly. Admission charge. Approximately 100 dealers. Market is restricted to fine art, quality collectibles, and true antiques. This is a great source market for those in the trade. Food available, rest rooms, h/a, ample parking, and lots of walking. Space from $40. *Contact* Chamber of Commerce, 10708 (914) 337-6040.

BROOKLYN

Avenue I Flea Market
1080 McDonald Ave.

Thursday, Friday, 12 p.m.–10 p.m., Saturday, 10 a.m.–9 p.m., Sunday, 10 a.m.–6 p.m. Average attendance is 10,000, holiday weekends over 50,000. Indoor market with approximately 600 dealers. Antiques, collectibles, art, and new merchandise available. Great place for budget shopping. Snack bar, rest rooms, h/a, limited parking. Space from $75 per weekend. *Contact* Joe Nova, 1080 McDonald Ave., 11230 (718) 338-8234.

Canarsie Flea Market
(718) 649-8855

Thursday–Sunday. New and used merchandise, gifts, clothing, prints, books, imports, and some collectibles.

Indoor Flea Market
6012 Farragot Rd.
(718) 251-5756

Sunday, March–October. New and used merchandise, clothing, gifts, electronics, and some collectibles available.

Bay Ridge Flea Market
88th St. between 4th and 5th Aves.
(718) 238-6967

Saturday, Sunday. New and secondhand merchandise, imports, overruns, jewelry, clothing, sports collectibles, and tools available.

Regina Center Flea Market
(718) 232-4340

Sunday, June–September. New and used desirable merchandise, imports, jewelry, electronics, housewares, clothing, including lots of sportswear, bric-a-brac for work, home, and play available.

Seventh Avenue Flea Market
P.S. 321
180 Seventh Ave.

Saturday, Sunday. Outdoor market with approximately 25 dealers. *Contact* Fred Stern (718) 833-9864.

BUFFALO

GEX Flea Market
1050 Walden Ave.

Saturday, Sunday. New and used merchandise, imports, manufacturers' overruns, sportswear, tools, electronics, decorator items, gifts, and garage sale bric-a-brac available.

Riverside Flea Market
827 Tonawanda St.

Friday, Saturday, Sunday. New and used merchandise, garage sale items, collectibles, crafts, art, and produce available. Snack bar, rest rooms, ample parking. *Contact* Bob Nix (716) 493-2566.

Super Flea and Farmers Market
2500 Walden Ave.
(716) 685-2902

Saturday, Sunday. New and used merchandise, crafts, collectibles, decorator items, produce, packaged food. Snack bar, rest rooms, h/a. Ample parking.

CALLICOON

Callicoon Flea Market
Main St.
Rte. 17B, west of Monticello

Saturday, Sunday, 9 a.m.–5 p.m. Antiques, collectibles, nice glassware, architectural items, and new merchandise available. This market is located in a very scenic and historic town. Great area to spend a weekend. Snack bar, rest rooms, ample parking. *Contact:* Carol Kay, Box 278, 12723 (845) 887-5411.

CAPE VINCENT

Cedar Point Flea Market
Rte. 12
(315) 658-2538

Friday, Saturday, Sunday, May–September. New and used merchandise, antiques, collectibles, housewares, clothing, jewelry, tools, crafts, and produce available. Food available, rest rooms, h/a, ample parking.

CAYUGA LAKE

Pennyless Pat's Flea Market
Rte. 90

Saturday, Sunday, July and August, 9 a.m. until dark. Outdoor market with approximately 50 dealers. Lots of secondhand garage sale merchandise, collectibles, and new items of all kinds available. Snack bar, ample parking. Lots of antique and specialty shops in the local area. *Contact* Pate Deles (315) 253-9844.

CHEEKTOWAGA

Super Flea & Farmers Market
2500 Walden Ave.

Saturday, Sunday, 9 a.m.–6 p.m. Approximately 400 dealers. Antiques, collectibles, crafts, new and used merchandise, giftware, sportswear, household items, and produce available. One of the area's better and more interesting markets. Good attendance but expect to do a lot of walking to see everything. Food available, rest rooms, h/a, ample parking. Space from $10 per day. Inside and outside spaces available. *Contact* Ronald Wagner, 2500 Walden Ave., 14225 (716) 685-2902 or 685-2902.

Airport Plaza Flea Market
Union and Genesee Rds.
(716) 531-5897

Sunday, April–October. Antiques, collectibles, new and used merchandise, and locally made crafts available. Food available, rest rooms, h/a, ample parking.

CLARENCE

Antique World & Market Place
10995 Main St.
Rte. 5

Sunday, 8 a.m.–4 p.m. Average attendance 5–8,000. Approximately 800 dealers. Excellent market for antiques and collectibles. Market has three large buildings with one devoted entirely to antiques. Also collectibles, furniture, jewelry, clothing, toys, new and used merchandise, crafts, trading cards, and fresh produce available. This is a great source market for those in the trade. Food available, rest rooms, h/a, ample parking with $1 charge. Lots of walking required to see everything, dress accordingly. Inside and outside spaces available from $15 per day. *Contact* Katy Toth, 10995 Main St., 14031 (716) 759-8483, fax (716) 759-6167. E-mail: antiques@pcom.net.

CLAVERACK

Bryant Farms Antique and Flea Market
Rtes. 9H and 23

Saturday, Sunday, 8 a.m.–3 p.m. Indoor/outdoor market. Indoors year-round and outdoors weather permitting. Approximately 25 dealers. Ample free parking. *Contact* Giulio DeLaurentis (518) 851-9061 or (212) 851-3817.

COOPERSTOWN

Milford Flea Market
State Rte. 28.
From Binghamton, I-88 to Exit 17 Rte. 28 North
Market is on right just past traffic light in Milford. From the NYS thruway, Exit 30, Rte. 26 south, 12 miles south of Cooperstown

Daily. Average daily attendance 100–300. Approximately 30 dealers. Reservations required. Space $80 per month. Inside space only. New and used merchandise, antiques, and collectibles. *Contact* Sally (607) 286-9839.

CORAM

Coram Drive-In Theater Flea Market
Long Island

Sunday. Approximately 100 dealers. Antiques, collectibles, jewelry, new and used merchandise, art, and crafts available. Snack bar, rest rooms, h/a, ample parking. Space from $3.

EAST AVON

East Avon Downs Flea Market
Avon Downs, 1520 Rte. 15
(716) 226-8320

Sunday, May–October. Antiques, collectibles, furniture, jewelry, sports merchandise, clothing, housewares, art, and crafts available. Food available, rest rooms, h/a, ample parking, and lots of walking required.

EAST FARMINGDALE

Route 110 Flea Market
1815 Broadhollow Rd.
(516) 454-0405

Friday, Saturday, Sunday. Approximately 300 dealers. Large classic commercial market, wide range of new merchandise: hot and trendy as well as lots of housewares, necessities, sports-related, and decorator items. It's all here at severely discounted prices. Used merchandise, lots of collectibles, both new and older items, nostalgia, memorabilia, crafts, art, books, prints, paper goods, and produce also available. Snack bars, rest rooms, h/a, ample parking, and miles of walking. Good market for commercial vendors.

ELBA

Rowcliffe's Flea Market
6151 Oak Orchard Rd.
(716) 757-2791

Saturday, Sunday. Approximately 20 dealers. Used merchandise, garage sale junk, collectibles. Inside and outside space available. Space from $10 per day.

ELMIRA

The Antique Mart
Nichols Plaza
2071 Upper Lake Rd.
(607) 732-0338

Saturday, Sunday. Indoor market, primarily antiques, collectibles, glassware, fine and estate jewelry, furniture, advertising items, vintage clothing, etc. Snack bar, rest rooms, h/a. Ample parking.

FARMINGVILLE

Tri-County Flea Market
751 Horseblock Rd.
(516) 736-6400

Saturday, Sunday. New and used merchandise and classic flea market fare: collectibles, housewares, clothing, farm and country items, crafts, imports, T-shirts, gifts, produce. Snack bar, rest rooms, h/a. Ample parking.

FLORIDA

Fancy Flea Market

Saturday, Sunday. Indoor market. New merchandise, antiques, crafts and collectibles, garage sale bric-a-brac, tools, household items, and sundries.

FLUSHING

Bethpage Flea Market
(516) 931-8400

Friday, Saturday. New and used merchandise, antiques, collectibles, gifts, housewares, clothing, and jewelry available. Snack bar, rest rooms, h/a, ample parking.

Antique & Flea Market
136 38th Ave.

Saturday, 10 a.m.–10 p.m., Sunday, 10 a.m.–7 p.m. Approximately 50 dealers. Good selection of antiques, furniture, collectibles, jewelry, vintage clothing, art, prints, and books available. Snack bar, rest rooms, h/a, ample parking.

Busy Bee Compartment Store
37-11 Main St.

Wednesday, Thursday, 11 a.m.–7 p.m., Friday, 11 a.m.–8 p.m., Saturday, 10 a.m.–7 p.m., Sunday 11 a.m.–6 p.m. Indoor market with approximately 150 dealers. New merchandise only. All the lines that you would find at a discount store with even lower prices. Snack bar, rest rooms, h/a, ample parking. Monthly rentals only. *Contact* Pete Markowski (718) 961-4111.

GARDEN CITY

Megamarket
Roosevelt Field Shopping Center
711 Stewart Ave.

Friday, 12 p.m.–9 p.m., Saturday, Sunday 10 a.m.–6 p.m. Large, new indoor market with approximately 700 booths. Lots of new, name merchandise. Great selection of jewelry. All the merchandise is severely discounted with much better prices than you would expect to find at a discount chain. Large selection and variety of crafts. Snack bars, rest rooms, h/a, ample parking. Space by monthly rental only. *Contact* Alan Finchley, 711 Stewart Ave., 11530 (516) 745-0600.

HEBRON

Flea & Farmers Market
Six miles south of town
(518) 642-0715

Friday, Saturday, Sunday. Antiques, collectibles, lots of country collectibles, decorator items, used merchandise, garage sale junk, crafts, and produce available. Food available, rest rooms, h/a, ample parking.

HOPEWELL JUNCTION

Parkers Flea Market
Rte. 376

Sunday. Antiques, collectibles, new and used merchandise, crafts, and produce available. Inside and outside space available. Snack bar, rest rooms, h/a, ample parking.

HUDSON

Hudson Flea Market
Columbia and 7th Sts.

Sunday. Approximately 20 vendors. Collectibles, glassware, jewelry, and used merchandise available. Ample parking. Space from $15. *Contact* Judy Meyer, 430 Warren St., 12534 (518) 828-8413.

ITHACA

Martha's Flea Market
619 Five Mile Dr.

Saturday, Sunday. Antiques, collectibles, used merchandise, and garage sale items available.

Snack bar, rest rooms, h/a. Seasonal market. *Contact* Martha Mobbs (607) 272-3289.

Ithaca Farmers Market
Junction of 3rd St. and Rte. 13 at the steamboat landing
(607) 273-7109

Saturdays. Outdoor market.

KIRKLAND

Kirkland Seneca Antique Galleries Flea Market
Rte. 5

Saturday, Sunday. Antiques, collectibles, furniture, decorator items, art deco, prints, memorabilia, and nostalgia items available. Snack bar, rest rooms, ample parking.

LEVITTOWN

Tri-County Flea Market
3041 Hempstead Tpke.

Thursday, Friday, 12 p.m.–9 p.m., Saturday, 10 a.m.–6 p.m., Sunday, 10 a.m.–5 p.m. A four-story building with approximately 400 dealers. Good mix of antiques, collectibles, memorabilia, primitives, advertising items, new merchandise, sportswear, and housewares available. Special jewelry section with a great selection of fine and estate jewelry, over 40 dealers in this section. Snack bar, deli, rest rooms. *Contact* Barbara Eve, 3041 Hempstead Tpke., 11756 (516) 579-4500, fax (516) 579-6715.

LONG ISLAND

Yankee Peddler Flea Market
(516) 271-5817

Daily. Market is restricted to sale of antiques only. Both casual collector and serious investor will enjoy this market and all it has to offer in books, furniture, glassware, vintage clothing and jewelry, decorator items, dolls, clocks, lamps, china, toys.

Flea Market
Shoppers Village
(516) 486-5250

Thursday, Friday, Saturday, Sunday. Lots of new merchandise, imports, giftware, electronics, along with some garage sale junque. Sports cards and memorabilia, crafts.

Flea Market Long Island Merchandise Mart
(516) 567-7277

Thursday, Sunday. This market is heavy on new merchandise, household necessities, clothing, imports. Also secondhand, nearly new desirables.

East Meadow Flea Market
(516) 731-2260

Saturday, Sunday. New and used merchandise for the entire family for work, home, and play. Housewares, clothing, children's items, tools, electronics, sports memorabilia, collectibles.

Flea Market
Long Island Arena
(516) 499-0800

Wednesday, Friday, Sunday. A classic flea market with plenty of new, trendy merchandise and lots of nearly new junque at discounted prices. Sportswear, jewelry, automotive, tools, collectibles, crafts, decorator items.

LOWMAN

Lowman Flea Market
Rte. 17

Saturday, Sunday, April–November for outside space. Approximately 75 dealers. Held inside at Eastowne Mall, downtown Elmira on Baldwin St. (Sunday only), during the months of November–April. Snack bar and rest rooms. *Contact* Jim or Sandy Stage (607) 734-3670.

ALWAYS CALL BEFORE TRAVELING LONG DISTANCES!

MASSAPEQUA PARK

Busy B Mall Flea Market
5300 Sunrise Hwy.

Thursday–Monday, 10 a.m. until late. Call for current schedule. New merchandise only, all the lines you would find at a discount store except at much lower prices. Snack bar, rest rooms, h/a, ample parking. Monthly rentals only. *Contact* Nancy Krokowski, Box 144, 11762 (516) 799-9090.

MAYBROOK

Maybrook Swap 'N Shop
Rte. 208

Saturday, Sunday, 8 a.m.–4 p.m. Approximately 100 dealers. Collectibles, new merchandise, lots of used and garage sale items, bric-a-brac, and some crafts available. Snack bar, rest rooms, h/a, ample parking. Space from $26. *Contact* Nick Perilli, Rte. 208, 12543 (845) 427-2715.

MIDDLETOWN

Middletown Drive-In Theater Flea Market
Rtes. 6 and 17
(845) 343-5551

Saturday, Sunday. Lots of new merchandise, used merchandise, garage sale items, collectibles, decorator items, crafts, and produce available. Snack bar, rest rooms, h/a, ample parking. Space from $3.

Vendors Outlet & Jewelry Exchange
Orange Plaza Mall
Rte. 211 East

Friday, Saturday, Sunday. New indoor market with approximately 120 booths. New name-brand merchandise severely discounted, fine jewelry. Space from $250 per month or $25 per day. Food court, rest rooms, h/a, ample parking. *Contact* Bill Sabia, Vendors Outlet, Rte. 211 East, 10940 (845) 344-2000.

MONSEY

Rockland Flea Market
Rte. 59
(845) 352-2637

Saturday, Sunday. Approximately 150 dealers. New merchandise, sportswear, housewares, sports merchandise, electronics, decorator items, giftware, jewelry, prints, crafts, and produce available. Snack bar, rest rooms, h/a, ample parking. Inside and outside spaces from $5. *Contact* E & P Promotions, Box 252, 10952 (845) 352-2637.

MONTICELLO

Montco Antique and Craft Flea Market
Rte. 17

Saturday, Sunday. This is a very pleasant market with a good selection of antiques and collectibles and a great assortment of locally made crafts and gift items. Food available, rest rooms, h/a, ample parking. *Contact* Al Bagon (845) 434-5513. Reservations recommended.

Flea Market
Monticello Raceway
Rtes. 17B and 17

Wednesday, Friday, Saturday, Sunday, 9 a.m.–5 p.m., Memorial Day–Labor Day weekend. Average attendance 5–15,000 per weekend. Market is for new merchandise only. Lots of upscale name-brand items here at drastically discounted prices. Electronics, sportswear, housewares, jewelry, a bargain hunter's bonanza. Full-service snack bar, rest rooms, h/a, ample parking. Approximately 150 spaces. Daily space $25 and up. Tables $5 and $7 per day. NYS Sales Tax certificate needed. *Contact* Alan Finchley, 42 Ohio Ave., Long Beach, 11561 (845) 796-1000, fax (516) 897-1800.

DAYS, DATES, AND MARKETS ARE SUBJECT TO CHANGE!

NEW YORK CITY

Traveler's alert: When in New York City I never drive, I take cabs or walk (depending on the neighborhood). For the most part there is no parking in NYC and actually very little room to drive on the streets. I highly recommend that you do not take your vehicle into New York City. Having worked a lot of shows in the Big Apple, at Javits Convention Center and the old Coliseum, I have only listed details about the markets of which I have firsthand knowledge. If you shop the markets in NYC and know of information we missed, send it to me and we will include it in the next edition. Also, a lot of markets require a New York City license before you will be allowed to set up. Go somewhere else.

Flea Market
370 Canal St.
(212) 282-9841

Saturday, Sunday. New merchandise, imports, name-brand clothing, stereo and electronic items, housewares, home furnishings, and some used merchandise available.

The Showplace
40 W. 25th St.
Between 6th Ave. and Broadway
Fax (212) 633-6064

Saturday, Sunday. New market with approximately 100 dealers located in a two-story building. Large selection of antiques and collectibles. No new merchandise. Space from $150 for the weekend. Food available, rest rooms, h/a. *Contact:* Kobi Barki, 40 W. 25th St., 10001 (212) 633-6063, fax 633-6064.

Flea Market
369 Canal St.
(212) 226-0680

Daily. New merchandise of every description from housewares to hardware, brand-name fashions and accessories, electronics, plants, paintings, toys, also nearly new and collectible items available.

The Glass House Bazaar
43 W. 13th St.

Saturday, Sunday. New and used merchandise with a bit of everything for the bargain-conscious shopper, from dust mops to name-brand jeans, videotapes to socket sets available.

Arts & Crafts Flea Market
42nd Street at 5th Ave.
(212) 751-4932

Friday. New merchandise, some used, including: imports, gifts, home furnishings, electronics, and collectibles. Nice selection of locally made crafts, including lots of ethnic crafts.

26th Street Indoor Antiques Fair
122 W. 26th St.
Between 6th and 7th Aves.

Saturday, Sunday, 9 a.m.–5 p.m. Large two-story facility with over 60 dealers inside. Market is restricted to antiques and collectibles. Lots of quality items here, including very fine estate jewelry and excellent furniture pieces. Snack bar, rest rooms, difficult parking. *Contact* Amos Balaish (212) 633-6010.

SoHo Antiques & Flea Market
465 Broadway

Saturday, Sunday, 9 a.m.–5 p.m. Outdoor market with approximately 75 dealers. Antiques, collectibles, memorabilia, glassware, silver, jewelry, crafts, lots of decorative art and folk art available. Very trendy market. Snack bar, rest rooms, parking is difficult. Several great restaurants in the neighborhood. Space from $70. *Contact* Ted Brachfeld, Box 337, Garden City, 11530 (212) 682-2000, fax (516) 742-4424.

Eleventh Street Flea Market
First Ave. between 11th and 12th Sts.

Saturday, Sunday. Outdoor market with approximately 25 dealers. Seasonal market open April through October. *Contact* Mary Help of Christians Church (212) 254-0058.

Fulton Street Plaza Flea Market
Cliff St. between Fulton and Beekman Sts.
Near the South Street Seaport

Wednesdays. Outdoor market with approximately 25 dealers. Sponsored by the Parks

Dept. and focus is on multicultural crafts. *Contact* (212) 809-5000.

The Garage Flea Market
112 W. 25th St.
Between Avenue of the Americas and Seventh Ave.

Saturday, Sunday, 8 a.m.–5 p.m. Indoor market with approximately 100 dealers. Antiques, collectibles, crafts, new and used merchandise, vintage clothing. Space from $75. Snack bar, rest rooms, h/a. Parking is difficult. *Contact* Michael Santulli, Box 7010 (212) 647-0707, fax (212) 463-7099.

Antique Flea & Farmers Market
Public School 183
419 E. 66th St.

Saturday. Approximately 150 dealers. Antiques, collectibles, crafts, and fine art available. Snack bar, rest rooms, parking is difficult. Inside and outside space available from $25. *Contact* PTA, 419 E. 66th St., 10021 (212) 737-8888 or 650-1429.

P.S. 44 Market
Public School 44
Between W. 76th and W. 77th Sts. on Columbus Ave.
(212) 721-0900
Fax (212) 721-6934

Sunday, 10 a.m.–5 p.m. Average attendance 12,000. Approximately 200 dealers. Antiques, collectibles, vintage clothing, glassware, jewelry, art deco, artwork, prints, crafts, new and used merchandise available. Food available, rest rooms, difficult parking. Space from $25. Must have city license. *Contact* Judith Gehrke, 162 W. 72nd St., 10023.

Annex Antique Fair & Flea Market
6th Ave. at 26th St.

Saturday, Sunday, 9 a.m.–5 p.m. Admission charge $1. Approximately 250 dealers. Saturday market is antiques and collectibles only. New merchandise is allowed on Sunday. The "in" market for the New York designer crowd. Lots of interesting people, booths, and merchandise at this market. Snack bar, rest rooms, no parking. Outdoor/indoor market. *Contact* Manager, Box 7010, 10116 (212) 243-5343, fax (212) 463-7099.

Walters World Famous Le Flea Market
252 Bleecker St. (Greenwich Village)
(212) 255-0175

Thursday–Sunday. Approximately 50 dealers, mainly permanent shops with very stylish, high-quality, and unique items.

Bowling Green Plaza Flea Market
Bowling Green Plaza, corner of Broadway and State Sts. in lower Manhattan
(212) 809-5000

Tuesday, Friday. Outdoor market with approximately 25 dealers. Sponsored by the Parks Dept and focus is on multicultural crafts.

The Grand Bazaar
25th St. between Broadway and Ave. of the Americas

Saturday, Sunday. Outdoor market with approximately 125 dealers. Great market to shop for interesting and unusual items, also close to the large Annex market. *Contact* Andrew Lackowitz (914) 273-1578.

Battery Park Flea Market
Battery Park on State St., at the waterfront
(212) 809-4900

Thursday. Outdoor market with approximately 25 dealers. Sponsored by the New York City Parks Department. Market focus is on multicultural crafts.

Jan Hus Flea Market
Jan Hus Church. 351 E. 74th St.
Manhattan's Upper East Side
(212) 288-6743

Saturday, Sunday.

The Annex at South Street Seaport
Burlington Slip, corner of South St.
Lower Manhattan

Thursday, Friday, Saturday, 11:30 a.m.–7 p.m. Outdoor market with approximately 75 dealers. Antiques, collectibles, gifts, imports, crafts, new and used merchandise. Space from $85 per day. Lots of food in the area, nice tourist area. Rest rooms. Parking is terrible. *Contact* Michael Santulli, Box 7010, 10166 (212) 534-3212, fax (212) 463-7099.

Spring Street Market
43 Spring St.
Corner of Wooster and Spring Sts.

Daily. Outdoor market with approximately 10–15 dealers. SoHo district. Lots of flea market and garage sale items here. *Contact* Irwin Yesselman (718) 273-8702.

Tower Records Flea Market
688 Broadway
Next to Tower Records at 4th St.

Saturday, Sunday. Outdoor market with approximately 50 dealers. *Contact* Irwin Yesselman (718) 273-8702 or (917) 860-1217.

P.S. 41 Schoolyard Flea Market
Greenwich Ave.
Between Sixth and Seventh Aves.
(212) 751-4932

Saturday. Outdoor market with approximately 15 dealers.

NORTH ROSE

Country Squires Flea Market
Rte. 41

Sunday. Approximately 500 dealers. This is a great market. Miles of booths with fine antiques, quality junk, new trendy merchandise. Great discounts. A shopper's and bargain hunter's paradise. Inside and outside spaces available. Good food, rest rooms, h/a, ample parking, and lots of walking. Excellent market for commercial vendors and professional shoppers. Space from $3. *Contact* Chuck Squires (315) 587-2689.

NORTH TONAWANDA

Super Flea & Farmers Market
100 Ridge Rd.
(716) 694-5441

Saturday, Sunday. New merchandise, sportswear, jewelry, decorator items, sports merchandise, electronics, housewares, some antiques, collectibles, art, prints, books, crafts, and used merchandise available. Snack bars, rest rooms, h/a, ample parking. Inside market.

PINE CITY

Flea Market
Rte. 328
(607) 739-2296

Sunday. New and used merchandise, garage sale items, antiques, collectibles, furniture, new and antique jewelry, clothing, housewares, crafts, and art available. Snack bar, rest rooms, h/a, ample parking. Indoor/outdoor market.

PLATTSBURGH

Bargaineer Flea Market
39 Bridge St.

Daily. Indoor market with approximately 10 dealers. Collectibles, antiques, and used items. Free admission. *Contact* John Silver (518) 561-3525.

PORT CHESTER

Empire State Flea Market
515 Boston Post Rd.
I-95, Exit 21, or I-287, Exit 12

Friday, 5 a.m.–9 p.m., Saturday, Sunday, 10 a.m.–6 p.m. Average weekend attendance 5,000. Approximately 150 exhibitors. New merchandise only. All the lines you would find at a discount store but at substantially lower prices. Great selection of upscale and high-dollar, name-brand items here at bargain prices. Snack bars, rest rooms, h/a, ample parking. Indoor market. Monthly rentals only. *Contact* Alan Finchley, 515 Boston Post Rd., 10573 (914) 939-1800 or (800) 220-7467, fax (914) 939-5046.

PRESTON HOLLOW

Preston Hollow Antique and Flea Market
Corner of Rtes. 145 and 81

Sundays, 9 a.m.–4 p.m. Antique mall is open daily. Outdoor market with approximately 50 dealers. Antiques, collectibles, locally made crafts, new and used merchandise, furniture. Space from $20 per day. Snack bar, rest rooms, h/a. Free parking. *Contact* Dorothy Como, Rte. 1, Box 88, 12469 (518) 239-4251.

PULASKI

Hillside Markets Flea Market
Rte. 3, one mile north of Port Ontario,
I-81, Exit 36

Saturday, Sunday, 7 a.m.–4 p.m. Indoor market with approximately 100 dealers. Antiques, collectibles, new and used merchandise, produce. Space from $9 per day. Overnight camping available. Cafe, rest rooms, h/a. Market is located next to Lake Ontario in a very scenic area. *Contact* (315) 298-4085.

QUEENS

St. Nicholas of Tolentine Outdoor Flea Market
St. Nicholas of Tolentine Church
150-75 Goethals Ave.
(718) 969-3226 or 591-1815

Saturdays. Seasonal market open from March through November. Indoor market with approximately 75 dealers.

Elmhurst/Jackson Heights Flea Market
81-16 45th Ave.

Friday, Saturday, Sunday. Indoor market with approximately 100 dealers. Space from $10 per day. Reservations required. *Contact* H. Ingbar, 40-10 Junction Blvd., Corona, NY 11368 (212) 426-9500.

Bingo Hall Flea Market
117-09 Hillside Ave.

Sundays. Indoor market. *Contact* David Gross (718) 847-1418.

ROCHESTER

Collector's Marketplace
1439 Buffalo Rd.

Sunday, May–October. New and secondhand merchandise and bric-a-brac. Aisles of booths full of bargains on everything from electronics to sweatshirts, pet supplies, prints, sports memorabilia, antiques, and collectibles. Ample parking.

SARATOGA SPRINGS

Stan's Flea Market
Rte. 9, three miles north of town

Saturday, Sunday. Seasonal market open April–October. Outdoor market with approximately 50 dealers. *Contact* Stanley Akers (518) 584-4339 or 584-6938.

SAYVILLE

Atlas Flea Market
5750 Sunrise Hwy. 11782

Indoor market, well stocked with wide variety, cosmetics, furniture, jewelry, clothing, electronics, 600 booths. Snack bars, rest rooms, h/a, ample parking. *Contact* Ziggy Attias (516) 244-5755. E-mail: Avattias@aol.com.

INFORMATION IS SUBJECT TO CHANGE—ALWAYS CALL FIRST!

SCHENECTADY

Dutch Mill Outdoor Antique Show, Crafts & Flea Market
3633 Carman Rd.
Approximately one mile west of New York State Thruway, Exit 25 on Rte. 146

Monthly, April–October, call for dates. Outside space only. *Contact* Jeannett Mastrianni, 3633 Carman Rd., 12303 (518) 355-3420.

White House Flea Market
952 State St., Rte. 5, I-87, Exit 25

Wednesday–Sunday. Indoor market with approximately 35 dealers. Snack bar, rest room, h/a. Ample parking. *Contact* Rudy Fecketter (518) 346-7851.

SENECA FALLS

Country Squires Flea Market
Hwy. 414
(315) 587-2689

Sundays. Good one-day market with mountains of bargain-priced new and used merchandise of all descriptions. Household furnishings, fashions, accessories, artwork, tools, and electronics available.

SOUTH OZONE PARK

Aqueduct Racetrack Flea Market (Queens)

Saturday, Sunday, except during racing season, 7:30 a.m.–4 p.m. Over 2,000 dealers. One of the area's major markets. Lots of great stuff for bargain hunters. Excellent market for commercial vendors. Lots of professional high-quality dealer setups here. Market is open during the Christmas season. If you're looking for great prices on new merchandise for your own use, this is the place to shop. Food available, rest rooms, h/a, ample parking. Space from $35 per day. *Contact* M. Cannava, 257 Hempstead, Elmont, 11003 (517) 775-2100 or 775-8774.

SPRING VALLEY

Spring Valley Flea Market
122 E. Central Ave.
I-87, Exit 14

Friday, 5 a.m.–10 p.m., Saturday, 10 a.m.–9 p.m., Sunday, 10 a.m.–7 p.m. Indoor market with approximately 500 dealers. New merchandise, everything you would find at Wal-Mart but at substantially lower prices. Great selection of upscale and high-dollar, name-brand items at severely discounted prices. Snack bar, rest rooms, h/a, ample parking. Space from $105 per week. *Contact* Al Bonadonna, 122 E. Central Ave., 10977 (845) 356-1100.

STORMVILLE

Stormville Airport Antique Show & Flea Market
Rte. 216

Monthly, call for dates, dawn to dusk. Approximately 600 dealers. Good well-attended market for all types of merchandise. Spaces 20×20 from $60. Camping available on space. Reservations recommended. *Contact* Pat Carnahan, Box 85, 12582 (845) 221-6561.

SYRACUSE

Midler Court Variety Mart
400 N. Midler Ave.
(315) 437-8877

Saturday, Sunday. Approximately 450 dealers. Large commercial market with a wide range of merchandise; new, used, antiques, collectibles, art, crafts, and gifts available. Snack bars, rest rooms, h/a, ample parking, and lots of walking.

VALLEY STREAM

Valley Stream Flea Market
700 W. Sunrise Hwy.
Sunrise Cinema
(516) 825-6469

Saturday. Approximately 300 dealers. Antiques, lots of furniture, many different booths of collector lines, jewelry, vintage clothing, art deco, art, prints, and paper goods available. Food available, rest rooms, h/a, ample parking, and lots of walking.

WOODSTOCK

Saturday Flea Market
Maple Lane
(914) 679-6744

Saturday, 8 a.m.–6 p.m. Great bargain prices on classic flea market merchandise. New and used goods including: electronics, televisions, stereos, videos, clothing, housewares, and jewelry. *Contact* John Mower, Box 556, 12498.

YONKERS

Yonkers Raceway Flea Market

Sunday, seasonal market, Open March through Christmas. 9 a.m.–4 p.m. Admission $2 per car. Average attendance 20,000. Approximately 500 dealers. Good market for commercial vendors. New merchandise market. Food stands, rest rooms, h/a, ample paved parking, lots of walking, good security. Space from $40. Outside market. No outside food sales allowed. *Contact* Marty McGrath, Yonkers Raceway, 10704 (914) 968-3898 or 968-4200, fax (914) 968-1121.

Main Street Flea Market
566 Sawmill River Rd.
(914) 476-1339

Saturday, Sunday. A classic flea market with all lines of housewares, home furnishings, clothing, jewelry, tools, and artwork available.

DAYS, DATES, AND MARKETS ARE SUBJECT TO CHANGE!

NORTH CAROLINA

ALBEMARLE

Albermarle Flea Market
Stony Gap Rd.
Hwy. 52, south of town

Friday, Saturday, 11 a.m.–10 p.m., Sunday, 1 p.m.–9 p.m. Approximately 50 dealers. Indoor market located in a former skating rink. Collectibles, primitives, advertising items abound; glassware, new and used merchandise, and lots of garage sale items available. Snack bar, rest rooms, ample parking. Space from $18. Reservations required. *Contact* Lyman Jones, Rte. 1, Box 3167, Mt. Gilead, 27306 (704) 982-5022.

ANDREWS

Hillbilly Mall
Hwy. 197/74 Bypass
(828) 321-2386

Saturday, Sunday, 8 a.m. until dark. Market has 100,000 sq. ft. indoors. Snack bar, rest rooms, h/a. Ample free parking.

ASHEVILLE

Smiley's Flea Market & Antique Mall
I-26, Exit 13, north approximately one mile

Friday, Saturday, Sunday. Antique mall is open daily with flea market outside on weekends. Approximately 400 spaces. Well-attended, interesting market with lots of everything, especially local crafts. Snack bar, rest rooms, h/a, ample parking. Covered space from $5 per day. Requires NC vendor's license, $5. *Contact* Manager, Box 458, Fletcher, 28732 (704) 684-3532.

Dreamland Drive-In Theater Flea Market
South Tunnel Rd., Rte. 74

Wednesday, Friday, Saturday, Sunday, 7 a.m.–4:30 p.m. Approximately 400 dealers. Antiques, collectibles, crafts, limited new merchandise, lots of used and secondhand items, great selection of primitives and advertising items available. Snack bar, rest rooms, h/a, ample parking. Space from $4. *Contact* Dusty Pless, Box 5936, 28801 (704) 255-7777.

BAKER'S CREEK

Aunt Fanny's Flea Market
Hwy. 74
(704) 586-1413

Friday, Saturday, Sunday.

BOONE

Wildcat Flea Market
Hwy. 421 East, eight miles east of town

Friday, Saturday, Sunday, 8 a.m.–5 p.m. Approximately 50 dealers offer collectibles, antiques, new merchandise, sportswear, used merchandise, and garage sale items. Market conducts public auctions on Saturday evening starting at 7 p.m. Snack bar, rest rooms, h/a, ample parking. Space from $5. Market located in a very scenic area and is a real fun family event. *Contact* Kevin Richardson (704) 264-7757.

NOTE: Many markets will require you to obtain a North Carolina vendor's license before setting up and selling. You can usually purchase the license at the market.

CHARLOTTE

Cook's Plaza
Statesville Rd., Hwy. 21 North
Across the street from the Metrolina Expo
(800) 505-5121 or (910) 661-0610

Friday, Saturday, Sunday. New market. Antiques, collectibles, new and used merchandise available. Snack bar, restaurant, rest rooms, h/a, ample parking. Food vendors welcome. Space from $50 for weekend. Reservations required. *Contact* Manager, Box 459, Rural Hall, NC 47045.

Metrolina Expo Flea Market
7100 Statesville Rd.
Hwy. 21 North, 10 minutes from downtown
I-77, Exit 16A, Sunset Rd., first exit north off I-85 and I-77 intersection

Monthly. Usually the first Saturday and the preceeding Thursday and Friday. Admission $3. Average attendance 12,000. Approximately 800–1,500 dealers. Primarily antiques, collectibles, primitives, and crafts. There are always some nice-quality Civil War items at this market. One of the largest and finest markets in the Southeast. This is a great "source" market for dealers and shopkeepers. Food available, rest rooms, h/a, ample parking. Space starts at $10. Camping with showers available. *Contact* Aileen Lisk, Box 26652, 28221 (800) 824-3770 or (704) 596-4643.

Shopper's Fair Flea Market
4500 Tyron St.
I-85, Exit 41
(704) 596-9007

Friday, 1 p.m.–7 p.m., Saturday, 9 a.m.–6 p.m., Sunday, 1 p.m.–6 p.m. Indoor market with approximately 250 dealers offering antiques, collectibles, crafts, art, new and used merchandise, sportswear, electronics, sporting goods, and housewares. Great market for the budget-conscious buyer. Snack bar, h/a.

CHEROKEE

Uncle Bill's Flea Market
Hwy. 441 North and 74
(704) 586-9613

Saturday, Sunday, April–November. Approximately 150 dealers. Indoor/outdoor market with some covered spaces. Ample parking. Space from $8 per day. Camping available. New market with antique mall open daily, flea market on weekends, weather permitting. *Contact* Bean Seay.

DALLAS

I-85 Flea Market
3867 Dallas-High Shoals Hwy.

Saturday, Sunday, 8 a.m.–4 p.m. Indoor/outdoor market with approximately 400 dealers. Antiques, collectibles, furniture, electronics, jewelry, crafts, livestock, new and used merchandise, produce, tools, and toys. Space from $12 per day outside and $20 inside. Snack bars, rest rooms, h/a. *Contact* David Stewart, Box 402, 28034 (704) 922-1416, fax (704) 922-4525.

DEEP GAP

Wildcat Flea Market
Hwy. 421
Seven miles east of Boone

Friday, Saturday, Sunday, 8 a.m.–5 p.m. Market is located deep in the Blue Ridge Mountains. Approximately 70 dealers offer crafts, antiques, collectibles, new and used merchandise. Great place to spend the day or weekend. Market conducts an auction on Saturday night. Restaurant, rest rooms, ample parking. Space from $5 per day. *Contact* Kevin Richardson, Rte. 7, Box 43, Boone, 28607 (828) 264-7757.

DILLSBORO

441 Flea Market
Hwy. 441, one mile south of town

Friday, Saturday, Sunday. Approximately 20 dealers. Outdoor market with some sheds. Lots of collectibles, secondhand junk, tools, housewares, and garage sale items available. Snack bar, rest rooms, ample parking. Space from $5 per day. *Contact* Padgett McCoy, Box 414, Sylva, 28779 (704) 586-6768.

DURHAM

Flea Market
2523 East Club Blvd.
Starlite Drive-In Theater
I-85, Exit 179

Saturday, Sunday, 8 a.m.–4 p.m. Outdoor market with approximately 75 dealers. Collectibles, memorabilia, guns, primitives, crafts, art, decorator items, always plenty of tobacco collectibles, new and used merchandise available. Snack bar, rest rooms, h/a, ample parking. *Contact* Kathy Bednarz (919) 688-1037.

EDEN

Eden Flea Market
122 N. Van Buren Rd.
Hwy. 14 North

Friday, 1 p.m.–7 p.m., Saturday, 8 a.m.–6 p.m., Sunday, 8 a.m.–5 p.m. Average daily attendance 1,500. Approximately 50 dealers. New merchandise, jewelry, sportswear, electronics, housewares, tools, sports merchandise, used merchandise, country collectibles, produce, and crafts available. Food available, rest rooms, h/a, ample parking. Inside and outside space available from $5 daily outside, $25 per week inside. Electricity available. No campground. *Contact* Phillip McCollum (336) 627-9440 or 623-2111.

FAYETTEVILLE

Raeford Road Flea Market
5207 Raeford Rd.
Rte. 401

Friday, Saturday, Sunday, 7:30 a.m.–5 p.m. Average daily attendance 5,000. Approximately 100 dealers. Outdoor market. New and used merchandise, sportswear, electronics, housewares, and lots of secondhand garage sale items available. Good assortment of collectibles and memorabilia at this market. Snack bars, rest rooms, h/a, ample parking. Space from $3 on Friday, $4 for Saturday and $4 for Sunday. No outside food or drinks sales allowed. Near Ft. Bragg and Pope AFB. *Contact* Camille Leonardo, 912 Hemlock Dr., 28304 (910) 425-8053.

U.S. Flea Market Mall
504 N. McPherson Church Rd.
(910) 868-5011

Friday, Saturday, Sunday, 10 a.m.–7 p.m. Indoor market with approximately 500 spaces. Market has many fine antiques and overall a very high quality of goods. The majority of the booths here are well stocked with the latest in new merchandise, severely discounted. Space from $20 per day. Snack bars, Asian and regular restaurants, clean rest rooms, h/a, ample parking. Camping available. *Contact* Manager, Box 35065, 28303.

FLETCHER

Smiley's Flea Market & Antique Mall
I-26, Exit 13
One-half mile north on U.S. Hwy. 25

Friday, Saturday, Sunday, 8 a.m.–5 p.m. Antique Mall open daily April–December. Flea Market open year-round. Approximately 250 dealers outside. Good selection of antiques, collectibles, primitives, country items, memorabilia, quality glassware and silver, new merchandise, electronics, music, housewares, and used merchandise available. Good all-around market and a very worthwhile stop. Snack bar, rest rooms, h/a, ample parking. Spaces are 10×10 and start at $10. Camping, water, and electricity available. *Contact* Wade McAbee, Box 458, 28732 (828) 684-5651.

FOREST CITY

74 By-Pass Flea Market
180 Frontage Rd.
74 Bypass and Hwy. 221-A

Friday, Saturday, Sunday. Approximately 250 spaces. New merchandise, electronics, housewares, tools, leather, tapes, some antiques and collectibles available here. Snack bar, rest rooms, and showers available, h/a, ample parking. *Contact* Gary Hardin, 180 Frontage Rd., 28034 (828) 245-7863.

FRANKLIN

Franklin Flea & Craft Market
199 Highlands Rd.
One mile from downtown
(828) 524-6658

Friday, Saturday, Sunday, April–November. Approximately 90 covered booths and eight permanent stores. Crafts, antiques, collectibles, jewelry and gemstones, new merchandise, souvenirs, and locally produced food items available. Snack bar, rest rooms, h/a. Space from $20 for the weekend. *Contact* Manager, 867 Highlands Rd., 28734.

FUQUAY

Carolina Gold Leaf Flea Market
Hwy. 55 East
(919) 552-4143

Wednesday, Saturday, Sunday, 7 a.m.–5 p.m. Average daily attendance 7,500. Approximately 175 dealers. Indoor market (building was formerly a tobacco warehouse). Lots of collectibles, glassware, pottery, jewelry, souvenirs, tobacco collectibles, primitives, and kitchenware available. Food available, rest rooms, h/a, ample parking. Space from $14. *Contact* Bill Alexander, Box 607, 27526.

GASTONIA

Great American Flea Market Mall
761 Linwood Rd.
(704) 864-3130

Friday, Saturday, Sunday. Antiques, collectibles, silver, jewelry, linens, glassware, pottery, memorabilia, Civil War items, books, art, prints, used merchandise, vintage clothing, and crafts available. Snack bar, rest rooms, h/a, ample parking.

GOLDSBORO

Goldsboro Flea Market
2102 Wayne Memorial Dr.

Saturday, Sunday, 8 a.m.–5 p.m. Indoor/outdoor market with approximately 250 dealers. Antiques, collectibles, crafts, vintage clothing, glassware, jewelry, silver, and new and used merchandise available. Snack bar, rest rooms, h/a, ample parking. This is a clean, friendly, well-managed market. Space from $10 outside. *Contact* Keith Hartzog (800) 282-FLEA or (919) 736-4422.

Country Junction Flea Market
Hwy. 70 West between Rosewood and Princeton Sts.
(919) 735-5307

Friday, Saturday, Sunday. Great country market with lots of desirable country and farm collectibles, along with a lot of junk. Food available, rest rooms. Space from $6.

GREENSBORO

Super Flea Market
Greensboro Coliseum
1921 W. Lee St.
(336) 373-8515

Saturday, 8 a.m.–5 p.m., Sunday, 10 a.m.–5 p.m. Admission $1.50. Average weekend attendance 8–10,000. Indoor market with approximately 400 dealers. Market is heavy on antiques and collectibles and limited new merchandise. This is a good source market for shopkeepers, dealers, collectors, and decorators. Worth the drive. Snack bar, rest rooms, h/a, ample paid parking. Space for $40 for the weekend. *Contact* William Smith, 703 Simpson St., 27401.

Greensboro Flea Market
4000 McConnel Rd.

Saturday, Sunday. Indoor/outdoor market with approximately 150 dealers. Collectibles, crafts, art, jewelry, silver, and new and used merchandise available. Snack bar, rest rooms, h/a, ample parking. *Contact* Calvin White (336) 697-2707.

GREENVILLE

Poor Man's Flea Market
Hwy. 264 between Greenville and Washington

Saturday, Sunday. Used merchandise, garage sale items, farm and ranch items, prepackaged food, produce, and locally made crafts available. Food available, rest rooms.

Flea Market
Fairgrounds
(919) 758-6916

Saturday, Sunday. New and used merchandise, antiques, collectibles, clothing, housewares, crafts, and produce available. Rest rooms, h/a, ample parking.

Augusta Road Drive-In Theater Flea Market
Junction of I-85 and Hwy. 25
(919) 277-9846

Friday, Saturday, Sunday. New merchandise, sportswear, western wear, electronics, jewelry, housewares, used merchandise, farm items, collectibles, crafts, and produce available. Outdoor market. Snack bar, rest rooms, h/a, ample parking.

HAMPTON

Vintage Village
I-77 and U.S. Hwy. 421 South
(336) 468-8616

Friday, Saturday, Sunday. Average weekend attendance 9,000. Antiques, collectibles, glassware, pottery, fine jewelry, silver, coins, vintage clothing, country collectibles, used merchandise, decorator items, books, art, prints, and Civil War items available. Snack bar, rest rooms, h/a, ample parking. Site has 160 indoor spaces 12×10. Covered outside spaces.

HICKORY

Thunderbird Drive-In Theater Flea Market
3451 Springs Rd.

Saturday, Sunday, 8 a.m.–4 p.m. Market averages 250 dealers offering antiques, collectibles, crafts, and used and new merchandise. Snack bars, rest rooms, h/a, ample parking. Outdoor/indoor market with some covered spaces. Space from $5 per day. *Contact* Jim Springs, 3451 Springs Rd., 28601 (828) 256-7669.

Hickory Livestock Sale & Flea Market
Sweet Water Rd. one-half mile north of Hwy. 64 and Rte. 70

Thursday, 5 a.m. until dark. Outdoor market with approximately 300 dealers. Antiques, collectibles, crafts, primitives, lots of used and secondhand items, and limited new merchandise available. Market conducts livestock auctions weekly. Nice cafe, good down-home cooking here, rest rooms, h/a. This is a classic southern market that is a real education to visit. Space from $7 per day. *Contact* George Hahn, 1958 Kool Park Rd. NE, 28601 (828) 256-2673 or 324-7354.

Flea Market
I-40 Trade Lot
I-40, Exit 113, Connley Springs exit

Friday, Saturday, 6 a.m.–5 p.m. Outdoor market. Antiques, collectibles, primitives, advertising items, farm items, antique toys, coins, silver, jewelry, livestock, new merchandise, sportswear, housewares, and lots of secondhand merchandise available. Snack bar, rest rooms, h/a, ample parking. Space from $5 per day. *Contact* George Hahn, 951 Cloninger Mill Rd. Northeast, 28601 (828) 256-2673.

HIGH POINT

Westchester Flea Market
2200 Westchester Dr.
Hwy. 68

Saturday, Sunday, 8 a.m.–5 p.m. Indoor market with approximately 250 dealers. Crafts, collectibles, fishing items, new and used furniture, and secondhand merchandise available. Snack bar, rest rooms, h/a, video arcade, ample parking. Space from $15. *Contact* Brenda Mauldin (910) 884-5063.

JACKSONVILLE

Cinema Drive-In Theater Flea Market
Belfork Rd.

Friday, Saturday, Sunday. Admission charge. Approximately 150 dealers. Large commercial market with lots of new merchandise, surplus, closeouts, prepackaged food, used merchandise, farm items, collectibles, crafts, and produce available. Snack bar, rest rooms, h/a, ample parking. Space from $5. *Contact* Bill Jensen, Box 5043, 28540 (919) 353-0911.

The Market Place
174 College Plaza
(919) 455-3889 or 347-2747

Saturday, Sunday. New and used merchandise, country collectibles, glassware, silver, jewelry, housewares, clothing, farm items, crafts, collectibles, and produce available. Snack bar, rest rooms, ample parking. Outside market with covered spaces. Camping and electricity available.

JAMESTOWN

Westchester Flea
715 W. Main St.
Jamestown Shopping Center, 27282

Saturday, Sunday, 9 a.m.–5 p.m. Heated and air-conditioned. Space of 10x12 with one table, $15 per day. Electricity available. Free parking. *Contact* (336) 454-5706, fax (336) 454-5934. E-mail: wcfleamkt@aol.com.

KANNAPOLIS

Koco's Flea Mall
485 S. Cannon Blvd.

Friday, Saturday, Sunday, 10 a.m.–6 p.m. Indoor market with approximately 70 dealers, 50,000 sq. ft. Antiques, collectibles, jewelry, sportswear, new and used merchandise, locally made crafts, gifts, and imports. Snack bars, rest rooms, h/a. Space from $8 per table. *Contact* Manager, 485 S. Cannon Blvd., 28083 (704) 938-9100.

KERNERSVILLE

Farm City Flea Market
4348 Kernersville Rd.

Friday, Saturday, Sunday, 8 a.m.–5 p.m. Indoor/outdoor market with approximately 200 dealers. Collectibles, memorabilia, crafts, new and used merchandise, furniture, and housewares available. Snack bar, deli, rest rooms, h/a, ample parking. *Contact* Tommy Chandler (919) 784-4440.

KILL DEVIL HILLS

Indoor Flea Market
306 W. Lake Dr.

Saturdays. Indoor market with approximately 25 dealers. Contact Fred Bear (252) 441-8830.

LEXINGTON

Farmers & Flea Market
Old Hwy. 64 West

Tuesday, Wednesday, daylight until dark. Average daily attendance 3,000. Market averages 250 vendors. Real country market with old-time atmosphere and lots of good stuff—and some not so good. Market is open on Monday for wholesale only. Tax ID required to purchase wholesale. Approximately 100 wholesalers set up selling various lines of merchandise at wholesale. Food available, rest rooms, ample parking. Camping and electricity available. Space from $15. Indoor and outdoor space available. *Contact* Tim Fritts, Rte. 15, Box 1357, 27292 (336) 248-2157 or 248-2222 for wholesale market; fax (336) 246-8693.

Davidson Farmers Livestock & Flea Market
Old Hwy. 64
(336) 248-2173

Open all day Tuesday and half day Wednesday. Used merchandise, garage sale items, treasures and trash, farm items, lots of tack, new merchandise, prepackaged food, clothing, housewares, produce, livestock, and pets. Food available, rest rooms, ample parking, lots of walking.

LUMBERTON

Traders Station Flea & Farmers Market
W. 5th St.
I-95, Exit 14 or 17
(919) 738-4519

Wednesday–Sunday. Approximately 200 vendors. Antiques, collectibles, silver, jewelry, glassware, pottery, memorabilia, Civil War items, books, art, crafts, prints, new merchandise, and some great collector lines here. Restaurant, rest rooms, h/a, ample parking. Outdoor/indoor market.

ALWAYS CALL AHEAD TO VERIFY DATES AND INFORMATION

MONROE

Sweet Union Flea Market
402 Hwy. 74 West

Saturday, Sunday, 8 a.m.–5 p.m. Indoor/outdoor market with approximately 250 dealers. Antiques, collectibles, new and used merchandise, garage sale items. Space from $10 per day. Snack bar, rest rooms, h/a. Ample free parking. *Contact* Manager, 402 Hwy. 74 West, 28110 (704) 283-7985.

MORGANTOWN

Jamestown Flea Market
Jamestown Rd.
I-40, Exit 100

Saturday, Sunday, 7 a.m.–5 p.m. Average daily attendance of 4,500. Market averages 250 dealers. Good selection of merchandise here including crafts, collectibles, new and used furniture, collectibles, coins, silver, jewelry, lots of new merchandise, and secondhand items. Snack bar, rest rooms, h/a, ample parking. One of the area's better markets. Space from $10 per day. Camping available. *Contact* P.W. Patton, Box 764, 28655 (704) 584-4038.

MT. AIREY

Greyhound Flea Market
2134 W. Pine St. Hwy. 89

Saturday, Sunday. Indoor market with approximately 25 dealers in a 20,000-sq.-ft. new building. *Contact* Nancy Dixon (336) 789-0417.

Mountain Man Flea Market
Hwy. 52

Sunday. Antiques, collectibles, farm and ranch collectibles, Civil War items, black powder items, toys, primitives, and a good assortment of early collectibles available. Food available, rest rooms.

MURPHY

Decker's Flea Market
Junction of Rtes. 19 and 129

Saturday, Sunday, 7 a.m.–3 p.m. Market is located in the mountains of western North Carolina. Indoor/outdoor market with approximately 100 dealers. Antiques, collectibles, primitives, livestock, new and used merchandise. Space from $5. Good food available, rest rooms. *Contact* Jerry Decker, Box 453, 28906 (828) 837-5753.

NEW LONDON

Shady Acres Flea Market
Hwy. 49

Friday, Saturday, Sunday, 7 a.m.–4 p.m. Outdoor market with approximately 100 dealers. Collectibles, some antiques, new merchandise, housewares, furniture, and lots of secondhand merchandise available. Snack bar, rest rooms, h/a, ample parking. Space from $8 per day. *Contact* Floyd Goins, Box 928, Denton, 27239 (704) 869-5386.

OLD FORT

Catawba Trading Lot
Catawba River Rd.
I-40, Exit 173

Friday, Saturday, Sunday, 7:30 a.m. until dark. Approximately 150 dealers. Antiques, collectibles, memorabilia, primitives, country items, vintage clothing, farm items, glassware, and antique toys available. No new merchandise. Snack bar, rest rooms, h/a, ample parking. Outdoor market with some covered spaces. *Contact* Phillip Lowery, Box 269, 28762 (704) 668-4737 or 668-4511.

RALEIGH

Raleigh Flea Market Mall
1924 Capital Blvd.

Saturday, Sunday, 7 a.m. until dark. Average weekend attendance 12,000. Approximately 200 vendors indoors and outdoors. Antiques, collectibles, country items, primitives, memorabilia, collectible glassware, silver, fine and costume jewelry, new merchandise, sportswear, electronics, videos, and housewares available. Indoor market is housed in an 85,000-square-foot building, heated and air-conditioned. Snack bars, rest rooms, h/a, ample paved parking. Space from $10 daily. Reservations recommended. Overnight camping welcome. *Contact* Wayne or Doug Brown, 1924 North Blvd., (919) 839-0038 or 856-0021, fax 856-0021.

Watson's Flea Market
1436 Rock Quarry Rd.
I-40, Exit 30
(919) 832-6232

Saturday, Sunday. Average daily attendance of 2,500. Approximately 150 dealers. New and used merchandise, antiques, collectibles, silver, coins, vintage clothing, and jewelry available. Restaurant, clean rest rooms, h/a, ample parking. Space from $3. Indoor and outside space available. Camping available. This is a very pleasant, clean, friendly, and well-managed market. *Contact* Ebern Watson, 27611.

Flea Market
Fairgrounds
2200 Atlantic Ave.
Raleigh Beltway, Exit 10

Saturday, Sunday, 7 a.m.–5 p.m. Indoor market with approximately 125 dealers. Antiques, collectibles, furniture, crafts, produce, lots of bric-a-brac, used items, and garage sale merchandise available. Good selection of new merchandise here. Space from $13 per day outside. *Contact* Joan Long, Box 33517, 27636 phone and fax (919) 829-3533.

RANDLEMAN

Randleman Flea Mall
Hwy. 220, Randleman Exit

Friday, Saturday, Sunday. Antiques, collectibles, silver, coins, vintage clothing, Civil War items, books, art, prints, new merchandise, used merchandise, and crafts available. Snack bar, rest rooms, h/a, ample parking.

REIDSVILLE

Flea Market
Fairgrounds
Hwy. 14
(919) 349-6536

Friday, Saturday, Sunday. Collectibles, coins, glassware, silver, sports cards, sometimes antiques, decorator items, new and used merchandise, crafts, and produce available. Food available, rest rooms, h/a, ample parking.

ROANOKE

158 Flea Market
I-95, Exit 173 West
(919) 535-4242

Saturday, Sunday. Indoor/outdoor market with approximately 20 vendors. Market is mainly collectibles, secondhand items, and a great selection of locally made country crafts. Ample parking. Space from $4.

ROCKINGHAM

Flea Fair USA
Westside Shopping Center
120 Caroline St.
(910) 895-0250

Friday, Saturday, Sunday, 6 a.m.–6 p.m. Market averages 250 dealers. New merchandise, used merchandise, good selection of country collectibles, antiques, and some very well-stocked booths here. Indoor/outdoor market. Snack bar, rest rooms, h/a, ample parking. Space from $7.50 per day outside. New market.

INFORMATION IS SUBJECT TO CHANGE—ALWAYS CALL AHEAD TO AVOID DISAPPOINTMENT

ROCKY MOUNT

Antiques & Crafts Flea Market
2532 N. Raleigh St.
(252) 443-0376

Saturday, Sunday. Antiques, collectibles, furniture, silver, jewelry, new and used merchandise, and a great selection of locally made country crafts available. Food available, rest rooms, h/a.

ROCKY POINT

Flea Market
Hwy. 117

Friday, Saturday, Sunday, 10 a.m.–5 p.m. Indoor/outdoor market with approximately 10 dealers. Some collectibles, crafts, lots of used and garage sale items here. These are the kind of places we find a treasure. No food. *Contact* Joe Stallings (910) 675-3023.

SALISBURY

Webb Road Flea Market
905 Webb Rd.
I-85, Exit 70

Saturday, Sunday, 8 a.m.–5 p.m. Outdoor/indoor market with approximately 300 dealers. Antiques, collectibles, memorabilia, primitives, country items, crafts, art, new merchandise, sportswear, jewelry, used merchandise, and tools available. One of the area's larger and better markets. Snack bar, rest rooms, h/a, ample parking. Space from $60 for the weekend. Camping, showers, and electricity available. *Contact* John Nash, 905 Webb Rd., 28146 (704) 857-6660.

STATESVILLE

Statesville Flea Market
1441 N. Center St.
Hwy. 115, I-40, Exit 150

Saturday, Sunday, 9 a.m.–6 p.m. Outdoor/indoor market. Collectibles, crafts, housewares, garage sale items, surplus, and new merchandise available. Restaurant, rest rooms, h/a, ample parking. Space from $15 per day. *Contact* George Turnage (704) 878-6426.

Sharon's Discount Flea Market
Hwy. 21, I-40, Exit 151, I-77, Exit 54

Daily. Indoor market with approximately 50 dealers. *Contact* Sharon Fuller (704) 838-0948.

THOMASVILLE

Eleven Acre Flea Market
825 Julian Ave.
I-85, Exit 103

Friday, Saturday, Sunday, 5 a.m.–5 p.m. Indoor/outdoor market with some covered spaces. Market averages 200 dealers. Collectibles, farm items, coins, crafts, advertising items, housewares, memorabilia, primitives, new merchandise, electronics, and used and garage sale items available. Space starts at $10 outside. Snack bar, rest rooms, h/a, ample parking. *Contact* Andrew Pope, 9 College St., 27360 (336) 472-0244 or 476-9566, fax (910) 472-0244.

WEAVERVILLE

Jupiter Flea Market
20 Old Jupiter Rd.
Hwy. 19-23, Jupiter Exit

Friday, 12 p.m.–9 p.m., Saturday, Sunday, 7:30 a.m.–4:30 p.m. Indoor/outdoor market with approximately 300 dealers. Collectibles, primitives, farm items, and new and used merchandise available. Snack bar, rest rooms, ample parking, but a long walk to the market. Space from $10 per day. Market is located in an old schoolhouse. *Contact* Steve Neshem (704) 645-6116.

WILMINGTON

Starway Flea Market
2346 Carolina Beach Rd.
Rte. 421

Friday, 8 a.m.–8 p.m, Saturday, 6 a.m.–4 p.m., Sunday, 7 a.m.–4 p.m. Indoor/outdoor market with approximately 150 dealers. Collectibles, memorabilia, primitives, country and farm items, decorator items, new merchandise, and lots of used items available. Snack bar, rest rooms, h/a, ample parking. Space from $5 on Friday outside. *Contact* Doyle Penley (910) 763-5520.

WINSTON-SALEM

Cook's Flea Market
5721 University Pkwy.
Junction of Hwys. 52 and 8
(910) 661-0610 or 661-0999

Saturday, Sunday. Market averages 300 dealers. Acres of new and used merchandise, antiques, collectibles, and lots of stuff. Restaurant with good food, clean rest rooms, h/a, ample parking. Indoor market. Space from $34 for the weekend. Reservations required. Camping and electricity available. Friendly, well-managed market. *Contact* Manager, Box 459, Rural Hall, 47045.

Cook's Flea Market 2
4263 N. Patterson Ave.
(910) 661-0610 or 661-0999

Saturday, Sunday. Approximately 300 dealers. Antiques, collectibles, and new and used merchandise available. Snack bars, rest rooms, h/a, ample parking. Space from $25 per weekend. Reservations required. Food vendors welcome. *Contact* Manager, Box 459, Rural Hall, 47045.

NORTH DAKOTA

BISMARCK

Dakota Midwest Flea Market & Antique Show
Mandan Community Center

Monthly. Call for dates. Antiques, collectibles, glassware, furniture, dolls, toys, vintage clothing, jewelry, books, country primitives, Victorian-era items, new and used merchandise of the general garage sale variety available. Food available, rest rooms, h/a, ample parking. New market. *Contact* Leo Mattern, 2738 Gateway Dr., No. 8, 58501 (701) 258-5623.

GRAND FORKS

Flea Market & Craft Show
South Forks Plaza Pavilion
1700 S. Washington

Friday, Saturday. Average attendance 1,500. New and used merchandise, collectibles, crafts, gifts, imports, decorator items, and jewelry available. Held indoors—new market. Snack bar, rest rooms. Electricity available; 150 dealer spaces. *Contact* Leo Saucedo (701) 772-8121.

Greater Grand Forks Area Flea Market
Fairgrounds

Every fourth Saturday. Antiques, collector items, country primitives, Victorian-era items, glassware, heirloom offerings of all kinds. Also plenty of garage-sale-type bric-a-brac and new necessities like household goods, home furnishings, and clothing available. Snack bar, rest rooms, h/a, ample parking.

MANDAN

Midwest Flea Market & Antique Show
Mandan Community Center
901 Division St.
I-94, Exit 152

Every first weekend, 9 a.m.–5 p.m. Admission charge $1. Approximately 75 dealers, indoors, with antiques, collectibles, art, crafts, new, and some used merchandise. Snack bar, rest rooms, h/a, ample parking. Space from $15 per day. *Contact* Bruce Skogen, 2512-93rd St. SE, Bismarck, 58504 (701) 223-6185.

MINOT

Magic City Flea Market
State Fairgrounds
Hwy. 2

Every second weekend, 9 a.m.–4 p.m. Admission $1. Average attendance 3,000. Approximately 125 dealers. Indoor market with some outdoor spaces during the summer. Antiques, collectibles, and crafts as well as new and used merchandise of all kinds and descriptions available. This is the area's leading flea market. Snack bar, rest rooms, h/a, ample parking. Space from $10 per day. *Contact* Richard Timboe, Box 1672, 58702 (701) 852-1289 or 838-1150.

OHIO

AKRON

Akron Antique Market, Fairgrounds
Junction of State Rte. 91 and East Howe Rd.

Quarterly. Admission charge. Market is held 4 times per year, call for exact dates. Indoor market with approximately 200 dealers. Antiques, collectibles, fine line of quality smalls, coins, stamps, vintage clothing, and glassware. Space from $50. Snack bar, rest rooms, h/a. Paid parking. *Contact* Luck Pro, Box 5473, 44334 (216) 867-6724.

ALLIANCE

Farmers Auction & Flea Market
Rte. 62
Eighteen miles northeast of Canton

Saturday, Sunday, 9 a.m.–5 p.m. Approximately 50 dealers. Average attendance 500–1,000. New merchandise, antiques, collectibles, and a large selection of new furniture available. This is a real pleasant country market. Mark your map so you don't miss this one. Snack bar, rest rooms, h/a, ample parking, and overnight parking available. Space from $20. *Contact* George Pilla, 1500 S. Mahoning Ave., 44601 (216) 823-2302 or 823-8242.

AMHERST

Jamie's Flea Market
Rte. 113
See South Amherst listing.

Wednesday, Saturday.

ALWAYS CALL BEFORE TRAVELING LONG DISTANCES!

ANDOVER

Pymatuning Lake Drive-In Flea Market
South of town
(440) 293-7757

Sunday. Admission charge. Approximately 400 dealers. Large, classic midwestern flea market with a great selection of collector lines, small antiques, primitives, sometimes loads of antique furniture, a wide range of new and used merchandise. Food available, rest rooms, h/a, ample parking, and lots of walking. Space from $2.75.

ASHTABULA

Tannery Hill Farmers Flea Market
Main Ave. Extension

Friday, Saturday. Average weekend attendance 15,000. Approximately 200 dealers offer used merchandise, collector items, jewelry, housewares, and clothing. Space from $5. *Contact* Arthur Eronson, Box 592, 44004 (440) 998-6211.

BEACH CITY

Shady Rest Flea Market
Hwys. 250 and 93

Sunday, April–October, daylight until dark. Outdoor market with approximately 100 dealers. New merchandise, lots of used garage sale items and bric-a-brac available. Snack bar, rest rooms, h/a, ample parking. Space from $6 per day. *Contact* Mildred Miller, 1762 Johnstown Rd. Northeast, Dover, OH 44622 (216) 343-9508.

BLOOMFIELD

Bloomfield Auction & Flea Market
Rte. 87
One-half mile west of town

Thursday, 6 a.m.–4 p.m. Indoor and outdoor market with approximately 150 dealers offering crafts, antiques, collectibles, new and used merchandise, and produce. Lots of Amish goods, food, and buggies here. Snack bar, rest rooms, h/a, ample parking. Space from $6. *Contact* Bill Herman, Box 51, Kinsman, 44428 (216) 875-4403.

BOWLING GREEN

Wood County Indoor & Outdoor Antiques & Flea Market
Fairgrounds
(419) 352-1861 or 352-0969

Every second weekend. Antiques, collectibles, country primitives, Victorian-era items, dolls, toys, glassware, advertising items, furniture, used desirables of all descriptions, handcrafted treasures, and some reproductions available. Snack bar, rest rooms, h/a, ample parking.

Bowling Green Flea Market
Junior Fair Building
Rte. 64 and Poe Rd.

Saturday, Sunday. Antiques, collectibles, furniture, jewelry, vintage clothing, kitchen collectibles, advertising items, and new and used merchandise available. Food available, rest rooms, h/a, ample parking. Inside and outside market. Camping available.

BROOKLYN

Memphis Flea Market
Memphis Triple Drive-In Theater
10543 Memphis Ave.

Wednesday, Saturday, Sunday. Admission charge. Large outdoor market with approximately 400 dealers. Lots of new merchandise here, used merchandise, garage sale items, new collector lines, crafts, produce. Snack bar, rest rooms, h/a. Ample free parking. Contact William Applearth (216) 941-2892.

CAESAR CREEK

Caesar Creek Flea Market
Junction of I-71 and State Rte. 73 near Wilmington

Saturday, Sunday. Admission charge. Average daily attendance of 5,000. Approximately 350 dealers. One of the area's better markets. Antiques, crafts, and lots of new and used merchandise available. Snack bar, rest rooms, h/a, ample parking. This is a real clean, friendly market with a great selection and variety of booths. Camping available, market open to food vendors. *Contact* Allen Levin, 7763 Rte. 73, Wilmington, 45171 (513) 382-1669 or 223-0222.

CANTON

Old Stark Antique Faire
Stark County Fairgrounds
305 Wertz Ave.
(216) 478-1602

Monthly. Indoor/outdoor market. Approximately 200 dealers. Strong antique, collectibles, and smalls market. Snack bar, rest rooms, h/a. Ample free parking.

CINCINNATI

Finneytown Flea Market
1047 W. Northbend Rd.
(513) 681-7250

Friday, Saturday, Sunday. Indoor market. New merchandise, electronics, housewares, decorator items, home furnishings, jewelry, sports merchandise, children's items, used merchandise, garage sale items, and collector items available. Snack bar, rest rooms, h/a, ample parking.

Paris Flea Market
Ferguson Hills Drive-In Theater
2310 Ferguson Rd.
(513) 223-0222 or 451-1271

Saturday, Sunday, 7 a.m.–4 p.m. Average attendance 9,000. Approximately 250 dealers offer lots of new merchandise, imports, gifts, housewares, electronics, sportswear, some antiques and collectibles, crafts, and produce. One of the area's better flea markets. Always a great opportunity to find some real treasures or super buys at this market. Snack bar, rest rooms, h/a, ample parking. Space from $4.50. *Contact* Ferguson Hills Drive-In, 2310 Ferguson Rd., 45238.

Peddlers Flea Market
4344 Kellogg Ave.
East of downtown on Ohio River
(513) 871-3700

Saturday, Sunday. Average attendance 5,000. Approximately 400 dealers. Large commercial market with lots of new merchandise, used merchandise, farm collectibles, a wide variety of collector lines, crafts, and produce available. Snack bars, rest rooms, h/a, ample parking, and lots of walking here. Inside and outside space available from $22. *Contact* Manager, Peddlers Flea Market, 4344 Kellogg Ave.

Stickers Grove Flea Market
Rte. 128
One mile south of Ross
(513) 733-5885

Thursday, June–September, 9 a.m.–5 p.m. Approximately 100 dealers offer antiques, furniture, collector lines, new and used merchandise. Food available, h/a, ample parking. *Contact* Ohio Valley Promotions, 9468 Reading Rd., 45215.

Turtle Creek Flea Market
I-75 and State Rte. 63

Saturday, Sunday. New merchandise, souvenirs, sportswear, housewares, sports cards, jewelry, secondhand merchandise, some collectibles. Snack bar, rest rooms, h/a, ample parking. Inside, covered, and outside space available. New market, not recommended for commercial vendors. A smaller, local market.

Traders World
601 Union Rd.
Off I-75, Exit 29

Saturday, Sunday. New market with inside and covered spaces. Good attendance. Primarily new merchandise and crafts at this market. Large selection of discounted surplus, closeouts on new, personal, and household merchandise. *Contact* Traders World, Box 99, Monroe, 45050.

Village Flea Market
2095 Seymore Ave.
(513) 351-3151

Saturday, Sunday. Indoor/outdoor market. Approximately 20 dealers.

CIRCLEVILLE

Pickaway County Flea Market
U.S. Rte. 22 East
(740) 474-2085

Monthly, call for dates. Approximately 90–100 dealers. Antiques, always a great selection of collector lines, and country and farm collectibles. Country primitives, new and used merchandise, and garage sale items also available. Food available, rest rooms, h/a, ample parking. Space from $10. Reservations recommended. Camping with showers and electricity available. *Contact* John or Melissa Rodgers, Box 93, Williamsport, 43164.

CLEVELAND

I-X Center Super Flea Mall
I-X Center
6200 Riverside Dr.

Monthly. Contact James Kostas (216) 265-2623. Call for current schedule.

Memphis Drive-In Theater Flea Market
10543 Memphis Ave.
(216) 941-2892

Saturday. New merchandise, housewares, electronics, jewelry, clothing, children's items, sportswear, sports merchandise, used merchandise, and garage sale junk available. Snack bar, rest rooms, h/a, ample parking.

Clark Avenue Flea Market
5109 Clark Ave.

Thursday–Sunday, 11 a.m.–6 p.m. Indoor/outdoor market with approximately 60 dealers. Antiques, collectibles, jewelry, glassware; indoors is mostly permanent shops with some nice-quality items. Excellent restaurant, clean rest rooms, h/a. Clean, friendly market. Outside space from $4. *Contact* Fred Scafe (216) 398-5283.

Lee Road International Market
4115 Lee Rd.
(216) 491-9058

Saturday, Sunday. Indoor market. New merchandise, closeouts, surplus, decorator items, and gift items available. Good shopper's market.

The Bazaar
4979 W. 130th St.
Corner of Brook Park Rd. and W. 130th St.

Friday, Saturday, Sunday, 10 a.m.–6 p.m. Primarily permanent dealers on a monthly basis. Lots of collectibles and secondhand items available. *Contact* John Grace (216) 362-0022.

COLUMBIANA

Theron's Country Flea Market
1641 Columbiana-Lisbon Rd.
Rte. 164
(216) 482-4327

Sunday, 9 a.m.–5 p.m. Approximately 50 dealers. Inside and outside spaces. Market is composed primarily of antiques and collectibles. Good selection of smalls here. Market conducts general household auctions on Saturday nights. Several small antique and collectible shops within the facility. Country restaurant, rest rooms, h/a, ample parking. *Contact* Manager, 1641 Columbiana-Lisbon Rd., 44408.

COLUMBUS

The South Drive-In Theater Flea Market
3050 S. High St.
Rte. 40, one mile east of Reynoldsburg

Wednesday, Saturday, Sunday, 7 a.m.–2 p.m. Approximately 400 dealers. Large outdoor market with mostly new and used merchandise, and garage sale dealers. Space $5 on Saturday or Sunday, 50 cents on Wednesday. *Contact* Doug Hott, 865 King Ave., 43212.

Livingston Court Flea Market
3575 E. Livingston Ave.
(614) 291-3133 or 231-7726

Friday, Saturday, Sunday, 10 a.m.–7 p.m. Large outdoor market with approximately 350 dealers. New and used merchandise, lots of bric-a-brac, some antiques, collectibles, and crafts available. Snack bars, rest rooms, h/a, ample parking. Space from $15 per day. *Contact* Doug Hott, 865 King Ave., 43212

Rainbow's Giant Amos Indoor Flea Market
3454 Cleveland Ave.

Friday, Saturday, Sunday, 10 a.m.–7 p.m. Approximately 225 dealers. Large indoor market with primarily new merchandise, electronics, sportswear, housewares, tools, jewelry, clothing, and new collectibles available. Snack bar, rest rooms, h/a, ample parking. Space from $16 per day. *Contact* Doug Hott, 865 King Ave., 43212 (614) 262-0045 or 291-3133.

Antiques & Collectibles Show
Ohio State Fairgrounds
I-71, Exit 17th Ave. West
(740) 569-4112
Fax (740) 569-7595

Monthly. Usually third weekend of month. Large, quality market with over 1,000 dealers. Antiques and collectibles only. Usually third weekend of the month. One of the better-quality antique events in the country. For those in the trade this is a great source market. Food available, rest rooms, h/a, ample parking with $3 charge. Inside space from $75. Outside from $54. *Contact* Don Scott, Box 60, Bremen, 43107 (740) 569-4112, fax 569-7595.

Swap Shop & Flea Market
CCC Twin Drive-In Theater
1375 Harrisburg Pike
(614) 275-4444

Saturday, Sunday. New and used merchandise, garage sale items, home furnishings, household goods, clothing, collectibles, crafts, and produce available. Snack bar, rest rooms, h/a, ample parking.

Westland Indoor Flea Market
4170 W. Broad St.
(614) 298-7122 or 291-3134

Friday, Saturday, Sunday, 10 a.m.–7 p.m. New market. Large indoor market with primarily new merchandise, electronics, sportswear, sports items, housewares, tools, some collectibles, and used merchandise available. Snack bar, rest rooms, h/a, ample parking. Space from $17 per day. *Contact* Doug Hott, 865 King Ave., 43212.

CUYAHOGA FALLS

Oakwood Antiques & Collectibles Market
3265 Oakwood Dr.

Friday, Saturday, Sunday. Indoor/outdoor market with approximately 10 dealers. Small market with mostly secondhand and garage sale items; some collectibles and decorator items available. Snack bar, rest rooms, ample parking. Space from $10 per day. *Contact* Bill Kern (330) 673-4762 or 923-7745.

DAYTON

Dayton Traffic Circle Flea Market
3700 Keats

Friday, Saturday, Sunday, 10 a.m.–5 p.m. Average attendance 4,000. Approximately 400 dealers offer new merchandise, housewares, sportswear, electronics, jewelry, children's items, tools, sports merchandise, decorator items, and gift items. Snack bar, rest rooms, h/a, ample parking. Inside and outside space available. *Contact* Jerry Richie, 3700 Keats, 45414 (513) 275-4759.

Paris Flea Market
6201 N. Dixie Dr.
Dixie Drive-in Theater

Saturday, Sunday, 7 a.m.–4 p.m. Admission charge. Average daily attendance 1,500. Approximately 50 dealers in outdoor market offer a good selection of antiques and collectibles, crafts, and new and used merchandise. Snack bars, rest rooms, h/a, ample parking. Space from $10. *Contact* Gary Castle, 6201 N. Dixie Dr., 45414 (937) 890-5513.

DELAWARE

Country Bazaar
Hwy. 23
I-480 and I-71
(614) 275-4444 or 291-3133

Sunday, 10 a.m.–6 p.m. Approximately 150 vendors. Antiques, collector lines, furniture, silver, coins, sports cards, fine and costume jewelry, vintage clothing, lots of country collectibles, and decorator items available. Food available, rest rooms, h/a, ample parking. Inside and outside space from $6 daily. Most inside spaces rented to sellers on a monthly basis. This is one of the area's better all around markets. *Contact* Doug Hott, 865 King Ave., 43212.

Kingman Drive-In Theater Flea Market
Rte. 23 North
Approximately eight miles north of I-270
(740) 548-4202

Sunday, March–October, 7 a.m.–3 p.m. Admission charge. Approximately 200 dealers offer new merchandise, crafts, produce, some antiques, and a good selection of collectibles. Snack bar, rest rooms, h/a, ample parking. Space from $10. *Contact* Dale Zinn, 865 King Ave. 43212, (740) 548-4227.

DOVER

Dover Flea Market
120 N. Tuscarawas Ave.
(330) 364-3959

Saturday, Sunday. New merchandise, sportswear, housewares, jewelry, sports merchandise, clothing, children's items, used merchandise, decorator wares, collectibles, and primitives available. Snack bar, rest rooms, h/a, ample parking. *Contact* H. Ricer (330) 364-3959, 44633.

EATON

Preble County Flea Market
Fairgrounds
Rte. 122
(513) 456-4709

Every first weekend. Approximately 75 dealers offer antiques, collectibles, farm and country collectibles, silver, coins, jewelry, and vintage clothing. Food available, rest rooms, h/a, ample parking. Inside and outside space available. Eaton is also the home of the Preble County Pork Festival, one of Ohio's better special events. The festival is always held in early September. *Contact* Myron Peer.

ELYRIA

Halls Flea Market
41957 N. Ridge Rd.
Rte. 254

Friday, Saturday, Sunday, 10 a.m.–6 p.m. Average daily attendance 500–1,000. Approximately 150 dealers. Good selection of new merchandise, lots of used items, many collector booths, crafts, produce, and country and farm collectibles available. Food available, rest rooms, h/a, ample parking. Inside and outside space available from $5. Overnight parking and camping nearby. *Contact* Connie Hall, 41957 N. Ridge Rd., 44035 (216) 324-4166 or 233-8613.

FERNALD

Web Flea Market
7500 New Haven Rd.

Saturday, Sunday. Approximately 300 dealers. Large, classic midwestern market with a great selection of new and used merchandise. Many booths of collector lines, silver, glassware, primitives, advertising items, housewares, clothing, fashion accessories, and giftware. Food available, rest rooms, h/a, ample paved parking, and lots of walking. Inside and outside spaces available. *Contact* Marge Weber, 3411 Spring Grove Ave., Cincinnati, 45225 (513) 738-2678.

FRANKLIN

Schome Flea Market
8862 Dayton Oxford Rd.

Saturday, Sunday. Admission charge. Average daily attendance 1,500. Approximately 125 dealers. New merchandise, used merchandise, garage sale items, farm items, clothing, and housewares available. Snack bar, rest rooms, h/a, ample parking. Space from $5. *Contact* Frank Sublett, 45005 (937) 746-0389.

FREMONT

Fremont Flea Market
Fairgrounds
Four miles south of tpke., Exit 6

Every second weekend, 10 a.m.–5 p.m. Average daily attendance 1,500. Approximately 90 dealers. Primarily used merchandise, lots of bric-a-brac, some collectibles, and new merchandise available. Snack bar, rest rooms, h/a, ample parking. Camping available on-site. Market held second Saturday and Sunday of every month. Inside and outside space available from $13 daily, tables $2. Reservations recommended. This market conducts several special events during the year. Call for brochure. *Contact* Gary Kern, 821 Rawson Ave., 43420 (419) 332-1200 or 332-6937.

HARTVILLE

Hartville Flea Market
788 Edison St.
Rte. 619 East from I-77
North of Canton

Monday, Thursday, 7 a.m.–6 p.m. Average attendance 10,000. Approximately 800–1,000 vendors. A wide-open marketplace with lots of new merchandise and a good selection of small antiques, collectibles, sports items, and memorabilia available. Snack bar, rest rooms, h/a, ample parking. Space from $6 on Monday; this is the big day at this market. Indoor and outdoor space available. *Contact* Marian Coblentz, 788 Edison St., 44632 (330) 877-9860.

HUBBARD

Hubbard Liberty Flea Market
Rte. 304

Wednesday, Saturday, Sunday. Approximately 100 dealers. New merchandise, clothing, housewares, children's items, jewelry, sports merchandise, collector lines, crafts, gifts, and used merchandise available. Snack bar, rest rooms, h/a, ample parking. *Contact* Mel Revelis (330) 534-9855.

HUBER HEIGHTS

Brandt Pike Flea Market
Marion Meadows Shopping Center
6123 Brandt Pike

Friday, Saturday, Sunday, 9 a.m.–5 p.m. New and used merchandise, lots of garage sale booths, collectibles, and locally made crafts. Market is in an interesting city of all-brick homes, only such town in America. *Contact* Ron Kronenberger, 45424 (513) 236-5003.

LIMA

Lima Antique Show & Flea Market
Fairgrounds

Saturday, Sunday, May–September. Admission charge. Approximately 50 dealers. Antiques, collectibles, silver, jewelry, sports cards, vintage clothing, primitives, and advertising items. Excellent market for antique shopping. Food available, rest rooms, h/a, ample parking. Indoor market. *Contact* Aubrey Martin, 716 S. Main St., 45804 (419) 228-1050.

MANSFIELD

Mansfield Flea Market
County Fairgrounds

Monthly, call for dates. Admission charge. Approximately 300 dealers. Primarily antiques and collectibles. This is always a buyer's market with lots of quality items at great discount prices. Usually held last weekend of the month. Snack bar, rest rooms, h/a, ample parking. Indoor market with space from $30 for the weekend. *Contact* J. Stark, 784 Vernon Rd., Columbus, 43209 (419) 237-3689.

MARENGO

Straw Factory Flea Market
637 Rte. 61
Junction of I-40 and I-71
(419) 258-FLEA

Saturday, Sunday. Average daily attendance 2,000. Approximately 50–60 dealers. New merchandise, surplus, closeouts, clothing, housewares, jewelry, used merchandise, collectibles, good selection of collector lines, decorator items, and advertising items available. Food available, rest rooms, h/a, ample parking. Indoor/outdoor market with space from $6 per day. Market is adding a new exhibit building.

MARIETTA

Flea Market
Hilltop Speedway
Rte. 7

Sunday. Antiques, collectibles, new and used merchandise, farm and country collectibles, clothing, jewelry, home furnishings, and decorator items available. Food available, rest rooms, h/a, ample parking.

MARION

Antique Show & Flea Market
Fairgrounds

Periodically, call for schedule. Antiques, collector lines including country and Victorian-era items, railroad items, clocks and watches, advertising items, china, vintage jewelry, furniture, and decorator items available. *Contact* Ronald Hilbert, Box 67, Unionville Center, 43077 (614) 873-4552.

MEDINA

Antique & Collectible Market
Fairgrounds
735 Lafayette Rd.
U.S. Hwy. 42
(330) 723-6083

Sunday. Admission charge. Approximately 150 dealers. This is a great midwestern antique market with a wide range of collector booths. Many quality items here. Food available, rest rooms, h/a, ample parking, and lots of walking. Space from $16. Overnight parking okay.

MONROE

Traders World
Junction of I-75 and State Rte. 63, Exit 29
(513) 424-5708

Saturday, Sunday. Admission charge. Average daily attendance 8,000. There are 500 inside spaces and 200 outside spaces. Large, anything-goes commercial market. Merchandise from antiquity to hot, new, and trendy. Acres of booths and merchandise. Food available, rest rooms, h/a, ample parking, and miles of walking. Space from $11 per day outside. Market has lots of special promotions and live entertainment. One of the area's better markets. *Contact* Darren Foster, 320 Garver Rd., 45050.

MONTPELIER

Flea Market & Auction
619 Main St.
State Rte. 107

Every first Saturday, Thursday. Approximately 50 dealers. New and used merchandise, closeouts, surplus, housewares, children's lines, home furnishings, clothing, jewelry, collectibles, and lots of garage sale items available. Food available, rest rooms, h/a, ample parking. *Contact* Sam Kunsman, 316 N. Emmet St., Bryan, 43506 (419) 636-1635 or 485-9963.

NORTH BLOOMFIELD

North Bloomfield Auction & Flea Market
Approximately one mile west of Bloom Center on Hwy. 87
(330) 876-7233

Thursday, 9 a.m.–4 p.m. Average attendance 1,000. Approximately 200 dealers. New and used merchandise, clothing, collectibles, housewares, and garage sale items available. Food available, rest rooms, h/a, ample parking. Inside and outside space available from $10. *Contact* Jo Herman, Box 51, Kinsman, 44428.

NORWALK

Fireland Public Market
Rte. 20 East

Monday, 8 a.m.–5 p.m. Average attendance 1,000. Approximately 30 dealers offer new and used merchandise, lots of garage sale booths, collectibles, decorator items, crafts, and produce. Food available, rest rooms, h/a, ample parking. Space from $5. Inside and outside space available. *Contact* Victor Mooney, Rte. 20, Laylin Rd., 44857 (419) 499-2086.

ALWAYS CALL BEFORE TRAVELING LONG DISTANCES!

OBERLIN

East Oberlin Flea Market
43433 U.S. Rte. 20 East
Two miles east of Oberlin

Friday, Saturday, Sunday. Indoor market with approximately 100 dealers who offer new merchandise, lots of surplus, closeouts, clothing, children's lines, sports merchandise, housewares, jewelry, and gift items. Market has a pleasant department store atmosphere. Food available, rest rooms, h/a, ample parking. Space from $5. Camping nearby. *Contact* Dewey Served, 43433 U.S. Rte. 20, 44074 (440) 774-4312 or 775-1395.

PAINESVILLE

Fairgrounds Flea Market
Fairgrounds
1301 Mentor Ave.
On Rte. 20

Saturday, Sunday. Average daily attendance 2,000. Approximately 80 exhibitors. Antiques, collectibles, jewelry, silver, coins, farm and country collectibles, crafts, and produce available. Food available, rest rooms, h/a, ample parking. Space from $8. *Contact* Jim or Dick (440) 352-7373.

PATASKALA

Red Barn Flea Market
10501 Columbus Expwy. Park
Hwy. I-70

Friday, Saturday, Sunday, 10 a.m.–6 p.m. Excellent market with a good mix of vendors. This is a very interesting market to browse and poke around in. I have found some real treasures here at terrific prices. Snack bar, rest rooms, h/a, ample parking. Inside and outside market with space from $5. *Contact* Dave Smith, 43062 (740) 927-1234.

INFORMATION IS SUBJECT TO CHANGE—ALWAYS CALL FIRST!

PERRYSBURG

Lakeview Hall Flea Market
Lakeview Hall
26879 Lakeview Dr.
Perrysburg/Freeman Exit

Sunday, 7 a.m.–4 p.m. Approximately 20 dealers with an average attendance of 100. Used merchandise, garage sale items, sometimes new merchandise, and collectibles. Overnight parking. Space from $16. *Contact* Carol Hauder, 203 Edgewood Dr., 43551 (419) 874-5013.

Antique & Flea Market

Every second Sunday. Open May through October. General line of antiques and collectibles. Food available. Inside and outside space from $25. *Contact* Lynn Savial, 23260 Dunbridge Rd., 43551.

PIKESTON

Pikeston Flea Market
U.S. Hwy. 23 South
(614) 289-2593

Friday, Saturday, April–October, 6 a.m.–5 p.m. New and used merchandise, clothing, children's items, housewares, jewelry, collectibles, crafts, and produce available. Food available, rest rooms, h/a, ample parking.

PROCTORVILLE

Proctorville Flea Market
Rte. 7

Friday, Saturday, Sunday, 8 a.m.–5 p.m. Indoor and limited outdoor market with approximately 200 dealers. Antiques, collectibles, crafts, coins, new merchandise, housewares, sportswear, tapes, and lots of used garage sale merchandise available. Snack bar, rest rooms, h/a, ample parking. Space from $20 per day inside and $3 outside. *Contact* Todd Rilely, Rte. 4, Box 541, 45669 (740) 886-7606.

REYNOLDSBURG

40 East Drive-In Theater Flea Market
Rte. 40, one mile east of town
(614) 291-3133

Sunday. Admission charge. Approximately 100 dealers. New merchandise, electronics, sportswear, housewares, jewelry, sports merchandise, children's lines, used merchandise, crafts, collectibles, and produce available. Outdoor market. Snack bar, rest rooms, h/a, ample parking. Space from $3. *Contact* Rainbow Theaters, 865 King Ave., Columbus, 43212.

RICELAND

Wooster Bargain Barn
Rte. 30 East
Seven miles east of Wooster

Wednesday, Sunday. New merchandise, surplus, closeouts, clothing, children's items, housewares, and collectibles available. Snack bar, rest rooms, h/a, ample parking. Inside and outside space from $4 per day. *Contact* Luther Hothem, 531 N. Market St., 44691 (216) 682-9058 or 264-3854.

ROGERS

Rogers Community Auction & Open Air Market
45625 Rte. 154 West
Eight miles east of Lisbon

Friday, 7 a.m. until dark. Large commercial market with average summer attendance of 20,000. Approximately 900 dealers. Outdoor and indoor market with a great variety of items. Excellent all-around market with a fun, upbeat atmosphere. This is a great market for the dealer, shopkeeper, or decorator—an excellent source market. Good food, rest rooms, h/a, ample parking, and lots of walking. Auction starts at 6 p.m. (general retail consignment auction). Space from $12. *Contact* Rogers Open Air Market, 44455 (330) 227-3233.

ROSS

Strickers Grove Flea Market
Rte. 128, one mile south of town

Thursdays, 8 a.m.–1 p.m. Indoor and outdoor market with approximately 50 dealers. Good selection of small antiques, collectibles, crafts. Lots of primitives, advertising items, and used merchandise. Space from $11 per day. Snack bar, rest rooms, h/a. *Contact* Gladys Jordan, 9468 Reading Rd., Cincinnati, OH 45215 (513) 733-5885.

SOUTH AMHERST

Jamie's Flea Market
Rte. 113 46585 Telegraph Rd.
Approximately one mile west of Rte. 58

Wednesday, Saturday, Sunday, 8 a.m.–5 p.m. Indoor/outdoor market. Market has a wide range of goods and is one of the area's oldest. Good selection of antiques and collectibles along with lots of locally made crafts. Average daily attendance 5,000. Approximately 150 dealers. Snack bar, rest rooms, h/a, ample parking, and lots of walking. Space from $5 per day. *Contact* John Mayfield, 44001 (440) 986-5681 or 986-4402.

SPRINGFIELD

Springfield Antique Show & Flea Market
Clark County Fairgrounds
I-70, Exit 59

Monthly, call for dates. Admission charge. Has 6–800 dealers inside and outside. Emphasis here is on quality antiques. This is an excellent market for the advanced collector, dealer, or shopkeeper. Food available, rest rooms, h/a, ample paved parking. *Contact* Bruce Knight, P.O. Box 2429, 45501 (937) 325-0053 or 568-4266.

Freedom Road Center Flea Market
1100 Sunset Ave.

Friday, Saturday, Sunday. Indoor market with approximately 25 dealers. *Contact* Elizabeth Kish (513) 322-5555.

STRAUSBERG

Garver Flea Market
134 N. Wooster Ave.
U.S. Hwy. 21

Sunday, 8 a.m.–5 p.m. Average attendance 2,000 with approximately 100 dealers offering antiques, collector lines, silver, coins, sports cards, jewelry, and new and used merchandise. Food available, rest rooms, h/a, ample parking. Space from $9. Overnight parking okay. *Contact* Vic Gessner, 134 N. Wooster, 44680 (330) 878-5664.

TIFFIN

Tiffin Flea Market
Seneca County Fairgrounds
Southwest side of Tiffin off State Rte. 53, 224, or 18

Saturday, Sunday, April–October. Admission charge. Average weekend attendance 5–10,000. Approximately 100 dealers. Antiques, collectibles, and new and used merchandise available. Good food here. Rest rooms, h/a, ample parking. Overnight camping available. Inside and outside space from $8. Tables $5 per weekend. Reservations recommended. *Contact* Mr. and Mrs. Don Ziegler, 6627 S. State Rte. 173, Bloomville, 44818 (419) 983-5084.

Tiffin Mall Flea Market
870 W. Market St.
Rte. 18
(419) 447-1866

Saturday, Sunday. New and used merchandise, decorator items, art, prints, jewelry, and collectibles available. Snack bar, rest rooms, h/a, ample parking.

TOLEDO

Bassett Flea Market
600 Bassett St.

Saturday, Sunday. Approximately 150 dealers. Wide variety of new merchandise, used merchandise, farm items, crafts, collectibles, and produce available. Snack bar. Camping available. *Contact* Al Cartier (419) 729-0601.

Outdoor Flea Market
5260 Telegraph Rd.

Saturday, Sunday. Used merchandise, garage sale items, plenty of bric-a-brac, housewares, home furnishings, imports, and novelties available.

Toledo Trade Market
1258 W. Alexis Rd.

Friday, Saturday, Sunday. New merchandise, lots of hot new trendy items, collectibles, silver, decorator items, and glassware available at this indoor market. Snack bar, rest rooms, h/a, ample parking. *Contact* Mike Tatro, 43611 (419) 478-1001.

Giant Outdoor Flea Market
Westgate Shopping Center parking lot
Secor Rd.

Wednesday, Saturday, Sunday. New and used merchandise, garage sale items, tools, electronics, imports, crafts, collectibles, and produce available. Food available.

Big B's Flea Market
7200 Airport Hwy.

Friday, Saturday, Sunday. Approximately 50 dealers offering used merchandise, garage sale items, new merchandise, surplus, imports, crafts, collectibles and produce. Food available. Space from $10 per day. *Contact* Marge Buckley (419) 865-6669.

Farmers & Flea Market
1500 Navarre Ave.

Saturday. Used merchandise, garage sale items, housewares, home furnishings, clothing, children's items, farm items, and collectibles available. Food available.

Flea Market
Langolis Auction House
640 N. Lallendorf Rd.
(419) 698-3412

Saturday, Sunday. New and used merchandise, closeouts, surplus, electronics, housewares, clothing, used furniture, and jewelry available. Food available, rest rooms, h/a, ample parking.

TORONTO

Tri-State Jockey Lot Flea Market

Friday, Saturday, Sunday. Approximately 150 dealers with an average daily attendance of 4–5,000. Large commercial market with lots of new merchandise, used merchandise, mountains of garage sale junk, collectibles, housewares, children's items, jewelry, crafts, and produce available. Food available, rest rooms, h/a, ample parking. Inside and outside space from $10 per day. *Contact* Dan Calabreese, Box 120, 43964 (614) 537-9241.

TROY

Flea Market
1375 Union St.
(513) 339-9387

Saturday, Sunday, 9 a.m.–5 p.m. Used and new merchandise, housewares, home furnishings, imports, surplus goods, crafts, and collectibles available. Snack bar, rest rooms, h/a, ample parking.

URBANA

South Point Flea Market
Junction of Rtes. 35 and 68
(937) 652-4691

Friday, Saturday, Sunday. Antiques, collectibles, crafts, sports cards, toys, pictures, old tools, and lots of miscellaneous items available.

Antique Show & Flea Market
Fairgrounds

Monthly, first weekend, 9 a.m.–5 p.m. Indoor/outdoor market with approximately 150 dealers inside, and during the summer approximately 150 dealers outside. Market features quality antiques and collectibles and is an excellent all-around event. Snack bar, rest rooms, h/a, ample parking. *Contact* Howard Goddard, 934 Amherst Dr., 43078 (937) 653-6013 or 788-2058.

VALLEY VIEW

Flea Market Bazaar
5300 W. Canal Rd.
(216) 524-9260

Saturday, Sunday. Used merchandise, housewares, clothing, children's items, and garage sale items available. Snack bar, rest rooms, h/a, ample parking.

WADSWORTH

Wadsworth Flea Market
Blue Sky Drive-In Theater
959 Broad St.
(330) 334-1809

Sunday, 7 a.m.–1 p.m. Large open-air market, seasonal, spring through fall. Books, school supplies, computers, software, gifts, crafts, antiques, collectibles, clothing, and furniture available. Snack bar, rest rooms, ample parking with 75-cent charge (admission free). Space from $7.50.

WALDO

Flea Market
Jessie's Auction House

Every second Sunday. New and used merchandise, closeouts, surplus, children's items, clothing, jewelry, and housewares available. Snack bar, rest rooms, h/a, ample parking.

WALNUT CREEK

Amish Flea Market
I-77 at Dover Exit
(330) 893-2836
Fax (330) 893-3523

Thursday, Friday, Saturday, 9 a.m.–5 p.m. Covered market with approximately 250 vendors. Glassware, antiques, quilts, baked goods, furniture, produce, collectibles, odds and ends, and a great selection of locally made Amish crafts, quilts, and furniture. Food available, rest rooms, h/a, ample parking. Market is located in the heart of Amish country and is a great place to spend a weekend. *Contact* Ben Mast, Box 172, 44687.

WARREN

Warren Flea Market
428 S. Main St.

Tuesday–Saturday, 8 a.m.–5 p.m. New and used merchandise, collectibles, decorator items, and lots of bric-a-brac available. Snack bar. Indoor and outdoor space available. *Contact* Alfred Raghanti, 44481 (330) 399-8298.

Skyway Drive-In Flea Market
Levit Rd.

Sunday. Used merchandise, garage sale items, new merchandise, home furnishings, decorator items, collectibles, crafts, and produce available. Snack bar, rest rooms, h/a, ample parking.

WASHINGTON COURT HOUSE

Washington Court House Flea Market
Fairgrounds
Rtes. 3 and 22
213 Fairview Ave.
(740) 335-5865 or 335-5345
Fax (740) 335-6940

Monthly. Admission charge. Approximately 1,000 dealers. A lot of everything here. This market runs the gamut of goods and it could take the entire weekend to see it all. Large truckloads of new surplus merchandise, quality antiques, and collectibles. Good food, rest rooms, h/a, ample parking, but can be difficult due to crowds and lots of walking. Space from $6. *Contact* Coy & Stookey, 134 E. Ohio St., 43160 (614) 278-2721. Washington Court House also hosts an annual citywide festival and flea market. This popular event is known as "Ohio's Favorite Flea Market."

WESTCHESTER

Flea Market
Queen City Speedway

Sunday. Antiques, collectibles, new and used merchandise, household goods, fashions and fashion accessories, and imports available. Snack bar, rest rooms, h/a, ample parking.

WILMINGTON

Caesars Creek Flea Market
See Caesar Creek listing.

Saturday, Sunday.

XENIA

Heartland Flea Market
457 Dayton Ave., Rte. 35

Saturday, Sunday. Indoor market with approximately 50 dealers. *Contact* Jason May (937) 372-6699.

YOUNGSTOWN

Austintown Flea Market
5370 Clarkins Dr.
I-80 and Rte. 46

Saturday, Sunday, 9 a.m.–5 p.m. Used merchandise, garage sale items, collector lines, glassware, and jewelry available. Food available. *Contact* Sally Shipley, 44515 (216) 799-1325.

Four Seasons Flea & Farmers Market
Rte. 422 and McCartney Rd.
(216) 744-5050

Wednesday, Saturday, 8 a.m.–5 p.m. New and used merchandise, clothing, housewares, children's items, jewelry, farm items, produce, and collectibles available. Food available, rest rooms, h/a.

DAYS, DATES, AND MARKETS ARE SUBJECT TO CHANGE!

OKLAHOMA

BARTLESVILLE

Dave's Bartlesville Flea Market
American Legion Bldg.
Hwy. 75 North

Every first and third Saturday. New merchandise, collectibles, Indian art, jewelry, and crafts available. Indoor and outdoor market with space from $10. *Contact* Dave Whiteturkey, Box 3203, 74006 (918) 333-6762.

BROKEN BOW

Ed's 259 Trading Post
Hwy. 259 North

Friday, Saturday, Sunday. Secondhand merchandise, household goods, electronics, imports, souvenirs, and novelties available. Snack bar, rest rooms.

Mountaineer Trade Days
Beavers Bend State Park
Hwy. 259

Every first weekend. New and used merchandise, black powder supplies, archery and sporting items, Indian art, crafts, and jewelry available. Food available, rest rooms, ample parking. This marketplace is located in a beautiful setting.

DEL CITY

Cherokee Flea Market and Snack Bar
3101 S.E. 15th St.

Daily. Indoor/outdoor market with approximately 25 dealers. Mostly used merchandise and garage sale items here, occasionally some antiques and also good buys on new merchandise. I have set up at this market many a time to make some weekday money. Snack bar, rest room. *Contact* K. O. Jose (405) 677-4056.

ELK CITY

Flea Market
Lil Opera Country Music Hall grounds
Hwy. 66 West
(580) 526-3873

Saturday, Sunday. New and used merchandise, western and Indian collectibles, jewelry, art, clothing, collectibles, and ranch items available. Snack bar, rest rooms, h/a, ample parking.

Blessed Bargains Flea Market
3306 S. Hwy. 66
(580) 225-4194

Friday, Saturday, Sunday, 7 a.m.–5 p.m. Inside/outside market featuring lots of western and Indian merchandise at Blessed Bargains. Space from $5 per day. Camping and electricity available. Market is open to food vendors.

ENID

Enid Flea Market
1821 S. Van Buren
(918) 744-1386

Friday, Saturday, Sunday, 9 a.m.–6 p.m. Average attendance 600. Outdoor market with antiques and collectibles, new and used merchandise, farm items, crafts, produce, and garage sale items. Space from $15 for the weekend. Reservations required. *Contact* Cody Smith, 1821 S. Van Buren, 73701.

LAWTON

Lawton Flea Market
1130 E. Gore St.
(580) 357-0626

Saturday, Sunday. Used merchandise, some new and imports, home furnishings, clothing, western and Indian collectibles available. Snack bar.

MUSKOGEE

Good Stuff Flea Market
2541 S. 32nd St.
(918) 682-9226

Daily. Indoor/outdoor market with approximately 25 dealers.

NORMAN

Town & Country Flea Market
209 W. Main St.
(405) 360-1015

Saturday, Sunday. New merchandise, gifts, jewelry, decorator items, collectibles, and used merchandise available. Snack bar, rest rooms, h/a, ample parking.

OKLAHOMA CITY

Mary's Flea Market
N.E. 23rd St. and Midwest Blvd.

Saturday, Sunday, daylight to dark. Approximately 250 dealers. Outside market with some covered spaces. Collectibles, used, and large amounts of new merchandise available. Good market for the traveling dealer. One of the area's better markets. Snack bars, cafe, rest rooms, h/a, ample parking, and live entertainment. This is the marketplace where I began my career. *Contact* Dennis Sizemore, 7905 N.E. 23rd St., 73141 (405) 427-0051.

Country Antique Flea Market
State Fairgrounds
N.W. 10th Street and May Ave.

Monthly, call for dates. Approximately 250 dealers. Lots of antiques, collectibles, furniture, jewelry, quilts, and crafts available. Snack bar, clean rest rooms, h/a, ample parking. Space from $45. This is always a fun market for sellers or buyers to visit. Clean, friendly, upbeat country atmosphere. *Contact* Dot Buchanan (405) 354-1664.

Flea Market & Antique Show
State Fairgrounds
N.W. 10th St. and May Ave.

Monthly, call for dates. Admission charge. Approximately 100 dealers. Good selection of antiques, collectibles, and lots of western collectibles here. Snack bar, rest rooms, h/a, ample parking. *Contact* Ted Lefler, Rte. 1, Box 9BB, Benton, KS 67017 (316) 744-3866.

AMC Flea Market Mall
1001 N. Pennsylvania Ave.
N.W. 10th St. and Pennsylvania

Saturday, Sunday, 9 a.m.–6 p.m. Indoor/outdoor market with approximately 200 dealers. Mostly new merchandise, imports, gifts, some antiques and collectibles, and some crafts available. Lots of discounted salvage goods here. Restaurants, clean rest rooms, h/a, ample parking. Space from $44 per weekend. *Contact* Nick Adams, 1001 N. Pennsylvania Ave., 73107 (405) 232-5061.

SuperFlea Flea Market
2600 S. I-35 Service Rd.
I-35, South 19th St. Exit
(405) 794-2481

Saturday, Sunday, 9 a.m.–7 p.m. New merchandise, electronics, jewelry, sportswear, children's goods, lots of hot new trendy items, used merchandise, crafts, and collector lines available. Snack bar, rest rooms, h/a, ample parking.

PONCA CITY

Flea Market of Ponca City
2108 N. Ash St.
(580) 762-6501

Saturday, Sunday. Average daily attendance of 3,000 with approximately 75 dealers at this indoor/outdoor market. New and used merchandise, garage sale items, western wear, western and Indian collectibles available. Snack bar, rest rooms, h/a, ample parking. Space from $12.

Fran's Flea Market
3501 N. 14th St.
(580) 762-6501

Saturday, Sunday.

SAPULPA

Sapulpa Flea Market
800 Block West Dewey St.
Rte. 66
(918) 224-4802

Friday, Saturday, Sunday, 8 a.m.–5 p.m. New merchandise, used merchandise, garage sale items, farm items, western and Indian collectibles, and jewelry available. Snack bar, rest rooms, h/a, ample parking.

TULSA

Tulsa Flea Market
Fairgrounds, Exchange Centers I and II
I-44, Yale Exit to 21st St.

Saturday, 8 a.m.–5 p.m. Primarily antiques, collectibles, and a few crafts with very limited new merchandise. One of the best markets in the area. Great market for collectors, shopkeepers, and decorators. Snack bar, rest rooms, h/a, ample parking. *Contact* Louis Larry, Box 4511, 74159 (918) 744-1113 or 744-1386.

Flea for All
6921 E. Admiral
(918) 936-1386

Saturday. Indoor market with lots of secondhand items and garage sale merchandise, acres of bric-a-brac, some new merchandise, and collectibles available. Snack bar, rest rooms, h/a, ample parking. Mostly permanent dealers with small attendance. Space from $10.

Great American Flea Market & Antique Mall
9212 E. Admiral Place

Friday, Saturday, Sunday, 10 a.m.–6 p.m. Approximately 150 dealers at this indoor/outdoor market with lots of new merchandise, imports, gifts, some antiques, collectibles, used merchandise, and crafts available. Snack bar, rest rooms, h/a, ample parking. Antique mall is open Tuesday–Sunday with a nice general line of antiques and collectibles. Space from $30 per weekend. Camping available on premises. New market. *Contact* Manager, 9212 E. Admiral Place, 74115 (918) 492-3476 or 834-6363.

Admiral Flea Market
9401 E. Admiral
(918) 834-9259.

Friday, Saturday, Sunday. Indoor/outdoor market with approximately 250 dealers.

VINITA

Eastern Oklahoma Antiques Flea Market
Junction of Hwys. 60, 66, and 69
(918) 256-2423

Saturday, Sunday. Antiques, collector lines, furniture, good selection of primitives, and advertising items available. Good market for bargain hunting. Food available, rest rooms, h/a, ample parking.

WAGONER

Main Street Flea Market
108 S. Main St.
(918) 485-5496

Wednesday–Sunday, 9 a.m.–5 p.m. Antiques, collectibles, secondhand merchandise, home furnishings, housewares, clothing, jewelry, gifts, and crafts available. Rest rooms, ample parking. *Contact* Gerald Holland.

ALWAYS CALL AHEAD TO VERIFY DATES AND INFORMATION

YUKON

Route 66 Traders Market
3201 Richland Rd.
I-40 and Exit 132 or 136, on the Frontage Rd. (Oklahoma City)

Friday, Saturday, Sunday. New outdoor market with 200 covered and 100 open booths. Nice, new modern facility, special events, food court, ample parking, h/a, rest rooms, ATM machine, 29 acres. Space from $8.50 per day. *Contact* Jerald Ashby, 3201 N. Richland Rd., 73099 (405) 752-1752 or 530-3366, fax (405) 752-9229. E-mail: jashby@telepath.com.

INFORMATION IS SUBJECT TO CHANGE—ALWAYS CALL AHEAD TO AVOID DISAPPOINTMENT

OREGON

BEAVERTON

Beaverton Flea Market
11595 S.W. Canyon Rd.
(503) 644-4062

Saturday, Sunday. New and used merchandise, home furnishings, housewares, clothing, decorator items, collectibles, crafts, sports memorabilia, and produce available. Snack bar.

BEND

Deschutes Flea Market
65005 N. Hwy. 97
(503) 536-1467

Friday, Saturday, Sunday, 9 a.m.–5 p.m. Outdoor market with approximately 50 dealers offering lots of secondhand and garage sale items, crafts, and some new merchandise. Snack bar, rest rooms, h/a, ample parking. Space from $10.

CLOVERDALE

The Red Barn Flea Market
33920 Hwy. 101 South
(503) 392-3973

Saturday, Sunday. Collectibles, glassware, jewelry, used merchandise, and garage sale items available. Small outdoor market, camping available. Food vendors welcome.

CORVALLIS

Heart of the Valley Flea Market
Fairgrounds

Every first Saturday, 10 a.m.–5 p.m. Admission charge. Indoor market with approximately 50 dealers. Market features antiques and collectibles. Some new merchandise, used items, crafts, and new collectibles. Good selection of Pacific Northwest country collectibles here. Snack bar, rest rooms, h/a, ample parking. Space from $10 per day. *Contact* Ilene Smith, 1010 N.W. 9th St., 97330 (541) 758-3019.

EUGENE

Piccadilly Flea Market
Fairgrounds
796 W. 13th St.

Sunday, 10 a.m.–4 p.m. Admission charge. Indoor market with approximately 300 dealers. Wide range of merchandise here. This is one of the area's largest and best markets. Great selection of new, severely discounted merchandise for home and individual needs. Snack bars, rest rooms, h/a, ample parking. Space from $17. Reservations recommended. *Contact* Suzanne Jackson, Box 2364, 97402 (541) 683-5589.

Eugene Flea Market
(541) 683-2573 or 687-1963

Every first Sunday. Antiques, collectibles, primitives, farm and ranch collectibles, lots of western and Indian art, jewelry, silver, coins, sports cards, vintage clothing, and kitchen wares available. Food available, rest rooms, h/a, ample parking.

HILLSBORO

Banner Flea Market
4871 S.E. Tualatin Valley Hwy.

Friday, Saturday, Sunday, noon–5:30 p.m. Indoor/outdoor market with approximately 20 dealers. Space from $5 per day. Rest rooms.

Contact Betty Hansen, 4871 S.E. Tualatin Valley Hwy., 97123 (503) 640-6755.

KLAMATH FALLS

Linkville Flea Market
Fairgrounds
6th St., two miles from downtown

Monthly, 9 a.m.–5 p.m. Admission charge. Approximately 100 dealers. New merchandise, limited antiques, collectibles, art, and crafts available. Market usually conducts two shows a month during the holiday season. Snack bar, rest rooms, h/a, ample parking. Space from $8 per day. *Contact* Elizabeth Boorman, 5420 Cottage St., 97603 (503) 884-4352.

LINCOLN BEACH

Aunt Rosie's Flea Market
4040 Coast Hwy. 101
Three miles north of Depot Bay, six miles south of Lincoln City

Saturday, Sunday, 10 a.m.–5 p.m. Approximately 15 dealers. Antiques, collectibles, new and used merchandise. Snack bar, restrooms. Seasonal market. Space from $8 per table, 70 tables available. Reservations recommended. Camping for vendors only. Electricity available. Free parking. *Contact* Bob or Stephen Fischer, Box 1357, Depot Bay, 97341 (503) 764-3782.

LINCOLN CITY

Stuffy's Lincoln Flea Market
1309 N. 12th St.
(541) 994-7711

Saturday, Sunday, 9 a.m.–5 p.m. Indoor market with approximately 40 dealers offering collectibles, new and used merchandise, books, and housewares. Snack bar, rest rooms, ample parking.

ALWAYS CALL BEFORE TRAVELING LONG DISTANCES!

MEDFORD

Phoenix Trade Mart
3846 Pacific Hwy.

Saturday, Sunday. New merchandise, electronics, sportswear, children's items, housewares, jewelry, tools, used merchandise, collector lines, and decorator items available. Snack bar, rest rooms, ample parking. Inside and outside space from $4.

PORTLAND

Portland Saturday Market
(503) 222-6072

Saturday. Held outdoors under the west end of the Burnside Bridge. Market is heavy on decorator items and crafts. Some collectibles and used merchandise available. Market has food, rest rooms, and entertainment. *Contact* Paul Verhoeven, 108 W. Burnside, 97209.

MKC Flea-O-Rama
Multnomah Kennel Club
223rd between Gilshaw and Halsay Sts.
(503) 666-8969

Saturday, Sunday. New and used merchandise, lots of garage sale bric-a-brac, housewares, home furnishings, and pet supplies available. Food available, rest rooms, h/a, ample parking.

No. 1 Flea Market
17420 S.E. Division St.
I-85, Exit 181st St. then east

Saturday, Sunday, 9 a.m.–5 p.m. Indoor/outdoor market with approximately 150 dealers. Antiques, collectibles, memorabilia, primitives, farm items, tools, new merchandise, crafts, fine, costume, and vintage jewelry, and used merchandise available. Snack bar, rest rooms, h/a, ample parking. *Contact* Lee Richardson, 17420 S.E. Division St., 97236 (503) 761-4646.

Saturday Flea Market
Memorial Coliseum
(503) 246-9996

Saturday. New and used merchandise, lots of bric-a-brac, collectibles, crafts, and produce available. Food available, rest rooms, h/a, ample parking. Space from $5.

Flea Market
Memorial Coliseum
(503) 282-6467

Sunday. Admission charged. Household goods, clothing, jewelry, decorator items, and crafts available. Food available, rest rooms, h/a, ample parking. Space from $7.50.

Barr's Flea Market
1225 N. Marine Dr.
I-5, Exit 307

Saturday, Sunday, 8 a.m.–3 p.m. Indoor market with approximately 300 dealers. Good selection of antiques, collectibles, primitives, crafts, coins, new merchandise, housewares, sportswear, sports-related merchandise, Pacific Northwest Indian and Eskimo items and artifacts available. Snack bars, rest rooms, h/a, ample parking. Tables from $5. Reservations required. *Contact* Sandy Barr, 1225 N. Marine Dr., 97217 (503) 283-6993 or 283-9565.

Springer's Flea Market
18300 S.E. Richey Rd.

Saturday, Sunday. Average attendance 3,000 per day. Indoor market with approximately 125 dealers. New and used merchandise, surplus, housewares, clothing, electronics, children's items, art, prints, books, collector lines, and decorator items available. Snack bar, rest rooms, h/a, ample parking. Space from $9 per day. *Contact* Ramona Rettinger, 18300 S.E. Richey Rd., 97236 (503) 665-3568.

Weekend Market Place
9100 N. Vancouver Ave.
(503) 286-5514

Saturday, Sunday. Approximately 150 dealers offer a good selection of new merchandise, used merchandise, garage sale booths, crafts, collectibles, and produce. Snack bar, rest rooms, h/a, ample parking. Space from $8.

Salvage Sally's Weekend Bazaar
2330 S.E. 82nd Ave.
(503) 777-5058

Saturday, Sunday. Admission charge. Average daily attendance 1,500. Approximately 250 dealers at this large market with lots of surplus, closeouts, new merchandise, clothing, housewares, and used merchandise available. Snack bar, rest rooms, h/a, ample parking. Space from $8. Camping and electricity available. Market is open to food vendors.

RICKERALL

Rickerall Flea Market
Hwy. 99 West
Fairgrounds
(503) 623-9711 or 623-3048

Every first Sunday. Antiques, collectibles, furniture, silver, coins, sports cards, jewelry (fine and estate), vintage clothing, Indian art, jewelry, and artifacts available. Food available, rest rooms, h/a, ample parking.

SALEM

Salem Flea Market
Fairgrounds
Silverton Rd. and 17th St.

Every first and fourth Sunday, 9:30 a.m.–4 p.m. Admission charge $1. Approximately 400 dealers. Show is heavy on antiques and collectibles. This market is far and away the area's finest, with some real quality booths. For anyone in the trade on the West Coast, this is a great source market. Prices here make the trip worthwhile. Snack bars, rest rooms, h/a, ample paved parking. Space from $10 per day. The Salem Flea Market produces several special events to go along with their monthly market. Call for information. *Contact* Karen or Greg Huston, Box 20805, 97307 (503) 393-1261.

INFORMATION IS SUBJECT TO CHANGE—ALWAYS CALL FIRST!

Big Red's Flea Market
3545 Portland Rd. Northeast
I-5, Exit 258, south one mile

Saturday, Sunday, 9:30 a.m.–5 p.m. Indoor and outdoor market with approximately 200 dealers. Wide range of antiques, collectibles, primitives, memorabilia, and a good selection of new and used merchandise available. This is one of those markets where opportunities to find treasures abound. Snack bar, rest rooms. Space from $8 per day. *Contact* Duke Whitney, 1203 Dearborn Rd. Northeast, 97303 (503) 362-1252.

Portland Road Flea Market
3046 Portland Rd. Northeast

Saturday, Sunday. Approximately 200 dealers. Large commercial market with a wide selection of new and used merchandise, antiques, collectibles, crafts, and produce available. Snack bar, rest rooms, h/a, ample paved parking. Space from $7. *Contact* Betty Martin (503) 581-2810.

PENNSYLVANIA

ADAMSTOWN

Antique Flea Market
Rte. 272
One mile north of PA Tpke., Exit 21
(717) 267-2177 or 267-8444

Thursday–Sunday, 7:30 a.m.–5 p.m. Over 1,500 dealers. Market features high-quality antiques and fine collectibles. This is the place for storekeepers and decorators to shop. This market conducts many special events. It is one of the nation's finest and largest antique markets. Great food here, rest rooms, h/a, ample parking, and lots of walking. Indoor and outdoor market. Space from $20 per day. Food vendors welcome.

Black Angus Antique Mall
Rte. 222
PA Tpke., Exit 21

Sunday, 8 a.m.–5 p.m. Large complex with antique mall, outdoor pavilions, restaurant. Quality antiques and collectibles, a collector's paradise. This is another market that conducts lots of special events. Call for dates and information about them. The antique mall is open daily and has over 250 booths. Flea market held on Sunday has approximately 100 dealers. This is one of my favorite marketplaces. Great food on premises, rest rooms, h/a, ample parking. *Contact* Carl Barto, Box 880, 19501 (717) 484-4385 or (717) 569-3536.

DAYS, DATES, AND MARKETS ARE SUBJECT TO CHANGE!

Green Hills Antique Market
Rte. 568
(717) 856-7034

Friday, Saturday, Sunday. Antiques, furniture, lots of country collectibles, primitives, Victorian-era items, vintage clothing, jewelry, coins, dolls, toys, glassware, and china available. Great all-around selection of booths here. Food available, rest rooms, h/a, ample parking.

Renninger's No. 1 Market
Rte. 272

Sunday, 7:30 a.m.–4 p.m. Average daily attendance 5,000. Approximately 400 dealers. Market features high-quality antiques and collectibles. One of the country's leading antique source markets. Renningers No. 1 has many special weekend promotions. This is a don't-miss market stop. Plenty of food here, rest rooms, h/a, ample parking, but a lot of walking is required. Indoor/outdoor market. Space from $15. Reservations highly recommended. *Contact* Manager, Renninger's Promotions, 27 Bensinger Dr., Schuylkill Haven, PA 17972 (570) 385-0104 or (877) 385-0104.

ALLENTOWN

Fairgrounds Flea Market
Fairgrounds
(610) 433-7541

Thursday, 11 a.m.–7 p.m., Friday, 8 a.m.–9 p.m., Saturday, 8 a.m.–6 p.m. Antiques, collectibles, primitives, Amish and farm collectibles, crafts, packaged food goods, and used merchandise available. Snack bars, rest rooms, h/a, ample parking.

ANNVILLE

Lebanon Valley Antique Depot
1251 E. Main St. Hwy. 422 East
Antique Mall and flea market.
(717) 867-4400

Antique mall is open daily, 9 a.m.–5 p.m. Flea market is open Saturday and Sunday, 9 a.m.–5 p.m. Approximately 160 antique dealers in mall. Market is heavy on antiques and collectibles. Air-conditioned. Ample parking, h/a, rest rooms, cafe.

ASHLAND

Hi-Way Drive-In Flea Market
Hi-Way Drive-In Theater
(717) 874-1719

Saturday. Collectibles, used merchandise, garage sale items, farm items, packaged food, clothing, children's items, housewares, crafts, and produce available. Snack bar, rest rooms, h/a, ample parking.

BARNSVILLE

Lakeside Flea Market
Lakeside Park
Rte. 54
(717) 467-2405

Sunday. Approximately 30 dealers offer antiques, furniture, collectibles, silver, coins, glassware, primitives, and advertising items. Snack bar, rest rooms. Indoor market. Space from $8. *Contact* Lakeside Park, Rte. 54, 18214.

BELLEVILLE

Belleville Flea Market
Belleville Livestock Market
655 S. Penn St.
(717) 935-2146

Wednesday. Antiques, collectibles, used merchandise, bric-a-brac, home furnishings, household goods, electronics, gifts, farm items, tack, and produce available. Great old-time country atmosphere here. Market also open on Tuesday during summer months.

BEN SALEM

Farmers & Flea Market
Philadelphia Park Racetrack
PA Tpke., Exit 28

Sunday, daylight until dark. Large outdoor market with approximately 4–500 dealers. Antiques, collectibles, crafts, lots of new merchandise, used merchandise, garage sale items, and produce available. Snack bars, rest rooms, h/a, lots of walking required. Space from $25. *Contact* Janice Ackerman, Box 387, Voorhees, NJ 08043 (609) 795-8393 or 795-4686.

BLOOMSBURG

Pioneer Village Sales Flea Market
Rte. 1 North
I-80, Exit 80, three miles south
(570) 784-5008

Saturday, Sunday, April–November, 9 a.m.–5 p.m. Indoor/outdoor market with approximately 50 dealers set up in what used to be an old tourist-type western town. New merchandise, souvenirs, gift items, and collectibles available. Snack bar, rest rooms, ample parking. Space from $6 per table.

CEDARS

Up Country Flea Market
Cedars Country Store
Rte. 73

Every third Saturday, May–October, 8 a.m.–4 p.m. Approximately 150 dealers offer antiques, crafts, fine art, collectibles, primitives, and antique toys. Cafe, snack bar, rest rooms, h/a, ample parking. Outdoor market with space from $9. Reservations required. *Contact* Linda Freed, Box 173, 19423 (215) 584-1490.

CHADDS FORD

Pennsbury Chadds Ford Antique Mall & Flea Market
640 E. Baltimore Pike, 19317
(610) 388-1620

Thursday–Monday, 10 a.m.–5 p.m. (upper level); Saturday, Sunday, 10 a.m.–5 p.m. (lower level only). Two-level facility. Market is heavy on quality antiques and collectibles. Monthly rentals only. Rest rooms. Snack bar. Air-conditioned, h/a. Ample parking. *Contact* Alfred Delduco, 640 E. Baltimore Pike, 19317.

CHAMBERSBURG

Famous Antique & Flea Market
1495 Lincoln Way East
(717) 264-5916

Sunday. General line of antiques and collectibles, good selection. Primarily indoor antique shops with some outdoor space available.

Sunset Farmers Antiques & Flea Market
Sunset Drive-In Theater
Rte. 11
(717) 264-2855

Sunday. Antiques, furniture, collector lines in all nostalgia categories, quality decorator items, new and used merchandise, crafts, and produce available. Snack bar, rest rooms, h/a, ample parking.

COLLEGEVILLE

Power House Antique and Flea Market
45 First Ave., Rte. 29

Sundays. Indoor market with approximately 40 dealers. Lots of quality antiques and collectibles here. Rest room. h/a. *Contact* Janet McDonnell (610) 489-7388.

DALLASTOWN

Dallastown Collectibles Mall
1 W. Main St.

Sunday. Antiques, furniture, collector lines, quality decorator items, silver, fine jewelry, art pottery, glassware, art, prints, and books available. Snack bar, rest rooms. Inside and outside space from $7. Reservations required. *Contact* James Knisley (717) 244-6394.

DENVER

Adam's Antiques & Collectibles Market
2400 N. Reading Rd. PA Tpke., Exit 21, one-half mile north to Rte. 272

Sunday. Antiques, lots of quality collectibles, Civil War items, art, prints, books, jewelry, silver, coins, glassware, dolls, primitives, and art pottery available. Food available, rest rooms, h/a. Indoor and outdoor market open year-round. *Contact* R. Vigilante (717) 335-3116.

Barr's Antique World Auction
2152 N. Reading Rd.
Rte. 272 and PA Tpke.

Saturday, Sunday, 10 a.m.–5 p.m. Approximately 100 dealers. Good selection of quality decorator items and fine antique European furniture. Very upscale and trendy merchandise here. Auctions are conducted here on Monday starting at 4 p.m. Lots of quality items and routine flea market junk on the auction block at this sale. Snack bar, rest rooms, h/a, ample parking. Reservations required for inside spaces; outside space is on a first-come basis. Camping available on premises. *Contact* B. L. Barr, Box 242, 17517 (717) 267-2861.

Shupps Grove Flea Market
Rte. 897
One mile south of Adamstown, two miles north of Lancaster
(717) 484-4115

Saturday, Sunday. Antiques, collector lines, furniture, Civil War items, glassware, silver, coins, vintage clothing, and fine and estate jewelry available. Food available, rest rooms, ample parking. Space from $60 for the weekend, reservations recommended. This market conducts several special events during the year. Market management is very rulebound and cranky. *Contact* Shupps Grove, 1686 Dry Tavern Rd., 17517. Reservations only (717) 949-3656.

DEVON

Outdoor Antiques Flea Market
Rte. 202, Devon Exit
(215) 688-0369

Saturday, Sunday. Antiques, furniture, collector lines in many categories, jewelry, silver, country primitives, and Victorian-era items available. Food available, rest rooms, h/a, ample parking.

DICKSON CITY

Circle Drive-In Flea Fair
Circle Drive-In Theater
12 Salem Ave. (Rte. 6)
I-81, Exit 57A
(570) 876-1400
Fax (570) 282-7299

Sunday, March–December, 7 a.m.–4 p.m. Average daily attendance 15,000 with approximately 500 dealers. This is a large, classic commercial market. A wide range of new merchandise, used merchandise, antiques, collector lines, crafts, packaged food, country and Amish crafts, produce, and pets available. Food available, rest rooms, h/a, ample parking, and lots of walking. Space from $10. Camping available. Well-attended market. *Contact* Michael Delfino, 12 Salem Ave., Carbondale, PA 18407.

DILLSBURG

Indoor & Outdoor Flea & Antique Market
Haar's Drive-In Theater
185 Logan Rd.
One mile north on Rte. 15
(717) 432-3011

Sunday. New and used merchandise, garage sale items, farm items, antiques, collector lines, crafts, and produce available. Snack bar, rest rooms, h/a, ample parking. Market is also open on Tuesday and Friday evenings. *Contact* Elwood Haar, 17019.

DOUGLASVILLE

Antiques, Crafts & Flea Market
Douglas Commons Trade Square
Rte. 422 and Maple Dr.
(215) 385-3061

Saturday, Sunday. Good selection of nice antiques, country and Amish crafts, and general flea market merchandise available. Food available, rest rooms, h/a, ample parking.

DUNCANNON

Old Sled Works Flea Market
722 N. Market St.
Fifteen miles northwest of Harrisburg, off Rtes. 22 and 322 or 11 and 15

Saturday, Sunday, closed during winter. Antique and collectible market with a great selection of locally made crafts. Approximately 125 dealers. Market features a 1950s soda fountain, a sled museum, and an old-time penny arcade with over 50 machines. Good food here. Rest rooms, ample parking, h/a.

DUNCANSVILLE

Duncansville Antique Depot
1401 Second Ave., Rtes. 22 and 764

Saturday, Sunday, 9 a.m.–5 p.m. Mall is open daily, 9 a.m.–5 p.m. Both markets are heavy on antiques and collectibles. Antique mall has approximately 200 antique dealers and flea market has approximately 250 dealers. Space from $30 per weekend inside and $12 outside. H/a, ample parking, rest rooms, cafe. *Contact* Tom George, Box 111, 16635 (814) 696-4000 or (800) 281-4001.

ALWAYS CALL AHEAD TO VERIFY DATES AND INFORMATION

ELIZABETHTOWN

Trading Post Flea Market
451 W. High St.

Saturday, Sunday. Approximately 250 dealers offer new merchandise, electronics, housewares, sportswear, sports merchandise, tools, jewelry, toys, used merchandise, antiques, collectibles, glassware, coins, sports cards, crafts, and produce. Snack bar, rest rooms, h/a, ample parking. Reservations recommended. *Contact* Tony Szafranic (717) 838-5278.

EPHRATA

Green Dragon Farmers Market
955 N. State St. (Rte. 272)
(717) 738-1117

Friday, 9 a.m.–10 p.m. Indoor/outdoor market with approximately 250–300 dealers. Wide variety of merchandise, crafts, antiques, food, bakery, etc. Unusually strong attendance for this market. Excellent one-day affair. Auction on Friday with livestock and housewares. This is a don't-miss market. Lots of walking is required to see it all, so dress comfortably. Great food, rest rooms, h/a; parking is difficult. Take my word for it, the Green Dragon Market is definitely worth the stop. Space from $25. *Contact* Green Dragon, 955 N. State St., 17522.

GILBERTSVILLE

Zerns Farmers Market
Rte.73
(610) 367-2899

Friday 2 p.m.–10 p.m., Saturday 11 a.m.–10 p.m. Indoor and outdoor market with approximately 350 dealers. Antiques, collectibles, memorabilia, primitives, crafts, new and used furniture. Several specialty shops here. Lots of treasures here. Market located in the heart of Amish country. Shops, restaurant open daily. Greatest shoofly pie in the area is served here. Rest rooms, h/a; parking can be difficult. Space from $25. Reservations required. *Contact* Zerns, Rte. 73, 19525.

GREENSBURG

Greengate Flea Market
Rte. 30
Next to the Greengate Mall

Sunday, April–October, 7 a.m.–3 p.m. Outdoor market with approximately 75 dealers. New merchandise, used and garage sale merchandise, some antiques and collectibles, furniture, crafts, and produce available. Snack bar, rest rooms, h/a, ample parking. Space from $15. New market. *Contact* Carol Craig, 214 Kenneth St., 15601 (724) 837-6881.

HARRISBURG

Silver Springs Antique & Flea Market
Rte. 11 West

Sundays. Approximately 150 dealers. Antiques, furniture, collector lines, lots of farm and country collectibles and primitives. Civil War items, used merchandise. Snack bar, rest rooms. Ample parking. *Contact* Anna Smith (717) 763-7633 or 249-8378.

HAZEN

Warsaw Flea Market
Rte. 28
Approximately one mile north of Hazen

Every first Sunday, May–October, daylight until dark. Approximately 300 dealers with an average daily attendance of 10–12,000. Outdoor market with mostly antiques, collectibles, primitives, and produce available. This is a classic country market that takes you back 100 years. Clean, friendly, well-managed market. Space from $15. Overnight parking available. *Contact* Warsaw Volunteer Fireman's Association, Rte. 1, Box 76C, 15825 (814) 328-2536 or 328-2528.

INFORMATION IS SUBJECT TO CHANGE—ALWAYS CALL AHEAD TO AVOID DISAPPOINTMENT

HULMEVILLE

Old Mill Flea Market
Fricke's Mill
Junction of Bellevue Ave. and Hulmeville Rd., I-95, Exit 1

Thursday, Friday. Indoor market. Lots of quality antiques and collectibles here. Snack bar, rest room. Market is located in an old 1800s mill. *Contact* Kathy Loeffler (215) 757-1777.

JONESTOWN

Frog Hollow Flea Market
N. Hwy. 72
(717) 865-0799

Saturday, Sunday, 8 a.m.–3 p.m. Indoor market featuring new and used merchandise and some collectibles. Snack bar, rest rooms, h/a, ample parking.

KULPSVILLE

Kulpsville Antique and Flea Market
1375 Forty Food Rd., Rte. 63

Saturday, Sunday. Indoor market with approximately 50 vendors. Snack bar, rest rooms, h/a. *Contact* Dawn Myers (215) 361-7910.

KUTZTOWN

Renninger's No. 2 Flea Market
740 Novel St.

Friday, 12 p.m.–8 p.m., Saturday, 8 a.m.–5 p.m. Approximately 300 dealers at this large, excellent antique market. Dutch farmers' market here also. Renningers also has many special events during the year. Some draw as many as 1,500 dealers. Always large attendance at this market. Lots of Amish furniture, antiques, quilts, and folk art available. Great food, rest rooms, h/a, ample parking, and miles of walking. *Contact* Renningers, 27 Bensinger Dr., Schuylkill Haven, 17972 (570) 385-0104 or (610) 683-6848, fax (570) 385-0605.

LANCASTER

Jockey Lot Flea Market
Rte. 272, twelve miles south of Lancaster

Thursday–Monday. Nice selection of antiques and collectibles here. Snack bar, rest rooms, h/a. *Contact* Rhoda Fisher (717) 284-4984.

LANGHORNE

Roosevelt Drive-In Theater Flea Market

Saturday, Sunday. Average attendance 10,000 with approximately 150 dealers. New merchandise, sportswear, toys, housewares, jewelry, electronics, tools, clothing, used merchandise, produce, and garage sale items available. There are always some good collector booths here, along with a good selection of locally made crafts. Snack bar, rest rooms, h/a, ample parking. *Contact* Norm Shore, 48 Fallenrock Rd., Levittown, 19056 (215) 943-0670.

LATROBE

Latrobe Flea Market
Rte. 30 at Shopping Plaza

Sunday. Approximately 125 vendors offer antiques, collectibles, sports cards, silver, coins, vintage clothing, used merchandise, garage sale items, and new merchandise. Snack bar, rest rooms, h/a, ample parking. Space from $12. *Contact* Carol Craig, 640 Diamond Ave., Indiana, PA 15701 (412) 463-7887.

LEBANON

Sunset Flea Market
1650 N. 7th St.
Seven miles off Rtes. 22 and 78 on 343 South

Sunday. Outdoor market that opens at daylight and goes until dark. Markets has new blacktop and is one of the area's largest. Good variety of merchandise here. Good selection of food here, rest rooms, h/a, ample parking. Food vendors can sell at this market with prior reservations. Regular space from $7. Food vendors from $25. *Contact* Andy (717) 273-2516.

LEESPORT

Leesport Farmers Market & Auction
Rte. 61
Seven miles north of Redding or six miles south of I-78 on Rte. 61, north end of town

Wednesday, 7 a.m.–3 p.m., Sunday, 9 a.m.–8 p.m. Average attendance of 5,000 with an average of 250 dealers. Large, well-established, classic old-time market. Lots of crafts and collectibles at this market. Great market for Pennsylvania Dutch items. Market conducts many special events and holds a weekly livestock auction. Good food available, rest rooms, h/a, ample parking. Outdoor and indoor spaces from $10. *Contact* Bill Weist, P.O. Box B, 19533 (610) 926-1307.

LEOLA

Meadowbrook Farmers Market & Antique Center
345 W. Main St.
Four miles east of Lancaster

Friday, 9 a.m.–8 p.m., Saturday, 8 a.m.–5 p.m. Indoor market with approximately 150 dealers. Antiques, super selection of collectibles, furniture, crafts, new merchandise. Large, spread-out complex with lots of walking and a great variety of goods. Excellent variety of food, rest rooms, h/a, ample parking. *Contact* Frank Suraci, 345 W. Main St., 17540 (717) 656-2226.

LEWISBURG

Route 15 Flea Market Center
Rte. 15, two miles north of town, I-80, Exit 30-A, four miles south

Wednesday–Sunday, 10 a.m.–6 p.m. Large indoor/outdoor market with approximately 500 dealers. Antiques, collectibles, new and used merchandise, produce, crafts. Space from $30 per day. Restaurant, good food here, rest rooms, h/a. Ample free parking. *Contact* Sandy Keister, Box 73, West Milton, PA 17886 (570) 568-8080 or 568-0452, fax (717) 568-8080.

MANHEIM

Old Mill Flea Market & Antiques
Off Rte. 7 on Graystone Rd.

Tuesday. Average attendance of 5,000 with approximately 70 dealers. Antiques, furniture, art, books, Civil War items, fine jewelry, quality decorator items, used merchandise, country crafts, and collectibles available. Good food available, rest rooms, h/a, ample parking. Space from $10. *Contact* Carol Headings, Rte. 7, Box 110, 17545 (717) 898-7443 or 898-8591.

Root's Country Market and Auction
705 Graystone Rd. (off Rte. 7)

Tuesdays, 9 a.m.–9 p.m. Indoor/outdoor market with approximately 200 dealers. Antiques, collectibles, lots of used and garage sale items. Good food served here. Rest rooms, h/a. Ample parking. *Contact* Thomas Longnecker, 705 Graystone Rd. 17545 (717) 898-7811.

MARSHALLS CREEK

Pocono Antique Bazaar & Flea Market
Rte. 209 North
I-80, Exit 52, north five miles on
U.S. Hwy. 200
(717) 223-8640

Saturday, Sunday, 9 a.m.–5 p.m. Average daily attendance 5,000. Antiques, collectibles, crafts, and new and used merchandise available. Snack bar, rest rooms, h/a, ample parking. Has 300 outdoor spaces and 200 indoor spaces from $25. *Contact* Kevin Hoffman, Box 248, 18335.

ALWAYS CALL BEFORE TRAVELING LONG DISTANCES!

R & J Flea World
I-80 at Exit 52

Saturday, Sunday, 9 a.m.–5 p.m. Indoor/outdoor market with average attendance 20,000 daily and approximately 500 dealers. Large commercial market. Antiques, collectibles, lots of new and used merchandise, produce, locally made crafts, gifts, imports. Space from $25. Ample parking. *Contact* Ruth Tiburzi, Box 1221, 18335 (717) 223-0690.

MCKEY'S ROCK

McKey's Rock Plaza Shopping Center Flea Market

Sundays. Average attendance 10,000. Approximately 150 dealers. Antiques, collectibles, new and used merchandise, garage sale items, crafts. Food available, rest rooms, h/a. Open April through October. Space from $7 plus $5 city tax. Ample parking. *Contact* Wyette Isaacson, 1236 S. Megley Ave., Pittsburgh, PA 15217 (216) 521-9127.

MEADOWLANDS

Antiques Fair Race Track Flea Market
Racetrack
I-79, Exit 8, twenty-five miles south of Pittsburgh
(412) 228-3045

Saturday, Sunday. Approximately 700 vendors. Large wide-open commercial market with a little bit of everything here, from fine antiques to garage sale junk to "camp" art. Lots of food, rest rooms, h/a, ample paved parking, with lots of walking.

MECHANICSBURG

Antiques World Flea Market
Rte. 15 and Winding Hill Rd.
(717) 766-4030

Saturday. Antiques, furniture, wide range of collector items, great decorator finds, fine jewelry, vintage clothing, Civil War items, and art available. Food available, rest rooms, h/a, ample parking.

Silver Springs Flea Market
6416 Carlisle Pike
Rte. 11 West

Sunday, 7 a.m.–3 p.m. Approximately 500 vendors. Antiques, crafts, farm goods, collectibles, and new merchandise available. Indoor and outdoor space from $10. *Contact* Silver Springs Flea Market, 6416 Carlisle Pike, 17005 (717) 766-7215 or 766-9027.

MENGES HILLS

Colonial Valley Flea Market
Rte. 116, ten miles west of York

Sundays, 8:30 a.m.–4:30 p.m. Indoor/outdoor market. Antiques, collectibles, crafts, new and used merchandise. Market has petting zoo. They also hold several antique and classic car shows, call for schedule. Space from $8 outside and $10 inside. Ample parking. *Contact* Betty Staines, Box 34, Menges Mills, PA 72346 (717) 225-4811 or (410) 472-2701.

MIDDLETOWN

Saturday Market
3751 E. Harrisburg Pike
Rte. 230

Saturday, 5:30 a.m.–6 p.m. Average weekend attendance of 10,000 at this indoor/outdoor market with approximately 300 dealers. New and used merchandise, sportswear, imports, antiques, collectibles, and advertising items available. Snack bar, rest rooms, h/a, ample parking. One of the area's larger markets. Space from $11. Reservations recommended for inside space. *Contact* Rod Rose, 3751 E. Harrisburg Pike, 17507 (717) 944-2555.

MONTGOMERYVILLE

309 Drive-In Flea Market
Rtes. 309 and 63

Sunday. Approximately 200 dealers at this outdoor market offer antiques, collectibles, produce, and new merchandise. Snack bar, rest rooms, h/a, ample parking. Space from $10. *Contact* Robert Langetta, 1114 Rte. 313, Perkasie, 18944 (215) 249-9692.

MORGANTOWN

Clocktower Plaza Flea Market
Junction of Rtes. 23 and 10, PA Turnpike, Exit 22
(610) 286-0611

Friday. Approximately 150 dealers, equally divided between inside and outside. Antiques, collectibles, used merchandise, primitives, advertising items, and farm items available. Snack bar, rest rooms, h/a, ample parking. Space from $8. *Contact* Manager, Market Place, Rte. 23, 19543.

NAZARETH

Antique Shows & Flea Market
Rtes. 191 and 248

Sunday. Approximately 200 dealers offer a nice selection of antiques, collector lines, glassware, furniture, silver, coins, military and Civil War memorabilia, art, prints, books, primitives, crafts, and decorator items. Food available, rest rooms, h/a, ample parking. Inside and outside space available. *Contact* Al Loquasto (215) 865-3880.

NEW CASTLE

Michelangelo's Flea Market
Rte. 422
Five miles west of town
(412) 654-0382

Sunday, 7 a.m.–5 p.m. Indoor and outdoor market with approximately 300 dealers. Quality-oriented market with antiques, collectibles, and decorator items available. Market conducts many special events during the year. They did not sponsor the infamous computer virus by the same name. Great selection of food here, rest rooms, h/a, ample parking. Space from $7. *Contact* Michelangelo's, Rte. 1, Box 211, Edinburg, 16116.

NEW HOPE

Rices Market Place
6326 Green Hill Rd.
(215) 297-5993 or 297-8722

Tuesday, 6:30 a.m.–2 p.m. Admission charge. Average daily attendance 5,000. Inside and outside space available with over 1,000 dealers weekly. One of the East Coast's larger and finer weekday markets. If you have the time to spend the day walking past the hundreds of booths, you will find what you are looking for. All types of items sold at this market, a little bit of everything. Lots of good country crafts here. Plenty of good food, rest rooms, h/a, ample parking. Space from $20. Camping available. *Contact* Manager, 18938.

Country Host Flea Market
Rte. 202

Saturday, 7 a.m.–2 p.m., Sunday, 6 a.m.–4 p.m. Outdoor market with approximately 25 dealers. Collectibles, crafts, and new and used merchandise available. Snack bar, clean rest rooms. Seasonal market. Space from $10 per day. *Contact* Robert Mazaleski, Country Host Flea Market, Rte. 202, 18938 (215) 862-3111.

NEW KINGSTON

Gateway Drive-In Theater Flea Market
133 Logans Ferry Rd.

Sunday. New merchandise, electronics, sportswear, housewares, jewelry, used merchandise, garage sale items, lots of good collector booths, antiques, crafts, country collectibles, and gifts available. Snack bar, rest rooms, h/a, ample parking. *Contact* Alice Laporte (412) 336-9724.

NEW OXFORD

The Golden Carriage Flea Market
Hwy. 305
Five miles east of Gettysburg

Saturday, Sunday. Antiques, collectibles, Civil War items, farm and country collectibles, used merchandise, decorator items, and crafts available. Food available.

Flea Market
Hwy. 94
(717) 624-2362

Saturday, Sunday. This indoor market features new and used merchandise, collectibles, antiques, furniture, art, prints, books, and jewelry. Snack bar, rest rooms, ample parking.

NEWRY

Leighty's Flea Market
Rte. 220
Two miles south of Altoona
(814) 695-9120 or 695-5151
Fax (814) 696-8543

Saturday, Sunday, 7 a.m.–5 p.m. Antiques, collectibles, primitives, crafts, new and used merchandise, and housewares available. Market is located on 29 acres and has inside and outside space available from $8. *Contact* Leighty's, Rte. 220, 16665.

NORTH VERSAILLES

Super Flea Market Place
Eastland Mall
833 E. Pittsburgh Blvd.
Rte. 30
(412) 673-3532
Fax (412) 673-4015

Saturday, Sunday, 8 a.m.–5 p.m. Average daily attendance of 7,500 with approximately 200 dealers. Good selection of antiques and collectibles. This market conducts many special events during the year. Call for schedule. Good market for the commercial vendor. Many other stores and shops located in this mall. Restaurant, nice rest rooms, h/a, ample parking. Indoor/outdoor space available from $8. *Contact* Ed Williams, 15137

OAKFORD

Neshaming Flea Market
(215) 364-1311

Saturday, Sunday. New and used merchandise, garage sale items, collectibles, home furnishings, household goods, imports, crafts, produce. Food available.

PARKSBURG

Wrights Flea Market
Rte. 10
(215) 857-9660

Tuesday, Sunday. Collectibles, used merchandise, garage sale items, imports, gifts, clothing, fashion accessories, farm items, crafts, and produce available. Food available.

PAXINOS

Paxinos Flea Market
Junction of Rtes. 61 and 487
Three miles from Koebel's Amusement Park
(717) 648-9695

Saturday, Sunday. Approximately 200 dealers outside and 25 inside. Good mix of merchandise here, antiques, collectibles, new and used merchandise, crafts, and country collectibles. Nice snack bar, rest rooms, h/a, ample parking. Indoor/outdoor market and some covered spaces. Space from $5.

PEKIOMENVILLE

Pekiomenville Flea Market & Auction
Rte. 29

Monday. Approximately 300 dealers offer a large and varied selection of antiques, furniture, collector lines, fine decorator items, jewelry, Civil War items, art, books, prints, country primitives, Victorian-era finds, advertising items, imports, and reproductions. Food available, rest rooms, h/a, ample parking. Inside and outside space available from $8 to $10. Camping on premises. One of the area's better markets. *Contact* Robert Landis, Box 14, 18074 (215) 234-4733.

PHILADELPHIA

Spectrum Outdoor Flea Market
Parking lot at Spectrum Stadium
(215) 947-8149

Thursday, 8 a.m.–3 p.m. Outdoor market with sportswear, cosmetics, clothing, electronics, videos, games, plants, crafts, linens, toys, and jewelry available. Large selection of new merchandise here. Food, rest rooms, h/a, ample parking with $1 charge.

Bargain Depot Mini-Mall & Flea Market
Intersection of Grant Ave. and Blue Grass Rd. at Northeast Philadelphia Market Place
(215) 969-8838

Wednesday, Saturday, Sunday, 8 a.m.–3 p.m. Food, rest rooms, h/a, ample parking.

Quaker City Flea Market
Tacony and Colony Sts.
Two blocks south of the Tacony-Palmyra Bridge

Saturday, Sunday, 8 a.m.–4 p.m. Approximately 200 dealers offer crafts, antiques, books, collectibles, good jewelry, produce, and a wide selection of new merchandise. Inside and outside space available from $15. *Contact* K. Williams, Tacony and Colony Sts., 19135 (215) 744-2022.

PITTSBURGH

Wildwood Peddlers Village
2330 Wildwood Rd.

Sunday, 6 a.m.–4 p.m. Average daily attendance 5–8,000 with approximately 300 dealers offering lots of antiques, collectibles, and a good mix of new merchandise. Good food, clean rest rooms, h/a, ample parking. Area's best market for commercial vendors. Space from $12. Inside and outside space available. Overnight parking. *Contact* George Rutledge, 2330 Wildwood Rd., Wildwood, 15091 (412) 487-2200.

Keystone State Grand Flea Market
(412) 232-3338

Saturday, Sunday. New merchandise, used merchandise, housewares, clothing, collectibles, crafts, and produce available. Food available, rest rooms, h/a, ample parking.

Pittsburgh Flea Market
West Park, Allegheny Commons

Sunday, 8 a.m.–4 p.m. Average attendance of 5,000 with approximately 150 dealers. Antiques, collectibles, crafts, new merchandise, used merchandise, garage sale items, and produce available. Food available, rest rooms, h/a, ample parking. Space from $7, $1 for electricity. *Contact* Webb Koying, 601 Ridge Ave., 15212 (412) 323-7229.

Panther Hollow Flea Market
Boundary St. and I-376
(412) 461-1160

Saturday, Sunday. Approximately 200 dealers. Crafts, collectibles, country and farm items, used merchandise, garage sale items, and new merchandise available. Food available, rest rooms, h/a, ample parking. Outdoor market with space from $12 per day. Food vendors welcome.

Flea Mart
Washington County Fairgrounds
(412) 361-9272

Monday–Saturday. New and used merchandise, garage sale items, home furnishings, housewares, farm items, tack, collectibles, crafts, and produce available. Food available, rest rooms, h/a, ample parking.

PULASKI

Pulaski Flea Market
Rte. 551
(412) 658-4923 or 654-4012

Thursday, 5 a.m.–1 p.m. Average attendance of 2,000 with approximately 100 dealers. Antiques, crafts, collectibles, new and used merchandise, lots of Amish crafts and food here. Indoor/outdoor market. Space from $4. *Contact* Lyle Koening, 130 Valhahla Dr., New Castle, 16105.

QUAKERTOWN

Quakertown Flea & Farmers Market
201 Station Rd. east of Rte. 309
One-half mile south of town

Friday, Saturday, 10 a.m.–10 p.m., Sunday, 11 a.m.–5 p.m. Approximately 500 dealers offer antiques, collectibles, furniture, primitives, new merchandise, used and garage sale merchandise, lots of farm items, and toys. Great selection of Amish and country crafts. Several restaurants, grocery store, meat market, and delis all on the market's grounds. Tremendous selection of food here. Rest rooms, h/a, ample parking. There are four buildings plus the outside area completely filled with dealers. It could take the full three days to see the entire market. Covered and open spaces from $10. *Contact* John Chism, 201 Station Rd., 18951 (215) 536-4115.

SAYLORSBURG

Blue Ridge Flea Market
Blue Ridge Drive-In Theater
Rte. 33
(717) 992-8044

Saturday, Sunday, 7 a.m.–5 p.m. Approximately 150 dealers. Large selection of new merchandise, lots of used merchandise, and bric-a-brac. Sometimes quality antiques, lots of collector lines, crafts, produce, and country, and farm items available. Food available, rest rooms, h/a, ample parking. Outdoor market with space from $7. Camping nearby.

SCHUYKIL HAVEN

The Original Renninger's Market
Flea Market and Farmers Market
(717) 336-2177 or (215) 267-2177

Saturday, Sunday.

SCRANTON

Giant Indoor Flea Market
710 Capouse Ave.
(717) 346-8777

Sunday. New merchandise, lots of hot new trendy items, housewares, clothing, children's goods, tools, jewelry, sports merchandise, used merchandise, collectibles, decorator items, gifts, crafts, produce, and packaged food available. Food available, rest rooms, h/a, ample parking.

Circle Flea Fair
Circle Drive-In Theater
Scranton-Carbondale Hwy.
Rte. 6
(717) 876-1400 or 489-5731

Saturday, Sunday, March–December, 7 a.m.–4 p.m. Average daily attendance 10,000 with approximately 400 dealers. This is a very clean market with an excellent variety of vendors and items. Good food, clean rest rooms, h/a, ample parking. Outdoor market with space from $15. Camping nearby.

SHADY GROVE PARK

Antiques & Collectibles Flea Market
Rte. 897
(215) 484-4225

Saturday. This is an excellent country antiques and collectibles market that will take you back in time 100 years. A bit of everything nostalgic. Good chance to find some real treasures at this market. Food available, rest rooms.

SINKING SPRING

Willow Glen Flea Market
Willow Glen Park
From Hwy. 422, turn onto Park Ave. at Springs Car Wash
(610) 376-0539

Sunday, 5 a.m.–1 p.m. New outdoor market with some pavilion and approximately 500 spaces (20×20). Space $10. Outdoor with some pavilions.

SOLEBURY

Rices Sale & Country Market
Green Hill Rd.
(215) 297-5808

Tuesday. New and used merchandise, housewares, children's items, clothing, collectibles, crafts, and produce available. Food available. Indoor and outdoor market.

SOUDERBURG

Mertz Flea Market
Rte. 30

Saturday, Sunday. Used merchandise, garage sale items, collectibles, home furnishings, housewares, imports, clothing, farm items, sports memorabilia, crafts, and produce available. Food available.

SYBERTSVILLE

Halls Antique Flea Market
Rte. 93
(717) 788-1275

Sunday. Approximately 90 dealers offer antiques, a good assortment of collector lines, Civil War items, books, art, prints, jewelry, coins, silver, glassware, art pottery, country primitives, Victorian-era finds, and crafts. Food available.

TAMAQUA

Hometown Farmers & Flea Market
Rte. 54

Wednesday, 8 a.m.–8 p.m. Average daily attendance of 7,500 with approximately 200 dealers outside and 100 inside. Large classic country market with lots of country and farm collectibles, antiques, a good variety of collector booths, crafts, gifts, souvenirs, and decorator items. Food available, ample parking. Indoor/outdoor and covered spaces available from $20. Camping nearby. *Contact* Robert Dunn, Rte. 1, Box 1371, New Ringold, PA 17960 (717) 668-2630.

309 Market Place
Rte. 309 and Rte. 54
Two miles north of town
(570) 668-2630

Saturday, Sunday. Used merchandise, new merchandise, household goods, home furnishings, decorator items, crafts, collectibles, and produce available. Food available.

Blue Mountain Flea Market
Rte. 309 South
(570) 386-2034

Saturday. Collectibles, crafts, used merchandise, garage sale bric-a-brac, souvenirs, imports, and country primitives available. Food available.

TANNERSVILLE

Pocono Peddler Village
Rte. 611 and I-80, Exit 45
(717) 629-6366

Saturday, Sunday, 9 a.m.–5 p.m. Nice market with lots of collectibles, small antiques, good selection of arts and crafts items. Over 60 dealers. Snack bar and rest rooms, ample parking, and camping nearby. Indoor/outdoor market. *Contact* Ralph Reifinger, Rte. 611, 18372.

TAYLOR

Flea Market
S. Keyser Ave.
(717) 347-3996

Sunday. Antiques, collectibles, farm items, bric-a-brac, home furnishings, housewares, imports, tools, electronics, toys, children's goods, and crafts available. Food available.

WANTICOKE

Flea Market
136 E. Main St.
(717) 735-2955

Saturday, Sunday. New and used merchandise, collectibles, silver, jewelry, crafts, and country collectibles available. Food available, rest rooms. Indoor market.

WASHINGTON

Al's Flea Market
37 Woodside Dr.
(412) 228-2219

Saturday, Sunday, 9 a.m.–3 p.m. New and used goods of all kinds, imports, sportswear, collectibles, jewelry, home furnishings, and crafts.

Flea Market
Fairgrounds
(412) 225-0961

Saturday, Sunday. A bargain hunter's haven with booths full of new and not-so-new merchandise of every price and description. Housewares, clothing, tools, electronics, imports, antiques, and collectibles available.

WEST MIDDLESEX

Mentzer's Antique Flea Market
Rte. 18 at I-80
Exit 1N

Wednesday, Saturday, Sunday, 9 a.m.–5 p.m. Approximately 75 dealers. Market located in the heart of Amish country. Good selection of antiques, collectibles, glassware, silver, primitives, advertising items, and antique toys. Great selection of Amish and Pennsylvania Dutch items, crafts, and food. Good food, rest rooms, h/a, ample parking. Outdoor and indoor market with space available from $30. *Contact* Fred Mentzer, 101 N. Sharon Rd., 16159 (412) 528-2300.

WEST MIFFLIN

Woodlands Flea Market
Woodlands Drive-In Theater
526 Thompson Run Rd.
(412) 462-4370
Fax (412) 462-4334

Saturday, Sunday, March–April, 7 a.m.–3 p.m. Average attendance 10–15,000. Large indoor/outdoor market with over 300 dealers. Antiques, collectibles, crafts, new and used merchandise available. Food, rest rooms, h/a, ample parking. Space from $8. Reservations required. *Contact* Woodlands Flea Market, 526 Thompson Run Rd., 15122.

INFORMATION IS SUBJECT TO CHANGE—ALWAYS CALL FIRST!

RHODE ISLAND

ASHAWAY

Ashaway Flea Market & Garage Sale
Ashaway Recreation Center

Saturday, Sunday, 10 a.m.–4 p.m. Indoor/outdoor market with approximately 25 dealers most weekends. Mostly garage sale type of sellers with lots of secondhand and bric-a-brac. Ample parking. Space from $10 per day. *Contact* John Marley, 1 Juniper Dr., 02804 (401) 377-4947.

CHARLESTOWN

Flea Market
General Stanton Inn
4115-A Old Post Rd.
Rte. 1A

Saturday, Sunday, March–November, 7 a.m.–4 p.m. Indoor market with approximately 200 dealers. Antiques, collectibles, crafts, art, and new merchandise available. Space from $25. Market is located in a historic inn. *Contact* Janice Falcone, Rte. 1, Box 222, 02813 (401) 364-8888, fax (401) 364-3333.

EAST GREENWICH

Rocky Hill Flea Market
Rocky Hill Fairgrounds
1408 Division Rd.
Corner of Division Rd. and Rte. 2

Sunday, April–December, 5 a.m.–4 p.m. Approximately 200 dealers. One of the area's better markets. Lots of new merchandise and great bargains. Sportswear, imports, electronics, sports-related merchandise, antiques, collectibles, and crafts available. Snack bars, clean rest rooms, h/a, ample parking. Space from $17 per day. *Contact* Gary E. Hamilton, 1408 Division Rd., 02818 (401) 888-4114.

PAWTUCKET

American Flea Market
Narragansett Racetrack
(401) 726-0081

Saturday, Sunday. Approximately 400 dealers. Large commercial market with a wide range of goods. New merchandise, surplus, closeouts, large variety of new personal and household items, used merchandise, antiques, many collector lines, crafts, and produce available. Snack bar, rest rooms, h/a, ample parking.

PORTSMOUTH

Tex's Auction House & Flea Market
1678 E. Main St.

Friday, Saturday, Sunday. New and used merchandise, bric-a-brac, clothing, housewares, jewelry, crafts, collectibles, and produce available. Snack bar, rest rooms, h/a, ample parking. *Contact* Henry Violette.

PROVIDENCE

Big Top Flea Market
120 Manton Ave.

Saturday, Sunday. Approximately 120 dealers in this indoor market offer new merchandise, housewares, electronics, sportswear, jewelry, sports merchandise, used merchandise, collector lines, decorator items, and crafts. Snack bar, rest rooms, h/a, ample parking. *Contact* Howard Brynes (401) 274-0060.

TIVERTON

Route 177 Flea Market
1560 Bulgar Marsh Rd.

Saturday, Sunday, 8 a.m.–5 p.m. New and used merchandise available at this indoor/outdoor market along with garage sale items, antiques, collectibles, decorator items, and crafts. Snack bar, rest rooms, h/a, ample parking. Space from $15. *Contact* Tom Ouelette, 8 Campton Ave., 02878 (401) 624-9354.

WARWICK

Rocky Point Flea Market
1 Rocky Point Ave.

Saturday, Sunday, April–October, 9 a.m.–4:30 p.m. Approximately 150 dealers. One of the better Rhode Island markets with a good selection of antiques, collectibles, new and used merchandise, and crafts available. Entertainment, snack bar, rest rooms, h/a, ample parking. Space starts at $28 for the weekend. Reservations required. Inside and outside space available. *Contact* Angelo Russo, 1 Rocky Point Ave., 02889 (401) 737-8000.

WOONSOCKET

Blackstone Valley Flea Market
401 Clinton St.

Friday, 1 p.m.–8 p.m., Saturday, Sunday, 9 a.m.–5 p.m. Large, well-established, and very popular indoor/outdoor market with approximately 200 dealers. Antiques, collectibles, new and used merchandise, great selection of locally made crafts, and gifts available at this market. Snack bar, rest rooms, h/a, ample parking. Space from $25 for the weekend. *Contact* Edward Perkins, Box 1361, Westport, MA 02790 (401) 762-9101 or (508) 677-2244.

Woonsocket Flea Market
6 Davidson Ave.
Junction of Rte. 22 and Davidson Ave.

Saturday, Sunday, 9 a.m.–5 p.m. Admission charge 50 cents. Indoor market with approximately 250 booths. Wide range of merchandise from new and used to antiques and collectibles. Market has a large staple food department. Cafe, snack bar, rest rooms, ample parking. Credit cards accepted. *Contact* Joseph Moranto, 6 Davidson Ave., 02790 (401) 762-3101.9

SOUTH CAROLINA

AIKEN

Pops Flea & Farmers Market
I-20, Exit 22

Friday, Saturday, Sunday, 8 a.m.–6 p.m. Average daily attendance of 7,500 with approximately 125 dealers. Antiques, collectibles, new and used merchandise, bric-a-brac, decorator items, and crafts available. Snack bar, clean rest rooms, h/a, ample parking. Camping available. Indoor, outdoor, and covered space from $5 per day. *Contact* Ray Cornett, 112 W. Frontage Rd., 29801 (803) 642-0071.

BEAUFORT

Laurel Bay Flea Market
Route 170, twenty miles from Hilton Head

Saturdays, dawn to dusk. New and used merchandise, some collectibles, primitives, furniture, produce, crafts. Approximately 75 dealers. Space from $5 per table. Rest rooms, no food on premises. *Contact* Kathleen McTeer, Box 1653, 29901 (803) 521-9794.

BELTON

Anderson Jockey Lot & Farmers Market
4530 Hwy. 29
Ten miles from Anderson, between Greenville and Anderson
(864) 224-2027 or 224-2279
Fax (864) 231-6927

Saturday, 7 a.m.–6 p.m., Sunday, 9 a.m.–6 p.m. Indoor/outdoor market with some covered spaces. Average weekend attendance of 30–40,000. Approximately 2,000 dealers. Little bit of everything here. Lots of nice items at bargain prices. This market has many professional dealers with great booths. This is a classic wide-open southern market. A great place to shop or sell. A market that in many ways makes you long for times gone by. Restaurant, snack bar, rest rooms, h/a, ample parking. Camping nearby. Space from $6 per day. *Contact* Manager, 4530 Hwy. 29N, 29627.

CHARLESTON

Palmetto State Flea Market
7225 Rivers Ave.
(843) 553-8030 or 883-3091

Saturday, Sunday, 8 a.m.–6 p.m. Average daily attendance of 8,000-plus with approximately 350 dealers. Good selection of merchandise with wide variety. Nice crafts and country decorator items here. Snack bars, clean rest rooms, h/a, ample parking. Indoor/outdoor market with space from $10 outdoors. Camping available on premises. *Contact* Ken Childress.

Low Country Flea Market & Collectibles Show
Municipal Auditorium
77 Calhoun St.

Every third weekend, 9 a.m.–6 p.m. Admission charge $2. Indoor event with approximately 100 dealers. Lots of quality antiques including furniture and collectible items in many fields. For shopkeepers and vendors this is a great source market—very attractive pricing. Snack bar, rest rooms, h/a, ample parking. Space from $55 for the weekend. *Contact* Nelson Garrett, 605 Johnnie Dodds Blvd., Mt. Pleasant, 29464 (843) 849-1949 or 577-7400, fax (843) 849-1949.

COLUMBIA

The Barnyard Flea Market
4414 Augusta Rd.
Hwy. 1; I-26, Exit 11A, or Exit 58 from I-20
(800) 628-7496 or (803) 957-6570

Friday, Saturday, Sunday, 8 a.m.–6 p.m. Indoor/outdoor market with approximately 500 dealers. Lots of goodies here. Four large buildings and about 100 dealers outside. New and used merchandise, antiques, collectibles, primitives, advertising items galore, crafts, sporting, hunting, and fishing items, jewelry, and lots of clothes available. This is one of those markets full of treasures waiting to be discovered. Great variety of food, rest rooms, h/a, ample parking, RV park. Space from $10 per day. *Contact* Barnyard Flea Market, 4414 Augusta Rd., 29211.

Airport Flea Market
Hwys. 215 and 302
(803) 955-9111

Friday, Saturday. Average daily attendance of 1,500 and approximately 150 dealers. New merchandise, electronics, sportswear, housewares, jewelry, sports merchandise, outdoor items, used merchandise, lots of garage sale bric-a-brac, antiques, collectibles, lots of new collector lines, crafts, packaged food, produce, and pets and pet supplies available. Snack bar, rest rooms, h/a, ample parking. Space from $5. Most spaces are covered.

U.S. 1 Flea Market
3500 Augusta Rd.
I-26, Exit 11A or Exit 58 from I-20
(800) 447-3522, (800) 447-FLEA, or (803) 796-9294

Friday, Saturday, Sunday, 8 a.m.–5 p.m. Inside/outside market with an average daily attendance of 10,000 and approximately 350 dealers. This is a wide-open marketplace with a little bit of everything. A classic southern market with a great upbeat country atmosphere. Great variety of food here, rest rooms, h/a, ample parking, and lots of walking. Camping available on-site. On Wednesday they conduct a wholesale market open to wholesale buyers only. Space from $5 to $10 outside. *Contact* Richard Hood, Box 1457, 29071.

FLORENCE

Florence Flea Market
4001 E. Palmetto St.
Junction of Rtes. 327 and 76

Saturday, Sunday, dawn to dusk. Estimated attendance 18,000 per weekend. A good mixture of new and used merchandise. Lots of nice country crafts. Good food, rest rooms, ample parking. Camping available on-site. There are 400 covered spaces. Space from $8. *Contact* Chuck Davis, 4001 E. Palmetto St., 29506 (843) 669-5303 or 667-9585.

GREENVILLE

Greenville Flea Market
Fairgrounds
1300 White Horse Rd.
I-85, Exit 44 North

Saturday, Sunday, 5 a.m.–5 p.m. Indoor/outdoor market with over 500 dealers. Wide range of antiques and collectibles. Lots of quality country items and primitives. Advertising items, farm items, antique toys, and new and used merchandise also available. Good food, clean rest rooms, h/a, ample parking. Great country market that is a pleasure to visit. Space from $8 per day. *Contact* Paul Baker, 1300 White Horse Rd., 29605 (864) 295-1183.

LADSON

Coastal Carolina Flea Market
Junction of College Park and Hwy. 78
I-26, Exit 203

Saturday, Sunday, 8 a.m.–6 p.m. This market has an average daily attendance of 5,000 and approximately 200 outside exhibitors and 400 dealers inside. Antiques, collectibles, cards, memorabilia, primitives, farm items, and antique toys available. Many quality dealer booths here. Lots of new merchandise, sportswear, electronics at great prices. Great food, rest rooms, h/a, ample parking. Camping available. Indoor and outdoor space available from $10. *Contact* Michael Masterson, Box 510, 29456 (843) 797-0540, fax (843) 797-0541.

LEXINGTON

Smiley's Flea Market
Hwy. 302, nine miles south of Columbia Airport
(803) 955-9111

Thursday–Sunday. Indoor/outdoor market. Nice selection of antiques, collectibles, new merchandise, new collectibles, sportswear, gifts, imports and locally made crafts. Snack bar, rest rooms, h/a.

The Barn Yard Flea Market
Hwy. 1
South at Oak Grove
(803) 957-6570 or (800) 628-7496

Friday, Saturday, Sunday. New and used merchandise, bric-a-brac, country collectibles, collector lines, crafts, and produce available. Snack bar, rest rooms, h/a, ample parking. *Contact* Dick Stewart, 4414 August Rd., 29072.

MYRTLE BEACH

Myrtle Beach Flea Market
Center South Shopping Center
3820 S. Kings Hwy.

Friday, Saturday, Sunday, 10 a.m.–4 p.m. Market is often open daily during tourist season. Indoor market with approximately 250 dealers. New merchandise, souvenirs, gifts, sportswear, jewelry, used merchandise, garage sale items, crafts, produce. Snack bar, rest rooms, h/a. Ample parking. *Contact* Judy Mode, 3820 S. Kings Hwy., 29577 (843) 477-1550.

Big Deals Bazaar and Flea Market
4761 Hwy. 501, six miles west of town

Saturday, Sunday, 10 a.m.–5 p.m. Seasonal market during winter months only. Often open daily. Indoor/outdoor market, approximately 100 dealers. Collectibles, new and used merchandise, furniture, garage sale items, crafts, gifts, and imports. Snack bar, rest rooms, h/a. Free parking. *Contact* Jan Watts, 4761 Hwy. 501, 29575 (800) 244-3325 or (843) 236-7474.

NORTH CHARLESTON

The Flea Market Depot
2935 Ashley Phosphate Rd.
(843) 552-4824

Friday, Saturday, Sunday, 8:30 a.m.–6 p.m. Indoor/outdoor market with approximately 200 dealers inside and 3–400 outside. Lots of new merchandise, glassware, housewares, electronics, tools, sportswear, collectibles, crafts, and some used merchandise available. Good food here, rest rooms, h/a, ample parking, and lots of walking. Space from $10.

NORTH MYRTLE BEACH

North Myrtle Beach Flea Market
Intersection of Hwy. 17 North and Hwy. 9
(843) 249-4701

Friday, Saturday, Sunday, 9 a.m.–5 p.m. Average daily attendance 8,000 with approximately 250 dealers. A good all-around market located in nice resort area. Plenty of varied, well-stocked booths. Good food, rest rooms, h/a, ample parking. Just a little over a mile to the beach. Indoor market with space from $10 per day. Camping and electricity available. *Contact* Jesse Medlock, Box 3467, 29582.

O.D. Flea Market
Kings Highway Plaza
523 N. Kings Hwy.
Rte. 17 North, I-95, exit Rte. 301

Sunday–Wednesday. Indoor market with approximately 100 exhibitors. Antiques, collectibles, vintage clothing, coins, crafts, fine art, new and used merchandise, and lots of sporting goods, especially golf items, available. Snack bar, rest rooms, h/a, ample parking. General retail auction on Wednesday at 7 p.m. Market hosts bingo on the weekends and Monday. Space from $8. *Contact* Albert Moyac, 523 N. Kings Hwy., 29582 (843) 249-4805.

ROCK HILL

Vendors Gallery Flea Market
Rock Hill Mall
2188 Cherry Rd.

Friday, Saturday, 8 a.m.–8 p.m., Sunday, 10 a.m.–6 p.m. Indoor/outdoor market with approximately 75 dealers. Collectibles, fine jewelry, cards, housewares, new and used merchandise, and new and used furniture available. Rest rooms, snack bar, h/a, ample parking. Space from $15 per day. *Contact* William Bailey, 2188 Cherry Rd., 29730 (803) 336-3992 or 366-6160.

SPRINGFIELD

Springfield Flea Market
Junction of Hwys. 3 and 4
One mile east of town

Monday, Saturday, 5 a.m.–2 p.m. Average daily attendance of 8,000-plus. Indoor and outdoor market with approximately 500 dealers. Great selection here with well-stocked booths. New merchandise, sportswear, electronics, housewares, jewelry, crafts, art, antiques, primitives, and collectibles available. Many quality specialty dealers with booths here. Lots of good food on premises, clean rest rooms, h/a, ample parking, and expect to do a lot of walking to see everything. Space from $5 outside. *Contact* Henry Cooper, Box 74, 29146 (803) 258-3192.

DAYS, DATES, AND MARKETS ARE SUBJECT TO CHANGE!

SUMTER

Shaw Flea Market
Hwy. 378 East
(803) 494-2635
Across the street from Shaw Air Force Base

Friday, Saturday, Sunday, 9 a.m.–6 p.m. Average daily attendance of 5,000-plus and approximately 75 dealers. Antiques, collectibles, coins, cards, crafts, art, and new and used merchandise available. Snack bar, rest rooms, h/a, ample parking. Outdoor and covered spaces available from $7. Food vendors okay by prior reservation. *Contact* Bob Kimber, 29154.

SURFSIDE BEACH

Hudson's Surfside Flea Market
1040 S. Kings Hwy.
(843) 238-0372

Friday, Saturday, Sunday, 7 a.m. until dark. Average daily attendance 7,000 with approximately 250 dealers. New merchandise, souvenirs, sportswear, lots of beach and water items, used merchandise, bric-a-brac, collectibles, collector lines in all categories, crafts, decorator items, and produce available. Snack bar, h/a, ample parking, and lots of walking. Outdoor market with covered spaces from $10. Camping available. Market located in high tourist area.

WESTMINSTER

Traders Junction
4265 Hwy. 11 South
(864) 882-3775

Saturday, Sunday, 7 a.m.–4 p.m. Indoor/outdoor market with approximately 100 dealers. Space from $10 per day. Snack bars, rest rooms, h/a. Market is located in a very beautiful scenic area. Ample free parking.

SOUTH DAKOTA

RAPID CITY

Rapid City Flea Market
Civic Center
444 Mount Rushmore Rd.

Monthly, call for dates, 9 a.m.–5 p.m. Indoor market with approximately 50–75 dealers offering antiques, collectibles, sports items, new merchandise, lots of secondhand items, and country crafts. Market always has a great selection of authentic Indian jewelry and art. Snack bar, rest rooms, h/a, ample parking. Space from $25. *Contact* Mrs. Robert Orlup, HC 1741, Deadwood, 57732 (605) 342-2524.

Blackhills Flea Market
550 Mount Rushmore Rd.
U.S. Hwy. 16

Saturday, Sunday, May–September, 7 a.m.–until dark. Indoor/outdoor market with approximately 125 dealers. Wide variety of collectibles, antiques, advertising items, farm items, good selection of locally made crafts, and new merchandise available. Lots of good food here, clean rest rooms, ample parking. Camping nearby. Very scenic market. Space from $10. *Contact* Deborah Cooley (605) 343-6477 or 348-1981.

ALWAYS CALL AHEAD TO VERIFY DATES AND INFORMATION

SIOUX FALLS

Flea Market
Fairgrounds, Expo Building
5th and Main Sts.

Every first weekend, 9 a.m.–5 p.m. Admission charge $1. Approximately 250 dealers at this indoor market. Nice overall market with a good selection of collectibles, new merchandise, used merchandise, and crafts. Clean rest rooms, snack bars, h/a, ample parking. Space from $30. *Contact* Ed Benson, Box 236, 57102 (605) 334-1312.

Cliff Avenue Flea Market
3515 N. Cliff Ave.

Daily. Small indoor market with approximately 12 dealers. Market closed on Wednesday. *Contact* Noami Carman (605) 338-8975.

YANKTON

Lewis & Clark Traders Market
Hwy. 52
One mile west of Gavins Point Dam

Friday, Saturday, Sunday. New and used merchandise, farm and ranch items, home furnishings, housewares, collectibles, western and Indian art and artifacts, crafts, and produce are available. Snack bar, rest rooms, h/a, ample parking. Has 75 spaces for $5 each. Camping and electricity available. *Contact* D. Larson, 800 East 4th, 57078 (605) 665-2231.

TENNESSEE

ATHENS

Shady Oaks Flea Market
625 Decatur Pike
Hwy. 30, I-75, Exit 49

Friday, Saturday, Sunday. Approximately 75 dealers offer antiques, collectibles, new and used merchandise, farm items, crafts, and produce. Snack bar, ample parking. *Contact* Chester Clark (615) 745-3975.

Athens Flea Market Mall
1637 Decatur Pike
Hwy. 30, I-75, Exit 49

Friday, Saturday, 9 a.m.–7 p.m., Sunday, 10 a.m.–5 p.m. Approximately 250 dealers at this well-stocked and well-attended market. Good range of merchandise here, antiques, collectibles, crafts, new merchandise, used merchandise. Plenty of food, rest rooms, h/a, ample parking. Indoor and outside space available. Overnight camping on premises. *Contact* Norman Barker, P.O. Box 515, Etowah, 37331 (615) 263-7414.

BAXTER

Baxter Flea Market
6051 Flea Market Rd.
Rte. 3, Baxter-Gainsboro Rd.
I-40, Exit 280

Saturday, Sunday, 8 a.m.–5 p.m. A wide selection of merchandise here. New and used goods, imports, antiques, and collectibles. Market has a separate section for the sale of animals. Outdoor market with covered spaces from $7 per day. Camping available. *Contact* Mary Hall (931) 868-5152.

BELLS

Bells Market Place
Rte. 1

Friday, Saturday, Sunday. New and used merchandise, lots of bric-a-brac, country collectibles, collector items, crafts, and decorator items available. Snack bar, rest rooms, ample parking. Inside and outside space available. Electricity and camping available. *Contact* Barbara Williams (901) 663-2919.

CAMDEN

The Ole Sun Flower Flea Market & Antique Mall
Hwy. 641 North
(901) 584-0912 or 584-3935

Friday, Sunday, 8 a.m.–10 p.m. Approximately 75 dealers outside and approximately 80 shops, stores, and booths indoors. Lot of good antiques, collectibles, and memorabilia here. Food available, rest rooms, h/a, ample parking. Indoor/outdoor market. It conducts a retail consignment auction on Tuesday and Friday starting at 6 p.m.

INFORMATION IS SUBJECT TO CHANGE—ALWAYS CALL AHEAD TO AVOID DISAPPOINTMENT

NOTE: Tennessee has a state dealer's registration fee of $45 per year; $15 per quarter; $5 per month. Severe penalties are imposed for violating this statute. Market operators have the necessary forms, and you may pay the fee at the market. The state also charges vendors from $1 to $2 per day to set up.

CHATTANOOGA

Chattanooga Indoor Flea Market
210 E. 21st St.
I-24, Exit 181
(423) 684-7017

Saturday, Sunday. New and used merchandise, antiques, furniture, collector lines, primitives, farm items, and decorator items available. Snack bar, rest rooms, h/a, ample parking. Reservations for space are recommended.

East Ridge Flea Market
6725 Ringold Rd.

Saturday, Sunday, 9 a.m.–6 p.m. Indoor/outdoor market with approximately 150 dealers. Antiques, collectibles, some nice spreads of quality smalls here. New and used merchandise. Space from $23 per 10x10 per day. Restaurant, rest rooms, h/a, RV park across the street. Ample free parking. *Contact* Ginger Long, 6725 Ringold Rd., 37412 (423) 894-3960.

CLARKSVILLE

Clarksville Fairgrounds Flea Market
Fairgrounds
Bypass on Hwy. 48 South
(931) 648-2320 or 647-2273

Wednesday. Approximately 75 dealers offer antiques, collectibles, crafts, new and used merchandise, and lots of bric-a-brac. Snack bar, rest rooms, h/a, ample parking. Indoor/outdoor market with space from $8 per day. *Contact* Ray Reed.

Kraft Street Flea Market
161 Kraft St.
(931) 648-9201

Friday, Saturday, Sunday. Used merchandise, garage-sale-type bric-a-brac, home furnishings, decorator items, imports, sports memorabilia, and collectibles are offered at this indoor market.

Clarksville Gigantic Flea Market
1600 Ft. Campbell Blvd., Two Rivers Mall

Every third weekend, Friday, 3 p.m.–7 p.m., Saturday, 9 a.m.–7 p.m., Sunday, 11 a.m.–5 p.m. Indoor market. Antiques, collectibles, new and used merchandise, new sportswear, electronics, crafts, produce, gifts, and imports. Approximately 300 dealers. Average attendance is 25,000 for the weekend. Space from $95. Reservations required. Snack bars, rest rooms, h/a. Ample parking. *Contact* Michael Epperson, Sale-A-Rama, 254 Seville St, #3, Florence, AL 35360 (800) 672-8988 or (256) 764-6400, fax (256) 764-6481

CLEVELAND

Flea Hollow
64 Bypass
I-75, Exit 20

Saturday, Sunday, 8 a.m. until dark. Approximately 75 dealers at this indoor/outdoor market with some covered spaces outside. Antiques, collectibles, primitives, farm items, and new and used merchandise available. Snack bar, rest rooms, h/a, ample parking. Space from $6. Camping available. *Contact* A. Goins (423) 476-4133 or 476-8894.

CLINTON

7 Acre Flea Market
Drive-In Theater
Hwy. 25 West
(615) 525-6666

Thursday–Sunday. New and used merchandise, lots of bric-a-brac, farm items, country collectibles, collector items, crafts, produce, pets and pet supplies, and decorator items available. Snack bar, rest rooms, h/a, ample parking.

ALWAYS CALL BEFORE TRAVELING LONG DISTANCES!

COOKEVILLE

Flea Town Mall
Burgess Falls Rd. and I-40

Saturday, Sunday. Average daily attendance over 2,000 with approximately 250 dealers. Market has pony rides, petting zoo, entertainment, and train rides. The Flea Town Mall also hold auctions on Tuesday and Thursday. Good food in cafe on premises, rest rooms, h/a, ample parking. Indoor/outdoor market with covered spaces from $3 to $15. Camping available. *Contact* Buddy Franklin, 38501 (931) 432-4097.

CROSSVILLE

Crossville Flea Market
Hwy. 70 North
I-40, Exit 317

Saturday, Sunday, 7 a.m.–3 p.m. Approximately 400 dealers. Excellent old-time market with a wide range of goods. Antiques, collectibles, primitives, advertising items, coins, paper goods, new merchandise, electronics, sportswear, housewares, crafts, and art available. Snack bar, clean rest rooms, h/a, ample parking. Fun upbeat family atmosphere here. Indoor/outdoor market with some covered space from $6. *Contact* Mary Brown, Box 3037, 38557 (931) 484-9970, fax (931) 707-1339.

DICKSON

Log Cabin Antiques and Flea Market
1635 Hwy. 46. I-40, Exit 172

Every first Saturday. Outdoor market with approximately 25 dealers. *Contact* Wayne Harris (615) 446-4438.

DIXON

Dixon Flea Market
I-40, Exit 317
(615) 484-9970 or 484-4083

Saturday, Sunday. Average daily attendance is over 10,000. Mountains of collectibles to be found here. Civil War items, tobacco items, advertising items, antiques, used merchandise, and crafts available. If it's in the collector field, it's probably here. Great fun shopping at this market. Nice cafe on premises, rest rooms, h/a, ample parking. Outdoor market with covered spaces from $3. Camping, electricity, and showers available. Billed as Tennessee's largest weekly flea market.

DYERSBURG

Dyer County Flea Market
Fairgrounds
Hwy. 51

Saturday, Sunday. Approximately 100 dealers at this indoor/outdoor market. Antiques, collectibles, furniture, and lots of good collector booths here. Good items, great pricing at this market. A good dealer's market. Check it out if you are in the area. Food available, rest rooms, h/a, ample parking. Camping available. Inside and outside covered spaces. *Contact* Wesley Frazier, Rte. 2, Box 54B, 38024 (401) 286-4784.

FRANKLIN

Franklin Flea Market
2nd Ave. and Franklin Rd.
(615) 794-0313

Wednesday. Antiques, collectibles, furniture, used merchandise, housewares, clothing, crafts, livestock, produce, pets and pet supplies, and lots of farm items available. Food available, rest rooms, ample parking.

Franklin Farmers & Flea Market
Corner of 4th Ave. and Hillsboro Rd.
(615) 256-7531

Wednesday, Friday, Saturday. Antiques, collectibles, furniture, lots of used merchandise and farm items, livestock, pets, produce, and packaged food available. Snack bar, rest rooms, ample parking.

GALLATIN

Depot Square Flea Market
Old Depot, downtown

Saturday, Sunday. Approximately 300 spaces at this indoor market. New merchandise, souvenirs, sportswear, housewares, electronics, sports merchandise, used merchandise, some great collector booths, glassware, art pottery, silver, coins, Civil War and military items, and jewelry available. Snack bar, rest rooms, h/a, ample parking. *Contact* Jon King (615) 452-1981 or 452-1983.

HOHENWALD

Natchez Trader Flea Market
Hwy. 48 South
Nine miles from town

Every second and fourth weekend, 8 a.m.–5 p.m. Outdoor market with approximately 50 dealers. Collectibles, primitives, country items, crafts, and lots of used and secondhand merchandise available. Snack bars, rest rooms, h/a, ample parking. Camping available. Space from $7.50 per day. *Contact* James Franks, Rte. 1, Box 259, 38462 (931) 796-5623.

HUMBOLT

Antique City Mall Flea Market
Hwy. 45

Thursday–Sunday, 8 a.m.–5 p.m. Indoor/outdoor market. Collectibles, new and used merchandise, and lots of garage sale items here. Snack bar, rest rooms, h/a, ample parking. Space from $30 for the weekend. *Contact* George Hensley, Rte. 2, 38343 (901) 784-1544.

INFORMATION IS SUBJECT TO CHANGE—ALWAYS CALL FIRST!

First Monday Trade Days
Fairgrounds
(901) 855-2981

Every first weekend. Antiques, collector lines, furniture, miles of used merchandise and farm items, produce, livestock, packaged food, and new merchandise available. Food available, rest rooms, h/a, ample parking.

HUNTINGTON

Carroll Country Flea Market
Hwy. 70 East
(901) 986-9628

Every first weekend. Antiques and collectibles, new and used merchandise, farm items, produce, and crafts available. Food available, rest rooms, h/a, ample parking.

JACKSON

Friendly Frank's Flea Market
Hwy. 45 South
One mile south of town

Every first weekend, 9 a.m.–6 p.m. Indoor/outdoor market with approximately 200 dealers. Antiques, collectibles, farm items, toys, primitives, advertising items, crafts, and new and used merchandise available. Snack bars, rest rooms, h/a, ample parking. This is one market that lives up to its name, lots of really pleasant folks here. Space from $55 for the weekend. *Contact* Frank Mulliken, Box 328, Cordova, 38088 (901) 755-6561.

JONESBORO

Jonesboro Flea Market
Livestock Market
2627 Hwy. 11 East
Five miles west of Jonesboro

Sunday. Approximately 200 dealers exhibit at this large classic southern market, where on a given day, you are apt to find anything and everything. Great collector booths with many quality items. Good down-home food here, rest rooms, h/a, ample parking, and miles of walking. Space from $7 per day. *Contact* John Crawford, Box 413, 37659 (423) 753-4241.

KINGSPORT

Traders Village Mall
2745 E. Stone Dr.

Saturday, Sunday, 8:30 a.m.–5:30 p.m. New and used merchandise, home furnishings, housewares, tools, jewelry, antiques, collectibles, decorator items, and crafts available at this indoor market. Snack bar, rest rooms, h/a, ample parking. *Contact* Phil Mann, 37660 (423) 288-8204.

KNOXVILLE

Family Craft & Flea World
I-40 at Cherry St.

Saturday, Sunday. New indoor market. Great selection of locally made craft and gift items. New merchandise, lots of modern collectibles, and decorator items available. Snack bar, rest rooms, h/a, ample parking.

River Breeze Flea Market
6110 Ashville Hwy.
(423) 522-5404

Saturday, Sunday, March–November. New and used merchandise, garage sale items, crafts, produce, and collectibles available at this outdoor market. Snack bar, rest rooms, h/a, ample parking.

Knoxville Fairgrounds Antique Flea Market
Fairgrounds
I-40, Exit 392

Every third weekend, 9 a.m.–5 p.m. Admission charge $3. Estimated attendance 4,000 with approximately 300 dealers. An excellent market for antiques, collectibles, crafts, and new and used merchandise. Good source market for antique shop dealers. Many dealers who set up booths here are very well stocked and will wholesale at good prices. Snack bars, clean rest rooms, h/a, ample parking. Indoor/outdoor market with space from $70 for the weekend. *Contact* Ralph Green, Box 50096, 37950 (800) 588-3728 or (423) 588-1233.

Green Acres Flea Market
Hwy. 129
I-40, airport exit
(423) 681-4433

Saturday, Sunday, 8 a.m.–5 p.m. Large indoor/outdoor market with approximately 300 dealers. Good selection of antiques, collectibles, primitives, memorabilia, coins, paper goods, vintage clothing, jewelry, new merchandise, housewares, electronics, sportswear, and used merchandise available. Snack bar, rest rooms, h/a, ample parking.

Seymour Flea Market
Hwy. 441
(423) 579-FLEA

Friday, Saturday, Sunday. New and used merchandise, home furnishings, decorator items, clothing, collectibles, farm items, crafts, and produce available. Snack bar, rest rooms, ample parking.

KODAK

Great Smokies Craft Fair & Flea Market
220 Dumplin Valley Rd. West, on I-40

Friday, Saturday, Sunday, 10 a.m.–6 p.m. Indoor market daily. Indoor/outdoor on weekends. New merchandise, lots of new collector lines, souvenirs, and gifts available. Market is great for local crafts, large selection of locally made items. This is a clean, upbeat, family-type market. It is one of the nicest and most friendly markets in the country. Food available, clean rest rooms, h/a, ample parking. *Contact* Charlie Atchley, 220 Dumplin Valley Rd. West, 37644 (423) 932-3532, fax (423) 932-3534.

LAWRENCEBURG

U.S. 64 Flea Market
Hwy. 64
Midway between Lawrenceburg and Pulaski
(931) 363-6562

Saturday, Sunday. Outdoor market. A good mix of vendors with a wide variety of items. Camping available. Market open to food vendors. *Contact* Morris Williams.

Deerfield Flea Market
4140 Hwy. 64 West, nine miles west of town
(931) 766-5908

Friday, Saturday, Sunday, 8 a.m.–5 p.m. New indoor/outdoor market with approximately 100 dealers. Heated and air-conditioned. Snack bar, rest rooms, h/a. RV hookups.

LEBANON

Parkland Flea Market
902 Castle Hts.
Hwy. 231 South; I-40, Exit 238

Saturday, Sunday, March–December, 7 a.m.–5 p.m. Average weekend attendance of 8,000 with approximately 150 dealers. Antiques, collectibles, primitives, and new and used merchandise available. Snack bar, rest rooms, h/a, ample parking. Indoor/outdoor market with 300 spaces from $10, open for 17 years. *Contact* Perry Lanius, Rte. 4, Box 532, 37087 (615) 449-6050.

LEWISBURG

Lewisburg Antique & Flea Market
Hwy. 31A
Three miles north of town
(615) 359-5939 or 359-8593

Saturday, Sunday, 8 a.m.–4 p.m. Approximately 25 dealers offer collectibles, used and new merchandise, crafts, and produce. Indoor/outdoor and covered space available from $5. Camping available. No food, rest rooms.

LOUISVILLE

Green Acres Flea Market
Hwy. 129

Saturday, Sunday, 6 a.m.–5 p.m. Indoor/outdoor market with approximately 500 dealers. Antiques, collectibles, primitives, farm items, and lots of new and used items available. Plan an all-day stop at this market. Restaurant, rest rooms, h/a, ample parking. Space from $10. *Contact* Linda Kidd, 908 Hillside Dr., 37777 (423) 681-4433, fax (423) 681-1091.

LYNNVILLE

Flea Market
Hwy. 31 North
(615) 527-3119

Every first weekend. Antiques, collectibles, new and used merchandise, lots of garage sale items, farm items, produce, and crafts available. Food available, rest rooms, h/a, ample parking.

MEMPHIS

Mid-America Trade Mart

Saturday, Sunday. New merchandise, sportswear, toys, electronics, jewelry, housewares, tools, sports merchandise. Used merchandise, garage sale items, new and older collector items, crafts, produce. Snack bar, rest rooms, h/a. Ample parking. *Contact* Richard Underwood, 2150 Covington Pike, 38128 (901) 372-1437.

Mid-South Flea Market
Fairgrounds

Saturday, Sunday. This market is held on the first, second, and fourth weekends monthly, except during fair month. Companion market held on third weekend. Approximately 200 dealers. Wide variety of goods at this indoor/outdoor market. Many traveling sellers add to the variety here. Good food, rest rooms, h/a, ample parking. Space from $50 per weekend. Tables available $5 per weekend. Has 24-hour security. Camping on premises. *Contact* Coleman-Simmons Promotions, Box 4077, 38104 (901) 725-0633. Third-weekend market *contact* Mike Hardage (901) 276-3532 or 755-6561.

Cleveland Street Flea Market Mall
438 N. Cleveland
(901) 276-3333

Saturday, Sunday, 8 a.m.–4 p.m. Indoor market with approximately 25 dealers. Ample free parking.

The Market Place
4780 Summer Ave.

Friday, Saturday, Sunday. New merchandise, used merchandise, garage-sale-type items, collectibles, and crafts available at this indoor market. Snack bar, rest rooms, h/a, ample parking. *Contact* Steve Rowland, 38122 (901) 683-0882.

Lamar's Flea Market
Hwy. 61 South and W. Raines Rd.
(901) 789-3175 or 785-6261

Daily. Lots of new merchandise and a good selection of collector booths. Good all-around market. Snack bar, rest rooms, h/a, ample parking. Reservations recommended for Friday–Sunday.

Midtown Flea Market
2018 Court Ave.
(901) 729-9059

Friday, Saturday, Sunday. New and used merchandise, garage sale items, home furnishings, household goods, clothing, imports, gift items, crafts, produce, and collectibles available. Snack bar, rest rooms, h/a, ample parking.

DAYS, DATES, AND MARKETS ARE SUBJECT TO CHANGE!

MONTEAGLE

I-24 Flea Market
Hwy. 41
I-24, Exit 134
(931) 924-2227

Sunday. Antiques, collectibles, new and used merchandise, quilts, pet supplies, tools, children's goods, fashion accessories, farm items, crafts, and produce available. Food on premises.

MONTEREY

Volunteer Flea Market Mall
Industrial Park
(615) 839-3432

Saturday, Sunday. New and used merchandise, garage sale items, farm items, crafts, collectibles, and produce available. Snack bar.

MORRISTOWN

I-81 Flea Market
I-81, Exit 8
(615) 587-9430

Saturday, Sunday. New and used merchandise, lots of bric-a-brac, farm items, crafts, collectibles, and produce available. Food available, rest rooms, h/a, ample parking.

MURFREESBORO

Murfreesboro Flea Market
2353 S. Church St.
(615) 848-1053

Tuesday–Saturday. Average daily attendance 500 with approximately 75 dealers. New merchandise, used merchandise, garage sale items, farm items, collector lines, decorator items, gifts, and crafts available. Snack bar, rest rooms, h/a, ample parking. Indoor/outdoor market. Space from $5. Camping nearby.

NASHVILLE

Big Star Flea Market
2500 Gallitan Rd.
(615) 228-7600

Daily. New merchandise, imports, sportswear, gifts, souvenirs, collectibles, used merchandise, and garage-sale-type bric-a-brac available.

Expo Antique & Flea Market
Fairgrounds
Expo Building, I-24, Exit 66A

Monthly, Friday, 3 p.m.–8 p.m., Saturday, 9 a.m.–6 p.m., Sunday, 10 a.m.–4 p.m. Snack bar, rest rooms, h/a. Ample parking. *Contact* Stewart Promotions, 2950 Breckenridge Lane, #4-A, Louisville, KY 40220 (502) 456-2244

Northwest Flea Market
1734 Jefferson St.

Monday, Friday, Saturday. Approximately 25 vendors at this indoor/outdoor market. Antiques, collectibles, new and used merchandise, and crafts available. *Contact* Vincent Jiles (615) 327-3628.

Nashville Flea Market
1364 Murfreesboro Rd.
Former Zayer's Store
(615) 360-7613

Friday, 4 p.m.–9 p.m., Saturday, 9 a.m.–6 p.m., Sunday, 10 a.m.–6 p.m. New indoor market. Mainly new and secondhand merchandise. Lots of new collectibles available. Large bird and pet market here. This is a local market not recommended for commercial vendors. Public auctions on Friday at 7 p.m. Snack bar, rest rooms, h/a, ample parking.

Nashville Fairgrounds Flea Market
Tennessee State Fairgrounds

Every fourth weekend, Saturday, 7 a.m.–6 p.m., Sunday, 7 a.m.–5 p.m. Strong attendance at this market. Excellent market for all types of merchandise. One of the largest flea markets in the U.S.A. Also, one of the country's best antique and collectible markets. Perhaps some of the best prices you will find on antiques anywhere. If you are a serious collector/investor, shopkeeper, or decorator, this is one of the country's leading source markets. A colorful and fun market to attend for buyer or seller. It uses the entire state fairgrounds: buildings, barns, grounds. Good food, restaurant, rest rooms, h/a; parking can be a nightmare here, and *lots of walking required* is an understatement. Inside and outside space from $75 for the weekend. Camping available. Reservations recommended. *Contact* Mary Snyder, Box 40208, 37204 (615) 383-7636 or 862-5016.

Metro Farmers Market
618 Jackson St.
(615) 360-7613

Friday, Saturday, Sunday. New merchandise, used merchandise, lots of garage sale items, farm items, crafts, and collectibles available. Food available, rest rooms. Farmers' market open daily. *Contact* James Witty, 37219 (615) 360-7613.

Nashville Junction Flea Market
3030 Dickerson Pike
(615) 262-3532

Saturday, Sunday. New merchandise, gifts, souvenirs, sportswear, jewelry, housewares, used merchandise, and collectibles available. Snack bar, rest rooms, h/a, ample parking.

Interstate Flea Market
Buchanan Rd.
I-24, Exit 89
(615) 895-4632 or 754-9757

Thursday–Sunday. Indoor/outdoor market with a good mix of merchandise, and a nice selection of antiques. Food vendors by reservation.

ALWAYS CALL AHEAD TO VERIFY DATES AND INFORMATION

Trinity Flea Market
120 Trinity Lane
I-65, Exit 87A

Friday, Saturday, Sunday. Outdoor market with approximately 30 dealers offering secondhand items, collectibles, crafts, produce, and new merchandise. Space from $12. *Contact* Juanita Ellis, 150 W. Trinity Lane, 37207 (615) 228-9131.

OAK RIDGE

Flea Market
School parking lot
(423) 483-7938

Saturday, Sunday. Used merchandise, bric-a-brac, clothing, gifts, farm items, country crafts, and collectibles available. Food available, rest rooms, ample parking.

OCOEE

Ocoee Flea Market & Campgrounds
Hwy. 411
(615) 338-8101

Daily, March–October. New merchandise, souvenirs, used merchandise, collectibles. Convenience store, rest rooms, and ample parking.

OLD HICKORY

Flea Market
Hadley Blvd.

Saturday, Sunday. New and used merchandise, home furnishings, housewares, clothing, sports memorabilia, farm items, bric-a-brac, crafts, and collectibles available.

PARIS

Flea Market
Fairgrounds
(901) 782-3396

Every second weekend. Antiques, collectibles, crafts, new and used merchandise, clothing, fashion accessories, jewelry, and home furnishings available. Food available, rest rooms, h/a, ample parking.

ROCK ISLAND

Hank Walters Flea Market
Hwy. 30

Saturday. Used merchandise, garage sale items, children's goods, tools, electronics, farm items, crafts, collectibles, and produce available.

ST. BETHLEHEM

M&M Flea Market
1690 Guthrie Hwy.
Hwy. 79 North

Tuesday–Sunday. Collectibles, and new and used furniture available. Food available, rest rooms. *Contact* Peggy Miller (615) 552-1952.

SAXTON

Trading Post Flea Market
Hwy. 51

Thursday–Sunday. New merchandise, souvenirs, sportswear, housewares, jewelry, used merchandise, garage sale items, and crafts available. Snack bar, rest rooms, h/a, ample parking.

SMYRNA

Gels Flea Market
Rte. 102
(615) 459-7471

Saturday, Sunday. Used merchandise, garage sale items, farm items, primitives, clothing, imports, gifts, collectibles, tools, electronics, and crafts available. Snack bar, rest room.

Granny's Flea Market
Hwys. 41 and 70 South
(615) 459-0805

Wednesday, Saturday, Sunday. Average daily attendance of 500 with approximately 40 dealers. New and used merchandise, garage sale items, farm items, collectibles, and decorator items. Snack bar, rest rooms, h/a, ample parking. Indoor/outdoor and covered space from $7. Camping available.

SODDY DAISY

Soddy Indoor Outdoor Market
Hwy. 27
(615) 322-2864

Saturday, Sunday. Approximately 50 dealers offer antiques, collectibles, farm and country collectibles, primitives, toys, used merchandise, and lots of garage sale items. Snack bar, rest rooms, ample parking. Space from $3.

SOUTH FULTON

South Fulton Flea Market
Hwy. 45 East
One mile south of city

Every second Friday, Saturday, Sunday. Average attendance of 5,000 per weekend with approximately 75 vendors. Antiques, collectibles, furniture, glassware, silver, coins, vintage clothing, jewelry, toys, primitives, advertising items, used merchandise, farm items, and bric-a-brac. Snack bar, rest rooms, h/a, ample parking. Space from $5 per day. Tennessee tax number required. County license also required. This city hosts one of the country's best spring events—the International Banana Festival. Yes, Virginia, they used to not raise bananas in Tennessee. *Contact* Ray Alford, Box 157, 38257 (901) 479-0077 or 469-5663.

SPARTA

Cherry Creek Flea Market
Rte. 1
(931) 738-3440

Saturday, Sunday. Used merchandise, garage sale items, farm items, collectibles, crafts, and produce available. Snack bar, rest rooms.

SPRINGFIELD

Highway 41 Flea Market
2862 Hwy. 41
Five miles south of town

Saturday, Sunday, 7 a.m.–5 p.m. Approximately 150 dealers at this indoor/outdoor market with some covered spaces outside. Antiques, collectibles, glassware, silver, crafts, used merchandise, new merchandise, and farm items and equipment. Snack bar, rest rooms, h/a, ample parking. Camping available. Market open to food vendors. Space from $10 per day. *Contact* Cecil Spender, 2862 Hwy. 41 S., 37171 (615) 643-4736.

Springfield Grand Central Flea Market
100 10th St.
(615) 382-0717

Saturday, Sunday. Indoor market with approximately 40 dealers. New and used merchandise, crafts, and collectibles available. Snack bar, rest rooms, ample parking. New market. Space from $15 per weekend. Market open to food vendors.

SWEETWATER

Sweetwater Flea Market
Sweetwater Livestock Auction Grounds
Hwy. 11
(423) 337-9535

Wednesday. Used merchandise, clothing, housewares, bric-a-brac, antiques, collectibles, primitives, crafts, and produce available. Food available, rest rooms, ample parking.

Fleas Unlimited Flea Market
I-75 and Hwy. 68 West
I-75, Exit 60
(423) 337-3532
Fax (423) 337-4694

Saturday, Sunday, 8 a.m.–5 p.m. Antiques, collectibles, coins, crafts, art, new and used merchandise, housewares, electronics, sportswear, and lots of secondhand items available. Food available, rest rooms, h/a, ample parking.

Camping available. Indoor/outdoor market with some covered spaces. Approximately 400 dealers. Space from $20 outside. *Contact* Fleas Unlimited, 121 County Rd. 308, 37874.

TAZEWELL

Dogwood High Flea Market
Hwy. 25 East
One mile east of city
(615) 626-3759

Friday, Saturday, Sunday. New and used merchandise, garage sale items, farm items, clothing, housewares, collectibles, crafts, and produce available. Food available, rest rooms.

TELFORD

Dee's Antique Flea Market
Hwy. 11 East
(423) 753-4241

Sunday. Approximately 300 dealers exhibit at this large country antique and collector market with a good selection of furniture and a great selection of collector booths full of everything from Civil War items to campaign buttons. This is a treasure hunter's bonanza. Food available, rest rooms, h/a, ample parking, and lots of walking.

TRENTON

Gibson County Flea Market
Fairgrounds

Every first Sunday and Monday. Average weekend attendance of 5,000 with approximately 150 dealers. This market has a good variety of merchandise, is clean and well managed. A very wholesome family atmosphere here. Food available, rest rooms, ample parking. Space from $5 outside or inside. *Contact* Paul Flowers, Redwood Dr., 38382 (901) 692-4060 or 855-2981.

TRIBUNE

Tribune Antique Mall Flea Market
Junction of Hwys. 31 and 41A
(615) 395-7140

Saturday, Sunday. General line of antiques and collectibles, glassware, furniture, paintings, coins, country and Victorian-era items, vintage jewelry, dolls, and toys available. Snack bar, rest rooms, h/a, ample parking.

INFORMATION IS SUBJECT TO CHANGE—ALWAYS CALL AHEAD TO AVOID DISAPPOINTMENT

TEXAS

ABILENE

Flea Market
Old Abilene Town
3300 E. I-20
Exit 390 I-20 East

Every second weekend. Antiques, collectibles, crafts, and lots of western and Indian collectibles. Food available, rest rooms, ample parking. *Contact* W. S. Smith, Rte. 8, Box 896, 79601 (915) 675-6588.

Elmdale Flea Market & Antique Shop
5423 Hwy. 80E
(915) 673-8623

Tuesday–Sunday. New merchandise, used and garage-sale-type finds, antiques, and collectibles, glassware, books, country primitives, and Victorian items available.

ALAMO

All Valley Flea Market
Junction of Cesar Chavez and Expressway 83

Saturday, Sunday, dawn to dusk. Admission 25 cents. Primarily new merchandise imports, gift items, some antiques and collectibles, lots of locally made and Mexican crafts. Indoor and outdoor market with approximately 500 dealers. Average attendance during the winter is 30,000 shoppers and 15,000 during the summer. Space from $12.50 per day. Food available, rest rooms, showers, camping, RV hookups, h/a. Ample free parking. *Contact* David Villegas, 501 N. Bridge St. #528, Hidalgo, TX 78557 (956) 781-1911, fax (956) 781-1911 or 787-8071.

AMARILLO

T-Anchor Flea Market
1401 W. Ross Blvd.

Saturday, Sunday, 9 a.m.–5 p.m. Average daily attendance of 5,000 with approximately 100 dealers. Good selection of merchandise here. Collectibles, primitives, advertising items, new merchandise, used merchandise. Snack bar, rest rooms, h/a, ample parking. Indoor/outdoor market with space from $10 per day. Camping with electricity available. *Contact* Claudia Blythe, Box 32282, 97120 (806) 373-0430.

Old I.C.X. Flea Market
I-40, Ross St. exit
Corner of 6th and Ross Sts.

Friday, Saturday, Sunday, 9 a.m.–6 p.m. Average daily attendance of 2,000 with approximately 75 dealers. Collectibles, jewelry, and new and used merchandise available. Large amounts of collectibles here. New indoor/outdoor market. Inside facility is air-conditioned. Snack bar, clean rest rooms, h/a, ample parking. *Contact* Shirley Roberts, 513 S. Ross St., 79104 (806) 373-3215.

ARKANSAS PASS

Shrimp Capital Flea Market
1242 N. Commercial St. Rte. 35
(512) 758-5812

Friday, Saturday, Sunday. New merchandise, imports, electronics, sports merchandise, clothing, jewelry, used merchandise, farm and ranch items, collectibles, crafts, and produce available. Snack bar, rest rooms, h/a, ample parking. Space from $5, inside and outside space available. *Contact* Mary Manning.

AUSTIN

Barton Springs Collectible Market & Trailer Court
1600 Barton Springs Rd.

Friday, Saturday, Sunday. Antiques and collectibles only. Market not open to new merchandise. Outdoor market with plenty of shade. Nice area with some interesting antique shops nearby. Snack bar, rest rooms, h/a, ample parking. *Contact* Lillie Mae Williams, 11704 N. Lamar, 78753 (512) 836-4966.

Austin Country Flea Market
9500 Hwy. 290 East
Five miles east of I-35 on 290 East

Saturday, Sunday, 10 a.m.–6 p.m. Average weekend attendance of 20,000. This is a classic southwestern market with 400 spaces. Lots of new merchandise, western and cowboy clothing and gear, collectibles, coins, sportswear, and housewares. Lots of food here, rest rooms, h/a, ample parking. Paved and covered spaces from $35 per weekend. Overnight camping available on premises. One of the largest markets in the area. Reservations recommended. *Contact* Buz Cook, 9500 Hwy. 290 East, 78724 (512) 928-2795.

City-Wide Garage Sale
City Coliseum
Intersection of Riverside Dr. at Bouldin Ave.
I-35, Riverside Dr. Exit

Monthly, call for exact dates. Saturday, 10 a.m.–5 p.m., Sunday, 11 a.m.–5 p.m. Admission $2.75. Approximately 125 vendors. Antiques, collectibles, used and garage sale merchandise available. No new merchandise or crafts allowed. Food available, rest rooms, h/a, ample parking. Space from $85. *Contact* Christopher Dwyer, 512 E. Riverside Dr., No. 104, 78704 (512) 441-2828 or (877) 840-3829.

BALLINGER

Ballinger Community Flea Market
Community Center
1000 10th St.

Every third weekend. Approximately 40 dealers offer antiques, collectibles, new and used merchandise, housewares, clothing, farm and ranch items, western wear and collectibles, crafts, produce, livestock, and packaged food. Food available, rest rooms. *Contact* Buddy McQueen (915) 365-3262.

BAYTOWN

Baytown Common Market
1801 Docker Dr.
Five miles south of I-10 on Spur 330
(Docker Dr.)

Friday, Saturday, Sunday, 9 a.m.–6 p.m. Approximately 50 vendors at this indoor/outdoor market. Antiques, collectibles, lots of western items here, new and used merchandise available. This market has a craft show on the third weekend of the month and public auctions on Friday starting at 7:30 p.m. Snack bar, rest rooms, ample parking. Space starts at $8 outside. *Contact* Guy Miles, 2500 E. James, H15, 77520 (409) 383-2585.

BEAUMONT

West End Flea Market & Antique Village
8615 College St.
Old Hwy. 90 at Major Dr. off I-10

Wednesday–Sunday. Average attendance 5–7,000 per weekend. Market features antiques, jewelry, and collectibles. Space from $5 daily. Inside and outside space available. Camping on-site. *Contact* Vallie Couch, 8615 College, 77707 (409) 866-1948.

ALWAYS CALL BEFORE TRAVELING LONG DISTANCES!

BONHAM

Bonham Trade Days
605 Hunter, Hwy. 82
(903) 583-4811

Every first Monday.

BOWIE

Second Monday Trade Days
Hwy. 81 North
Second Monday Trade Grounds
(940) 872-1680

Every second Monday. Approximately 600 dealers. Excellent outdoor market with strong attendance. Ideal market for the commercial vendor. Lots of new and used merchandise. Jewelry, antiques and livestock here. This is a real fun market for the entire family. Good food, rest rooms, h/a, ample parking.

Trade City
408 Pelham St.
Across the street from Second Monday Trade Grounds

Every second Monday. Approximately 150 spaces. New and used merchandise, farm and ranch items, collectibles, imports, and crafts available. Food on premises. Rest rooms, electricity, and water available. Inside, covered and enclosed space available. *Contact* Dallas Hutson, Box 1446, 76230 (940) 872-3082.

BROWNSVILLE

Super Flea Market
1647 Price Rd.

Friday, Saturday, Sunday. New merchandise, truckloads of Mexican imports, crafts, used merchandise, collectibles, clothing, fashion accessories, and tools available. Food on premises, rest rooms. *Contact* Dr. Santiago Gonzales, Box 4030, 78420.

BUFFALO

Buffalo Gap Flea Market
Old Settlers Grounds
Rte. 89
Six miles south of Abilene

Every third Monday, March–November, 7 a.m.–10 p.m. This large outdoor market features approximately 250 dealers. A wide range of goods makes the Buffalo Gap marketplace a shopper's bonanza. Antiques, collectibles, primitives, new and used merchandise available. Classic wide-open Texas market. This market is open late into the evening. A pure country adventure. Good food available, rest rooms, ample parking, and lots of walking. Space from $14 for the weekend. *Contact* John Brollis, Box 575, 79508 (915) 572-3327.

BURLESON

All American Texas Flea Market
South of Burleson on I-35 West Exit 32
(817) 641-1004 or 783-5468

Friday, Saturday, Sunday, 7 a.m. until dark. Inside and outside market with approximately 250 dealers. Lots of collectibles, memorabilia, primitives, advertising items, tools, crafts, art, and new and used merchandise available. Food concessions on premises. Rest rooms, ample parking. Camping on-site. Space available from $25 per weekend.

CANTON

First Monday Trade Days
First Monday Trade Grounds
(903) 567-6556
Fax (903) 567-1753

Held weekend of first Monday, daylight to well after dark. Parking charge $3. With 5,000 dealers, this market is so Texas-sized big that one can get lost while walking around the grounds. If you are a serious collector/investor, antique dealer, or decorator, this is a "must stop" market. This market also conducts many popular special events. Sellers can camp in their selling space. Electricity and water available. Showers on grounds. Lots of great food, plenty of rest rooms. This market is so big that on one Sunday afternoon when the crowds are the largest I actually became lost and it took over one hour to find my way back to my space. A tremendous amount of walking is required, and you still won't be able to see everything in one weekend. It has the reputation of being one of the nation's premier flea markets. Sales reported good for all types of merchandise. This place has it all. It has always been my wife's favorite market. Evenings here are campfires, country musicians, gossip and fellowship: almost movielike. Sunday is the major day at this market. Historians consider Canton to be home to America's first flea market. Space from $50. Reservations highly recommended. *Contact* City of Canton, Box 245, 75103 (903) 567-6556, fax (903) 567-1753.

CLEBURNE

I-35 West Flea Market
Hwy. 917; I-35, Exit 30
I-35 West Access Rd.
(817) 783-2282

Friday, Saturday, Sunday. Indoor/outdoor market with approximately 100 exhibitors. Collectibles, memorabilia, country and western items, new merchandise, sportswear, and crafts available. Snack bar, rest rooms, ample parking. Market is open to food vendors by prior reservation. Space from $20 for the three days. *Contact* Manager, Rte. 4, Box 480, 76031.

CLEVELAND

Olde Security Square Flea Market
18431 Hwy. 105

Saturday, Sunday, March–December, 10 a.m.–6 p.m. Average weekend attendance 2,000 with approximately 250 dealers. Indoor/outdoor and covered space. Wide range of merchandise here, collectibles, primitives, lots of new merchandise and western items available. Snack bar, rest rooms, h/a, ample parking. Camping available. Space from $3 outside per day. *Contact* Chamber of Commerce, Box 1733, 77327 (281) 592-6017.

COLDSPRING

Courthouse Square Trade Days
Courthouse Square in Old Town

Every fourth Saturday, dawn to dusk. Seasonal market, March–November. Outdoor market with approximately 50 dealers. Sponsored by the Heritage Society. Ample parking. *Contact* Jane Guissinger (409) 653-2009.

CONROE

Weekend Trader Flea Market
2418 N. Frazier, 77303
Located one mile west of I-45 on Hwy. 75, north of North Loop 336. Take North Loop Exit 336 if traveling north on I-45 and turn left on Hwy. 75. If traveling south on I-45, take the League Line Road exit and turn right on Hwy. 75.

Saturday, Sunday, 8 a.m.–5 p.m. New market. Approximately 40 spaces, with room to expand. Tools, used merchandise. Space from $10 per day. Ample parking, rest rooms. Friendly, pleasant country market. *Contact* Don Moran, 2418 N. Frazier, 77303 (713) 441-9167, 441-1004, fax (713) 441-9168.

CORPUS CHRISTI

Corpus Christi Flea Market
2202 Joyce St.
(512) 851-2015

Friday, Saturday, Sunday. Approximately 75 dealers offer new merchandise, gifts, souvenirs, imports, used merchandise, collectibles, jewelry, and clothing. Food available, rest rooms. Inside and outside space available.

Flea Market
Trade Center Factory Outlet
2833 South Padre Island Dr.
(512) 854-4943

Friday, Saturday, Sunday, 10 a.m.–7 p.m. Indoor market with an average daily attendance of 4,000. Approximately 100 dealers offer new merchandise, sportswear, housewares, electronics, collectibles, coins, crafts, and memorabilia. Several specialty shops here in the market. Snack bar, rest rooms, h/a, ample parking. Camping available. This is the largest indoor market in the area. *Contact* Manager, 78415.

DALLAS

The Quality Antique Fair & Flea Market
Big Town Exhibition Hall
Big Town Plaza
2323 Big Town Blvd.
(601) 892-5650
Fax (601) 892-1434

Saturday, Sunday. Antiques, furniture, collectibles, lots of western and Indian items, and a great selection of fine jewelry. Food available, rest rooms, h/a, ample parking. *Contact* Antique Flea Mkt., 231 W. Georgetown St., Crystal Springs, MS 39059.

DJ's Antique Market
Lochwood Mall
(214) 324-4427

Saturday, Sunday. Antiques, collectibles, antique furniture, glassware, dolls, coins, paper and advertising items, military memorabilia, and art pottery available. Food available, rest rooms, ample parking.

Lone Star Bazaar
10724 Garland Rd.
(214) 324-1484 or 324-4427

Friday, 12 p.m.–6 p.m., Saturday, Sunday, 10 a.m.–6 p.m. Outdoor market with approximately 50 dealers. Lots of new and used merchandise and some collectibles available. Food available, rest rooms, h/a, ample parking.

The Market Place of DeSoto
719 N. Hampton Rd.
(214) 223-7372

Saturday, Sunday. Antiques, collectibles, western and Indian items, farm and ranch items, and used merchandise available. Food on premises, rest rooms, ample parking.

Fair Park Flea Market
Fairgrounds, Grand Place Bldg.

Monthly, 9 a.m.–5 p.m. Admission charge $1. Quality antique flea market with wide selection. Some great western and Indian items here. Monthly event. Food available, rest rooms, h/a, ample parking. *Contact* Texas State Fair Main Office.

Big T Bazaar
4515 Village Fair Dr.

Thursday–Monday. Large indoor market with approximately 150 dealers. Lots of new merchandise, housewares, jewelry, furniture, sportswear, electronics, and some collectibles. This is a great market for shopping for personal needs and household goods. Plenty of food, rest rooms, h/a, ample parking. *Contact* Kenneth Lee (214) 372-9173.

Super Trade Days
Royce City and I-30 Village
(214) 635-9501

Saturday, Sunday. New merchandise, sportswear, western wear, electronics, jewelry, housewares, used merchandise, garage sale items, tools, imports, farm and ranch items, and crafts available. Food available, rest rooms, h/a, ample parking.

Bargain City Bazaar
735 N.W. Moreland

Friday, Saturday, Sunday, 10 a.m.–7 p.m. Indoor market with approximately 150 dealers. Lots of new items here, some collectibles, cards, and western items available. *Contact* Brady Bryant, 735 N.W. Moreland, 75211 (214) 330-8111.

DENTON

380 Flea Market
4200 E. University
Three miles east of town

Friday, Saturday, Sunday. Approximately 200 dealers. Antiques, furniture, collectibles, art, western and Indian items, used merchandise, farm and ranch items, crafts, and produce available. Good food, rest rooms, ample parking. Market has a special antique flea market on the fourth weekend each month. *Contact* John Lillard, 76201 (940) 566-5060 or 383-1064.

Denton Flea Market Mall
3105 Ft. Worth Dr.
Hwy. 377
(940) 566-0060

Saturday, Sunday. Approximately 150 vendors offer new merchandise, used garage-sale-type merchandise, antiques, collectibles, and western items. Food available, rest rooms, ample parking. Indoor/outdoor market with space from $2. Camping and electricity available.

DIBOL

Olde Frontier Town Traders Market
Hwy. 59, five miles south of Lufkin
(409) 632-8696

Daily. Indoor/outdoor market with some covered spaces. Approximately 50 dealers. Space from $5. Food vendors welcome. Snack bar, rest rooms, h/a.

EL PASO

Ascarte Drive-In Theater Flea Market
6701 Delta Dr.

Saturday, Sunday, 5 a.m.–6 p.m. Large outdoor market with approximately 350 dealers. Wide range of goods at this market. Mostly new, imports, and discounted merchandise. Good pickings for shrewd buyers. Bring a big truck and plenty of green money. Snack bar, good food, rest rooms, h/a, ample parking. *Contact* Artemio Juarez, 79905 (915) 779-2503, fax (915) 779-8265.

Bronco Swap Meet
8408 Alameda Ave.
(915) 858-5555

Saturday, Sunday, 8 a.m.–4 p.m. Large commercial outdoor market with approximately 300 dealers. Mountains of new merchandise and imports, used merchandise, garage sale items, and lots of Mexican crafts. Snack bar, rest rooms, h/a. Ample free parking.

El Paso International Flea Market
1500 E. Palsane
(915) 533-1605

Friday, Saturday, Sunday. Mountains of Mexican imports, new and used merchandise, home furnishings, household goods, imports, crafts, lots of produce, and collectibles available. Snack bars, rest rooms.

FT. STOCKTON

Ft. Stockton Trade Day
I-10 and Hwy. 1053
(915) 336-2933

Every first weekend. Antiques, collectibles, furniture, new and used merchandise, farm and ranch items, livestock, produce, and crafts available. Food on premises, rest rooms, ample parking. Outdoor market with space from $10. Camping available on premises. Market open to food vendors.

FT. WORTH

The Market Center
4950 Hwy. 337 South

Friday, Saturday, Sunday. Approximately 75 dealers offer new merchandise, western wear, electronics, housewares, jewelry, used merchandise, collectibles, crafts, and produce. Food available, rest rooms. *Contact* Ray Hayes (817) 244-2330.

Ft. Worth Flea Market
Will Rogers Memorial Center
3301 W. Lancaster
(817) 335-0734

Saturday, Sunday. Antiques, collectibles, lots of western and Indian jewelry, art, and collectibles here. Food available, rest rooms, h/a, ample parking.

University Drive-In Theater Flea Market
Hwy. 199

Saturday, Sunday. New merchandise, imports, clothing, jewelry, electronics, tools, sports and western wear, used merchandise, garage sale items, crafts, collectibles, and produce available. Snack bar, rest rooms.

Barn Flea Market
Will Rogers Complex, Cattle Barn 1
(817) 473-0505

Saturday, Sunday. Antiques, collectibles, new and used merchandise, farm and ranch items, crafts, and produce available. Snack bars, rest rooms, h/a, ample parking.

GALVESTON

Flea Marketeers Mall
4621 Ft. Crockett Blvd.

Thursday–Sunday. New merchandise, imports, clothing, electronics, jewelry, housewares, used merchandise, crafts, and collectibles available. Snack bar, rest rooms.

GARLAND

Vikon Village Flea Market
2918 S. Jupiter Rd.
(214) 271-0565 or (972) 271-0565

Saturday, Sunday, 10 a.m.–7 p.m. Excellent indoor market with approximately 150 dealers. Wide range of merchandise, lots of new items, sportswear, furniture, housewares, some collectibles. This is a very pleasant market for shoppers. I have found some real treasures here. Food available, rest rooms, h/a, ample parking. *Contact* Manager, 2918 S. Jupiter Rd., 75041.

GRAND PRAIRIE

Traders Village Flea Market
2602 Mayfield Rd.
(972) 647-2331 or 647-8205
Fax (972) 647-8585

Saturday, Sunday, 8 a.m. to dark. Inside, outside, and covered spaces. Over 2,000 selling spaces. Heavy attendance; this is a thoroughly professional market, the Tiffany of flea markets. Plenty of good food, rest rooms. Parking charge $2. Lots of walking here. Considered by many to be America's finest flea market, certainly the finest market in entire region. Reservations suggested. Many special events held in conjunction with the market. This is a great market for bargain-conscious shoppers. For sellers it is a good place to sell or buy at wholesale. It is always an excellent source market for new merchandise and imports. There are quite a few direct importers who have booths here. On the lighter side, this market has little Cushman beer carts that bring beer (and soft drinks) around to your booth. Those little carts are a most welcome sight coming down the row on a hot Texas summer day! *Contact* Manager, 2602 Mayfield Rd., 75051.

GREENVILLE

Traderama
State Hwy. 34

Every second and fourth weekend. Approximately 50 dealers offer new merchandise, mountains of used and garage sale merchandise, farm and ranch items, crafts, collectibles, antiques, produce, and livestock. Food available, rest rooms. Space from $4.

INFORMATION IS SUBJECT TO CHANGE—ALWAYS CALL FIRST!

GUN BARREL CITY

Gun Barrel Flea Market
1307 W. Main St.

Saturday, Sunday, 8 a.m.–5 p.m. Indoor/outdoor market with approximately 50 dealers. Antiques, collectibles, primitives, crafts, western, and ranch items. Indian jewelry, produce, gifts, and imports. Space from $8. Food available, rest rooms. RV hookups, camping. *Contact* Lorene Bowles, 1307 W. Main St., 75147 (903) 887-1000.

HALTOM CITY

Country Fair Indoor Flea Market Mall
4051 Denton Hwy.
One mile south of Loop 820 on Hwy. 377, Exit 19

Thursday–Sunday. Average attendance of 1,000 daily with approximately 50 dealers. New merchandise, crafts, collectibles, and used merchandise available. Good selection of all types of merchandise here. Snack bars, rest rooms, ample parking. Space from $20 daily or $130 monthly. Reservations recommended. No outside food concessions allowed. *Contact* Leo Lamp, 4051 Denton Hwy. (817) 831-4425.

HARLINGEN

All Valley Flea Market
H Street and Expwy. 77

Saturday, Sunday. Approximately 100 dealers offer new merchandise, mostly Mexican imports, crafts, jewelry, housewares, collectibles, and produce. Food available, rest rooms. Space from $2. *Contact* Harvey Bruns, P. O. Drawer 908, Mission, 78572.

HOUSTON

The White Elephant Flea Market
15660 E. I-10 Freeway East, Channel View Exit

Saturday, Sunday, 7:30 a.m.–5:30 p.m. Large indoor/outdoor market with approximately 350 dealers. Furniture, jewelry, electronics, collectibles, and lots of used and garage sale items available. Snack bar, rest rooms, h/a, ample parking. Space from $12. *Contact* Ruth McDaniel, Box 209, 77530 (713) 452-9022.

The Houston Flea Market
6116 Southwest Freeway
Rte. 59

Saturday, Sunday, 8 a.m.–6 p.m. Indoor/outdoor market with approximately 250 dealers. Good selection of goods at this flea market with lots of new merchandise, western and cowboy items, farm and ranch items and supplies, home furnishings, clothing, tools, and electronics. Also plenty of collectibles and memorabilia. Food, rest rooms, h/a, ample parking. Space from $45 per weekend. *Contact* Mary Wright, Box 573007, 77257 (713) 782-0391, fax (713) 781-0642.

Traders Village
7979 N. Eldridge Rd.

Saturday, Sunday, 8 a.m. until dark. Indoor/outdoor market with over 500 dealers. Wide range of merchandise at this market makes this a bargain hunter's paradise. Perhaps the area's finest market. Always good entertainment and many special events each weekend. Lots of food, rest rooms, and plan for lots of walking. Ample parking with a charge of $2. Space from $20 per day. *Contact* Charles Portales, 7979 N. Eldridge Rd., 77041 (281) 890-5500, fax (281) 890-6568. E-mail: tvh@flash.net.

Trading Fair II
5512 S. Loop
I-610, Crestmont Exit on Loop 610

Friday, Saturday, Sunday, 10 a.m.–6 p.m. Indoor market with approximately 400 dealers. Worlds of new merchandise, imports, gifts, trendy desirables, new collectibles, antiques and collector items, memorabilia, crafts, and costume and fine jewelry available. Food, rest rooms, h/a, ample parking with a charge of $1. *Contact* W. S. Henkle, 5515 S. Loop E., 77033 (713) 731-1111, fax (713) 731-1121.

JEWETT

Flea Market of Jewett
Hwy. 79

Every second Saturday, dawn to dusk. Outdoor market with approximately 150 dealers. Antiques, collectibles, primitives, farm and ranch items, livestock, locally made crafts. New and used merchandise. Gifts and imports. Space from $18 per weekend. Reservations required. Lots of good food, rest rooms. *Contact* Dana Sullivan, Box 762, Centerville, TX 75833 (903) 536-7689.

JUSTIN

156 Speedway Flea Market & Auction
9539 Industrial, 7624, Hwy. 156 between Justin and Hwy. 114

Saturday, Sunday. Contact Nancy McCullar (940) 648-8812 or 464-3164.

LAREDO

Bordertown Flea Market
359 E. Hebbronville Hwy.
Three miles east of city
(956) 726-1186

Thursday–Sunday, 7 a.m.–6 p.m. Average daily attendance 2,500 with approximately 200 dealers. NAFTA hard at work here. Mountains upon mountains of Mexican imports. Sellers—if you want to be an importer without crossing the border, just bring a big truck and lots of green money to this market. Food available, rest rooms, ample parking. Outdoor and covered space from $10 under cover and $7 open. Camping available on-site. This market is located three miles from the Mexican border.

LOCKHART

Lockhart Flea Market
Brownsboro Rd.

Saturday, Sunday, 8 a.m. until dark. Outdoor market with covered booths and approximately 150 dealers. Antiques, collectibles, lots of used merchandise available. Country entertainment, food, rest rooms, ample parking. Space from $15 per weekend. Camping and electricity available. Market open to food vendors. *Contact* Henrietta Kaufman (512) 398-4901.

LUBBOCK

National Flea Market
1808 Clovis Rd.

Wednesday–Sunday, 9 a.m.–5 p.m. Average daily attendance of 500 with approximately 150 dealers. Indoor, outdoor, and covered spaces. New merchandise, sportswear, electronics, housewares, some antiques, collectibles, and crafts available. Snack bar, rest rooms, h/a, ample parking. Space from $15 outside. *Contact* Debi Grant, 1808 Clovis Rd., 79415 (806) 744-4979, fax (806) 744-4979 or 744-0164.

Lubbock Flea Market
2323 Ave. K

Saturday, Sunday, 7 a.m.–5 p.m. Inside and outside spaces with approximately 300 dealers. New merchandise, sportswear, sports-related merchandise, lots of western and cowboy clothing and items, collectibles, country primitives, and a good selection of used items here. Food, rest rooms, h/a, ample parking. Space from $5. *Contact* Bert Thrush (806) 747-8281.

MATHIS

Mathis Bazaar
213 E. San Patricio North
(512) 547-6031

Friday, Saturday, Sunday, 6 a.m.–9 p.m. Approximately 150 dealers offer new and used merchandise, farm and ranch items and supplies, western and tack items, collectibles, crafts, antiques, and produce. Good food, rest rooms. This market is located in the center of a great vacation and resort area. Auctions held here on Tuesday. Space from $5 per day.

MCALLEN

The Flea Market
2400 S. 23rd St.
(956) 687-4513

Saturday, Sunday, 7 a.m. until dark. Market is seven miles from the Mexican border. Mountains of Mexican imports, produce, lots of used merchandise, garage sale items, and western collectibles available. Approximately 400–500 dealers with average daily attendance of 5,000. Food on premises, rest rooms.

First Sunday Flea Market
Villa Real Convention Center
Benson Rd., Hwy. 83

Every first Sunday, daylight until dark. Admission charge 50 cents. Approximately 250 dealers. This flea market is strong on antiques and collectibles. Great selection of western and Indian art, jewelry, and collectibles. Food available, rest rooms, h/a, ample parking. *Contact* Hilda Reyes, Box 1099, Alamo, 78516 (956) 781-1911.

MCKINNEY

Third Monday Trade Days
Third Monday Trade Grounds
Hwy. 380 West
(972) 542-7174

Every third Monday, 8 a.m. until dark. Approximately 600 dealers. Excellent outdoor market for all types of merchandise. This is a large, well-managed market with a wide range of merchandise. It is a classic, wide-open Texas flea market in every sense. Shoppers will find everything from fine art and antiques to worn-out junk all mixed together. Lots of walking. It's an all-day adventure here, with treasures and bargains aplenty. Good food, rest rooms. Space from $35 per weekend. *Contact* Manager, 3rd Monday Trade Day, 4550 W. University Dr., 75070 (972) 562-5466, fax (972) 562-5466. E-mail: darrell@tmtd.com.

MERCEDES

Valley of Mercedes Flea Market
Expwy. 83, mile marker 2 West
Between Mercedes and Westlake
(956) 781-1911 or 565-2751
Fax (956) 787-8071

Saturday, Sunday, 6 a.m.–until dark. Indoor/outdoor market with approximately 400 dealers. Good selection here, lots of new merchandise, imports, sportswear, jewelry, crafts, art, collectibles, coins, advertising items, and primitives available. Good food, rest rooms, ample parking with a charge of 25 cents. Lots of walking. Space from $4.50, 6.00 shaded space outside. *Contact* Sylvia Villegas, 21 Coma, No. 115, Hidalgo, 78577.

MIDLAND

Rankin Highway Flea Market
2840 Rankin Hwy.

Friday, Saturday, Sunday, 7:30 a.m.–6 p.m. Approximately 50 dealers at this indoor/outdoor market offer new merchandise, electronics, jewelry, housewares, western wear, used merchandise, collector lines, and crafts. Food available, rest rooms. Space from $5 per day outside. Camping available. *Contact* Joseph Romine (915) 684-5060.

NACOGDOCHES

Nacogdoches Trade Days
5001 N.W. Stalling Dr.

Every first and fourth weekend, dawn to dusk. Average daily attendance of 3,000 with approximately 275 dealers. All types of merchandise at this market with lots of western, cowboy, and farm and ranch items. Also, a good array of collectibles and memorabilia. If you are looking for a market with the feel of the old West, this rates as a real southwestern cowboy market. Lots of livestock sold here. Food vendors okay with prior reservation. A 12×30 space starts at

$20. Camping and electricity available. *Contact* Mickey Calvin, 1304 N.W. Stallings Dr., 75961 (409) 560-1287 or 560-1287.

ODESSA

Henry's Flea Market Mall
7715 Andrews Hwy.

Saturday, Sunday. Average daily attendance to 2,000 with approximately 50 dealers. Antiques, furniture, collector lines, jewelry, new and used merchandise. Lots of western memorabilia. Snack bar, rest rooms, grocery store. Camping and hookups available. No outside food or beverage sales allowed. Inside and outside spaces. *Contact* Frances Henry, 7715 Andrews Hwy., 79765 (915) 366-8189.

PASADENA

Pasadena Flea Market
5400 Spencer
(713) 998-8510

Friday, Saturday, Sunday. Inside and outside market with approximately 100 dealers. New merchandise, western wear, housewares, electronics, sports merchandise, sportswear, jewelry, collector booths, crafts, and nostalgia items available. Snack bar, rest rooms. Space from $15 per weekend. Camping available on premises.

Captain Flea Market
1001 E. Shaw Ave.

Saturday, Sunday, 10 a.m.–6 p.m. Indoor/outdoor market with approximately 150 dealers. Collectibles, lots of western and cowboy items, new merchandise, sportswear, electronics, housewares available. Several specialty shops here. This flea market has three good restaurants, rest rooms, h/a, ample parking. Space from $10. *Contact* Bob Scanlon, 1001 E. Shaw Ave., 77506 (713) 477-9137.

PEARLAND CITY

Cole's Flea Market & Antique Village
1014 N. Main St.
Rte. 35 and Telephone Rd.
(281) 485-2277

Saturday, Sunday, 7:30 a.m.–6 p.m. Inside and outside spaces with approximately 5–600 dealers. Antiques, collectibles, furniture, glassware, crafts, and lots of new merchandise available. Food available, rest rooms, h/a, ample parking with a $1 charge. Space starts at $40 for the weekend. *Contact* Manager, 1014 N. Main St., 77581.

PHARR

All Valley Flea Market
807 E. Hwy. 83

Saturday, Sunday. Approximately 300 dealers at this large commercial market. Lots of new merchandise, imports, collectibles, crafts, produce, livestock, and mountains of used merchandise of every variety available. Snack bar, rest rooms, ample parking. Space from $2.50 per day.

PROGRESSO

Progresso Flea Market
Approximately one mile north of Progresso International Bridge
(512) 565-1702

Wednesday–Monday. Average attendance of 6,000 on weekends and approximately 200 dealers on weekends. Mountains of Mexican imports and produce. Sellers, if you have a big truck and lots of green money, you can become an importer without crossing the border. Food available, rest rooms, ample parking. Space from $4 daily. Camping available on premises.

DAYS, DATES, AND MARKETS ARE SUBJECT TO CHANGE!

ROCKPORT

Pirate's Cove Flea Market
Austin St., downtown.

Friday, Saturday, Sunday. Outdoor market with approximately 20 dealers. *Contact* Maryjane Knight (361) 790-8658 or (281) 337-1946.

SAN ANTONIO

Austin Highway Flea Market
1428 Austin Hwy.

Friday, Saturday, Sunday, 7:30 a.m. until dark. Approximately 150 dealers offer antiques, collectibles, new and used merchandise, crafts, and produce at this outdoor market. Snack bar, rest rooms, h/a, ample parking. Space from $19. *Contact* Ed Barley, 1428 Austin Hwy., 78209 (512) 828-1488.

Eisenhauer Road Flea Market
3903 Eisenhauer Rd.

Indoor mall Monday–Friday, 12 p.m.–7 p.m.; outdoor flea market Saturday, Sunday, 9 a.m.–7 p.m. Indoor/outdoor market with approximately 200 exhibitors. Great selection of new merchandise here, electronics, sportswear, housewares, lots of discounted new merchandise, collectibles, memorabilia, and primitives available. Good food here, rest rooms, h/a, ample parking. Space from $15. *Contact* Pat Walker, 3903 Eisenhauer Rd., 78218 (210) 653-7592, fax (210) 657-1692.

Flea Mart
12280 Hwy. 16 South
(210) 624-2666

Saturday, Sunday, 10 a.m.–6 p.m. Admission charge $1. Average weekend attendance of 25,000 with approximately 600 dealers. Outdoor market with covered spaces. Great selection of goods here. Various types of food here for hungry shoppers. Clean rest rooms. Ample parking. The market has live entertainment, live music, and many family activities. Space from $35 per weekend. Camping available. *Contact* Tom Browning, 78224.

Northwest Flea Market
3600 Fredericksburg Rd.

Saturday, Sunday. Indoor air-conditioned market. New and used merchandise, imports, clothing, crafts available. Snack bar, rest rooms, h/a, ample parking. Space from $14. *Contact* James Maxwell, Northwest Flea Market, 3600 Fredericksburg Rd., 78201 (210) 736-6655.

SCHERTZ

Bussey's Flea Market
18738 I-35 North, Exit 175 or 177

Tuesday–Friday, 8 a.m.–5 p.m. (indoor shops); Saturday, Sunday, 7 a.m. until dark (flea market). Outdoor flea market on weekends with approximately 500 dealers. Wide range of goods here, lots of Western and cowboy items and apparel, crafts, art, collectibles, and coins available. Market is loaded with Mexican goods. Food, rest rooms, h/a, ample parking. *Contact* Harold Smith, 18738 I-35 N, 78154, (830) 651-6830.

SEVEN POINTS

Big Daddy's Traders Market
Hwy. 274
One mile south of Seven Points

Saturday, Sunday, 8 a.m.–6 p.m. Approximately 100 dealers. Indoor/outdoor market with covered spaces. Collectibles, crafts, new merchandise, sportswear, electronics, and housewares available. Snack bar, rest rooms, h/a, ample parking. Space from $22 for the weekend. *Contact* Jim Shafer, Box 43718, 75143 (903) 432-4911, fax (903) 778-2887.

ALWAYS CALL AHEAD TO VERIFY DATES AND INFORMATION

STEVENVILLE

The Chicken House Flea Market
Hwy. 377
(254) 968-0888

Saturday, Sunday. Approximately 200 dealers. New merchandise, sportswear, tools, jewelry, sports merchandise, toys, electronics, lots of Mexican imports, crafts, collector booths, sports cards, coins, silver, linens, and glassware available. Snack bar, rest rooms, ample parking. Indoor and outdoor under cover. Food vendors allowed at this market.

TEXARKANA

Great American Indoor Flea Market
2615 New Boston Rd.
(903) 793-7700

Tuesday–Sunday. Primarily an indoor market with lots of new merchandise, used merchandise, collectibles, and decorator items in permanent booths. Snack bar, rest rooms, ample parking. Limited outdoor space. Approximately 300 booths inside, with most rented on a monthly basis. This is the market where Ross Perot might have gotten his start.

TIOGO

Western Trade Days
Town Square

Every first weekend. Approximately 150 dealers. Wide selection of new merchandise including western wear and boots, used merchandise, farm items, garage-sale-type bric-a-brac, collectibles, crafts, and produce. Snack bar, rest rooms, h/a, ample parking. Inside and outside space available. *Contact* James Wendover, Box 176, 76271 (817) 437-2219.

INFORMATION IS SUBJECT TO CHANGE—ALWAYS CALL AHEAD TO AVOID DISAPPOINTMENT

VIDOR

I-10 Golden Triangle Flea Market
445 W. Freeway
Six miles east of Beaumont
(409) 769-4100

Friday, Saturday, Sunday, 8 a.m.–6 p.m. Average daily attendance of 10,000 at this large commercial market. New merchandise, mountains of used desirables, collectibles, antiques, crafts, and produce available. Snack bar, rest rooms, h/a, ample parking. Outdoor/indoor market. Camping available on premises.

WACO

Prices Unlimited Flea Market
2728 LaSalle and 2729 LaSalle
I-35 and LaSalle

Saturday, Sunday, daylight until dark. Approximately 400 dealers with an average attendance of 10,000 at these two sister markets. Collectibles, memorabilia, lots of new merchandise and used items available. Markets have two cafes and a beer garden. Rest rooms, h/a, ample parking. One of the better markets in the area. Space from $5. Camping available. No food or drink sales allowed by outside vendors. *Contact* Darrell Goetsch (254) 662-6616.

WAXAHACHIE

Waxahachie Flea Market
Howard Rd.
FM Rd. 877
(972) 937-4277

Saturday, Sunday, 10 a.m.–6 p.m. Indoor/outdoor market with approximately 50 dealers. Collectibles, crafts, new merchandise, and lots of used and garage sale items available. Snack bar, rest rooms, ample parking. Camping available. Food vendors welcome.

WEATHERFORD

First Monday Trade Days
Downtown
(817) 596-8586

Every first weekend, 7 a.m.–7 p.m. Classic outdoor Texas market. Antiques, collectibles, new merchandise, animals, lots of western and cowboy items, and used merchandise. Good food, rest rooms; parking is on street with lots of walking to see everything. Space from $30 per 12x25 space for the weekend. *Contact* First Monday, Box 1504, 76086.

WICHITA FALLS

Flea Market
2820 Holiday Rd.

Saturday, Sunday, 7 a.m. until dark. Average daily attendance is 3,000 with approximately 200 dealers. Indoor/outdoor and covered spaces. Collectibles, crafts, new and used merchandise, and lots of discounted and surplus items here. Space from $7. Camping and electricity available. *Contact* Jim Parish, 76301 (817) 767-9038 or 767-1712.

ALWAYS CALL BEFORE TRAVELING LONG DISTANCES!

WIMBERLEY

Wimberley Market Place
Ranch Rd. 12
Halfway between Wimberley and San Marcos

Every first and third weekend. Art, crafts, antiques, and quality flea market items here. Currently market has 250 spaces. Overnight camping and electricity available. *Contact* Terry Williams, P.O. Box 8, 78676 (512) 353-0300.

WINNIE

Old Time Trade Days
Hwy. 110
Hwy. 1663, Exit 829
Two miles west of Beaumont

Every first weekend, daylight until dark. Market is outdoors with covered spaces. Average attendance of 45,000 per weekend. Market always has over 500 dealers. This is another classic, wide-open Texas flea market. It is a good source market for market peddlers, shopkeepers, and decorators because many sellers will wholesale. Lots of great food here, rest rooms, h/a, ample parking with a charge of $2. Space from $25 for the weekend. Reservations recommended. Food vendors welcome. *Contact* Larry Tinkle, 14902 Hwy. 1663, 77665 (409) 892-4000 or 296-3300, fax (409) 296-3301.

UTAH

MIDVALE

Rocky Mountain Swap-A-Rama
8169 S. State St.
(801) 566-4335

Saturday, Sunday. New merchandise, souvenirs, used merchandise, good selection of collectibles, western and Indian items available. Food available, rest rooms, ample parking. Indoor market with outside vending during summer months.

OGDEN

Swap & Shop Meet
Exchange Rd.

Saturday, Sunday. Admission charge. Approximately 200 dealers offer antiques, collectibles, silver, jewelry, lots of western and Indian items, farm and ranch items, tack, and used merchandise. Food available, rest rooms. Space from $3. *Contact* John Elizondo, Box 9692, 84409.

RIVERDALE

Riverdale Flea Market
Motor View Drive Inn
5368 S. 1050 St.
(801) 394-1768

Saturday, Sunday, 7 a.m.–1 p.m. New and used merchandise, farm and ranch items, Western and Indian jewelry, art and collectibles, housewares, clothing, jewelry, crafts, and lots of primitives available. Food available, rest rooms. Space from $6. Outside space only. No reservations needed.

SALT LAKE CITY

Intermountain Independent Flea Market
3435 S. Main St.
(801) 255-4029

Saturday, Sunday. New and used merchandise, housewares, clothing, farm and ranch items, collectibles, and crafts available. Snack bar, rest rooms.

Redwood Swap Meet
3688 S. Redwood Rd. West
Redwood Drive-In Theater
I-15, Exit 33rd South, west to Redwood
(801) 973-6060

Saturday, Sunday, 8 a.m.–4 p.m. Admission charge 50 cents. Average attendance of 10,000 for the weekend. Approximately 400 dealers offer antiques, collectibles, crafts, primitives, good country and farm items, and new merchandise. Snack bar, rest rooms, h/a, ample parking. Space from $12 per day. *Contact* Manager, 3688 S. Redwood Rd. West, 84119.

Utah State Fairgrounds Swap Meet
Utah State Fairgrounds
155 North, 1000 West Fairgrounds
(801) 538-8440 or 322-4222

Saturday, Sunday. Admission charge. Average daily attendance of 3–5,000 with approximately 200 dealers. Antiques, collectibles, crafts, lots of western and Indian items here, new and used merchandise, along with a great selection of mountain man and black powder merchandise. Good food here, rest rooms, h/a, ample parking. Space from $7 per day.

VERMONT

BRATTLEBORO

Black Mountain Flea Market
Rte. 30
(802) 254-3848

Sunday. Good country antique and collector market located in a lovely area. Antiques, furniture, great selection of New England country decorator items, and collectibles. Food available, rest rooms.

CHARLOTTE

Charlotte Flea Market
Rte. 7
Between Burlington and Vergennes

Saturday, Sunday, April–November, 6 a.m.–6 p.m. Outdoor market with approximately 100 dealers. Nice market in a beautiful area. Good selection of antiques, collectibles, memorabilia, and interesting used merchandise and junk. Snack bar, rest rooms, h/a, ample parking. Space from $5 on Saturday and $10 for Sunday. *Contact* Larry Lavalette, Box 415, Shelburne, 05482 (802) 425-2844.

FAIRLEE

Railroad Station Flea Market
Rte. 5, I-91, Exit 15

Saturday, Sunday, May–October, daylight until dark. Lovely outdoor market located next to an old train station. Lots of good antiques and collectibles here. This a particularly nice stop because the market has neighboring antique and specialty shops. Space from $15. *Contact* Barry LeBarron, Box 57, 05045 (802) 333-4574.

MANCHESTER

Manchester Flea Market
Bromley Mountain Rd.
Junction of Rtes. 11 and 30
Three miles from junction of Rtes. 7, 11, and 30

Saturday, May–October, 9 a.m.–5 p.m. Average attendance of 2,000 with approximately 35–40 dealers. Lots of collectibles, secondhand items, fishing items, and some new merchandise. The market has a retail auction on Thursday. Food, rest rooms, h/a, ample parking. Space from $15. Reservations required. Outside space only. Camping available. *Contact* John Wessner, Rte. 1, Box 1960, 05255 (802) 362-1631.

NEWFANE

Newfane Flea Market
Rte. 30
Two miles north of city

Sunday, May through October. Approximately 75 dealers. Antiques, collectibles, crafts, produce, new and used merchandise available. Snack bars, rest rooms, ample parking. Space from $20. *Contact* Earl Morse, Box 5, 05345 (802) 365-4000.

RUTLAND

Vermont Craft Fair and Flea Market
State Fairgrounds. Rtes. 7 and 4
175 S. Main St.

Saturday, Sunday. Covered and outside space from $10. Walking distance of restaurants and motels. Rest rooms, ample parking, h/a. *Con-*

tact Chuck Wade, 175 S. Main St., 05701 (802) 492-2013. E-mail: vermontmarket@aol.com.

SALISBURY

The Flea Mart Center
Rtc. 7

Daily. With 25 dealers displaying antiques, collectibles, china, glassware, pottery, and jewelry. Lots of treasures are found here. Indoor market with permanent spaces. *Contact* Joyce McGettrick, Box 186, 05769 (802) 352-4424. E-mail: fleamart@together.net.

SOUTH HERO

South Hero Flea Market
Rte. 2
Champlain Islands off I-89

Saturday, Sunday, May–October. Indoor/outdoor market with approximately 50 dealers. Antiques, collectibles, and locally made crafts available. Gorgeous area. Worth visiting this market just to spend some time in the area. Space from $7 per day. *Contact* Charles Langlois, 21 Curtis St., Burlington 05401 (802) 864-5091.

WATERBURY CENTER

Waterbury Flea Market
Rte. 2
I-89, Waterbury Exit

Saturday, Sunday, May–October, daylight until dark. Outdoor market with approximately 75 dealers. Lots of collectibles, memorabilia, and new and used merchandise available. Snack bar, rest rooms, h/a, ample parking. *Contact* Reginald Erwin, 71 N. Main St., 05676 (802) 244-5916.

Stowe Road Flea Market
Stowe Rd.
Rte. 100
Four miles east of I-89
(802) 244-8817 or 244-8879

Saturday, Sunday, June–October, 8 a.m.–5 p.m. Approximately 40 dealers offer a good selection of collectibles, memorabilia, primitives, new and used merchandise, and used furniture. Good food here. Rest rooms, h/a, ample parking. Outdoor market with some covered spaces from $8. *Contact* Barbara or Richard Woodward, Box 10, 05677. Market is located three miles north of the Ben & Jerry's ice cream factory. Great place for a weekend.

WILMINGTON

Wilmington Antique and Flea Market
Junction of Rte. 9 and Rte. 100 East

Saturday, Sunday, May–October, dawn until dark. Outdoor market with approximately 100 dealers. Good selection of collectibles, memorabilia, souvenirs, coins, crafts, art, new and used merchandise, and furniture available. Always a lot of good buys at this market. Food available, rest rooms, h/a, ample parking. Camping with showers available. Space from $15 daily. *Contact* Sally Gore, P.O. Box 22, 05363 (802) 464-3345.

VIRGINIA

ALTA VISTA

First Saturday Trade Days
7th Street, downtown
(804) 369-5001

Every first weekend, Friday, 12 p.m.–4 p.m., Saturday, dawn until dark. Outdoor market with approximately 100 dealers. Good selection of collectibles, memorabilia, primitives, and lots of used and new merchandise available. Always a good selection of local country crafts. Good food, rest rooms, Park on the street or wherever, as parking can be difficult here. *Contact* Carl Davis, Box 333, 24517.

BRIDGEWATER

Mossy Creek Flea Market
205 S. Main St., Rte. 42

Thursday, Friday, Saturday. Indoor market with approximately 20 dealers. *Contact* Bruce Knicely (703) 828-3942.

BRISTOL

Carriers Flea Market
Hwy. 11 East
Approximately one mile from racetrack

Saturday, Sunday, 6 a.m.–5 p.m. Average daily attendance of 10,000 with approximately 100 dealers. Good selection and variety of new and used merchandise, secondhand garage-sale-type bric-a-brac, farm items and supplies, crafts, and produce. Many good collector booths here. Food available, rest rooms, h/a. Space from $4. Overnight parking. *Contact* J. W. Carrier, Rte. 1, Bluff City, TN 37618 (615) 538-7177.

CENTERVILLE

South Boston Mega Market
Halifax Rd.
Rte. 501

Friday, 12 p.m.–7 p.m., Saturday, 8 a.m.–5 p.m., Sunday, 9 a.m.–5 p.m. Approximately 100 dealers offer a good variety of new merchandise, used items, many collector booths, art, crafts, books, antiques, and furniture. Food available, rest rooms. Indoor/outdoor market. Space from $5 per day outside. *Contact* John Carter, 707 Corn Tassel Trail, Martinsville, 24112 (703) 638-7514.

EDINBURG

The Flea Market
Old Valley Pike, Rte. 11 to Landfill Road
(540) 984-8771

Friday, Saturday, Sunday, 9 a.m.–5 p.m. Indoor/outdoor market with some covered spaces. Approximately 50 dealers.

FREDERICKSBURG

Flea Market
U.S. Hwy. 1
South of town

Saturday, Sunday, 7 a.m.–5 p.m. Average daily attendance of 3,000 with approximately 50 dealers. Indoor/outdoor market. Collectibles, new merchandise, lots of sports-related items, and used wares available. Snack bar, rest rooms, h/a, ample parking. Space from $10. Camping available on-site. This market is located in a former motel. *Contact* Nick Dommissee, 10307 Bedford Ct., 22408 (540) 898-4685.

GLOUCESTER

Stagecoach Markets Antique Market
Rtes. 17 and 1420
(804) 693-3951

Saturday, Sunday. Has 45 antique shops and a large country outdoor flea and farmers' market. This is a great source market with lots of treasures at great prices. Food available, rest rooms.

HAMPTON

The Big Flea Market
Hampton Coliseum
(757) 431-9500 or 422-9500

Monthly. Large one-day show usually held on Saturday. Approximately 300 dealers selling quality antiques, collectibles, a nice selection of crafts, and new merchandise. *Contact* Flea Market, 544 Central Dr. No. 106, Virginia Beach, 23454.

HOPEWELL

Flea Market
Colonial Corner Shopping Center, exit from I-295

Saturday, Sunday. Antiques, collectibles, clothing, furniture, jewelry, flower arrangements.

LADYSMITH

Ladysmith Fleamarket
I-95, Exit 110

Saturday, Sunday, 9 a.m.–5 p.m. New indoor/outdoor market scheduled to open May 6 and 7. Situated on 100 acres 67,000 sq.-ft. building, heated and air-conditioned, 355 spaces inside, 1,800 spaces outside, 100 with electricity. Food court, rest rooms, h/a, ample parking. Space rate varies, and contracts for food are available. Market will feature antiques, crafts, collectibles, a farmers market, and general line of flea market merchandise.

LYNCHBURG

Fort Flea Market
7306 Timberlake Rd.
Hwy. 460 West
(804) 239-0619

Saturday, Sunday, 8 a.m.–4 p.m. Admission charge. Average daily attendance of 4,00 with approximately 300 dealers. Large well-established commercial market with a wide range of merchandise and dealers. Some great booths of quality items along with booths of garage sale junk. This is a fun, clean, interesting market where bargains and treasures abound. Food available, rest rooms, h/a, ample parking. Indoor/outdoor market with space from $7 per day.

NORFOLK

Flea Market of Norfolk
3416 N. Military Hwy.
(804) 857-7824 or 855-3331
Fax (757) 853-8393

Saturday, Sunday, 7 a.m. until dark. Indoor/outdoor market with approximately 50 dealers. Collectibles, crafts, and new and used merchandise available. Snack bar, rest rooms, h/a, ample parking.

PETERSBURG

South Side Station Flea Market & Mini Mall
5 River St.
I-95, Exit 52

Saturday, Sunday, 8:30 a.m.–5 p.m. Antiques, collectibles, crafts, fabrics, produce, and jewelry available. The majority of the indoor section of this market is open during the week, featuring a nice selection of antiques, collectibles, and crafts. Cafe, rest rooms, h/a. *Contact* Linda Murphy, Box 2820, 23804 (804) 733-5050, fax (804) 733-0667.

PORTSMOUTH

Airline Flea Fair
3535 Airline Blvd.
I-264, Greenwood West Exit

Thursday–Sunday. Indoor market with approximately 300 dealers. Antiques, collectibles, lots of memorabilia and country primitives, crafts, art, new and used merchandise, home furnishings, and furniture available. Some real interesting booths to poke through at this market. Snack bars, rest rooms, h/a, ample parking. Space from $5 per day on Thursday. *Contact* Philip Knight, 3535 Airline Blvd., 23701 (757) 488-3695.

RICHMOND

Bellwood Drive-In Theater Flea Market
9201 Jefferson Davis Hwy. I-95, Exit 64

Saturday, Sunday, 8 a.m.–4 p.m. Admission charge $1. Outdoor market with an average daily attendance of 3,000 and approximately 250 dealers. Antiques, collectibles, crafts, Civil War items, furniture, new merchandise, and used items available. Snack bar, rest rooms, h/a, ample parking. Space from $14. *Contact* Belinda Riddle, 9201 Jeff Davis Hwy., 23237 (804) 275-1187 or (800) 793-0707.

Flea Market
Fairgrounds

Monthly, call for dates. Saturday, 12 p.m.–7 p.m., Sunday, 12 p.m.–5 p.m. Admission charge $1.50. Large market with approximately 400 dealers. The offerings are heavy on antiques and collectible. Some new merchandise, imports, and reproductions. This is one of the area's better antique and collectibles markets. Snack bar, rest rooms, h/a, ample parking. Space from $70 for the weekend. *Contact* D'aore Promotions, 2125 Mecomas Way, #102, Virginia Beach, 23454 (757) 421-9500, fax (757) 427-8888.

Richmond Super Flea
5501 Midlothian Tpke.
(804) 231-6687
Fax (804) 231-3170
E-mail: ppn50010@aol.com

Saturday, Sunday, 9 a.m.–6 p.m. Wide range of new merchandise, used merchandise, garage sale items, outdoor items, housewares, clothing, jewelry, a good assortment of collectibles, crafts, and produce available. Food available, rest rooms. *Contact* Kathy or Fred Freiburger, 23225.

ROANOKE

Happy's Flea Market
5411 Williamson Rd.
Rte. 11
(703) 563-4474

Thursday–Sunday. Indoor/outdoor market with approximately 7–800 dealers. This is a large wide-open market with a wide range of merchandise from quality antiques to junk to new imports. Restaurant, snack bars, rest rooms, h/a, ample parking. Space from $9 per day. *Contact* Manager, 5411 Williamson Rd., 24012.

Lee Hi Drive-In Flea Market
1700 Apperson Dr.

Saturday, Sunday. Admission charge. Approximately 50 dealers offer collectibles, new and used merchandise, garage sale items, housewares, clothing, crafts, and produce. Food available, rest rooms, h/a, ample parking. Space from $3. *Contact* Ralph Hoskins (703) 389-5556.

The Peddlers Market
Civic Center, downtown
(703) 674-1349

Monthly, call for dates. Admission charge. Average daily attendance of 5,000 with approximately 200 dealers. Good market with lots of folk art, crafts, antiques, collectibles, and reproductions. Snack bar, rest rooms, h/a, ample parking. Space from $60 for the weekend. *Contact* Peddlers Market, Box 1590, Dublin, 24084.

STAUNTON

Verona Flea Market
Hwy. 11
(703) 886-9640

Thursday–Sunday. Approximately 150 dealers offer a great selection of new merchandise, used merchandise, garage sale items, farm items and supplies, antiques, good collector booths, crafts, and produce. Snack bar, rest rooms, h/a, ample parking.

TAZWELL

Tazwell Flea Market
Old Drive-In Theater
Hwy.19 and Rte. 460

Monday. Average attendance of 3–4,000 with approximately 300 dealers. This is a large classic southern market with a wide range of booths from professional quality to the garage sale variety. Always a lot of treasures and great deals at this market. Good food available, rest rooms, h/a, ample parking, and lots of walking. Space from $2. Camping available. *Contact* James Hughes, Box 864, 24651 (703) 988-5804.

TEMPERANCEVILLE

Shore Flea Market
Rte. 13
One-half mile south of Tyson Foods

Saturday, Sunday, April–November. Large outdoor market. Unable to give information about this market as I do not visit towns that begin with the word *temperance*. *Contact* William Miles (757) 824-3300 or 824-5020.

THORNBURG

Outdoor Flea Market
(703) 582-5755

Saturday, Sunday. New and used merchandise, garage sale items, antiques, furniture, collectibles, crafts, and produce available. Food available, rest rooms, h/a, ample parking.

VERONA

Verona Antique Market
Rte. 11, at the firehouse
(540) 248-3532

Thursday–Sunday. Indoor market with approximately 20 dealers.

WAYNESBORO

Skyline Drive-In Flea Market
Rte. 250 West

Saturday, Sunday, 7 a.m.–4 p.m. Outdoor market with approximately 50 dealers. Collectibles, crafts, lots of used and garage sale merchandise, and some new merchandise. Food, rest rooms, h/a, ample parking. *Contact* Melvin Twitchell (540) 942-1738.

WEYERS CAVE

Rocky's Antique Mall
I-81, Exit 60
(703) 234-8676

Thursday–Sunday. Average attendance 1,000 with an average of 150 dealers. General line of antiques, furniture, and collector items. Indoor mall with 40,000 square feet. Air-conditioned; food, clean rest rooms, h/a, ample parking. Camping available. Outside booths $5 daily.

INFORMATION IS SUBJECT TO CHANGE—ALWAYS CALL FIRST!

WHITE POINT

Shen Valley Flea Market
Rte. 522
(703) 869-7858 or 635-7023

Saturday, Sunday, March–December. Approximately 200 dealers at this outdoor market. Great summer market with lots of antiques, collector booths, new and used merchandise, farm items and supplies, jewelry, clothing, and housewares available. Food available, rest rooms, h/a, ample parking. Camping available on premises.

WINCHESTER

Shen Valley Flea Market
Rte. 522 South
(540) 869-7858 or 635-7023

Saturday, Sunday, 7 a.m. until dark. Outdoor market with approximately 250 dealers. Snack bar, rest rooms, h/a, camping available. Ample free parking.

ALWAYS CALL BEFORE TRAVELING LONG DISTANCES!

WASHINGTON

ABERDEEN

Grays Harbor Farmers Market & Crafts Fair
Broadway at Market St.
(206) 538-0696

Saturday. Large farmers' market, new and used merchandise, lots of garage sale items, collectibles, and a very large selection of locally made crafts available. Good food, rest rooms. *Contact* Farmers Market, Rte. 1, Box 333, 98520.

EVERETT

Puget Park Drive-in Theater Flea Market
13020 Meridian Ave. South

Saturday, Sunday, April–October, 9 a.m.–4 p.m. Admission charge $1. Outdoor market with approximately 200 dealers. Antiques, collectibles, always booths with Pacific Northwest Indian and Eskimo art and artifacts, crafts, and produce available. Food, rest rooms, h/a, ample parking. Space from $11. *Contact* Dan Sutton, 13020 Meridian Ave. South, 98204 (425) 337-1435 or 455-8100.

GRAHAM

Weekender Swap Meet
6200 296th East
(206) 847-9675

Saturday, Sunday. New and used merchandise, clothing, home furnishings, household goods, imports, garage sale items, farm items, collectibles, crafts, and produce available. Food available, rest rooms.

KENNEWICK

Kennewick Flea Market
310 N. Benton

Friday, Saturday, Sunday, 9 a.m.–5 p.m. Indoor market with approximately 75 dealers. Collectibles, coins, jewelry, country primitives, and new and used merchandise available. Snack bar, rest rooms, h/a, ample parking. *Contact* Bonnie Turcott (509) 586-9993.

LAMONA

Rendezvous Flea Market
Fairgrounds
(509) 784-6124

Every third weekend. Antiques, furniture, lots of nice collector booths here, including Pacific Northwest Indian and Eskimo art, jewelry, and artifacts, black powder supplies and accessories, and new and used merchandise. Food available, rest rooms, h/a, ample parking.

LYNWOOD

Swap Shop Drive-In Flea Market
17325 Hwy. 99
(425) 743-2294

Saturday, Sunday. New and used merchandise, garage sale items, home furnishings, clothing, imports, surplus, farm items, collector booths, crafts, and produce available. Snack bar, rest rooms, h/a, ample parking.

DAYS, DATES, AND MARKETS ARE SUBJECT TO CHANGE!

MIDWAY

Midway Swap Shop
240th St. and Pacific Hwy.
(206) 878-1802

Saturday, Sunday, 6:30 a.m.–4 p.m. New merchandise, souvenirs, jewelry, used merchandise, housewares, clothing, collectibles, produce, seafood, and crafts available. Snack bar, rest rooms, h/a.

PASCO

Pasco Farmers Market
Hwy. 12 and E. Lewis St.
Downtown
(509) 547-5035 or 547-7057

Thursday, Saturday, March–December, 6 a.m.–4 p.m. Average weekend attendance of 5,000 with approximately 250 dealers. One of the area's largest markets. Nice mix of merchandise. This marketplace has a good selection of antiques and collectibles. Lots of new merchandise, sportswear, housewares, auto items, and new and used furniture available. Food, rest rooms, h/a, ample parking. Camping available. Space from $5 per day. *Contact* Farmers Market, Box 550, 99301.

PUYALLUP

Swap Meet
Fairgrounds
(253) 588-8621

Saturday, Sunday. Antiques, furniture, collector booths, new and used merchandise, clothing, housewares, auto items, sports merchandise, and crafts available. Snack bars, rest rooms, h/a, ample parking.

ALWAYS CALL AHEAD TO VERIFY DATES AND INFORMATION

SEATTLE

Flea Market
Midway Drive-In Theater
Hwy. 99
(206) 878-2536

Saturday, Sunday. New and used merchandise, collector booths, marine and fishing gear, clothing, housewares, used furniture, and crafts available. Snack bar, rest rooms, h/a, ample parking.

Fremont Sunday Market
Corner of Evanston Ave. and North 34th in the central parking lot by the Fremont Bridge. One mile north of the Space Needle.

Sundays, 10 a.m.–5 p.m. Seasonal market open May–October. Indoor/outdoor market with approximately 150 dealers. New and used merchandise, some collectibles, locally made crafts, produce, lots of garage sale items, and bric-a-brac. Space from $25. Snack bar, rest rooms, h/a. *Contact* John Hegeman, 3416 Evanston, 98103 (206) 781-6776 or 784-2753.

SPANAWAY

Overnighter Swap Meet
6611 296th East

Saturday, Sunday. Used merchandise, garage sale items, and collectibles available. Food, rest rooms. Outside market with camping available. *Contact* Forest Haag (206) 847-9675.

SPOKANE

Auto Vue Drive-In Theater Flea Market
6800 Division St.
(509) 487-6171

Saturday, Sunday. Antiques, collectibles, new and used merchandise, clothing, housewares, marine and fishing items, crafts, and produce available. Snack bar, rest rooms, h/a, ample parking.

Swap Meet and Bargain Fair
Fairgrounds
(206) 588-8621

Monthly. Call for dates. Antiques, furniture, collectibles, new and used merchandise, housewares, clothing, jewelry, and crafts available. Snack bar, rest rooms, h/a, ample parking.

Sprague Drive-in Theater Swap Meet
I-90, Sprague Exit

Sunday. Antiques, great selection of collector booths, antique and used furniture, and new and used merchandise available. Lots of garage sale booths, farm items, fishing tackle, sports merchandise, and crafts here. Snack bar, rest rooms, h/a, ample parking.

TACOMA

Swap & Shop Flea Market
Starlight Drive-In Theater
84th St. and S. Tacoma Way

Tuesday, Friday, Saturday, Sunday, 8 a.m.–4 p.m. Indoor/outdoor market with approximately 300 dealers. Booths full of nice antiques and collectibles at this market. Crafts, fine art, and a good selection of Indian and Eskimo items. Nice fishing collectibles here, and new merchandise, sportswear, electronics, and cookware available. Indoor market is open throughout the week. Snack bar, rest rooms, h/a, ample parking. *Contact* Jack Cobb, 3827 S. Tacoma Way, 98499 (253) 588-8090, fax (253) 588-8929.

YAKIMA

Yakima Swap Meet & Farmers Market
Central State Fairgrounds
10th St. and Nob Hill Ave.
(509) 454-0212

Saturday, Sunday. Antiques, furniture, lots of collector booths, good selection of Pacific Northwest collectibles, new and used merchandise, and crafts available. Food, rest rooms, h/a, ample parking. Indoor and outdoor space available from $8. Tables $2. Reservations recommended. Overnight camping nearby with full hookups. License not required. *Contact* Yakima Swap Meet, P.O. Box 870, 98907.

Mead Avenue Flea Market
1104 E. Mead Ave.

Wednesday, Sunday, 10 a.m.–6 p.m. Indoor/outdoor market with approximately 100 dealers. Antiques, collectibles, sportswear, electronics, toys, and new and used merchandise available. *Contact* Roger Wilson, 1902 S. 11th St., 98903 (509) 457-6243 or 453-9983.

WEST VIRGINIA

BECKLEY

Beaver Creek Traders Village
I-64, Exit 125
(304) 253-4500 or 638-4700

Saturday, Sunday. Average daily attendance of 3,000 with approximately 100 dealers. New merchandise, electronics, sportswear, souvenirs, housewares, sports merchandise, tools, auto items, used merchandise, garage sale items, collector booths, crafts, and produce available. Snack bars, clean rest rooms, h/a, ample parking. Live musical entertainment. Outdoor market with space from $5. Camping available on premises.

BLUEFIELD

Bluefield Flea Market
Princeton Ave. Parking Building
Across from Amtrak Station

Saturday, March–November, 7 a.m.–5 p.m. Average daily attendance at this indoor market is 1,000 with approximately 150 dealers offering collectibles, crafts, art, lots of garage sale items, and new merchandise. Food, rest rooms, h/a. Overnight parking available. Space from $5. *Contact* Sharon Leffell, City Hall, 514 Scott St,. 24701 (304) 327-8031.

BRIDGEPORT

Old Ellis Drive-In Theater Flea Market
(304) 623-1640

Saturday, Sunday. Collector booths, antiques, silver, coins, sports cards, new and used merchandise, garage sale items, farm items, crafts, and produce available. Snack bar, rest rooms, ample parking.

CHARLESTON

Capitol Flea Market
Rte. 114 South
I-79, Exit 5; I-64, Exit 99

Friday, Saturday, Sunday, 8 a.m.–5 p.m. Indoor/outdoor market with approximately 150 dealers. This market has a good selection of country collectibles and primitives. Usually mining collectibles and Civil War/military items can be found here. Also new merchandise and new and used furniture available. Food, rest rooms, h/a, ample parking. *Contact* Frances Brown, 24 Meadow Brook Plaza, 25311 (304) 342-1626.

FAIRMONT

Fairmont Flea Market
500 Quincy St.
Rte. 19, downtown
(304) 366-3265

Friday, Saturday, Sunday, 9 a.m. until dark. Admission charge. Average weekend attendance of 1,000 with approximately 25 dealers. Secondhand items, collectibles, clothing, and primitives available. Snack bar, rest rooms, h/a, ample parking. Indoor market with space from $8.

HARPERS FERRY

Harpers Ferry Flea Market
Rte. 340 (Dual Hwy.) at Bloomery Rd.
One mile south of town
(304) 725-4141 or 725-0092

Saturday, Sunday, March–December, daylight until dark. Average weekend attendance of

2,500 with approximately 120 vendors. Good selection of country collectibles, farm items, memorabilia, primitives, glassware, new merchandise, and lots of used bric-a-brac available. Snack bars, rest rooms, h/a, ample parking. Largest market in the area. Outdoor market with space from $11 daily. Electricity and overnight camping available. No fruit or vegetable sales allowed. *Contact* Manager, 904 Oregon Trail, 25425.

HINTON

Bence Springs Flea Market
State Rtes. 3 and 12
Approximately 12 miles from Hinton

Saturday, Sunday, April–October. Approximately 200 dealers. Large old-time country market with lots of used merchandise, mining items, farm items, country collectibles, decorator items, new merchandise, antiques, and crafts available. Food available, rest rooms, h/a. Space from $3. Camping nearby. *Contact* Ashby Berkley (304) 466-2607.

HUNTINGTON

Ohio Valley Flea Market
404 W. 18th St.
Rte. 60 West

Friday, Saturday, Sunday. Market is held in the city's old bus barn. New and used merchandise, antiques, good selection of collector booths, and always mining and tobacco items available. Snack bars, rest rooms, h/a, ample parking. *Contact* William Erwin (304) 736-6830.

MARTINSBURG

I-81 Flea Market
I-81 at Springmills Rd., Exit 20

Friday, Saturday, Sunday, 8 a.m.–6 p.m. Average daily attendance of 3,000 with approximately 150 vendors outside. This market has good mix of merchandise, with several Amish and Mennonite vendors selling traditional crafts and food. Great selection of older collector items. Food available, rest rooms, h/a, ample parking. Food vendors welcome. Camping available. This market hosts several special events during the year. Note: This was formerly a large indoor/outdoor market; however, the building burned and is being rebuilt. Call for schedule and further information. *Contact* Betty Kline, Rte. 2, Box 230, 25401 (304) 274-3387 or 274-1313.

MILTON

Milton Flea Market
1215 U.S. Rte. 60
I-64, Exit 28

Saturday, Sunday, 8 a.m.–5 p.m. Indoor/outdoor market with approximately 300 dealers. Good selection of antiques, collectibles, memorabilia, country crafts, farm items, jewelry, and new merchandise available. Food, rest rooms, h/a, ample parking. Camping on-site. Space from $8 outside. *Contact* Boyd Meadows, Box 549, 25541 (304) 743-9862.

MORGANTOWN

Riverfront Antique & Flea Market
1389 University Avenue, Rte. 119

Thursday–Sunday. Indoor market with approximately 20 dealers. *Contact* Joan Evanoff (304) 292-9320.

Westover Drive-In Flea Market
Westover Drive-In Theater
Dupont and River Rd.

Sunday, March–December. Approximately 200 dealers. Large outdoor market with a good selection of merchandise, lots of new items, and good collectibles available. Food, rest rooms, h/a, ample parking. *Contact* Joseph Nevera (304) 983-2220.

PIPESTEM

Speedway Flea Market
Rte. 20 North at Drive-In
Nine miles north of Princeton
(304) 384-7382

Saturday, Sunday. Approximately 50 dealers offer new and used merchandise, lots of bric-a-brac, farm items, and crafts. Food available, rest rooms. Space from $4. *Contact* Sun Valley Market, Athens-Hinton, Star Rte., Box 175A, 27412.

WESTOVER

Indoor Flea Market
1389 University Ave.
(304) 292-9230

Thursday, Friday, Saturday, Sunday. New merchandise, clothing, electronics, jewelry, housewares, lots of new collectibles, used merchandise, and garage sale items available. Snack bar, rest rooms.

Westover Flea Market
Dupont and River Rd., 26505

Sundays. Antiques, collector booths, used merchandise, garage sale items, country and farm collectibles. Food available, rest rooms. Ample parking. Market open March–October. *Contact* Joe Nevers (304) 983-2220.

WHEELING

Antique Flea Market
Civic Center, downtown

Monthly, call for dates. Admission $1. Indoor market with approximately 150 dealers. Antiques, collectibles, art, crafts, and some new merchandise available. Snack bar, rest rooms, h/a, ample parking with a charge of $1. Space from $15. *Contact* Lela Karges (304) 233-7000.

WINFIELD

Flea Market
Winfield Riding Club
Rtes. 34 and 35
(304) 757-9040

Saturday, Sunday. New and used merchandise, bric-a-brac, antiques, collector booths, farm and country items, tack, jewelry, and crafts available. Food, rest rooms, h/a, ample parking.

INFORMATION IS SUBJECT TO CHANGE—ALWAYS CALL AHEAD TO AVOID DISAPPOINTMENT

WISCONSIN

ADAMS

Adams Flea Market
556 S. Main St.
Hwy. 13 South

Saturday, Sunday, 6 a.m. until dark. Approximately 50 dealers. Inside and outside spaces. Antiques, collectibles, coins, vintage clothing, and jewelry available. Snack bar, rest rooms, h/a. Camping available. *Contact* Irene Steffen, 2151 Hwy. 13, 53910 (608) 339-3192.

CALEDONIA

7 Mile Fair Flea Market
2720 W. 7 Mile Rd.
I-94, 7 Mile Rd. Exit
Fifteen miles south of Milwaukee

Saturday, Sunday, 6 a.m.–5 p.m. Admission charge $1.25. Approximately 750 dealers at this large commercial market. Worlds of new and trendy merchandise, imports, and new collectibles available. Plenty of food, rest rooms, h/a, ample parking. Management does not wish this flea market referred to as a flea market, so when you're at their market, call it a fair. But by its very nature it really is a flea market and an exceptionally fine one at that. Outside space available from $25 for the weekend. *Contact* Scott Niles, 2720 W. 7 Mile Rd., 53108 (414) 835-2177, fax (414) 835-2968.

ALWAYS CALL BEFORE TRAVELING LONG DISTANCES!

COLUMBUS

Sunday Flea Market
Downtown
(414) 623-3699

Sunday, June–September. Antiques, lots of collector booths, crafts, used merchandise, home furnishings, housewares, apparel, fashion accessories, and crafts available. Food available, rest rooms. *Contact* Chamber of Commerce.

EAU CLAIRE

The Golden Indoor/Outdoor Flea Market
Melby Rd., off Rte. 53
(715) 832-8605

Friday, Saturday, Sunday. Antiques, furniture (used and antique), many collector booths, jewelry, coins, sports cards, clothing, housewares, bric-a-brac, fishing collectibles, and used merchandise available. Snack bar, rest rooms, h/a, ample parking.

ELKHORN

Antique & Flea Market
Fairgrounds

Monthly, call for dates. Admission charge $1. Over 500 dealers inside and outside. Good market for antiques, primitives, and collectibles. This is a tremendous source market with literally hundreds of booths crammed full of desirable collector items. Food, rest rooms, h/a, ample parking, and lots of walking. *Contact* N. L. Promotions, Box 544, 53121 (262) 723-5651.

GREEN BAY

Northeastern Wisconsin's Biggest Craft Sale & Flea Market
Brown County Arena
1901 S. Oneida
Next to Lambeau Field

Monthly, 8:30 a.m.–3:30 p.m. Admission charge. Average daily attendance of 3,000 with approximately 300 dealers. Great selection of antiques, collectibles, fine jewelry, collectible glassware and silver, and some new and used merchandise available. Large selection of locally made crafts and gifts. This is probably my favorite Wisconsin market. I'm always able to find good wholesale buys here for resale. Snack bars, rest rooms, h/a, ample parking. Space from $14. Reservations required. Camping available. No outside food concessions allowed. *Contact* J. H. Van Stechhelman, Box 10566, 54307 (414) 494-9507 or 494-3401.

HAYWARD

Hayward Flea Market
Hwy. 27 and Country Rd. B

Tuesday, Wednesday, dawn to dark. Indoor and outdoor market with approximately 75 dealers. Good selection of collectibles, lots of used merchandise, and some new goods available. *Contact* Jan Thirty, 10556 N. Sunnyside Ave., 54843 (715) 634-4794.

JANESVILLE

Janesville Flea Market
3030 Prairie Ave., junction of Rte. 351 and Country Trunk G
(608) 755-9830

Saturday, Sunday.

INFORMATION IS SUBJECT TO CHANGE—ALWAYS CALL FIRST!

JEFFERSON

Jefferson Bargain Fair
Speedway Grounds
Hwy. 18
(414) 835-1168

Sunday, summer months only. Antiques, collector booths, mountains of used merchandise, clothing, furniture, farm items, fishing and marine items, auto items, a great selection of crafts, and decorator items available. Food available, rest rooms, ample parking.

KENOSHA

Bargain Showcase Indoor/Outdoor Market
8501 75th St.

Friday, Saturday, Sunday, 9 a.m.–5 p.m. New and used merchandise, lots of new fashion and decorator items, and newer collector lines available. Snack bar, rest rooms, h/a, ample parking. *Contact* Bill Utaski, 53241 (414) 697-9770.

Kenosha Flea Market
5535 22nd Ave.

Friday, Saturday, Sunday. New and used merchandise, collector booths, good selection of fishing collectibles, art, prints, jewelry, clothing, and housewares available. Snack bar, rest rooms, h/a, ample parking. Space from $15. *Contact* Beth Goll, 5535 22nd Ave., 53140 (414) 658-3532.

Mid City Outdoor Theater Flea Market
Hwy. 32

Sunday. Antiques, collector booths, furniture, new and used merchandise, clothing, housewares, sports and fishing items, farm items, crafts, and produce available. Snack bar, rest rooms, h/a, ample parking.

LADYSMITH

Van Wey's Community Auction & Flea Market
Rte. 2
Four miles west of town on Hwy. 8

Every fifth and twentieth of the month, April–October, 6:30 a.m. until dark. Average attendance of 3,500 with approximately 200 dealers. This is a classic country market that will take you back to an earlier time. Antiques, collectibles, primitives, farm items, new and used merchandise, and crafts available. Cafe, rest rooms, h/a, ample parking. Space from $8. Camping nearby. This market has been in existence since 1926. *Contact* Cecil Van Way, W10139 Van Wey Lane, 54848 (715) 532-6044 or 532-3661.

MADISON

The Forum Flea Market & Collectors Show
Dane County Expo Center

Monthly, 9 a.m.–4 p.m. Admission charge. One of the area's most popular markets with approximately 100 dealers. Indoor market featuring antiques and collectible items, with a wide range of quality items. This is a very clean, well-managed market that is always a pleasure to shop. Snack bars, rest rooms, h/a, ample parking. Space from $25. *Contact* Ed Haferman, Box 1361, 53701 (608) 837-5666 or 837-8531.

MENOMENEE FALLS

Starlite Swap-O-Rama
N. Fond du Lac Ave.
Hwys. 145 and 41
(312) 774-3900

Sunday, May–November. Approximately 75 dealers at this outdoor market offer antiques, collectibles, furniture, new merchandise, lots of used merchandise, bric-a-brac, farm items, clothing, and housewares. Food available, rest rooms, h/a, ample parking.

MILWAUKEE

Rummage-O-Rama
State Fair Park

Monthly, call for dates, 10 a.m.–5:30 p.m. Admission charge. There are over 500 dealers at this large indoor market. Usually held once a month, occasionally twice a month. This is a strong market with exceptional attendance. All types of merchandise can be found here. Many unique one-of-a-kind treasures and plenty of traditional flea market bric-a-brac. Always several pitchmen/demonstrators here selling the latest in kitchen and trendy gadgets. Many of the products seen on late-night TV were introduced at this market. Lots of new items, collectibles, and more. Food, rest rooms, h/a, ample parking. Camping available. Space from $68 to $84 for the weekend. *Contact* J. Rasner, Box 510619, New Berlin, 53151 (414) 521-2111.

Mega Market
7793 W. Appleton Ave.
(414) 464-8277

Saturday, Sunday. Admission charge. New merchandise, tools, fishing tackle, electronics, housewares, sportswear, toys, jewelry, sports merchandise, lots of new collectible lines, and decorator items available. Snack bar, rest rooms, h/a, ample parking.

MONTELLO

Granite City Antique Mall & Flea Market
145 Clay St.
(608) 297-7925

Saturday, Sunday. Average daily attendance of 3–5,000 with approximately 50 dealers. Flea market merchandise new and used, antiques, collectibles, and crafts available. Indoor/outdoor, the flea market here is in operation on weekends, and permanent shops inside are open during the week. Snack bars, rest rooms, h/a, ample parking. Camping available. Space from $12.

Candy's Flea Market
Hwy. 22
Six miles south of Montello

Saturday, Sunday, May–October. Average attendance of 200 with approximately 25 dealers. New and used merchandise, lots of bric-a-brac, antiques, collector booths, and crafts available. Snack bar, rest rooms, h/a. Inside and outside space from $5 daily. *Contact* Candy Howell, Rte. 1, Box 175A, 53949 (608) 297-2489.

MUKWONAGO

Mukwonago Flea Market

(414) 363-2003 or (262) 363-2003

Third weekend in July, August; 2nd weekend in September, 8 a.m.–5 p.m. Over 6,000 vendors. Sponsored by the American Legion.

NEW LONDON

Flea Market
Pin River Amusement Park
(414) 726-4302

Saturday, Sunday, summer months only. New merchandise, souvenirs, novelties, used merchandise, and crafts available. Food available, rest rooms.

PRINCETON

Princeton Flea Market
City Park
(414) 295-3877

Saturday, May–October. New merchandise, trendy fashion items, used merchandise, lots of garage sale booths, collectibles, and crafts available. Food available, rest rooms. *Contact* Chamber of Commerce.

RHINELANDER

North Town Trade Center
3846 Shawnee Lane
North on Hwy. 17 to Chippewa Dr., turn right, then one block

Saturday, Sunday. Approximately 150–200 dealers at this indoor market. New merchandise, gifts, electronics, fishing tackle, auto items, tools, sportswear, housewares, sports merchandise, jewelry, toys, used merchandise, garage sale items, antiques, collector booths, and crafts available. Snack bar, rest rooms, h/a, ample parking. Space from $7 daily or $14 for the weekend. Camping available on premises. Prior approval needed for any food or beverage sales. *Contact* Ernest or Michael Feight (715) 369-3068.

ST. CROIX FALLS

Pea Picking Flea Market
Hwys. 8 and 35
Five miles east of town

Saturday, Sunday, 6 a.m.–5 p.m. Inside and outside market with approximately 75 dealers. Collectibles, country and farm items, crafts, and used furniture available. Lots of local food items, cheese, etc. Space from $8 daily. *Contact* Judy Hansen, 1938 Little Blake Lane, Luck, 54853 (715) 857-5479.

SHAWANO

Shawano Flea Market
Fairgrounds
Hwy. 29

Sunday, April–mid-November, daylight until 5 p.m. Admission charge $1. Approximately 200 dealers at this large outdoor market. Antiques, collectibles, new merchandise, crafts, and produce are just some of the variety that this popular market has to offer. Clean, friendly, well-managed market. Food available, rest rooms, h/a, ample parking. Delightful tourist area with many interesting shops and attractions. This market holds several special weekend antique events; call for current schedule. *Contact* Bob Zurko, 211 W. Green Bay St., 54166 (715) 526-9769, fax (715) 524-5675. E-mail: vatabat@aol.com.

WAUSAU

Marathon Park Indoor Flea Market
1810 Stewart Circle
(715) 359-9500

Saturday, Sunday, April–October. Lots of new merchandise, used merchandise, furniture, garage sale items, collector booths, crafts, and gifts available. Snack bar, rest rooms, h/a, ample parking.

WAUTOMA

Wautoma Flea Market
Junction of Rtes. 73 and 21

Saturday, Sunday, mid-April–November, 7 a.m. until dark. Approximately 20–25 dealers. Collectibles, crafts, furniture, used and garage sale items available. Outdoor market. Space from $8. Market is located in the center of a charming and beautiful vacation and fishing area. *Contact* Milton Sommer, Rte. 4, Box 42, 54982 (414) 787-2300 or 787-7787.

DAYS, DATES, AND MARKETS ARE SUBJECT TO CHANGE!

WEST ALLIS

Rummage-O-Rama
State Fair Park

Monthly. Usually held once a month. Occasionally twice a month. Strong market with exceptional attendance. For sellers, all types of merchandise goes well at this market. A don't-miss market. (*See Milwaukee listing*). *Contact* J. Rasner, Box 51619, New Berlin, 53151 (414) 521-2111.

WOODSTOCK

Woodstock Antique & Flea Market
Fairgrounds
(715) 526-9769

Monthly. Antiques, furniture, many fine-quality collector booths, used merchandise, farm items, auto items, fishing and marine items, some new merchandise. Crafts, local food items, produce. Food available, rest rooms, h/a. Ample parking.

WYOMING

CASPER

Tuckway's Flea Market
4040 Sam Howell Rd.
(307) 234-0756

Daily. Used merchandise, collectibles, bric-a-brac of all kinds, and western items available.

Casper Super Flea
Central Wyoming Fairgrounds Rte. 220

Monthly, 10 a.m.–5 p.m. Seasonal market June–October. Admission 50 cents. Approximately 50 dealers. Indoor market. Antiques, collectibles, new and used merchandise, farm and ranch items, western and Indian jewelry, crafts, and gifts. Space from $20 per table. Snack bar, rest rooms, h/a. Ample free parking. *Contact* Bruce Smith, 1625 S. Kenwood St., 82601 (307) 234-6663.

Eagle Hall Flea Market
Eagle's Hall. 306 N. Durbin
(307) 234-6663

Saturday, Sunday. Call for current schedule as market is rather erratic.

CHEYENNE

Tee Pee Flea Market
3208 S. Greeley Hwy.
(307) 635-8535

Daily, 10 a.m.–7 p.m. Indoor market with approximately 30 permanent booths. Collectibles, small antiques, and some new and used merchandise available.

Bart's Flea Market West
408 E. Lincoln
(307) 632-0063

Daily. Indoor market with approximately 40 dealers.

Avenues Flea Market
315 E. 7th Ave.

Daily. Indoor market with approximately 50 dealers. *Contact* Darla Wellman (307) 635-5600.

Bargain Barn Flea Market
2112 Snyder Ave.

Monday–Saturday, 10 a.m.–6 p.m., Sunday, 12 p.m.–5 p.m. Indoor market with approximately 25 permanent booths. Collectibles, crafts, and new and used merchandise available. *Contact* Bill Lucas, 3556 Concord Rd., 82001 (307) 635-2844.

Frontier Wholesale Flea Market
1515 Carey Ave.
(307) 634-4004

Daily, 10 a.m.–6 p.m. Indoor market with collectibles, glassware, crafts, and new and used merchandise available.

Downtown Flea Market
312 W. 17th St.
(307) 638-3751

Daily. Small indoor market with antiques, furniture, western collectibles, secondhand items, great home furnishings, and decorator items available.

Odds 'N' Ends Flea Market
1408 Greeley Hwy.
(307) 635-3126

Daily. Collectibles, souvenirs, glassware, western items, used merchandise, and home furnishings available.

GILLETTE

Razor City Flea Market
Energy Hall Complex

Saturday, Sunday. Approximate weekend attendance 2,000. Space from $25. Camping and electricity available. *Contact* Don Clemens, Box 3255, 82716 (307) 682-0372.

LARAMIE

Bart's Flea Market
2401 Soldier Springs Rd.
(307) 632-0004

Daily. Indoor market with approximately 25 dealers.

Golden Flea Gallery
725 Skyline Rd.
(307) 745-7055

Daily. Indoor market with approximately 100 dealers. Snack bar, rest room, h/a.

ATTENTION!!!

FLEA MARKET OWNERS AND MANAGERS:
CUSTOMERS AND VENDORS ARE LOOKING FOR YOU!!!

In order for your FREE listing to appear in our next update of *The Flea Market Shopper's Companion*, simply fill out the survey form below and and e-mail to fleamktusa@aol.com or return to:

Jim Goodridge
P.O. Box 744
Arnold, MO 63010

MARKET SURVEY

Days Held: ______________________________

City: ______________________ State ________

Name of Market: ______________________________

Street Address: ______________________________

Directions: ______________________________

____

Contact Person: ______________ Telephone # (_____)________

Address: ________________ City/State/Zip ____________

Vendor Information: ______________________________

____

Average Daily Attendance: __________ Number of Vendors: ______

Space cost: ______________ Tables Available: __________

Reservations: Recommended ______ Required ______ Not Necessary ______

Inside Space Available: Yes _____ Cost ______________ No______

Overnight Camping: Yes _____ Cost __________ Free _____ No______

Showers on site: Yes _____ No _____ Electricity Available: Yes _____ No_____

Basic Merchandise Make-Up: New _____ Used _____ Antique/Collectible_____

Merchandise restrictions or comments: ______________________

Restrictions & License: ______________________________

THERE IS NO CHARGE FOR YOUR LISTING. Thank you—Jim

YOU BE THE JUDGE

IN THE 10TH ANNUAL

"TOP 10 ALL-AMERICAN MARKETPLACE AWARD"

Cast your vote today and help us honor the "Top 10" markets who have shown outstanding service to the industry during the past 12 months.

OFFICIAL BALLOT

________ Yes, here's my vote for the "Top 10 All-American Marketplace Award"

Name of Market: ______________________________

Address: ______________________________

Phone #: (______) ______________________________

Comments: ______________________________

____

____

____

(If possible send brochure, literature, photos, etc., about market.)

Please e-mail your vote to fleamktusa@aol.com or mail your entries to:

Jim Goodridge
P. O. Box 744
Arnold, MO 63010